MART

SELECT EPIGRAMS

EDITED BY

LINDSAY AND PATRICIA WATSON

Senior Lecturers in Classics, University of Sydney

CAMBRIDGE
UNIVERSITY PRESS

CAMBRIDGE UNIVERSITY PRESS
Cambridge, New York, Melbourne, Madrid, Cape Town, Singapore, São Paulo

Cambridge University Press
The Edinburgh Building, Cambridge CB2 2RU, UK

Published in the United States of America by Cambridge University Press, New York

www.cambridge.org
Information on this title: www.cambridge.org/9780521554886

© Cambridge University Press 2003

First published 2003

A catalogue record for this publication is available from the British Library

ISBN-13 978-0-521-55488-6 hardback
ISBN-10 0-521-55488-8 hardback

ISBN-13 978-0-521-55539-5 paperback
ISBN-10 0-521-55539-6 paperback

Transferred to digital printing 2006

CONTENTS

PREFACE

All academic authors inevitably incur debts both to colleagues and to pre-decessors in the field. Among the latter we particularly single out the com-mentaries of Howell and Citroni on Martial book I, Grewing on 6 and Kay on II. The excellence of the works on I and II decided us at the outset to include in our selection only a single epigram from these two books. We have, on the other hand, commented on a number of epigrams from book 6: research on these was virtually completed when Grewing appeared. The commentary on Book 7 by G. Galán Vioque (English trans. by J. J. Zoltowski, Leiden 2002) reached us too late for it to be possible to take account of it. Because roughly half of Martial's fourteen books still await a published commentary, we have deliberately incorporated in the present work more secondary literature than is usual in the Cambridge Greek and Latin Classics series: it is hoped that this will be of assistance to future scholars of Martial.

On a personal level, especial thanks are due to Ted Kenney for prompt and invaluable criticisms of successive drafts; like all contributors to the series, we have benefited immensely from his superb Latinity and general encouragement. Dexter Hoyos and Lawrence Keppie offered helpful ad-vice on specific points. Papers on various epigrams were given at Sydney University SACAH seminars; we thank the audience on these occasions for their comments and suggestions. The bulk of the work for the present commentary was done in Oxford's Ashmolean Library, an institution where research is truly an unalloyed delight and the staff the essence of helpfulness.

It has been put to us that, in commenting on selected poems, we have overlooked a fundamental aspect of Martial's compositional technique, the structuring of the individual book as an organic whole (see introduc-tion, pp. 29–31). But we see it as our task to imbue readers with some of the enthusiasm which we entertain for Martial: and this purpose could best be served by selecting poems upon which we feel we have new and interesting things to say. We also see it as part of our brief to give a representative sample of Martial's oeuvre – something that a commentary on a single book might not do, given that these often have a specific and circumscribed emphasis.

The text printed in this edition represents our own, although we owe an enormous debt both to the OCT and to the Teubner text of Shackleton Bailey.

We dedicate this book to the memory of two Latinists who represented very different approaches to the subject but mutually respected each other: Harry Jocelyn, from whom PW first learned to appreciate the scholarly possibilities of Roman erotica, and who would have heartily approved at least of this aspect of our selection, and our friend Don Fowler, who would have been highly amused to find himself paired with a scholar of such radically opposite stamp.

ABBREVIATIONS

Adams, *LSV*	J. N. Adams, *The Latin sexual vocabulary*. London 1982
ANRW	*Aufstieg und Niedergang der römischen Welt.* Berlin 1972–
ARV	J. D. Beazley, *Attic red-figure vase-painters,* 2nd edn 1963
Becker, *Gallus*	W. A. Becker, *Gallus,* tr. F. Metcalfe, 5th edn London 1876
Blümner, *Technologie*	H. Blümner, *Technologie und Terminologie der Gewerbe und Künste bei Griechen und Römern.* Leipzig 1875–87
CGL	*Corpus glossariorum latinorum*
CHCL	*Cambridge history of classical literature* II (*Latin literature*) edd. E. J. Kenney and W. V. Clausen. Cambridge 1982
CIG	*Corpus inscriptionum graecarum.* Berlin 1828–77
CIL	*Corpus inscriptionum latinarum.* Berlin 1863–
CLE	F. Buecheler, ed., *Carmina latina epigraphica.* Leipzig 1895–7
D–S	C. Daremberg and E. Saglio, edd., *Dictionnaire des antiquités grecques et romaines.* Paris 1877–1919
Ditt. *Syll.*	W. Dittenberger, *Sylloge inscriptionum graecarum.* 3rd edn Leipzig 1915–24
FLP	E. Courtney, ed., *The fragmentary Latin poets.* Oxford 1993
Foerster	R. Foerster, ed., *Libanii opera.* Teubner text, Leipzig 1903–27
GLK	H. Keil, ed., *Grammatici latini.* Leipzig 1857–70
GP	A. S. F. Gow and D. L. Page, edd., *The Greek anthology. The garland of Philip and*

	some contemporary epigrams. 2 vols., Cambridge 1968
HE	A. S. F. Gow and D. L. Page, edd., *The Greek anthology. Hellenistic epigrams*. 2 vols., Cambridge 1965
Housman, *CP*	A. E. Housman, *Classical papers*. Cambridge 1972
IG	*Inscriptiones graecae*. Berlin 1873–1914
ILS	H. Dessau, *Inscriptiones latinae selectae*. Berlin 1892–1916
K–A	R. Kassel and C. Austin, edd. *Poetae comici graeci*. Berlin 1983–
K–S	R. Kühner and C. Stegmann, *Ausführliche Grammatik der lateinischen Sprache*. Darmstadt 1955
Kajanto	I. Kajanto, *The Latin cognomina* (Societas Scientiarum Fennica, Comm. Hum. Lit. 36.2) 1965
Latte, *RR*	K. Latte, *Römische Religionsgeschichte*. Munich 1960
LHS	M. Leumann, J. Hofmann, A. Szantyr, *Lateinische Grammatik* I–II. Munich 1965–77
LIMC	*Lexicon iconographicum mythologiae classicae*. Zurich 1981–
LSJ	H. Liddell, R. Scott, H. Stuart Jones, edd., *A Greek–English lexicon*. Oxford 1968
Marquardt, *Staatsverwaltung*	J. Marquardt, *Römische Staatsverwaltung*, 2nd edn Leipzig 1881–5
Marquardt-Mau	J. Marquardt, *Das Privatleben der Römer* 2nd edn ed. A. Mau. Leipzig 1886
N–H	R. G. M. Nisbet and M. Hubbard, *A Commentary on Horace Odes* I. Oxford 1970
Nissen	H. Nissen, *Italische Landeskunde*. 2 vols. Berlin 1883–1902
N–W	F. Neue and C. Wagener, *Formenlehre der lateinischen Sprache*. Berlin 1892–1905

OLD	*Oxford Latin dictionary.* Oxford 1970
Otto, *Sprichw.*	A. Otto, *Die Sprichwörter und sprichwörtlichen Redensarten der Römer.* Leipzig 1890
PGM	K. Preisendanz, ed. *Papyri graecae magicae.* 2nd edn Stuttgart 1973–4
PIR	*Prosographia Imperii Romani Saeculi I, II, III.* 2nd. ed. Berlin/Leipzig 1933–
Platner–Ashby	S. B. Platner and T. Ashby, *A topographical dictionary of ancient Rome.* London 1929
RAC	*Reallexikon für Antike und Christentum.* Stuttgart 1941–
RE	*Real-Encyclopädie der classischen Altertumswissenschaft.* Stuttgart 1893–
Richardson	L. Richardson, *A new topographical dictionary of ancient Rome.* Baltimore/London 1992
Roscher	W. Roscher, ed., *Ausführliches Lexicon der griechischen und römischen Mythologie.* Leipzig 1884–1937
SB	D. R. Shackleton Bailey, ed. and transl., *Martial: epigrams* Loeb Classical Library, 3 vols. Cambridge, Mass. and London 1993
SEG	*Supplementum epigraphicum graecum.* Amsterdam 1923–
S–W	A. N. Sherwin-White *The Letters of Pliny: a historical and social commentary.* Oxford 1985
Syme, *RP*	R. Syme, *Roman papers.* Oxford 1979–91
TLL	*Thesaurus linguae latinae.* Leipzig 1900–
Woodcock	E. C. Woodcock, *A new Latin syntax.* London 1959

References in **bold** figures are to the continuous numeration of the epigrams included in this edition. Those not in bold figures are to the standard numeration by book, epigram and line.

INTRODUCTION

1 LIFE OF MARTIAL

Our knowledge of M.'s life is derived mostly from the information provided
by the poet. Only for his retirement to Spain and his death there do we
have independent evidence in the form of the Younger Pliny's well-known
obituary (*Ep.* 3.21). In drawing inferences about the poet from the epigrams,
one must be careful to distinguish between 'facts' which there is no reason
to doubt, such as M.'s Spanish provenance, and comments which are either
not meant to be taken as autobiographical (e.g. allusions to a 'wife') or which
are susceptible of more than one interpretation (e.g. M.'s reasons for leaving
Rome). The point needs stressing, since modern descriptions of M.'s life
are based largely on a strictly biographical reading of the epigrams.

Marcus Valerius Martialis[1] was born in the Roman *municipium* of Bilbilis
in Spain (**19**.9n.) between AD 38 and 41.[2] His birth occurred in the month
of March: hence the name Martialis.[3] By nationality he was Celtiberian,
a racial mix of Celts and Iberians of Libyan origin which had long been
dominant in that part of Spain (10.65.3–4 *ex Hiberis | et Celtis genitus*). It is
clear from his name and those of his parents, Fronto and Flaccilla (**83**.1 n.),
that he came from a Spanish family which had attained Roman citizenship.
M.'s parents must have been comfortably off, at least by local standards,
for they provided him with a good education (**57**.8n.) and, if he enjoyed
the patronage of the Senecan circle (see below), he may have exploited
some sort of family connection, suggesting that the household was among
the ruling aristocracy of Bilbilis.[4]

Like all ambitious provincials, M. headed for Rome. It attests to the high
premium put on education in Spain that, when M. arrived in the city in 64,
many of the leading writers were of Spanish origin: Seneca the Younger, his

---

[1] Pliny refers to Valerius Martialis; for M.'s *praenomen*, cf. 1.5.2.

[2] The tenth book, of which we have the second edition, published in 98, contains
a poem for M.'s 57th birthday (10.24). It is uncertain whether this epigram also
appeared in the first edition of 95.

[3] As was customary, M. celebrated his birthday on the Kalends of his natal month:
cf. 9.52, 10.24, 12.60, H. Lucas, *CQ* 32 (1938) 5–6.

[4] Bilbilis received *municipium* status under Augustus, which meant that all the
magistrates and their families were full Roman citizens (L. A. Curchin, *Roman Spain*
(London/New York 1991) 66); it is likely that M.'s family fell into this category.

nephew Lucan, Quintilian and Columella. It is possible that M. was taken into the Senecan circle, though this has recently been called into question.[5] The location of M.'s farm at Nomentum, where Seneca and his family owned property, has sometimes been adduced in support of Senecan patronage, but it cannot be proved that M. obtained the property from them.[6]

It seems certain that M. was honing his skills as an epigrammatist between the date of his arrival in Rome and the appearance of his first published work, the *Liber de spectaculis*, written for the opening of the Colosseum in 80.[7] In all likelihood he circulated individual poems or small collections privately among potential patrons over a number of years, including them in the first two books of epigrams when these were published in 86–7.[8] This would explain M.'s introduction of himself in the first poem of book 1 as *toto notus in orbe Martialis | argutis epigrammaton libellis*.[9]

M. continued to live mostly[10] in Rome, where he published at regular intervals books 2–11, as well as a second edition of 10.[11] Various details of his life during these years can be regarded as certain. That he owned a house in Rome (**11**.2n.) and an estate at Nomentum (**14**.1 n.) is indisputable fact, though these residences were clearly not as humble as he claims. The town-house is first mentioned in book 9, dated to 94; in earlier years he tells us that he occupied a modest flat (1.117.7 *scalis habito tribus sed altis*; 108.3 *mea Vipsanas spectant cenacula laurus*). There is no reason to question the reality

[5] By M. Kleijwegt, *AC* 42 (1999) 105–19, who demonstrates the flimsiness of the evidence that M. enjoyed the patronage of Seneca.

[6] Sullivan (1991) 4, Saller (1983) 251, and Howell on 1.105, hold that M.'s farm was a gift from Seneca.

[7] This widely assumed date for the publication of the *Liber de spectaculis* has been questioned by Holzberg (2002) 40.

[8] In between the *De spectaculis* and the epigrams (books 1–12) he also published two books of short mottoes (books 13 and 14), the *Xenia* and the *Apophoreta*: cf. T. J. Leary, *Martial book XIV* (London 1996) 9–13.

[9] See esp. White (1974) and (1996), where he defends his case against Fowler, (1995). White thought that M. continued the practice of pre-circulation throughout his career, though Citroni (1988) 34 argues that, after M. began formal publication, the latter became the main means of circulating the epigrams.

[10] Apart from a stay in Gaul, whence book 3 was sent, and periods of respite at his Nomentan farm.

[11] M. Citroni, *ICS* 14 (1989) 201–23 gives the following chronology: bk 1 early 86, bk 2 86–7, bk 3 Autumn 87, bk 4 Dec. 88, bk 5 Dec. 89, bk 6 90–1, bk 7 Dec. 92, bk 8 Jan. 94, bk 9 Autumn 94, bk 10 (first ed.) 95, bk 11 Dec. 96, bk 10 (2nd ed.) 98. The widespread assumption of a second edition of book 10 which postdated the appearance of book 11 is attacked by Holzberg (2002) 144ff.

of this flat or its location; on the other hand, it must have been reasonably roomy, since he has a number of slaves, assuming that some, if not all, of those mentioned are real.[12] Ownership of slaves and (after 94) an urban house suggests that he was comparatively well off: he had obtained a tribunate and equestrian status (3.95.9–10), as well as the *ius trium liberorum* (see below), which allowed him to accept legacies from friends and patrons; income from poetry came via gifts from patrons rather than through royalties. M.'s financial position has been the subject of controversy: White argued that the equestrian census was sufficient for a decent existence, patronage being needed more as general support and for publicising his poetry; Saller that it was only a bare minimum and that M. relied on patronage to maintain his lifestyle.[13]

One question which has provoked extensive discussion is the poet's marital status.[14] Frequent allusions to a 'wife' have given rise to much speculation about whether or not M. was married at any stage. Despite a recent tendency to regard the poet as a confirmed bachelor,[15] it seems clear that in his early years he had one or more marriages: this is shown by his petition to the emperor for the *ius trium liberorum* on the basis that Fortune had not granted him offspring (**9a**.5), which suggests an infertile marriage, rather than a deliberate decision to remain single. M.'s marital status during the period after he began to publish his poems is less clear. Mutually contradictory allusions to a wife (e.g. **9b**.3, **69**.7) and to the absence thereof (11.19) and grossly insulting allusions to an *uxor* (e.g. 11.104) which would have been insupportable to a real person, suggest that the wife of the epigrams is a literary construct.

The broad outline of M.'s later years is certain. After 34 years in Rome (10.103.7–8), he retired in 98 to Spain, where he lived in Bilbilis in a villa provided by a patroness, Marcella (**17**); he died there, probably in 104 (Plin. *Ep.* 3.21). In 101 he had produced a book for the arrival in Spain of his fellow countryman and patron Terentius Priscus (book 12 *praef.*). This may not have been book 12 as we have it, but a shorter version

---

[12] Sullivan (1991) 27. The reality of all the slaves who appear in M. is assumed by Garrido-Hory (1981b); some, like Diadumenus (**52**), might be literary constructs, but no one doubts the factual existence of those for whom he writes epitaphs, like Erotion (**83**) or his secretary Demetrius (1.101).

[13] White (1975), Saller (1983). The latest discussion of the matter by P. M. W. Tennant *AC* 43 (2000), 139–56 treats the poems as autobiographical documents.

[14] See J. P. Sullivan, *CW* 72 (1979) 238–9, Watson (2003).

[15] E.g. Howell (1980) 4, (1995) 1–2; Kay (1985) 276–7.

which was filled out later, partly from earlier unpublished work, either by M. himself or by editors after his death.[16] So much for the basic facts, but accounts of M.'s last years usually include other details, based on a literal interpretation of certain epigrams in books 10 and 12. According to such accounts M., becoming increasingly tired of the client's life in Rome (cf. 10.70, 74), planned permanent retirement in Bilbilis, for which he had long felt a nostalgic attraction (cf. 1.49). Once there, his ideal of happiness was initially translated into reality (**19**), but he soon became disillusioned and missed the advantages of Rome which he had previously taken for granted (cf. **25**, 12 *praef.*). Ironically, the country, far from being a haven of tranquillity conducive to writing, came to represent a small-town lack of urban sophistication which was antithetical to poetic production. M. only began to compose again at the urging of his patron Priscus. Death prevented his returning to Rome, but this was not a realistic prospect in any case.

The above, canonised as the official version of M.'s final years, should not be accepted without reservation. For instance, M.'s real reason for returning to Spain could have been that he was so closely associated with Domitian's regime that he could not expect patronage from Nerva and Trajan, despite attempts to ingratiate himself (cf. 11.1–5, 12.4, **12** intro.). In that case, the epigrams expressing dissatisfaction with life in Rome and the delights of rural retirement would have been inserted into the second edition of book 10 as a front for the real situation.[17] Again, the conventional assumption of a period of beatitude upon M.'s return to Spain followed by a gradually supervening disillusionment is called into question by **19**, which is written in so parodic and at times unrealistic a spirit as to rule out any such sharp demarcation between the earlier and later stages of M.'s retirement (see **19**.18 intro.). The fact that book 12 contains many poems set in Rome and few with a distinctively Spanish setting, might bear out M.'s complaints in the Preface that the provincial atmosphere of Bilbilis stifled poetic composition, yet, as archaeological remains demonstrate, Bilbilis was a highly Romanised town, with a theatre and a bath complex. The Roman character of the book could be interpreted differently, i.e. that M. was planning to return to Rome: it would explain his intention to send his book to patrons there after its presentation to Priscus (cf. 12.2), as well as his anxiety that the book should not appear to be tainted with Spanishness.[18]

[16] See Howell (1998) 183.

[17] For this view, see for instance Sullivan (1991); *contra*, Howell (1998) 184–5.

[18] Cf. 12 *praef.* 25–7.

Nor should it be assumed that a come-back was impossible: despite the often-made assumption that M. sold his townhouse, it is just as likely that he rented it out to keep his options open should he change his mind about retirement.[19]

2 THE USE OF THE FIRST PERSON IN THE EPIGRAMS

M.'s poems are frequently written in the first person. Often this contributes to the building up of a persona which is part literary creation, part based on reality. On other occasions, the poet speaks with different voices which are temporarily adopted for purposes of individual epigrams. It is not always easy to distinguish between the various 'I's.

Of all M.'s character creations, the most successful is that of Martial himself. The persona can be summarised as follows. He is a poet of equestrian status whose *officia* as a client of rich patrons are so onerous that at times he scarcely has the leisure to pursue his craft. Since he does not receive from this 'job' sufficient rewards, his circumstances are impoverished; all he owns is a poor farm, to which he escapes periodically, and a modest town house in a noisy area of Rome. In a modicum of epigrams M. is himself a patron, issuing dinner invitations and subject to the not always welcome attentions of clients. To offset these disadvantages, there are pleasures: he enjoys dinner parties, friendships, sexual encounters, especially with young slave boys, and he revels in the fame which his poetry brings. He does not seek to harm individuals through his satire, but delights in holding up to ridicule the foibles and vices of society. His dream is of a simple lifestyle in the country, free from the burdens of the client and other disadvantages of the city.

The extent to which this persona resembles the real Martial cannot be known, but the question needs addressing because of a tendency among scholars to talk as if the two can be equated. Though most show healthy scepticism about such details as the poet's poverty, opinions and preferences expressed via the persona are often assumed to be the poet's own. For example, the frequent satirical attacks on women betray, according to Sullivan,

---

[19] The proceeds from the farm at Nomentum, which he did sell (10.92), along with Marcella's gift of an estate at Bilbilis (**17**) and the patronage of Terentius Priscus (12.3), could have provided M. with sufficient means to live, and his house in Rome would return a good rental income (**64**.3n.).

a deep-seated misogyny on the part of M. himself.[20] But these may be explained partly in terms of the sceptic tradition directed against women, and partly as demonstrating that the predominantly male audience for whom M. wrote appreciated anti-feminist humour. The clear sexual preference of the persona for boy slaves, on the other hand, may reflect that of the 'real' M., not so much because of the number of erotic poems addressed to these, as because of the lack of corresponding poems to women; as an epigrammatist he might have been expected to include both.[21]

Of greater interest is the extent to which the persona represents a consistent self-characterisation on M.'s part. Often, discrepancies are more apparent than real. For instance, although complaints about financial hardship do not cohere with M.'s often expressed wish to pursue a simple rural existence, it needs to be kept in mind that sustaining even a modest lifestyle in Rome was an expensive business: it is not inconsistent to imagine an idealised life in the country where pleasure costs little. Again, M.'s rôle as long-suffering client may be reconciled with his occasional pose as patron (e.g. **25**), if it is recalled that many must have been both client and patron at once.

M.'s self-portrait is, then, coherent in a general way. There are however inconsistencies of other sorts. For example, the Nomentan farm is sometimes depicted as completely unproductive (e.g. 7.31.8), while at other times it yields a variety of edibles, enough to furnish a reasonable dinner party (10.48).

M.'s financial position as 'poor' client, too, is varied to suit the context. Sometimes he appears not as relatively poor, but as lacking the wherewithal for a meal (e.g. 1.59). On the other hand, in 6.5 M. asks a friend for a loan of 100,000 sesterces to help with the purchase of an expensive country property (*rustica mercatus multis sum praedia nummis: | mutua des centum, Caeciliane, rogo* 1–2).

M. likes to present different aspects of the same subject. For instance, the client/patron relationship is shown both from the client's viewpoint and, less frequently, from the patron's. This can lead to inconsistencies. Though M. frequently complains about patrons' lack of generosity, regarding the standard dole of 100 *quadrantes* as a paltry reward, in 8.42, by contrast, a client is offered that very amount by M. himself in the rôle of patron. Whether we are meant to overlook the incongruity or whether a degree of irony is intended is unclear.

[20] Sullivan (1991).
[21] As did Catullus; and the *Palatine anthology* contains love epigrams addressed both to women (book 5) and to boys (book 12).

A second example of inconsistency is the group of epigrams on legacy hunters. At **58**, for instance, a *captator* is gleefully mocked for being taken in by a lady who fakes illness in order to encourage his attentions. Yet M. elsewhere adopts the persona of a *captator*, giving expensive gifts and complaining that the object of his attentions does not respond appropriately (e.g. 5.39). Again, M. sometimes criticises the captated for succumbing to the bribes of a *captator* (e.g. 11.44, 6.63). Elsewhere, however, he portrays himself as preyed upon by a legacy hunter whom he encourages to keep giving him gifts (9.88). And though he laughs at a man for desiring to marry a rich woman, attracted by her cough, which suggests terminal illness (1.10), he hints that he himself would not be unsusceptible to the charms of an old woman were she older (10.8 *nubere Paula cupit nobis, ego ducere Paulam | nolo: anus est. uellem, si magis esset anus*).

One way of interpreting the foregoing is to deny that there is a single persona, and to regard the persona as constantly changing to suit the context. But it is also possible to draw a distinction – though one that is not always clear – between M.'s self-characterisation in general and cases where a voice is momentarily adopted by the poet to suit an individual epigram. This explanation is applicable, for instance, in 10.8 just cited, where the I appears to be a fictitious construct extemporised for the purposes of the joke.

Sometimes the use of the first person as a temporary voice is more clear-cut; instances are 11.39 where the poet, speaking in the person of a young adult, complains to his interfering *paedagogus* that he is now fully grown, and 8.17, where the poet acts as an advocate. Defending a client's case in court was one of the duties of the patron, but not, as here, for direct financial remuneration (see **25**.3n.); M.'s voice is that of the professional advocate, the *causidicus*, a profession which he elsewhere rejects (e.g. 1.17, 5.16). In such cases, the use of the first person is no more than a rhetorical device, a more vivid and direct means of satire than a third-person narrative; it belongs to a longstanding tradition that stretches back to Archilochus.[22]

3 MARTIAL'S AUDIENCE

It is clear that the tastes and attitudes of his audience played a large rôle in the shaping of M.'s poems (cf. Sullivan (1991) xxii–xxiv). Somewhat less clear, however, is the composition of that audience.

[22] For bibliography, see D. E. Gerber, ed. *A companion to the Greek lyric poets* (Leiden 1997) 6.

M. claims that everyone in Rome knows and appreciates his poetry: *laudat, amat, cantat nostros mea Roma libellos, | meque sinus omnes, me manus omnis habet* (6.60. 1–2). As well, his fame spans the world: he is read in Britain (11.3.5) and Vindelicia (9.84.5), by centurions in Thrace (11.3.3–4) and by people of all age groups in Vienne (7.88).

Harris's thesis[23] of widespread illiteracy leads him to dismiss M.'s statements as mere convention. Moreover the relatively high cost of books would, he suggests, have put them out of range for the 'average' person.[24] But what M. is saying – albeit exaggeratedly – is that his works were widely known, not to the public at large, but to the reading public, that is those, predominantly from the senatorial and equestrian classes, who had the money and education to be consumers of poetry. Despite the conventionality of M.'s claim,[25] there is no need to dismiss it as untrue.

Horsfall[26] argued that the lower classes had access to literature through dramatic performances and recitations. It is unclear however to what extent ordinary people attended recitations of poetic works, and in any case M.'s poems were probably known primarily through the published books rather than recitations. M.'s addresses to his audience are to the reader, rather than the listener,[27] and in the passages where he claims wide popularity for his poetry the context is that of reading rather than listening (e.g. 7.88.3 cited below).

The audience which M. has in view when composing his epigrams is primarily, then, the upper-class reader.[28] His poetry is 'popular' in the sense that it is more widely read and enjoyed among the educated classes than pretentious tragedies and epics on hackneyed mythological themes.[29]

It is worth pointing out that M.'s readers included both women and men. In Vienne, for instance, he claims that *me legit omnis . . . senior iuuenisque puerque | et coram tetrico casta puella uiro* (7.88.3–4). In 3.86, the joke that *matronae*

---

[23] Harris (1989) esp. 225–7.   [24] Harris (1989) 225.   [25] See Kay on 11.3.3.

[26] 'Statistics or states of mind?', in M. Beard *et al.*, ed., *Literacy in the Roman world* (Ann Arbor 1991) 59–76.

[27] Cf. Howell on 1.1.4. W. Burnikel, 'Zur Bedeutung der Mündlichkeit im Martials Epigrammenbüchern i–xii', in G. Vogt-Spira, ed., *Strukturen der Mündlichkeit in der römischen Literatur* (Tübingen 1990) 221–34 exaggerates the importance of *recitatio* over published work.

[28] For the exclusiveness of the Roman reading public see also E. J. Kenney in *CHCL* ii 10.

[29] Cf. 4.49.10 *laudant illa* (sc. bombastic poems on mythological topics), *sed ista* (sc. M.'s epigrams) *legunt*. Cf. Citroni (1968).

will eagerly peruse the second (obscene) section of the book depends on the assumption of a sizeable female readership. A similar assumption underlies 11.16, in which a covert female fascination with the sexual content of M.'s epigrams is again taken for granted.

4 MARTIAL AND DOMITIAN

Epigrams in praise of Domitian are found throughout books 1–9; the first edition of the tenth book must also have contained a number of poems addressed to him which were replaced in the second edition (book 10 as we have it), published after the emperor's assassination. Apart from a number of poems thanking Domitian for his patronage or requesting further favours, the majority of the epigrams in which the emperor features are eulogistic. He is praised for his military successes, especially in book 8, dedicated to Domitian, where the centrality of the emperor reflects his renewed presence in the City after a period abroad.[30] The social legislation which he introduced in keeping with his position as *censor perpetuus* is given due prominence (e.g. **43**). Like Statius, M. played a rôle in promoting the imperial cult of Domitian: there are references to him as *dominus et deus* (see on **10**), frequent comparisons between the emperor and the gods, especially Jupiter (**12**.10n.) and Hercules (**15**.15n.), and mention of the cult of the Flavian dynasty (**15**.16n.).

M.'s flattery of Domitian has always offered cause for concern. The main problem is not so much its exuberance – Pliny the Younger's *Panegyric* of Trajan is no less extreme – but the fact that the emperor suffered a *damnatio memoriae* immediately after his assassination and has until fairly recently continued to receive a bad press. On the assumption that no one could really approve of such a monster, M. has been condemned as a grovelling hypocrite, this being borne out by the fact that in the books issued after Domitian's death M. admits to having flattered Domitian (e.g. 10.72.1–3), and favourably compares the new regime with the old (e.g. **12**).

In recent years two different arguments have been used in an attempt to rescue M.'s good name: (1) the traditionally unfavourable picture of Domitian derives from hostility on the part of the senatorial class, which suffered most under his reign.[31] He was not, however, regarded in the same

---

[30] See Coleman (1998).   [31] Cf. Waters (1964).

light by the common people and by the equestrian class, to which the poet belonged; thus M.'s praise of him could have been sincere; (2) M.'s eulogies of Domitian are expressed in deliberately ambiguous terms: while appearing outwardly to approve of the emperor, they contain a subversive undercurrent. On this hypothesis M. is absolved from the charge of hypocritically flattering an unworthy subject because the poet takes the opportunity to offer criticism of the emperor for those who choose to read between the lines.[32]

The second line of argument cannot be sustained. It defies credibility that Domitian, who was known to appreciate literature, could have been so obtuse as not to see what M. was up to. And it is equally incredible that M., to whom imperial patronage was so important, was prepared to take such a risk, especially as others had suffered under Domitian for their writings. If however the first alternative, that M. might have genuinely approved of Domitian, is correct, the poet is still open to condemnation for insincerity because of the retraction of his praise of the emperor after Domitian's death in an attempt to curry favour with Nerva and Trajan.

An important assumption of both arguments is that M.'s flattery of Domitian needs to be excused on moral grounds. But this is to impose an anachronistic viewpoint which ignores the workings of the patronage system in Rome. Under this system, anyone who desired favours from the emperor, or indeed any other patron, was obliged to flatter him. What the client really thought was irrelevant, nor was it relevant whether the patron believed what was said of himself. Both sides were simply playing a game, and to judge this by modern standards of morality is to condemn not M. himself, but the whole system of patronage which was an integral part of the fabric of Roman society.[33]

More interesting are two different questions: (1) Did M.'s flattery work, i.e. did he gain from the emperor the patronage that he desired? (2) How did he go about flattering the emperor, and are the results to be dismissed as lamentable, or are some at least of the epigrams about Domitian successful in their own right?

Opinion is divided on the first question.[34] Certainly M. was never on such intimate terms with the emperor as to be invited to dinner (contrast

---

[32] Szelest (1974a), Holzberg (1988), B. W. Jones, *The emperor Domitian* (London 1992) 106–7. The theory of deliberate subversiveness is explored especially by Garthwaite (1990) 13–22.

[33] See Darwall-Smith (1996) 271–3; Coleman (1998) 337–8.

[34] For arguments against M.'s receiving patronage from Domitian, see esp. Szelest (1974).

Statius). Only in the first book does he suggest any kind of personal relationship, when he makes Domitian himself address a joke to M. with the intimate use of his first name (1.5). After that, however, M. either approaches the emperor in a timid and diffident tone (e.g. 8.24, 6.1) or else through his freedmen (5.6 Parthenius, 7.99 Crispinus). On the other hand, M. claims that Domitian is accustomed to read and to praise his poetry (e.g. 4.27.1 *saepe meos laudare soles, Auguste, libellos*; cf. 5.6.18–19, **6**.14–15). Those who believe that he did not get patronage from Domitian dismiss such remarks as wishful thinking and point to unsuccessful appeals for help (e.g. 5.19, 6.10): in the case of the request for a water supply to M.'s town house (**11**) the absence of a poem thanking Domitian is used as evidence that the request was denied. But this is not conclusive (**11** intro.), and the fact that M. continued throughout Domitian's lifetime to address poems to him suggests that he had some hope of success. M. did receive the highly profitable *ius trium liberorum* from Domitian as well as Titus, though this does not prove that M. enjoyed special favour with Domitian, since Domitian ratified all the *beneficia* granted by his brother.[35]

In arguing that M.'s pleas for assistance from the emperor were rarely heard, Szelest adduces as evidence poems on Republican heroes (a touchy subject) or those on *caluities* (a matter about which the bald Domitian was apparently sensitive: cf. **72** intro.). But it is possible that, if M. did not receive patronage to the extent that he would have liked, it was not his fault but that of the genre in which he wrote. Pliny, though praising M.'s wit and ingenuity, is unconfident that his poetry will survive, and Domitian too might have thought that the lowly and ephemeral genre of epigram was not the ideal means of acquiring immortality for himself through verse (epigram seems not to have been included in Domitian's poetry competitions, in which Statius was a prominent winner).

To the second question posed above, a more definite answer can be proffered. Although many of the epigrams on Domitian might seem tedious to a modern reader, a considerable number are admirable for their compositional virtuosity, in particular, those epigrams where encomium is harnessed to wit.

Such pieces are scattered throughout books 1–10: Domitian, who is known to have had a sense of humour, no doubt welcomed these as a relief

---

[35] K. Coleman (in Grewing (1998b) 29–34) argues that because M. was a favourite of Titus, for whom he wrote the *De spectaculis* on the opening of the Colosseum, this might have alienated Domitian from M. and could explain his relatively ungenerous patronage of the poet.

from his usual diet of oleaginous eulogising. An early instance is **9b** in which M. feels able to jest flippantly on subjects of heartfelt importance to the emperor, marital legislation and maintenance of the civic birthrate. What M. is doing here is leavening encomium of the emperor with a well-known type of misogynistic humour which preaches that women are an evil necessity, a biological conduit for perpetuation of the human race which would ideally be dispensed with (see **9b**.4n.).

M.'s propensity for investing panegyric with humour may be further exemplified by an instance from a later book. In 8.21 he complains to the Morning Star of the tardiness of its rising, which is delaying the triumphant return to Rome of Domitian from his successful Danubian campaign. The epigram is a witty inversion of the so-called *alba* or dawn-song, in which an *amator* reproaches the dawn for its precipitate arrival that will perforce separate him from his mistress. But here the speaker's impatience with Phosphorus stems, not from his arrival, but from his non-arrival, and the expressions of longing which he expresses are not sexual in nature, but the rapturous *amor* of a patriot towards the emperor, whose ἐραστής (lover), in common with the citizenry, M. represents himself as being. As in **9b**, encomium of Domitian is encased in a frame which might seem humorously irreverent or mildly risqué. But Domitian, who was far from uncultured, must have appreciated the wit, otherwise M. would never have persisted: and in any case there was plenty of precedent for the wedding of panegyric with laughter.[36]

5   PERSONAL NAMES IN THE EPIGRAMS

M.'s use of personal names is one of the most striking features of the epigrams. Sometimes names are merely mentioned in passing, but more frequently, named individuals are the subject or the addressee of an epigram. They can be divided conveniently into the real and the fictional.

Epigrams may focus on historical characters, e.g. Fannius (**78**), or on contemporaries like the charioteer Scorpus (**28**) for whose existence there is independent inscriptional evidence. According to Sullivan (1991) 16, there are around 140 different identifiable friends and patrons in the epigrams. A number of these recur frequently throughout the corpus: Domitian apart,

[36] See further L. Watson, 'Martial 8.21, literary *lusus*, and imperial panegyric', *PLLS* 10 (1998) 359–72. The whole subject of wit in Martial's epigrams to Domitian has now been profitably addressed by Holzberg (2002): see especially 63–74.

among the most important are Flaccus (**53**. 1 n), Stella (cf. **13**, **14**), Faustinus (**4**.6n.) Aulus Pudens, and Julius Martialis (**18**.2n.). Some, like Stella, are known from other sources, others e.g. Flaccus,[37] are mentioned only by M., though there is no reason to doubt their reality.

Friends often appear as addressees of epigrams in which the poet airs his own views (e.g. **18**) or where the friend is invited to observe, or comment on, the behaviour of a third individual who is the subject of an attack. The effect is to engage the closer involvement of the reader, who can readily identify with the person addressed. The choice of addressee is random in the majority of such pieces, but this is not invariably so. For instance, it seems no coincidence that M. directed to his friend Flaccus an epigram (**15**) in which Maecenas, patron of Horatius Flaccus, plays a prominent rôle, while the use of Julius Martialis as the recipient of quasi-philosophic musings (e.g. **18**) might reflect the interests of that friend, or even recall in poetic form their real-life conversations.

Some of the friends or patrons addressed by M. are clearly fictitious.[38] This is certainly so when a named patron is the object of invective, e.g. Umber (**24**. 1 n.) and Caecilianus (**23**.2n.). Sometimes, too, the addressee of a satirical epigram is an obvious invention, e.g. Fabullus, whose name is chosen for its Catullan resonances (see **71**. 1 n.).

Fictitious named individuals are most commonly the targets of scoptic epigrams, on the principle that an anonymous addressee would diminish somewhat the sharpness of the satire. M. however makes it clear that these names do not represent real people. Of particular importance here is the prose preface to book 1: *spero me secutum in libellis meis tale temperamentum ut de illis queri non possit quisquis de se bene senserit, cum salua infimarum quoque personarum reuerentia ludant; quae adeo antiquis auctoribus defuit ut nominibus non tantum ueris abusi sint sed et magnis. mihi fama uilius constet et probetur in me nouissimum ingenium. absit a iocorum nostrorum simplicitate malignus interpres nec epigrammata mea scribat: improbe facit qui in alieno libro ingeniosus est.* Unlike his forebears – he has Catullus particularly in mind, as well as Lucilius – he will not attack even the lowliest persons by name, let alone the great. And the warning against maliciously reading into his epigrams an unintended meaning suggests that his personal names are not even meant as pseudonyms, but are used rather to portray character types (cf. 10.33.10 *parcere personis, dicere de uitiis*).[39]

---

[37] See Pitcher (1984).   [38] For fictitious names in M. see SB III 323–6.

[39] Despite the disclaimer, some did read the poems as personal attacks, e.g. 3.11.2, 9.95[b].3.

In disengaging his invective from reality, M. is of necessity disingenuous to some extent: his character portraits are no doubt based on personal observation of one or more individuals, even if his more elaborate creations like Zoilus are also influenced by literature. In general, however, M. avoids details which would identify a subject as real, though 'one must . . . wonder whether there was more than one rich cobbler in Bononia who put on public spectacles' (3. 16, 59, 99).[40]

Often a name is used on one occasion only, but some appear more frequently, inviting us to consider whether these are meant to allude to the same fictitious individual. An obvious yardstick is consistency of characterisation. Selius and Ligurinus, for instance, are invariably portrayed as a *captator cenae* and an inveterate reciter respectively, each featuring three times in the same book. Umber, on the other hand, at **24** and 12.81 plays the rôle of a patron who is stingy with gifts, but at 7.90.3 appears as a bad poet. In book 3, a series of epigrams placed close together (83, 87 (**29**), 97) concern a *fellatrix*, Chione, who refrains from vaginal intercourse (**29**). This character cannot be the same as the more sexually conventional Chione of 1.34,[41] nor the frigid[42] Chione in 11.60 who *non sentit opus*. The name Chione, then, is a typical appellation for a prostitute which M. suits to various contexts.

By contrast Zoilus, a name which M. uses more frequently than any other, is attacked for a number of vices, none of them contradictory, and it can be assumed that all allusions to him are to the same fictitious personage. This multi-faceted individual is M.'s most notable attempt at creating a believable character, as opposed to a mere representative of a character type. Zoilus appears in seven of the books, in books 2 and 11 often enough to constitute a cycle (see Barwick (1958) 302–3, Kay on 11.12 intro.). He exhibits the typical traits of the parvenu, most notably ostentation (e.g. **54**) and effeminacy. As with Trimalchio, his character is developed in the context of his appalling behaviour as host at a dinner party (**56**). There are sceptic epigrams about his sexual perversions (e.g. **56**, 2.42, 11.30, 6.91, 11.85), and he is ridiculed for his servile origins (e.g. 3.29, 11.12, 11.37, 11.54). The characterisation is also extended to include more original themes: for instance, in 11.54 he is depicted as stealing incense and spices from funerals, on the

[40] Sullivan (1991) 64. For a different view see Garthwaite (1998) 168–9.
[41] She is offered as an *exemplum* of 'normal' but discreet sex to an adulteress, Lesbia, who makes no attempt to hide her *furta*.
[42] For exploitation of the etymological resonances of the name cf. **75**.

basis that an ex-slave might well be a thief, while in **74** the physiognomic theory that vice is manifest in bodily flaws is exploited in a description of Zoilus as physically deformed, at least in Roman eyes.

Though the names of imaginary persons may have no special significance (e.g. Caelius in **73** or Tongilianus in **65**), more often, they are meaningful.[43] A name may be chosen for the sake of an etymological pun (e.g. Chione, **75**); play on names may even be the whole point of the poem, as with Paulinus/Palinurus in **76**. Sometimes a name indicates social status, e.g. Thais (**70**) suggests a prostitute, Vacerra a Celtic immigrant (**64**.2n.). In **44** – an epigram particularly rich in the clever use of nomenclature – a member of the upper classes invites ridicule by raising the seven children of his wife by various of their slaves. The use of typically aristocratic names for the couple – Cinna and Marulla – not only announces their social class but serves to underscore the disparity in status between the wife and her lovers.

The choice of a name appropriate to the vice for which the subject is attacked is common: examples include Philaenis (**50** and **84**), Sotades (**48**), Telesilla (**43**) and Linus (**69**). Alternatively, a name might be humorously unsuitable (κατ' ἀντίφρασιν) e.g. Chione (**75**), Ligurinus (**68**) or Lupercus (**47**).

Finally, a name may have literary associations: this is seen most often in epigrams which are Catullan in inspiration, such as the attack on Catulla (**40**) or on Fabullus (**31**) who, like Catullus himself in his invitation to Fabullus, provides the guests with ointment but leaves them hungry.

6 THE STRUCTURE AND STYLE OF THE EPIGRAMS

Analyses of M.'s formal structures and epigrammatic techniques generally start with Lessing's oft-repeated dictum that a Martialian epigram is typically built around the sequence *Erwartung-Aufschluss*: that is to say, a 'set-up' in which the reader's curiosity is aroused regarding a specific subject, and a 'conclusion', in which M. provides personal, often witty, comment thereon.[44] Hand in hand with this went the observation that M.'s epigrams exhibit a bipartite structure and characteristically end in some amusing or trenchantly expressed point (*sententia*). The brief 1.24, *aspicis incomptis illum, Deciane, capillis | cuius et ipse times triste supercilium, | qui loquitur Curios et assertoresque Camillos? | nolito fronti credere: nupsit heri*, will exemplify what Lessing

---

[43] For significant names in M. see Giegengack (1969).
[44] See conveniently Sullivan (1991) 222–4.

had in mind. This piece attacks one of M.'s favourite targets, the pathic homosexual who masquerades as the very embodiment of old-fashioned morality. Lines 1–3 'set up' the victim, drawing pointed attention (*aspicis?*) to his ostentatious advertisement of his uncompromising integrity, the first half of 4 proffers the observation that all is not as it seems, and the concluding *nupsit heri* explodes the carefully nurtured illusion; *nubere*, the *mot juste* for a women marrying a man, discloses that the purported paragon of virtue plays the female or receptive role in a same-sex relationship.

Seminal though Lessing's aperçus are, they have provoked as much dissent as approval. It is objected *inter alia* that *Erwartung* and *Aufschluss* are misleading terms, and that it is better to a speak of an 'objective' (first) and 'subjective' (second) part to the epigram;[45] that his insistence on a bipartite structure downplays the unity of a Martialian epigram and ignores the dynamic movement which enlivens and sustains it;[46] that Lessing's schema is predicated on the scoptic pieces for which M. is most famous and consequently does not fit the numerous epigrams of other types to be found in his *oeuvre* (especially the epideictic, declamatory and laudatory pieces);[47] that the sentiments roused by an epigram of M. are far more varied than the 'curiosity' which Lessing diagnosed as their driving force;[48] and that he failed to identify rhetorical theory and the contemporary taste for a rhetorical style as the inspiration for the 'point' which is M.'s chief glory.[49]

Yet despite these methodological shortcomings, Lessing was right in one irrefutable essential: the centrality of the conclusion to the working of M.'s epigrams.[50] As noted, these are typically rounded off with some incisive or amusing *bon mot*. This is true in particular of the short poems, though the longer pieces by no means lack such 'point' (sometimes, it must be conceded, rather factitiously appended).[51] A particularly effective instance of this closural technique is 4.69: *tu Setina quidem semper uel Massica ponis,* | *Papyle, sed rumor tam bona uina negat:* | *diceris hac factus caelebs quater esse lagona.* | *nec puto nec credo, Papyle, nec sitio.* Papylus serves only the best of wines, but M. must refuse his invitation to have a drink: it's not that he believes the reports

---

[45] Barwick (1959) 5.

[46] Citroni (1969), an important critique of Lessing and his influence, at 225, 238 and 242, Kay (1985) 7–9.

[47] Citroni (1969) 220, Howell (1980) 11, Sullivan (1991) 223–4.

[48] Citroni (1969) 226.   [49] Barwick (1959) 36.   [50] Cf. Citroni (1969) 222.

[51] E.g. 4.55, 8.49. An excellent treatment of various species of wit in Martial, especially the witty conclusion, is now found in Holzberg (2002) 86–97.

that they are lethal; he simply isn't thirsty. This is a nice example of M.'s often devastating irony and his tendency to collapse the boundaries of logic for humorous purposes:[52] the issue of the rumours and M.'s rejection of Papylus' invitation are presented, in a dead-pan fashion, as independent phenomena – a flagrant denial of the premise of 4.69, which strongly insinuates their interconnectedness.

Another illustration of the pointed or witty conclusion is 4.28, *donasti tenero, Chloe, Luperco | Hispanas Tyriasque coccinasque | et lotam tepido togam Galaeso, | Indos sardonychas, Scythas zmaragdos, | et centum dominos nouae monetae: | et quidquid petit usque et usque donas. | uae glabraria, uae tibi misella! | nudam te statuet tuus Lupercus.* M. here mocks that common butt of satiric humour, the woman who showers expensive gifts on a young gigolo in return for sexual services. Chloe has given so many costly cloaks, precious stones etc. to Lupercus that she will end up 'naked'; the adjective plays alike on its literal sense to effect a contrast with the abundantly well-clothed Lupercus and activates its transferred meaning 'stripped of cash', the result of Chloe's sexually driven extravagances. The particular focus of the humour is thus a pun: puns and word-play are one of the fundamental weapons in M.'s armoury of wit.[53] Equally characteristic is the use of a meaningful name to enhance that wit.[54] Lupercus, the male protagonist, recalls the Luperci, who at the festival of the Lupercalia ran largely unclothed round the Palatine: but, in a piece of comic inversion, the present Lupercus is generously provided with apparel, and it is Chloe, his benefactress, who will end up naked. Other aspects too of 4.28 are characteristic of M.'s epigrammatic technique: the repetition for emphasis at the end of a poem of a key phrase or a name,[55] a tendency to build up detailed catalogues (seen here only in embryonic form but capable of reaching imposing dimensions), and a taste for the striking verbal coinage,[56] in the present case *glabraria*, 'a lover of smooth young skin'.

M.'s endings depend in large measure on an effect of surprise.[57] One instance is 6.51, *quod conuiuaris sine me tam saepe, Luperce, | inueni noceam qua*

---

[52] Cf. Sullivan (1991) 242–4.

[53] Joepgen (1967), Sullivan (1991) 244–8, Grewing (1998a).

[54] Cf. n.42.

[55] E.g. 2.55, 11.23. Cf. P. Laurens, *L'abeille dans l'ambre* (Paris 1989) 270–2, 275–9.

[56] See 24–5 below.

[57] O. Gerlach, *De Martialis figurae ἀπροσδόκητον quae uocatur usu* (Diss. Jena 1911), who concludes (49) that M. used the device of the unexpected conclusion much more extensively, and in a far more varied fashion, than any of his predecessors.

ratione tibi. | *irascor: licet usque uoces mittasque rogesque* —| *'quid facies?'* inquis. *'quid faciam'? ueniam.* After the first three lines of this complaint against a patron who fails to invite M. to dinner we expect the poet to say that, even if Lupercus does come up with an invitation, he will refuse. Instead he states that he will come: thus will he better vent his anger upon one who evidently does not desire his company. Integral to the effect of surprise is an element of paradox, a device for which M. has a conspicuous predilection.[58] 5.42, a somewhat longer poem than those hitherto examined, offers an elegant instance. Here M. rounds off an itemised list of the various ways in which one's fortune can be lost (theft, house fire etc.) with the paradoxical observation *quas dederis, solas semper habebis opes*, only the money that you give away to your friends will be permanently yours (in the sense that the memory of your generosity will be everlasting).

M.'s status as a satirical humorist is unquestioned (whether in a spirit of social criticism or moral nihilism has been disputed).[59] Some of the means by which he attains that status have been examined above. Others may be briefly noticed, such as M.'s well-developed eye for the ridiculous, whether it be the absurd poetic conceit of calling Jupiter the mother of Dionysus (the god was born from Zeus' thigh: one might with as little sense call Semele his father, 5.72), the risible long-windedness of a pleader who requires seven water clocks and multiple glasses of water in order to speak (he could expedite matters by drinking from the clocks, 6.35) or the grotesque contortions engaged in by a social climber in order to assert a spurious claim to a place on the equestrian benches (5.14). This last piece exhibits a marked degree of hyperbole and satiric exaggeration, and this too is pivotal to M.'s thesaurus of wit:[60] 11.84, on a brutal barber, and 7.18, on Galla, who suffers from obstreperous vaginal farts (*poppysmata cunni*) during intercourse, are two instances among many. Another favoured technique is radical recontextualisation of the meaning of a word or phrase so as to subvert its apparent or commonly accepted sense: examples include 1.84 (the ironically named Quirinalis[61] redefines the meaning of *paterfamiliae* by fathering a brood of bastards on the female members of his *familia*, slave household),

[58] Cf. Sullivan (1991) 240–1.

[59] For the former position, cf. Holzberg (1986): for the latter, Seel (1961). Seel's views, though more trenchantly expressed, essentially echo those of Lessing: cf. Citroni (1969) 222. Holzberg (2002), in a complete recantation of his previous position, now regards Martial as a classic of wit, not moralising satire.

[60] Cf. Sullivan (1991) 248.   [61] Cf. Giegengack (1969) 67–8.

5.47 (Philo swears that he never dines at home: rightly so, since he does not dine, i.e. goes hungry, when he fails to secure an invitation) and 10.27 (Diodorus celebrates his birthday, *natalis*, in lavish style. How odd, since he was never born, *natus*; according to Roman law persons born into slavery had no legal existence). Closely related to such epigrams are those in which the initial thought is drastically derailed: the pattern may be illustrated by 2.56[62] where the reputation of a provincial governor's wife for rapacity and greed is nullified by the revelation that she is exceedingly liberal – of her sexual favours. Parody too is not alien to M.'s repertoire, though scarcely as prominent as in Juvenal; instances are 1.45, 1.50, 2.41 and 5.66.

'Point' in M. is often achieved by using figures of thought or speech.[63] Alliteration, for example, a feature of both the panegyric and the scoptic epigrams, is deployed with particular effectiveness in the latter to underline the satiric barb.[64] Thus in 1.37, *uentris onus misero, nec te pudet, excipis auro,* | *Basse, bibis uitro: carius ergo cacas*, the antiphonal *b*'s and *c*'s neatly mock the pretentiousness of Bassus' bowel habits, while in 1.19, *si memini, fuerant tibi quattuor, Aelia, dentes:* | *expulit una duos tussis et una duos.* | *iam secura potes totis tussire diebus:* | *nil istic quod agat tertia tussis habet* the repeated *t*'s in lines 3–4 sarcastically mimic the explosive force of Aelia's persistent coughing. In the following instance, 1.79, the alliteration may be allowed to speak for itself: *semper agis causas et res agis, Attale, semper:* | *est, non est quod agas, Attale, semper agis.* | *si res et causae desunt, agis, mulas.* | *Attale, ne quod agas desit, agas animam*. The epigram is mentioned here because it exemplifies another prominent feature of M.'s rhetorical style, the insistent repetition of words or phrases as a build-up to a satiric or pointed climax: other instances are 1.109, 2.4, 3.26, 4.39, **26**, 5.61, 7.10 and 9.97. Circumstantiality of detail is a pronounced feature of M.'s writing, and no reader can fail to be struck by his fondness for constructing elaborate inventories or comparisons (*cumulatio*), sometimes for encomiastic purposes (e.g. 3.58, **52**, 5.37, **30**, **18**), but more commonly for satiric ends,[65] as in 4.4, on the hypermalodorous Bassa. Finally in this connexion one may note Quintilian's categorisation (*Inst.* 8.5.5) of various classes of *sententia* used to effect a pointed conclusion: *sunt etiam qui decem genera fecerint . . . per interrogationem, per comparationem, infitiationem, similitudinem, admirationem et cetera huius modi*. All five categories named by Quintilian are employed by M., but of these his personal favourite was the

---

[62] Other examples: 7.90, 9.58.   [63] Sullivan (1991) 249.   [64] Adamik (1975).
[65] A detailed list in Kay on 11.21 intro.

sententia per interrogationem. This is evident from the number of epigrams which end with an incisively phrased question, sometimes buttressed by an apostrophe in the shape of *rogo.* Two examples are **78** *hostem cum fugeret, se Fannius ipse peremit. | hic, rogo, non furor est, ne moriare, mori?*, and 2.60, on Hyllus who 'fucks the wife of an armed tribune', but waxes indignant at the suggestion that he might be punished by castration: *'non licet hoc'. quid, tu quod facis, Hylle, licet?*

M. is by no means shy of protesting his popularity,[66] but tempers such claims by insistently playing down his poetic talents.[67] Among such gestures of artistic self-disparagement are 1.16, *sunt bona, sunt quaedam mediocria, sunt mala plura | quae legis hic: aliter non fit, Auite, liber.*[68] Though such affectation of modesty is a conventional posture, to which M. may have been led in particular by Catullus' trivialising of his literary output as *ineptiae* or *nugae*, it must be said that there is a good deal of justice in the poet's assessment of his work as uneven in quality. Many of M.'s epigrams will strike the modern reader as feeble,[69] forced,[70] frigid, or downright tedious,[71] and may have so struck the ancient reader, even granting that Greek and Roman occasional verse was receptive of much material that nowadays seems unfunny or offensive.[72] Accordingly, it should be possible to analyse with some semblance of objectivity why some epigrams do not seem to come off. In 4.36, for example, *cana est barba tibi, nigra est coma: tinguere barbam | non potes – haec causa est – et potes, Ole, comam*, not only is the joke extremely tired, but more importantly, it is sprung in the first line instead of being held over for greater effect until the second, as in M.'s more felicitous compositions. Similarly, the conclusion of 6.52, an epitaph for a young barber with a feathery touch, *sis licet, ut debes, tellus, placata leuisque, | artificis leuior non potes esse manu* is a piece of over-ingenious preciosity, particularly given the virtuoso manner in which M. elsewhere deployed the *sit tibi terra leuis* formula.[73] Likewise, few will relish encomiastic pieces such as 7.60, 8.36, 8.49, 8.78, and 9.64, which disappoint, not because they are addressed to Domitian, but on account of their vapid and adulatory hyperbole (9.65 shows that M. is capable of doing this kind of thing much better). Lastly, M's many epideictic pieces nowadays hardly fire the imagination. Despite a vogue

---

[66] Cf. 4.49.10, 6.82.3–5, Howell on 1.1.2.

[67] E.g. 9 *praef.* 5–9. Cf. Kay, intro to 11.1, Sullivan (1991) 59–63.

[68] Cf. 7.81, 90.   [69] Some personal non-favourites: 2.67, 3.59, 4.62.

[70] E.g. 2.35, 2.52, 4.47, 4.74.   [71] Such as 3.58 or 5.65.

[72] Cf. Nisbet (1998) 11.   [73] 5.37.9–10, **84**. 11–12.

in the first and second centuries AD for declamatory extemporisations, did they, one wonders, provoke the enthusiasm of any but their immediate recipients?

7 THE LANGUAGE OF THE EPIGRAMS

(i) *The popular character of M.'s language*

(a) *Obscenity*

The use of basic obscenities is the feature which most clearly distinguishes Latin epigram not only from the 'higher' Roman genres, but also from the Greek epigram.[74] The employment of obscenity is thus integral to M.'s establishing himself as the successor of Catullus and Marsus. It is this tradition which he himself invokes in justifying his use of the *lasciua uerborum ueritas*;[75] an apology occasioned not merely by conventional attitudes to obscenity (i.e. that it contravenes Roman *dignitas*, or is a sign of personal immorality on the part of the writer) but especially necessary in the light of Domitian's recent assumption of the censorship *in perpetuum*. A second, equally important reason for the prominence of obscenity in the epigrams is adverted to in 1.35.3–5 *hi libelli,* | *tamquam coniugibus suis mariti,* | *non possunt sine mentula placere.*[76] M.'s readers, in other words, have a taste for the sexually explicit, and pleasing them is a major factor in the poet's quest for popularity.

M. uses all the basic obscenities employed by Catullus as well as several others, e.g. *ceuere, cunnilingus* and *fellator*. At least some of these he may have introduced into Latin literature.[77] With two exceptions (see below), such vocabulary is found in every book. In the last third of book 3 and the whole of book 11, however, the frequency is significantly increased: this is linked

[74] On the contrast between Greek and Roman epigram in this respect, see A. E. Richlin, 'Sexual terms and themes in Roman satire and related genres' (Dissertation, Yale 1978), 102–3, Adams, *LSV* 219–20.

[75] See book 1 *praef. lasciuam uerborum ueritatem, id est epigrammaton linguam, excusarem, si meum esset exemplum: sic scribit Catullus, sic Marsus, sic Pedo, sic Gaetulicus, sic quicumque perlegitur.* On the *apologia*, see Sullivan (1991) 64–74.

[76] Cf. 3.69, where the linguistically chaste epigrams of Cosconius are said to be fit, unlike those of M., to be read only by schoolchildren.

[77] We cannot know the extent to which M.'s lost epigrammatic predecessors anticipated him, and the relative dates of M. and the *Carmina Priapea*, where obscenity is widely used, are uncertain, though it has recently been argued that the *Priapea* predate M.: cf. M. Kissel, *RhM* 137 (1994) 299–311, O'Connor in Grewing (1998b) 189.

in the case of book 11 to the relaxed atmosphere following the succession of Nerva (11.2.5–6). By contrast, obscene language is completely absent from books 5 and 8, a phenomenon closely associated with the dedication of these books to Domitian, whose rôle as *censor perpetuus* was thereby honoured.

The function of obscene language is twofold: it contributes in a general way to the everyday colouring of epigram, and it is employed in the context of invective to degrade and insult. The majority of M.'s obscene epigrams are directed against those who indulge in sexual practices which diverge from the accepted norm: these include oral sex, passive homosexuality, Lesbianism, and adultery. Obscene words are also used insultingly in non-sexual contexts such as attacks on physical abnormalities (e.g. 3.98 *sit culus tibi quam macer, requiris?* | *pedicare potes, Sabelle, culo*), or else for purely comic effect, as in **85**, with its unexpected use of *mentula* in the concluding line.

It is worth observing that obscene language is almost never employed for reasons of pornography, that is with the express purpose of producing sexual arousal in the reader, even though M. claims that this is one of its functions: cf. 11.16.5–8 *o quotiens rigida pulsabis pallia uena,* | *sis grauior Curio Fabricioque licet!* | *tu quoque nequitias nostri lususque libelli* | *uda, puella, leges*. A parallel may be drawn here with the use of obscenity in Aristophanic comedy, which has invective as its main aim, but produces the incidental effect of arousing the reader, albeit in a more transitory way than pornography proper.[78] On occasion, however, the aim of titillation is to the fore. In 3.68, which marks the end of the 'clean' part of the book, M. disingenuously warns his female readers about the sexual explicitness of the remaining epigrams (3–4). Far from discouraging these from perusing the second section of the book, however, M. goes to some pains to draw their attention to its obscene character, for instance, by the elaborate and unnecessarily long periphrasis for *mentula* (7–10). Finally, the closing couplet, *si bene te noui, longum iam lassa libellum* | *ponebas, totum nunc studiosa legis*, is a clear invitation to the *matronae* to continue reading. The game is continued in poem 86, where the pretence that *matronae* should keep away from poems containing obscene language is dropped altogether.

---

[78] Cf. Henderson (1991) 7–13. Kay (1985) 101 thinks M.'s remarks in 11.16 are not meant seriously; Richlin (n. 74) 106–7, by contrast, argues that M.'s attacks on sexual vices, being impersonal and conventional, are not true invective but designed solely to titillate. See also Holzberg (2002) 112–14.

(b)   Everyday language

The epigrams contain a substantial number of words which are mostly avoided in the more elevated genres of poetry, but are employed by prose writers such as Cicero (in the speeches) and Caesar. These include many adverbs, such as *cito, diligenter,* and *longius.* More striking is the employment of an extraordinarily large number of words from the everyday sphere; some of these are elsewhere found mainly in the lowlier genres (e.g. *caballus*), others M. may have introduced into poetry. Mundane words of foreign provenance abound, mostly Greek (e.g. *harpastum* 'handball' (**50**.4n.), *enterocele* 'intestinal hernia', *opthalmicus* 'eye doctor' (**61**.1 n.) but occasionally Spanish (e.g. *balux* 'gold-dust'), or Celtic/Gallic (e.g. *bardocucullus* = a type of hooded cloak, *draucus* 'a strong man'). In addition, M. often uses formations that are especially common in everyday speech: words with the suffix *-o* e.g. *ardalio,* terms for banausic occupations and trades ending in *-arius* or *-tor* (e.g. *salarius, balneator*), compound verbs like *perosculari,* and diminutives which are the popular term for some ordinary object, e.g. *flabellum,* 'fan', *aureolus* [*nummus*], a type of gold coin, or which have an emotional colouring e.g. *labellum, paruulus, lectulus.* There are also vulgar spellings e.g. *olla* for *aula* or *copo* for *caupo.*

Popular language not only makes an important contribution to the everyday flavour of the epigrams, but is also employed for other effects. A word-type associated with familiar speech may be invented for purposes of humour and satire, e.g. the desiderative form *cenaturire* at 11.77.3, where Vacerra, who spends all day in the public toilets in the hope of obtaining a dinner invitation, *cenaturit ... non cacaturit* 'wants to dine, not to shit'. *cacaturire* is attested in a Pompeian inscription; M. has apparently coined *cenaturire* by analogy for the sake of an alliterative pun.[79]

Less elevated language may equally be used to mirror the style of everyday discourse. For instance, in 1.3, where the poet addresses his book in the tone of a master giving advice to a young slave, the informality is reinforced by the use of colloquial expressions, e.g. *crede mihi, nasum rhinocerotis habent, i fuge,* and everyday words such as *sophos,* found only in M. and Petronius. In **56**, familiar language is employed freely in order to match by its vulgar flavour both Zoilus' boorish manners and his sexual tastes; it may also suggest the lowliness of the social class from which he originated. The piece contains an abundance of words with a colloquial or everyday

[79] Sullivan (1991) 230 n.25, Kay *ad loc.*

colouring, many of which make their entry into literature with M., e.g. *galbinatus, tractatrix,* and *rhoncus.* The neologism *sciscitator* (**56**.16n.), coined on the analogy of words ending in *-tor* and used to designate a slave's occupation, is particularly amusing.

(*ii*) The language of invective and satire

Several word-groups which are very common in M. are elsewhere associated with invective and satire, both in the 'lower' genres of poetry and prose and sometimes also in more elevated texts like Cicero's speeches. These include the deflationary diminutive, as well as formations with the suffixes *-atus* and words in *-arius,* or in *-tor/-trix,* which suggest excessive devotion to a vice or habit. Here M.'s ingenuity is especially prominent and many of his usages in these categories, as far as we can tell, are his own coinages. Examples include *putidula* (**39**.4n.), *galbinatus* (**56**.5n.), *infantaria* (**71**.3n.) and *sudatrix* (**19**.5n.).

M. also obtains witty or satiric effects by employing words which are in themselves unremarkable in a new sense, or by placing them in a novel combination with another word. At **32**.16, for instance, *longa,* in the unusual sense of 'extended at full length', vividly describes the hand of the gluttonous diner Santra, who stretches under the table as far as he can reach in order to steal table scraps from the floor. *nouae iuncturae,* among the most remarkable aspects of M.'s innovatory uses of language, include *cana pruna* (**24**.7n.), *lippa ficus* (**32**.12n.) and *carnifices pedes* (**36**.10).

Figures of speech are also found in satiric contexts. For instance Laietanian wine, which was known for its inferior quality, is referred to by metonymy as *faex Laietana* (1.26.9), literally 'Laietanian dregs'.[80] M. has many innovatory uses of metaphor e.g. *aluta* (lit. 'soft leather'), of a limp and impotent penis (11.60.3), and the topographical *gemina Symplegas culi,* 'the twin clashing rocks (Symplegades) of your bum', a colourful description of a steatopygic woman (11.99.5).

Finally, M. is fond of witty word-play of various sorts. A good example is **76** *minxisti currente semel, Pauline, carina.* | *meiere uis iterum? iam Palinurus eris,* which conjoins two common types, one involving proper names, the other the etymological pun in *currente carina* (see *ad loc.*).[81]

[80] Cf. **24**.6n.   [81] Cf. n.53.

(iii)   Poetic language

Just as M.'s corpus contains a relatively large number of prosaic/familiar words, there is also a smaller percentage of 'poetic' vocabulary than in the higher genres. M.'s use of poetic words is for the most part unremarkable, with the prominent exception of adjectives derived from proper names, a type of word of which M. is especially fond.[82] In this area the poet's inventiveness is noteworthy, e.g. the epithet *Antenoreus* is used (1.76.2) for 'Patavian' because Antenor was the mythical founder of that city. New *iuncturae* include *Phaethontis gutta* for amber (4.32.1),[83] and the use of *Parrhasius* (poetic for 'Arcadian') with *domus* and *aula* to denote the imperial residence on the Palatine, the hill where the Arcadian Evander settled.[84]

Unsurprisingly, poetic language is most frequently employed by M. in epigrams with a more serious tone, such as the eulogistic pieces addressed to the emperor or other patrons, e.g. the description of the Spanish estate received from Marcella (**17**). But poetic language is also often used in satiric contexts for a mock-serious effect, and it is in this area that M. displays the greatest originality. For instance, Titius' over-sized *columna* (penis) is described as *tanta . . . | quantam Lampsaciae colunt puellae*,[85] while Selius is made to flatter a runner by praising his *Achilleos pedes* (**21**.4n.). At 5.41.2 an effeminate man is colourfully described as *concubino mollior Celaenaeo*, more effeminate than the castrated Attis, beloved of the Phrygian goddess Cybele. The mock elevation of the phrase *caluam trifilem semitatus unguento*, 'his bald pate with its three remaining hairs streaked with unguent', enhances the absurdity of a man's attempts at dissemblance (see **72**.2n.).

(iv)   Intertextuality

Frequently M. pays homage to his predecessor Catullus by the use of Catullan language (see on **31** and **40**). On other occasions, M. selects language which deliberately recalls a poetic predecessor in order to make a special point: the phenomenon has been discussed on **15** (Virgil) and on

---

[82] Approximately 125 different words used by M. come under this heading.

[83] An allusion to the mythical explanation of the origin of amber drops as the tears shed by Phaethon's sisters on his death.

[84] Cf. Virg. *A.* 11.31 *Parrhasius Euander*. M. must have been pleased with this creation since he uses the expression four times (7.56.2, 7.99.3, 8.36.3, **12**.1).

[85] 11.51.1–2: an allusion to the cult of Priapus at Lampsacus.

7, an attack on contemporary epic poets, where the choice of vocabulary strongly suggests that the specific target of the poem is Statius.

(v) Stylistic variation in the epigrams

The epigrams exhibit a diversity of language which matches the diverse range of tone and subject matter. In general, the stylistic register varies according to theme and content, the satiric epigrams being the least linguistically elevated, those for the emperor containing less popular language and a greater number of poetic words. Tone is also a key factor in determining word selection: thus pieces addressed to the emperor or other patrons in witty or playful mood admit a greater degree of less elevated language than is usual in this type of epigram.[86] Occasionally the 'low' stylistic level of the genre of epigram permits the use of unpoetic words even in epigrams where the mood and language are comparatively more elevated. For instance, in **11**, carefully composed in high-flown style (cf. 5n.), the unusual word *antlia* (4), an everyday term describing a device for drawing water, is intrusive.

8 THE METRES OF THE EPIGRAMS[87]

With the exception of twelve poems, M. uses three metres (i) the elegiac couplet (ii) the Phalaecean hendecasyllable (iii) the choliambic ('limping' iambic), also known as the scazon.

(i) The elegiac couplet

This is the metre of epigram *par excellence*, and the one most commonly employed by M.[88] It is the usual metre in adulatory poems addressed to the emperor and other patrons, likewise in epitaphic and deictic poems, though it is also routinely found in the satiric epigrams.

---

[86] E.g. 5.15, addressed to Domitian in playful tones, has the prosaic *nemo, sane* and *iste*. For a full treatment of M's language, see P. Watson, *Glotta* 2002 (forthcoming).

[87] Details of M.'s metres in Birt *apud* Friedländer (1886) 1 26–50, C. Giarratano, *De M. Val. Martialis re metrica* (Naples 1908), Sáez (1998).

[88] It is the predominant metre of books 13 and 14 and the *De spectaculis*. On average it is used in about 75 per cent of the epigrams, though the figure is lower for book 12, which contains an unusually high percentage of hendecasyllabic poems.

M.'s use of the metre is closest to Ovid, except that whereas Ovid almost invariably ends the pentameter with a disyllable, M. sometimes employs polysyllabic endings, thus throwing emphasis on the final word: e.g. **59**.2 *uxorem pascit Gellius et futuit.*[89] This practice, along with the occasional use of monosyllabic endings and elision, gives his couplets a stronger ending than those of Augustan verse. M., in sum, harnesses metre to context, the metrically striking ending enhancing the witty point with which the epigrams often conclude (cf. **59**.2 cited above).

(ii)   The hendecasyllable

The metre is common in the lighter genres of Greek and Latin poetry, including epigram.[90] M. however employs it with unusual frequency,[91] no doubt in imitation of his predecessor Catullus, who uses the metre in two thirds of the polymetrics 1–60.[92] Although the hendecasyllable was often associated with obscenity (Quint. *Inst.* 1.8.6, Plin. *Ep.* 4.14) M. follows Catullus[93] in employing it in a wide variety of contexts, not only in satiric epigrams (e.g. **37**, **68**, **73** and the parodic **26**), but also in more serious contexts, such as philosophising about the ideal life (**18**; cf. **19**), eulogy of a patron's baths (**30**) and poems concerning the emperor (**10**, **12**). It is interesting, however, that even though the hendecasyllable is not satiric *per se*, in pairs of related poems, where the first is a serious treatment of a theme and the second a witty variant, the elegiac couplet is often used in the first poem, the hendecasyllable in the second (cf. **9a/b** and 5.11 and 12).[94] On occasion, M.'s use of the hendecasyllable has a special significance,

---

[89] Cf. Raven (1965) 107–8, G. A. Wilkinson, *CQ* 42 (1948) 71.

[90] A history of its use in J. W. Loomis, *Studies in Catullan verse* (Leiden 1972) 34–42.

[91] Overall, it appears in 228 epigrams in books 1–12 – just under 20 per cent, though the figures vary considerably from book to book, ranging from round 10 per cent in books 3 and 9 to an exceptional 38 poems (39 per cent) in book 12. The average for books 1–11 is 17.7 per cent.

[92] In regarding Catullus as an epigrammatist, M. made no distinction between Catullus' polymetrics and the elegiac 69–116.

[93] Catullus uses it for invective (e.g. 16), a dedicatory poem (1), erotic poems (2, 3, 5, 7) and an invitation to dinner (13).

[94] Note also **86**, a mock epitaph, which is in hendecasyllables, rather than the usual metre for epitaphs, the elegiac couplet. These uses of the metre may arise from its association with informality, for which see L. Morgan, *PCPhS* 46 (2000) 99–120, esp. 115.

notably in epigrams where he pays homage to Catullus, such as **31**, **40** (see commentary) and 1.7 on Stella's pet dove.[95]

Whereas Catullus admits variation, especially in the first two syllables, in M. the pattern is fixed:[96]

$$— \; — \; —\cup\cup—\cup—\cup—\times$$

M. also avoids elision, again in contrast to Catullus, who has it on average once in every two lines.[97] When M. does employ the device, therefore, it often has particular import, as for instance at **31**.3 *res salsa est bene olere et esurire*, where the triple elision not only reinforces the Catullan flavour of the line but alludes specifically to the poem (Catullus 13) on which the epigram is based, which has twelve elisions in its fourteen verses.

(iii)   The scazon/choliambic ('limping' iambic)

This metre consists of an iambic trimeter in which the final short syllable is replaced with a long, effecting a 'limping close that calls a sneering halt to the line'.[98] It was associated particularly with the sixth-century BC Hipponax of Ephesos, to whose invective poetry the metre was specially suited. Later the scazon was employed by Greek and Latin poets for a wider variety of subject matter, though it retained its association with invective and satire.[99] Catullus, for instance, uses the metre eight times, mostly in contexts of invective, the notable exception being the Sirmio-poem (31).[100]

Like his predecessor, M. uses the scazon less frequently than his other major metres. It appears in 74 epigrams, i.e. just over 6 per cent of the total in books 1–12. The percentage of choliambic lines in the corpus is somewhat higher, however, since poems in the metre tend to be longer pieces.[101] In particular, scazons are employed in some of M.'s most prolonged and vivid attacks on individuals such as Zoilus (**56**), Santra (**32**) and Vacerra (**64**).

---

[95] For literary reminiscence determining metre, cf. 1.49, in the same metre as Horace's *Epodes* 1–10, where M.'s description of Bilbilis recalls the second *Epode*.

[96] For M.'s handling of the metre, which has been criticised as monotonous, see Raven (1965) 139, Ferguson (1970) 175.

[97] Ferguson (1970).

[98] See I. C. Cunningham ed., *Herodas Mimiambi* (Oxford 1971) 12.

[99] Cf. Loomis (n.90 above) 102–18, Kay on 11.61 intro.

[100] On Catullus' use of the scazon in 31, see Morgan (n. 94 above) 102–7.

[101] The 74 epigrams in scazons contain 778 lines, i.e. an average of more than 10 lines per poem. For a list of M.'s poems in scazons, see Raven (1965) 181.

The association of the metre with invective is thus maintained for the most part, but, as with Catullus' Sirmio poem, M. can on occasion employ the scazon in less expected places, such as two eulogies for Domitian at the beginning of book 9 (1 and 5).

Given that Hipponax, with whom the choliambic metre was especially associated, was particularly noted for his gross obscenity, one might have expected to find that M.'s scazons made a feature of obscene language. In fact, the opposite is the case. Scazons occur most often in book 5, from which obscenity is banished, while they are least common in the consciously sexual eleventh book. And in book 3 they are found mostly in the linguistically 'clean' first section, the main exceptions to this pattern being the poems on Zoilus (**56**) and on Vetustilla (3.93).[102]

The basic pattern used almost invariably by Catullus is:

$$\times - \cup - \quad \times \ - \cup - \cup - \ - \times$$

Catullus has a marked preference for spondees in both the first and third feet; this is also M.'s favourite scheme, used in 44 per cent of his choliambic verses.[103] M. however employs a much wider variety of patterns than his predecessor. In addition to the Catullan pattern shown above (which he uses in two thirds of his verses) he has 26 other variations, mostly involving the first half of the line, where dactyls, tribrachs and anapaests are found. A favourite pattern, for instance (used in 8 per cent of his lines) is anapaest + spondee + iambus.

9 THE STRUCTURE OF INDIVIDUAL BOOKS[104]

Within each book, the individual epigrams are arranged with care. The primary criterion is variety. Poems of equal length are juxtaposed comparatively rarely, while unusually long epigrams are often framed by shorter ones (e.g. 4.64, containing 36 lines, is preceded by a four-line epigram and followed by a single couplet). Similar variety is seen in the choice of metre, epigrams in the less-common metres being normally interspersed with

[102] Similarly, although hendecasyllables were connected with obscenity (Quint. *Inst.* 1.8.6, Plin. Ep. 4. 14), books 3 and 11 are among the books where they occur least frequently.

[103] For details of M.'s and Catullus' usage, see the table in Sáez (1998) 254.

[104] See most recently J. Scherf, 'Zur Komposition von Martials Gedichtbüchern 1–12', in Grewing (1998b) 119–38.

those in elegiacs; it is unusual to find two adjoining epigrams in hendecasyllables or scazons. The third area in which variety plays a rôle is content,
although on occasion epigrams on the same topic are grouped together for
special purposes, most notably in thematic pairings. Sometimes, as with
9a and **b**, the second poem complements the first, in other cases a pair of
epigrams constitutes different treatments of the same topic, such as the two
poems on the reciter Ligurinus (3.44 (**68**) and 45), or 3.56 and 57 (**66**) on
the water supply at Ravenna. One of M.'s longer pieces, the 32-line hexameter poem 6.64 (**6**), is immediately followed by an epigram (6.65) defending
both extended epigrams and the use of the hexameter. Another discussion
about the proper length of epigrams is **3**, where M. answers Cosconius'
criticism that his epigrams are too long by pointing out that even a couplet
by Cosconius is tedious. Not only is this epigram preceded by a two-line
poem but it is followed – unusually – by five epigrams consisting of single
couplets, a subtle means of demonstrating to Cosconius that M. is perfectly
capable of writing short epigrams as well as longer ones.

Each book has an overall structure, more apparent in some than others.
A sense of unity is often achieved by the appearance in the same book of thematic cycles, such as the 'lion and hare' epigrams of book 1.[105] Again, a book
may have a unifying theme, as for instance the praise of Domitian in book 8
or the Saturnalian licence associated with the new freedom under Nerva in
book 11;[106] in each case this is accompanied by linguistic propriety (absence
of obscenity in 8, preponderance of the same in 11). In general, the openings
of M.'s books tend to be more elaborate than the endings. The latter are
usually confined to a single poem announcing closure of the volume; in
some books (e.g. 5, 6, and 9) even this is absent. Openings are more important: they often serve a dedicatory function, and they may draw attention to
a distinctive feature of the book, e.g. 8.1 announces its purity of language;
such announcements are sometimes reinforced, as in 8, by a prose preface.

The unusual structure of book 3 is particularly interesting. It falls into
two clearly marked sections of unequal length, the first 68 poems containing
no explicitly sexual language,[107] whereas an abnormally large number of

---

[105] See Barwick (1958); on cycles in M. see also E. Merli in Grewing (1998b)
139–56.
[106] For unifying themes in other books, see Garthwaite (1993) for book 9, and the
same author in Grewing (1998b) 157–72 (book 5).
[107] They do however contain scatological indecency (*cacare* and *merda*): contrast
book 8 (addressed to Domitian) in which there is no obscenity of any kind.

obscene words is used in the remaining 32 epigrams. The change is signalled
in poem 69 (discussed earlier), where *matronae* are advised to discontinue
reading. M. then includes obscenities in virtually every poem thereafter, as
if to underline the linguistic difference between this and the earlier part of
the book. The difference is underscored even more strikingly by the strategic placing of poems on related topics in the two sections: themes treated
in veiled or metaphorical language in the first part of the book are repeated in the second, but with the addition of obscenity, affording a notable
contrast with the verbal purity of the corresponding epigrams in the first
section.[108]

10 THE WIDER TRADITION: MARTIAL AND EPIGRAM

An epigram (Greek *epigramma*, 'inscription') is properly a text, generally
brief, written down on stone or some other physical medium, such as a
drinking vessel. At an early stage the term came to be applied exclusively
to verse: by the fifth century BC (possibly earlier) the elegiac couplet was established as the metre of choice. The epigram was initially used for serious
and practical ends, for commemorative, dedicatory and, above all, sepulchral inscriptions. But one of the earliest surviving epigrams, probably from
the late eighth century, is humorous in character,[109] and the note of humour
or satire, which will become dominant in M., is sporadically sounded in
epigrams of the following centuries, such as Archilochus' elegiac quatrain
about the loss of his shield in battle (fr. 5 W). By the fourth century BC
fictional epigrams are being written. With the advent of the Hellenistic
period, epigram comes to be recognised as a literary genre in its own right,
and there was a simultaneous enlargement of its repertoire to include sym-
potic, hortatory and erotic themes: epigram now becomes receptive of the
most diverse kinds of subject matter. The epigrammatists of this period,
amongst whom the names of Asclepiades, Posidippus, Dioscorides and the
influential Callimachus stand out, have been preserved in the anthology
known as the *Garland of Meleager*, put together about 100 BC. Approximately
a century and a half later there followed a second anthology, the *Garland of
Philip*, containing the poets who were active in the intervening years. The

---

[108] Such pairs include 24/91, 32/76, 34/87, 51/72 and 67/78.
[109] Holzberg (2002) 20–1.

two *Garlands* form the core of the overlapping compilations known as the *Palatine anthology* and the *Planudean anthology*, collectively referred to as the *Greek anthology*, which constitutes our main surviving body of Greek literary epigram. In broad terms the *Garland of Meleager* has little in common with M., save for its sophisticated pungency and adoption of the Callimachean principle of ὀλιγοστιχίη, brevity, a watchword mostly, but not invariably, followed by M.[110] A closer relationship exists between M. and the writers represented in Philip's *Garland*, where the influence of rhetoric looms large, and a satirical strain begins to develop which reaches its apogee in M.[111] In a further sign of changing taste and accelerating adumbration of M.'s *oeuvre*, there occurs a prodigious development of narrative and epideictic epigram, often showing a pronounced taste for paradox or the sententious conclusion.[112] Also of relevance to M. is the marked growth in what may be styled 'courtly' epigram, reflecting the social position of Greek poets such as Crinagoras and Philodemus towards their Roman patrons. But it is with the practitioners of the immediately following era, the Neronian Lucillius and his follower Nicarchus, that the influence of Greek epigram upon M. becomes paramount.

Roughly 150 epigrams of Lucillius survive, nearly all of them satiric, and accordingly found in book 11 of the *Greek anthology*, which is in the main devoted to such material. It is with Lucillius that scoptic epigram becomes for the first time a recognised sub-category of the genre. Some 17 of M.'s epigrams trace their parentage to a Lucillian model.[113] Lucillius further significantly anticipates M. by attacking, not individuals,[114] but recognisable satiric or humorous types – the incompetent physician, the chronically slow runner, the thief, the insufferably bad poet, and so on. Central to Lucillian epigram is a large element of hyperbole, again a recognisably Martialian trait. Indeed the hyperbole at times verges on the surreal and can involve quite fantastic exaggeration, a tendency illustrated by *AP* 11.91,

[110] The dedicatory and epideictic epigrams of both *Garlands* may have inspired M.'s *Xenia* and *Apophoreta* (C. Salemme, *Orpheus* 8 (1987) 16–23).

[111] Thematic correspondences between the *Garland of Philip* and M. are noted by Sullivan (1991) 83–4.

[112] Laurens (1965) 322–3.

[113] Burnikel (1980). See conveniently Sullivan (1991) 88 n.17. Clear instances include *AP* 11.141 and M. 6.19, *AP* 11.257 and **60** and *AP* 11.239 and M. 4.4. A useful treatment of Martial and Lucillius now in Holzberg (2002) 101–9.

[114] Cf. the *praefatio* to book 1, further Sullivan (1991) 63–4.

'thin Stratonicus fixed on a reed a spike of corn and attaching himself to it by a hair hanged himself. And what happened? He was not heavy enough to hang down, but his dead body flies in the air above his gallows, although there is no wind.' As with M., 'point', particularly the pointed conclusion, is integral to Lucillian epigram (though it cannot be claimed as his original contribution to the genre).[115] One instance among many is *AP* 11.176, 'as he carried off winged Hermes, the servant of the gods, the Lord of the Arcadians, the cattle-rustler, who stood guard over this gymnasium, Aulus the night-thief said "often pupils are cleverer than their teachers"'. Like M., Lucillius often chose his names with an eye to humour, e.g. Olympicus the battered pugilist (*AP* 11.75–6) or the tiny Macron ('Tall': *AP* 11.95). More contentious is the recent suggestion that Lucillius was prepared to engage in light-hearted back-chat, verging on the cheeky, with Nero:[116] if so, there is a partial parallel with M., for whom addressing Domitian was by no means incompatible with humour. Of course there are also differences between Lucillius and M. It was implied above that Lucillian hyperbole goes further in its extravagance of detail than M.'s, which tends to rely rather on an overwhelming density of imagery. And it has frequently been noted that Lucillius' comic and satiric imagination is more intellectual, less emotionally engaged and less mordant than M.'s:[117] *AP* 11.160 and 249, which jest respectively on the subject of astrology and atomic theory, are good examples. Perhaps in consequence of this, Lucillius' epigrams are a great deal less amusing than M.'s.

The tendencies just noted in Lucillius are replicated in his poorly represented imitator and (possibly) close contemporary Nicarchus, but there is one significant addition, and that is his earthiness, a feature confirmed by some recently published epigrams from Oxyrhynchus (*POxy* 4502). *AP* 11.328, a sophisticated parody on the subject of τριπορνεία (triple penetration of a female) is a good example of a sexual humour which, barring the absence of explicit obscenities, has obvious affinities with M., but no real correlate in Lucillius.

---

[115] Nisbet (1998) 29–30 demonstrates this by analysing a recently published epigram of Posidippus (third century BC) which reads 'the Cretan Arcas, being deaf and unable to hear the crash of the waves on the beach or the booming of the winds, went straight home after making vows to Asclepius and found himself able to hear even words through bricks'.

[116] Nisbet (1998).   [117] E.g. by Laurens (1965) 335–6.

We now turn to the Latin epigrammatic tradition.[118] The earliest forays
in the field, metrical epitaphs for political luminaries and poets,[119] have
little detectable influence on M. The same goes for the earliest literary
epigrams, dating to the turn of the second and first centuries BC, written by
Q. Lutatius Catulus, Porcius Licinus and others, although one such piece,
by an otherwise unknown Papinius, does seem to underlie **39**.[120] The
Hellenistic tenor of these occasional verses leaps to the eye.[121] Of rather
more significance are pre-Catullan inscriptional *uersiculi*, one of which, in
its combination of sexual humour and explicit obscenity, looks forward
to M. The text runs: *hospes adhuc tumuli ni meias, ossa prec(antur).* | *nam, si uis
huic gratior esse, caca.* | *Vrticae monumenta uides, discede cacator.* | *non est hic tutum
culu(m) aperire tibi.*[122] The conjunction of the above two features is in fact a
distinctive marker of Latin epigram; it is visible, for example, in Octavian's
highly explicit attack on Fulvia's sexual habits quoted by M. in defence of
his own relish for *nuda uerba* (11.20), or the lengthy list of Roman grandees
who, according to the Younger Pliny (*Ep.* 5.3), dabbled in this kind of risqué
material.

The primary influence on M. has always been recognised as Catullus.[123]
The poet himself trumpeted that fact, mentioning the latter's name more
than twenty times and foregrounding his Catullan inheritance in significant programmatic contexts.[124] This stands in pointed contrast to M.'s
reticence concerning his debt to his Greek models, an omission which
has its origins in an enthusiastic championing of Roman literary self-
awareness and a characteristically Roman tendency, not shared by Greek
exponents of the genre, to utilise frankly sexual language in epigrammatic
contexts.[125] A little more surprising is M.'s silence regarding Catullus'

---

[118] The best treatment is by Kay 9–13.   [119] Cf. Kay 9–10.

[120] Quoted in the introduction to **39**.

[121] E.g. the epigram of Porcus Licinus (*apud* Kay 11) uses the same conceit as *AP*
9.15, a man so enflamed with love that he can kindle a literal fire.

[122] *CIL* IV 8899. A brief discussion in Courtney (1995) 368–9.

[123] Paukstadt (1876), Schulze (1887), Ferguson (1963), Swann (1994).

[124] Paukstadt (1876) 5–9.

[125] Cf. *praef.* I. 10–17 *lasciuam uerborum ueritatem, id est epigrammaton linguam, excusarem,
si meum esset exemplum. sic scribit Catullus, sic Marsus, sic Pedo, sic Gaetulicus, sic quicumque
perlegitur. si quis tamen tam ambitiose tristis est ut apud illum in nulla pagina latine loqui fas
sit, potest epistula uel potius titulo contentus esse. epigrammata illis scribuntur qui solent spectare
Florales* with Howell, 11.20.2 and 10.

fellow-neoterics, since they shared with Catullus a relish for punishing invective and sexual satire which in important ways foreshadows M. But presumably M. hit on Catullus as the most brilliant member of that loose poetic grouping.

The Catullan inheritance in M. can be broken down into a number of strands. An obvious factor is metre. Of the three verse-systems employed by M. in the majority of his epigrams, two, the hendecasyllable and the scazon, owe much to Catullus.[126] Also congenial to M. was the strongly personal flavour of Catullus' writings, which show an engaging readiness to talk frankly of his own and others' loves or hates, idiosyncrasies, sexual predilections, and prejudices: a pattern that is continued in M.'s epigrams, where the poet's voice, whether of M. himself or a fictional construct, is a constant and insistent presence, albeit tinged with a cool and sardonic objectivity which is alien to Catullus. Some of Catullus' most rancorous poetry is violently obscene,[127] liberally besprinkled with primary obscenities, and here too Catullan influence is of great importance for M. although, as has been noted, his predecessor's often startling obscenity is part of the broader Roman literary canvas. It has been posited that in the case of M.'s occasionally very extended epigrams, Catullan influence may be at work:[128] poems such as 76, of twenty-six lines, are pointed to. There is perhaps some truth in this, and it is certainly the case that Greek epigram as a whole eschews length; in defending his right to compose such pieces, M. however appeals, not to Catullus, but to the precedent of Domitius Marsus and Albinovanus Pedo (**3**). An indisputable debt is owed to Catullan vocabulary, in particular to descriptors such as *nugae, ludere, ioci* and *sal* which resonate with literary self-referentiality and mock-modesty. M. deploys these terms, exactly as Catullus had done, in order ironically to disclaim the possession of authentic poetic talent, and to disavow any ambitions to compose in the grander genres such as epic.[129] Style too represents a further inheritance from Catullus. Formal influences include Catullus' liking for *cumulatio*[130] and repetition, as in the brief 53 *Quid est, Catulle? quid moraris emori? | sella in curuli struma Nonius sedet, | per consulatum peierat Vatinius: | quid est, Catulle? quid moraris emori?*

---

[126] See above.   [127] D. Lateiner, *Ramus* 6 (1977) 15–32.
[128] Ferguson (1963) 8–9.   [129] Swann (1994) 47–64.
[130] E.g. 23.7–11, 25.1–4, 58b.1–6.

The most palpable evidence of Catullus' influence is M.'s constant echoing of Catullan poems: multiple echoes are often clustered in a single epigram.[131] This is far too large a subject to treat here, and the whole issue
of M.'s verbal and thematic adaptations to Catullan models is urgently in
need of a detailed intertextual study.[132] But some pieces which were particularly quarried by M. may be briefly noted: they include the two *passer*
poems,[133] the various epigrams on kissing, the dedication to Nepos which
prefaces the collection,[134] poem 13, *cenabis bene*, which M. imitated far more
widely than is generally realised, 85, *odi et amo*, which in combination with
93, was the source of the famous *non amo te Sabidi, nec possum dicere quare:* |
hoc tantum possum dicere, non amo te (1.32), and the important and profoundly
influential *apologia* for the use of verbal obscenity, 16, which M. several times
echoed, most famously at 1.4.8 *lasciua est nobis pagina, uita proba*. But these
are only the most obvious instances among many, and a close reading of
M. will disclose even more echoes or imitations of Catullus than have been
unearthed by the industrious Paukstadt.

As a coda to the above, it should be mentioned that M. names three
other Latin models in addition to Catullus – Domitius Marsus, Albinovanus Pedo and Cn. Cornelius Lentulus Gaetulicus. The last two are too
shadowy to call for notice here,[135] but it is of interest that Domitius Marsus
put out a collection of short poems or epigrams styled *Cicuta* ('Hemlock'),
the title suggesting a satirical vein which is abundantly exemplified in an
eight-line fragment on a pair of reprobates, Bavius and his *frater*. Also of
relevance to Domitius' poetic output was his prose work *De urbanitate*, 'On
Wit', his definition of which has been preserved by Quintilian: it runs
*urbanitas est uirtus quaedam in breue dictum coacta et apta ad delectandos mouendosque
homines in omnem affectum animi, maxime idonea ad resistendum uel lacessendum,
prout quaeque res ac persona desiderat* (*Inst.* 6.3.104). The relevance of this
to M.'s epigrams, particularly the insistence on compression and point,
and the effectiveness of *urbanitas* in satiric contexts, will be immediately
evident.[136]

---

[131] Paukstadt (1876) 12, 20.
[132] Treatments of M.'s imitation of Catullus do little more than note verbal sim-
ilarities or deal in vague generalities, and do not address the creative uses made by
M. of his Catullan template.
[133] Catullus 2 and 3, Ferguson (1963) 9.
[134] See conveniently Ferguson (1963) 11.
[135] The scanty facts are assembled by Sullivan (1991) 99–100.
[136] Cf. Ramage (1973) 100–6, Bardon (1956) 52–57, **3**.5n.

II CONCORDANCE

OCT/SB	THIS EDITION	OCT/SB	THIS EDITION
1.102	37	6.7	43
2.8	1	6.21	13
2.14	21	6.26	48
2.16	54	6.39	44
2.20	2	6.42	30
2.26	58	6.53	60
2.29	55	6.64	6
2.77	3	6.72	67
2.80	78	6.74	72
2.89	45	6.88	23
2.91/92	9a/9b	7.20	32
3.2	4	7.36	14
3.8	70	7.37	82
3.12	31	7.39	73
3.34	75	7.53	24
3.44	68	7.67	50
3.52	65	7.79	77
3.57	66	7.87	53
3.65	52	7.95	69
3.75	47	8.6	33
3.76	38	8.23	34
3.78	76	8.31	49
3.82	56	8.53	27
3.85	42	8.54	40
3.87	29	8.55	15
4.18	79	8.74	61
4.20	39	9.15	62
4.30	10	9.18	11
4.44	80	9.25	35
4.59	81	9.29	84
4.67	22	9.67	46
4.72	5	9.73	57
4.87	71	9.80	59
5.24	26	10.4	7
5.34	83	10.5	8

OCT/SB	THIS EDITION	OCT/SB	THIS EDITION
10.16	63	12.18	19
10.47	18	12.20	51
10.50	28	12.31	17
10.63	85	12.32	64
10.64	16	12.48	36
10.67	86	12.54	74
10.68	41	12.57	20
12.15	12	12.68	25

SELECT EPIGRAMS

1 (= 2.8)

Si qua uidebuntur chartis tibi, lector, in istis
    siue obscura nimis siue Latina parum,
non meus est error: nocuit librarius illis
    dum properat uersus annumerare tibi.
quod si non illum sed me peccasse putabis,   5
    tunc ego te credam cordis habere nihil.
'ista tamen mala sunt.' quasi nos manifesta negemus!
    haec mala sunt, sed tu non meliora facis.

2 (= 2.20)

Carmina Paulus emit, recitat sua carmina Paulus.
    nam quod emas possis iure uocare tuum.

3 (= 2.77)

Cosconi, qui longa putas epigrammata nostra,
    utilis unguendis axibus esse potes.
hac tu credideris longum ratione Colosson
    et puerum Bruti dixeris esse breuem.
disce quod ignoras: Marsi doctique Pedonis   5
    saepe duplex unum pagina tractat opus.
non sunt longa quibus nihil est quod demere possis,
    sed tu, Cosconi, disticha longa facis.

4 (= 3.2)

Cuius uis fieri, libelle, munus?
festina tibi uindicem parare,
ne nigram cito raptus in culinam

cordylas madida tegas papyro
uel turis piperisue sis cucullus.　　　　　　　　5
Faustini fugis in sinum? sapisti.
cedro nunc licet ambules perunctus
et frontis gemino decens honore
pictis luxurieris umbilicis,
et te purpura delicata uelet,　　　　　　　　10
et cocco rubeat superbus index.
illo uindice nec Probum timeto.

5　(= 4.72)

Exigis ut donem nostros tibi, Quinte, libellos.
　　non habeo sed habet bibliopola Tryphon.
'aes dabo pro nugis et emam tua carmina sanus?
　　non' inquis 'faciam tam fatue.' nec ego.

6　(= 6.64)

Cum sis nec rigida Fabiorum gente creatus
nec qualem Curio, dum prandia portat aranti,
hirsuto peperit deprensa sub ilice coniunx,
sed patris ad speculum tonsi matrisque togatae
filius et possit sponsam te sponsa uocare:　　　　5
emendare meos, quos nouit fama, libellos
et tibi permittis felices carpere nugas –
has, inquam, nugas, quibus aurem aduertere totam
non aspernantur proceres urbisque forique,
quas et perpetui dignantur scrinia Sili　　　　10
et repetit totiens facundo Regulus ore,
quique uidet propius magni certamina Circi
laudat Auentinae uicinus Sura Dianae,
ipse etiam tanto dominus sub pondere rerum
non dedignatur bis terque reuoluere Caesar.　　　　15
sed tibi plus mentis, tibi cor limante Minerua

acrius, et tenues finxerunt pectus Athenae.
ne ualeam, si non multo sapit altius illud,
quod cum panticibus laxis et cum pede grandi
et rubro pulmone uetus nasisque timendum 20
omnia crudelis lanius per compita portat.
audes praeterea, quos nullus nouerit, in me
scribere uersiculos miseras et perdere chartas.
at si quid nostrae tibi bilis inusserit ardor,
uiuet et haerebit totoque legetur in orbe 25
stigmata nec uafra delebit Cinnamus arte.
sed miserere tui rabido nec perditus ore
fumantem nasum uiui temptaueris ursi.
sit placidus licet et lambat digitosque manusque,
si dolor et bilis, si iusta coegerit ira, 30
ursus erit: uacua dentes in pelle fatiges
et tacitam quaeras, quam possis rodere, carnem.

7 (= 10.4)

Qui legis Oedipoden caligantemque Thyesten,
    Colchidas et Scyllas, quid nisi monstra legis?
quid tibi raptus Hylas, quid Parthenopaeus et Attis,
    quid tibi dormitor proderit Endymion,
exutusue puer pinnis labentibus, aut qui 5
    odit amatrices Hermaphroditus aquas?
quid te uana iuuant miserae ludibria chartae?
    hoc lege, quod possit dicere uita 'meum est'.
non hic Centauros, non Gorgonas Harpyiasque
    inuenies: hominem pagina nostra sapit. 10
sed non uis, Mamurra, tuos cognoscere mores
    nec te scire: legas Aetia Callimachi.

8 (= 10.5)

Quisquis stolaeue purpuraeue contemptor
quos colere debet laesit impio uersu,

erret per urbem pontis exul et cliui,
interque raucos ultimus rogatores
oret caninas panis improbi buccas.
illi December longus et madens bruma   5
clususque fornix triste frigus extendat:
uocet beatos clamitetque felices
Orciniana qui feruntur in sponda.
at cum supremae fila uenerint horae   10
diesque tardus, sentiat canum litem
abigatque moto noxias aues panno.
nec finiantur morte simplici poenae,
sed modo seueri sectus Aeaci loris,
nunc inquieti monte Sisyphi pressus,   15
nunc inter undas garruli senis siccus
delasset omnes fabulas poetarum:
et cum fateri Furia iusserit uerum,
prodente clamet conscientia 'scripsi.'

9a (= 2.91)

Rerum certa salus, terrarum gloria, Caesar,
    sospite quo magnos credimus esse deos,
si festinatis totiens tibi lecta libellis
    detinuere oculos carmina nostra tuos,
quod fortuna uetat fieri permitte uideri,   5
    natorum genitor credar ut esse trium.
haec, si displicui, fuerint solacia nobis;
    haec fuerint nobis praemia, si placui.

9b (= 2.92)

Natorum mihi ius trium roganti
Musarum pretium dedit mearum
solus qui poterat. ualebis, uxor.
non debet domini perire munus.

10 (= 4.30)

Baiano procul a lacu, monemus,
piscator, fuge, ne nocens recedas.
sacris piscibus hae natantur undae,
qui norunt dominum manumque lambunt
illam, qua nihil est in orbe maius.   5
quid quod nomen habent et ad magistri
uocem quisque sui uenit citatus?
hoc quondam Libys impius profundo,
dum praedam calamo tremente ducit,
raptis luminibus repente caecus   10
captum non potuit uidere piscem,
et nunc sacrilegos perosus hamos
Baianos sedet ad lacus rogator.
at tu, dum potes, innocens recede
iactis simplicibus cibis in undas,   15
et pisces uenerare delicatos.

11 (= 9.18)

Est mihi – sitque precor longum te praeside, Caesar –
    rus minimum, parui sunt et in urbe lares.
sed de ualle breui quas det sitientibus hortis
    curua laboratas antlia tollit aquas:
sicca domus queritur nullo se rore foueri,   5
    cum mihi uicino Marcia fonte sonet.
quam dederis nostris, Auguste, penatibus undam,
    Castalis haec nobis aut Iouis imber erit.

12 (= 12.15)

Quidquid Parrhasia nitebat aula
donatum est oculis deisque nostris.
miratur Scythicas uirentis auri

flammas Iuppiter et stupet superbi
regis delicias grauesque luxus: 5
haec sunt pocula quae decent Tonantem,
haec sunt quae Phrygium decent ministrum.
omnes cum Ioue nunc sumus beati;
at nuper – pudet, ah pudet fateri –
omnes cum Ioue pauperes eramus.   10

13 (= 6.21)

Perpetuam Stellae dum iungit Ianthida uati
    laeta Venus, dixit 'plus dare non potui.'
haec coram domina; sed nequius illud in aurem:
    'tu ne quid pecces, exitiose, uide.
saepe ego lasciuum Martem furibunda cecidi,   5
    legitimos esset cum uagus ante toros,
sed postquam meus est, nulla me paelice laesit:
    tam frugi Iuno uellet habere uirum.'
dixit et arcano percussit pectora loro.
    plaga iuuat: sed tu iam, dea, caede duos.   10

14 (= 7.36)

Cum pluuias madidumque Iouem perferre negaret
    et rudis hibernis uilla nataret aquis,
plurima, quae posset subitos effundere nimbos,
    muneribus uenit tegula missa tuis.
horridus, ecce, sonat Boreae stridore December: 5
    Stella, tegis uillam, non tegis agricolam?

15 (= 8.55)

Temporibus nostris aetas cum cedat auorum
    creuerit et maior cum duce Roma suo,
ingenium sacri miraris deesse Maronis
    nec quemquam tanta bella sonare tuba.

sint Maecenates, non deerunt, Flacce, Marones   5
   Vergiliumque tibi uel tua rura dabunt.
iugera perdiderat miserae uicina Cremonae
   flebat et abductas Tityrus aeger oues:
risit Tuscus eques paupertatemque malignam
   reppulit et celeri iussit abire fuga.   10
'accipe diuitias et uatum maximus esto;
   tu licet et nostrum' dixit 'Alexin ames.'
astabat domini mensis pulcherrimus ille
   marmorea fundens nigra Falerna manu,
et libata dabat roseis carchesia labris,   15
   quae poterant ipsum sollicitare Iouem.
excidit attonito pinguis Galatea poetae
   Thestylis et rubras messibus usta genas;
protinus ITALIAM concepit et ARMA VIRVMQVE,
   qui modo uix Culicem fleuerat ore rudi.   20
quid Varios Marsosque loquar ditataque uatum
   nomina, magnus erit quos numerare labor?
ergo ero Vergilius, si munera Maecenatis
   des mihi? Vergilius non ero, Marsus ero.

16 (= 10.64)

Contigeris, regina, meos si, Polla, libellos,
   non tetrica nostros excipe fronte iocos.
ille tuus uates, Heliconis gloria nostri,
   Pieria caneret cum fera bella tuba,
non tamen erubuit lasciuo dicere uersu   5
   'si nec pedicor, Cotta, quid hic facio?'

17 (= 12.31)

Hoc nemus, hi fontes, haec textilis umbra supini
   palmitis, hoc riguae ductile flumen aquae,
prataque nec bifero cessura rosaria Paesto,
   quodque uiret Iani mense nec alget holus,

quaeque natat clusis anguilla domestica lymphis,   5
    quaeque gerit similes candida turris aues,
munera sunt dominae: post septima lustra reuerso
    has Marcella domos paruaque regna dedit.
si mihi Nausicaa patrios concederet hortos,
    Alcinoo possem dicere 'malo meos'.   10

18 (= 10.47)

Vitam quae faciant beatiorem,
iucundissime Martialis, haec sunt:
res non parta labore sed relicta;
non ingratus ager, focus perennis;
lis numquam, toga rara, mens quieta;   5
uires ingenuae, salubre corpus;
prudens simplicitas, pares amici;
conuictus facilis, sine arte mensa;
nox non ebria sed soluta curis;
non tristis torus et tamen pudicus;   10
somnus qui faciat breues tenebras:
quod sis esse uelis nihilque malis;
summum nec metuas diem nec optes.

19 (= 12.18)

Dum tu forsitan inquietus erras
clamosa, Iuuenalis, in Subura
aut collem dominae teris Dianae;
dum per limina te potentiorum
sudatrix toga uentilat uagumque   5
maior Caelius et minor fatigant:
me multos repetita post Decembres
accepit mea rusticumque fecit
auro Bilbilis et superba ferro.
hic pigri colimus labore dulci   10
Boterdum Plateamque – Celtiberis

haec sunt nomina crassiora terris −:
ingenti fruor improboque somno
quem nec tertia saepe rumpit hora,
et totum mihi nunc repono quidquid   15
ter denos uigilaueram per annos.
ignota est toga, sed datur petenti
rupta proxima uestis a cathedra.
surgentem focus excipit superba
uicini strue cultus iliceti,   20
multa uilica quem coronat olla.
uenator sequitur, sed ille quem tu
secreta cupias habere silua;
dispensat pueris rogatque longos
leuis ponere uilicus capillos.   25
sic me uiuere, sic iuuat perire.

20 (= 12.57)

Cur saepe sicci parua rura Nomenti
laremque uillae sordidum petam, quaeris?
nec cogitandi, Sparse, nec quiescendi
in urbe locus est pauperi. negant uitam
ludi magistri mane, nocte pistores,   5
aerariorum marculi die toto;
hinc otiosus sordidam quatit mensam
Neroniana nummularius massa,
illinc balucis malleator Hispanae
tritum nitenti fuste uerberat saxum;   10
nec turba cessat entheata Bellonae,
nec fasciato naufragus loquax trunco,
a matre doctus nec rogare Iudaeus,
nec sulphuratae lippus institor mercis.
numerare pigri damna quis potest somni?   15
dicet quot aera uerberent manus urbis,
cum secta Colcho Luna uapulat rhombo.
tu, Sparse, nescis ista nec potes scire,

Petilianis delicatus in regnis,
cui plana summos despicit domus montes,   20
et rus in urbe est uinitorque Romanus
– nec in Falerno colle maior autumnus –
intraque limen latus essedo cursus,
et in profundo somnus et quies nullis
offensa linguis, nec dies nisi admissus.   25
nos transeuntis nisus excitat turbae,
et ad cubile est Roma. taedio fessis
dormire quotiens libuit, imus ad uillam.

21 (= 2.14)

Nil intemptatum Selius, nil linquit inausum,
    cenandum quotiens iam uidet esse domi.
currit ad Europen et te, Pauline, tuosque
    laudat Achilleos, sed sine fine, pedes.
si nihil Europe fecit, tunc Saepta petuntur,   5
    si quid Phillyrides praestet et Aesonides.
hic quoque deceptus Memphitica templa frequentat,
    assidet et cathedris, maesta iuuenca, tuis.
inde petit centum pendentia tecta columnis,
    illinc Pompei dona nemusque duplex.   10
nec Fortunati spernit nec balnea Fausti,
    nec Grylli tenebras Aeoliamque Lupi:
nam thermis iterumque iterumque iterumque lauatur.
    omnia cum fecit, sed renuente deo,
lotus ad Europes tepidae buxeta recurrit,   15
    si quis ibi serum carpat amicus iter.
per te perque tuam, uector lasciue, puellam,
    ad cenam Selium tu, rogo, taure, uoca.

22 (= 4.67)

Praetorem pauper centum sestertia Gaurus
    orabat cana notus amicitia,

dicebatque suis haec tantum deesse trecentis,
    ut posset domino plaudere iustus eques.
praetor ait 'scis me Scorpo Thalloque daturum,   5
    atque utinam centum milia sola darem.'
ah pudet ingratae, pudet ah male diuitis arcae.
    quod non uis equiti, uis dare, praetor, equo?

23 (= 6.88)

Mane salutaui uero te nomine casu
    nec dixi dominum, Caeciliane, meum.
quanti libertas constet mihi tanta, requiris?
    centum quadrantes abstulit illa mihi.

24 (= 7.53)

Omnia misisti mihi Saturnalibus, Vmber,
    munera, contulerant quae tibi quinque dies:
bis senos triplices et dentiscalpia septem;
    his comes accessit spongia, mappa, calix,
semodiusque fabae cum uimine Picenarum   5
    et Laietanae nigra lagona sapae;
paruaque cum canis uenerunt cottana prunis
    et Libycae fici pondere testa grauis.
uix puto triginta nummorum tota fuisse
    munera, quae grandes octo tulere Syri.   10
quanto commodius nullo mihi ferre labore
    argenti potuit pondera quinque puer!

25 (= 12.68)

Matutine cliens, urbis mihi causa relictae,
    atria, si sapias, ambitiosa colas.
non sum ego causidicus nec amaris litibus aptus,
    sed piger et senior Pieridumque comes;
otia me somnusque iuuant, quae magna negauit   5
    Roma mihi: redeo, si uigilatur et hic.

26 (= 5.24)

Hermes Martia saeculi uoluptas,
Hermes omnibus eruditus armis,
Hermes et gladiator et magister,
Hermes turba sui tremorque ludi,
Hermes, quem timet Helius, sed unum,   5
Hermes, cui cadit Aduolans, sed uni,
Hermes uincere nec ferire doctus,
Hermes suppositicius sibi ipse,
Hermes divitiae locariorum,
Hermes cura laborque ludiarum,   10
Hermes belligera superbus hasta,
Hermes aequoreo minax tridente,
Hermes casside languida timendus,
Hermes gloria Martis uniuersi,
Hermes omnia solus et ter unus.   15

27 (= 8.53)

Auditur quantum Massyla per auia murmur,
    innumero quotiens silua leone furit,
pallidus attonitos ad Poena mapalia pastor
    cum reuocat tauros et sine mente pecus:
tantus in Ausonia fremuit modo terror harena.   5
    quis non esse gregem crederet? unus erat,
sed cuius tremerent ipsi quoque iura leones,
    cui diadema daret marmore picta Nomas.
o quantum per colla decus, quem sparsit honorem
    aurea lunatae, cum stetit, umbra iubae!   10
grandia quam decuit latum uenabula pectus
    quantaque de magna gaudia morte tulit!
unde tuis, Libye, tam felix gloria siluis?
    a Cybeles numquid uenerat ille iugo?
an magis Herculeo, Germanice, misit ab astro   15
    hanc tibi uel frater uel pater ipse feram?

28 (= 10.50)

Frangat Idumaeas tristis Victoria palmas,
  plange, Fauor, saeua pectora nuda manu;
mutet Honor cultus, et iniquis munera flammis
  mitte coronatas, Gloria maesta, comas.
heu facinus! prima fraudatus, Scorpe, iuuenta   5
  occidis et nigros tam cito iungis equos.
curribus illa tuis semper properata breuisque
  cur fuit et uitae tam prope meta tuae?

29 (= 3.87)

Narrat te rumor, Chione, numquam esse fututam
  atque nihil cunno purius esse tuo.
tecta tamen non hac, qua debes, parte lauaris:
  si pudor est, transfer subligar in faciem.

30 (= 6.42)

Etrusci nisi thermulis lauaris,
  illotus morieris, Oppiane.
  nullae sic tibi blandientur undae,
  non fontes Aponi rudes puellis,
  non mollis Sinuessa feruidique   5
  fluctus Passeris aut superbus Anxur,
  non Phoebi uada principesque Baiae.
  nusquam tam nitidum uacat serenum:
  lux ipsa est ibi longior, diesque
  nullo tardius a loco recedit.   10
  illic Taygeti uirent metalla
  et certant uario decore saxa,
  quae Phryx et Libys altius cecidit.
  siccos pinguis onyx anhelat aestus
  et flamma tenui calent ophitae.   15
  ritus si placeant tibi Laconum,

contentus potes arido uapore
cruda Virgine Marciaue mergi;
quae tam candida, tam serena lucet
ut nullas ibi suspiceris undas   20
et credas uacuam nitere lygdon.
non attendis et aure me supina
iam dudum quasi neglegenter audis.
illotus morieris, Oppiane.

31 (= 3.12)

Vnguentum, fateor, bonum dedisti
conuiuis here, sed nihil scidisti.
res salsa est bene olere et esurire.
qui non cenat et unguitur, Fabulle,
hic uere mihi mortuus uidetur.   5

32 (= 7.20)

Nihil est miserius neque gulosius Santra.
rectam uocatus cum cucurrit ad cenam,
quam tot diebus noctibusque captauit,
ter poscit apri glandulas, quater lumbum,
et utramque coxam leporis et duos armos,   5
nec erubescit peierare de turdo
et ostreorum rapere liuidos cirros.
buccis placentae sordidam linit mappam;
illic et uuae collocantur ollares
et Punicorum pauca grana malorum   10
et excauatae pellis indecens uuluae
et lippa ficus debilisque boletus.
sed mappa cum iam mille rumpitur furtis,
rosos tepenti spondylos sinu condit
et deuorato capite turturem truncum.   15
colligere longa turpe nec putat dextra
analecta quidquid et canes reliquerunt.

nec esculenta sufficit gulae praeda:
mixto lagonam replet ad pedes uino.
haec per ducentas cum domum tulit scalas   20
seque obserata clusit anxius cella
gulosus ille, postero die uendit.

33 (= 8.6)

Archetypis uetuli nihil est odiosius Eucti
  – ficta Saguntino cymbia malo luto – ;
argenti fumosa sui cum stemmata narrat
  garrulus et uerbis mucida uina facit:
'Laomedonteae fuerant haec pocula mensae: 5
  ferret ut haec muros struxit Apollo lyra.
hoc cratere ferox commisit proelia Rhoecus
  cum Lapithis: pugna debile cernis opus.
hi duo longaeuo censentur Nestore fundi:
  pollice de Pylio trita columba nitet.   10
hic scyphus est in quo misceri iussit amicis
  largius Aeacides uiuidiusque merum.
hac propinauit Bitiae pulcherrima Dido
  in patera, Phrygio cum data cena uiro est.'
miratus fueris cum prisca toreumata multum,   15
  in Priami calathis Astyanacta bibes.

34 (= 8.23)

Esse tibi uideor saeuus nimiumque gulosus,
  qui propter cenam, Rustice, caedo cocum.
si leuis ista tibi flagrorum causa uidetur,
  ex qua uis causa uapulet ergo cocus?

35 (= 9.25)

Dantem uina tuum quotiens aspeximus Hyllum,
  lumine nos, Afer, turbidiore notas.

quod, rogo, quod scelus est mollem spectare ministrum?
    aspicimus solem, sidera, templa, deos.
auertam uultus, tamquam mihi pocula Gorgon   5
    porrigat, atque oculos oraque nostra tegam?
trux erat Alcides, et Hylan spectare licebat;
    ludere Mercurio cum Ganymede licet.
si non uis teneros spectet conuiua ministros,
    Phineas inuites, Afer, et Oedipodas.   10

36 (= 12.48)

Boletos et aprum si tamquam uilia ponis
    et non esse putas haec mea uota, uolo:
si fortunatum fieri me credis et heres
    uis scribi propter quinque Lucrina, uale.
lauta tamen cena est: fateor, lautissima, sed cras   5
    nil erit, immo hodie, protinus immo nihil,
quod sciat infelix damnatae spongia uirgae
    uel quicumque canis iunctaque testa uiae:
mullorum leporumque et suminis exitus hic est,
    sulphureusque color carnificesque pedes.   10
non Albana mihi sit comissatio tanti
    nec Capitolinae pontificumque dapes;
imputet ipse deus nectar mihi, fiet acetum
    et Vaticani perfida uappa cadi.
conuiuas alios cenarum quaere magister   15
    quos capiant mensae regna superba tuae:
me meus ad subitas inuitet amicus ofellas:
    haec mihi quam possum reddere cena placet.

37 (= 1.102)

Qui pinxit Venerem tuam, Lycori,
blanditus, puto, pictor est Mineruae.

38 (= 3.76)

Arrigis ad uetulas, fastidis, Basse, puellas,
    nec formosa tibi sed moritura placet.
hic, rogo, non furor est, non haec est mentula demens?
    cum possis Hecaben, non potes Andromachen!

39 (= 4.20)

Dicit se uetulam, cum sit Caerellia pupa:
    pupam se dicit Gellia, cum sit anus.
ferre nec hanc possis, possis, Colline, nec illam:
    altera ridicula est, altera putidula.

40 (= 8.54)

Formosissima quae fuere uel sunt,
    sed uilissima quae fuere uel sunt,
o quam te fieri, Catulla, uellem
    formosam minus aut magis pudicam!

41 (= 10.68)

Cum tibi non Ephesos nec sit Rhodos aut Mitylene,
    sed domus in uico, Laelia, Patricio,
deque coloratis numquam lita mater Etruscis,
    durus Aricina de regione pater;
κύριέ μου, μέλι μου, ψυχή μου congeris usque,   5
    pro pudor! Hersiliae ciuis et Egeriae.
lectulus has uoces, nec lectulus audiat omnis,
    sed quem lasciuo strauit amica uiro.
scire cupis quo casta modo matrona loquaris?
    numquid, quae crisat, blandior esse potest?   10
tu licet ediscas totam referasque Corinthon,
    non tamen omnino, Laelia, Lais eris.

42 (= 3.85)

Quis tibi persuasit nares abscidere moecho?
  non hac peccatum est parte, marite, tibi.
stulte, quid egisti? nihil hic tua perdidit uxor,
  cum sit salua tui mentula Deiphobi.

43 (= 6.7)

Iulia lex populis ex quo, Faustine, renata est
  atque intrare domos iussa Pudicitia est,
aut minus aut certe non plus tricesima lux est,
  et nubit decimo iam Telesilla uiro.
quae nubit totiens, non nubit: adultera lege est.   5
  offendor moecha simpliciore minus.

44 (= 6.39)

Pater ex Marulla, Cinna, factus es septem
non liberorum: namque nec tuus quisquam
nec est amici filiusue uicini,
sed in grabatis tegetibusque concepti
materna produnt capitibus suis furta.   5
hic qui retorto crine Maurus incedit
subolem fatetur esse se coci Santrae.
at ille sima nare, turgidis labris
ipsa est imago Pannychi palaestritae.
pistoris esse tertium quis ignorat,   10
quicumque lippum nouit et uidet Damam?
quartus cinaeda fronte, candido uultu
ex concubino natus est tibi Lygdo:
percide, si uis, filium: nefas non est.
hunc uero acuto capite et auribus longis,   15
quae sic mouentur ut solent asellorum,
quis morionis filium negat Cyrtae?

duae sorores, illa nigra et haec rufa,
Croti choraulae uilicique sunt Carpi.
iam Niobidarum grex tibi foret plenus 20
si spado Coresus Dindymusque non esset.

45 (= 2.89)

Quod nimio gaudes noctem producere uino,
    ignosco: uitium, Gaure, Catonis habes.
carmina quod scribis Musis et Apolline nullo,
    laudari debes: hoc Ciceronis habes.
quod uomis, Antoni: quod luxuriaris, Apici. 5
    quod fellas, uitium, dic mihi, cuius habes?

46 (= 9.67)

Lasciuam tota possedi nocte puellam,
    cuius nequitias uincere nemo potest.
fessus mille modis illud puerile poposci:
    ante preces totas primaque uerba dedit.
improbius quiddam ridensque rubensque rogaui: 5
    pollicita est nulla luxuriosa mora.
sed mihi pura fuit; tibi non erit, Aeschyle, si uis
    accipere hoc munus condicione mala.

47 (= 3.75)

Stare, Luperce, tibi iam pridem mentula desît,
    luctaris demens tu tamen arrigere.
sed nihil erucae faciunt bulbique salaces
    improba nec prosunt iam satureia tibi.
coepisti puras opibus corrumpere buccas: 5
    sic quoque non uiuit sollicitata Venus.
mirari satis hoc quisquam uel credere possit,
    quod non stat, magno stare, Luperce, tibi?

48 (= 6.26)

Periclitatur capite Sotades noster.
reum putatis esse Sotaden? non est.
arrigere desît posse Sotades: lingit.

49 (= 8.31)

Nescio quid de te non belle, Dento, fateris,
    coniuge qui ducta iura paterna petis.
sed iam supplicibus dominum lassare libellis
    desine et in patriam serus ab urbe redi:
nam dum tu longe deserta uxore diuque   5
    tres quaeris natos, quattuor inuenies.

50 (= 7.67)

Pedicat pueros tribas Philaenis
et tentigine saeuior mariti
undenas dolat in die puellas.
harpasto quoque subligata ludit
et flauescit haphe, grauesque draucis   5
halteras facili rotat lacerto,
et putri lutulenta de palaestra
uncti uerbere uapulat magistri:
nec cenat prius aut recumbit ante
quam septem uomuit meros deunces;   10
ad quos fas sibi tunc putat redire,
cum colyphia sedecim comedit.
post haec omnia cum libidinatur,
non fellat – putat hoc parum uirile –,
sed plane medias uorat puellas.   15
di mentem tibi dent tuam, Philaeni,
cunnum lingere quae putas uirile.

51 (= 12.20)

Quare non habeat, Fabulle, quaeris
uxorem Themison? habet sororem.

52 (= 3.65)

Quod spirat tenera malum mordente puella,
    quod de Corycio quae uenit aura croco;
uinea quod primis cum floret cana racemis,
    gramina quod redolent, quae modo carpsit ouis;
quod myrtus, quod messor Arabs, quod sucina trita,   5
    pallidus Eoo ture quod ignis olet;
gleba quod aestiuo leuiter cum spargitur imbre,
    quod madidas nardo passa corona comas:
hoc tua, saeue puer Diadumene, basia fragrant.
    quid si tota dares illa sine inuidia?   10

53 (= 7.87)

Si meus aurita gaudet lagalopece Flaccus,
    si fruitur tristi Canius Aethiope,
Publius exiguae si flagrat amore catellae,
    si Cronius similem cercopithecon amat,
delectat Marium si perniciosus ichneumon,   5
    pica salutatrix si tibi, Lause, placet,
si gelidum collo nectit Glaucilla draconem,
    luscinio tumulum si Telesilla dedit:
blanda Cupidinei cur non amet ora Babyrtae,
    qui uidet haec dominis monstra placere suis?   10

54 (= 2.16)

Zoilus aegrotat: faciunt hanc stragula febrem.
    si fuerit sanus, coccina quid facient?

quid torus a Nilo, quid Sidone tinctus olenti?
  ostendit stultas quid nisi morbus opes?
quid tibi cum medicis? dimitte Machaonas omnes.   5
  uis fieri sanus? stragula sume mea.

55 (= 2.29)

Rufe, uides illum subsellia prima terentem,
  cuius et hinc lucet sardonychata manus
quaeque Tyron totiens epotauere lacernae
  et toga non tactas uincere iussa niues,
cuius olet toto pinguis coma Marcellano   5
  et splendent uulso bracchia trita pilo,
non hesterna sedet lunata lingula planta,
  coccina non laesum pingit aluta pedem,
et numerosa linunt stellantem splenia frontem.
  ignoras quid sit? splenia tolle, leges.   10

56 (= 3.82)

Conuiua quisquis Zoili potest esse,
Summemmianas cenet inter uxores
curtaque Ledae sobrius bibat testa:
hoc esse leuius puriusque contendo.
iacet occupato galbinatus in lecto   5
cubitisque trudit hinc et inde conuiuas,
effultus ostro Sericisque puluillis.
stat exoletus suggeritque ructanti
pinnas rubentes cuspidesque lentisci,
et aestuanti tenue uentilat frigus   10
supina prasino concubina flabello,
fugatque muscas myrtea puer uirga.
percurrit agili corpus arte tractatrix
manumque doctam spargit omnibus membris;
digiti crepantis signa nouit eunuchus   15

et delicatae sciscitator urinae
domini bibentis ebrium regit penem.
at ipse retro flexus ad pedum turbam
inter catellas anserum exta lambentes
partitur apri glandulas palaestritis   20
et concubino turturum nates donat;
Ligurumque nobis saxa cum ministrentur
uel cocta fumis musta Massilitanis,
Opimianum morionibus nectar
crystallinisque murrinisque propinat,   25
et Cosmianis ipse fusus ampullis
non erubescit murice aureo nobis
diuidere moechae pauperis capillare.
septunce multo deinde perditus stertit:
nos accubamus et silentium rhonchis   30
praestare iussi nutibus propinamus.
hos Malchionis patimur improbi fastus,
nec uindicari, Rufe, possumus: fellat.

57 (= 9.73)

Dentibus antiquas solitus producere pelles
    et mordere luto putre uetusque solum,
Praenestina tenes decepti regna patroni,
    in quibus indignor si tibi cella fuit;
rumpis et ardenti madidus crystalla Falerno   5
    et pruris domini cum Ganymede tui.
at me litterulas stulti docuere parentes:
    quid cum grammaticis rhetoribusque mihi?
frange leues calamos et scinde, Thalia, libellos,
    si dare sutori calceus ista potest.   10

58 (= 2.26)

Quod querulum spirat, quod acerbum Naeuia tussit,
    inque tuos mittit sputa subinde sinus,

iam te rem factam, Bithynice, credis habere?
erras: blanditur Naeuia, non moritur.

59 (= 9.80)

Duxerat esuriens locupletem pauper anumque:
uxorem pascit Gellius et futuit.

60 (= 6.53)

Lotus nobiscum est, hilaris cenauit, et idem
inuentus mane est mortuus Andragoras.
tam subitae mortis causam, Faustine, requiris?
in somnis medicum uiderat Hermocraten.

61 (= 8.74)

Oplomachus nunc es, fueras opthalmicus ante.
fecisti medicus quod facis oplomachus.

62 (= 9.15)

Inscripsit tumulis septem scelerata uirorum
'se fecisse' Chloe. quid pote simplicius?

63 (= 10.16)

Dotatae uxori cor harundine fixit acuta,
sed dum ludit Aper: ludere nouit Aper.

64 (= 12.32)

O Iuliarum dedecus Kalendarum,
uidi, Vacerra, sarcinas tuas, uidi;
quas non retentas pensione pro bima

portabat uxor rufa crinibus septem
et cum sorore cana mater ingenti.   5
Furias putaui nocte Ditis emersas.
has tu priores frigore et fame siccus
et non recenti pallidus magis buxo
Irus tuorum temporum sequebaris.
migrare cliuum crederes Aricinum.   10
ibat tripes grabatus et bipes mensa
et cum lucerna corneoque cratere
matella curto rupta latere meiebat;
foco uirenti suberat amphorae ceruix;
fuisse gerres aut inutiles maenas   15
odor impudicus urcei fatebatur,
qualis marinae uix sit aura piscinae.
nec quadra deerat casei Tolosatis,
quadrima nigri nec corona pulei
caluaeque restes alioque cepisque,   20
nec plena turpi matris olla resina
Summemmianae qua pilantur uxores.
quid quaeris aedes uilicosque derides,
habitare gratis, o Vacerra, cum possis?
haec sarcinarum pompa conuenit ponti.   25

65 (= 3.52)

Empta domus fuerat tibi, Tongiliane, ducentis:
    abstulit hanc nimium casus in urbe frequens.
collatum est deciens. rogo, non potes ipse uideri
    incendisse tuam, Tongiliane, domum?

66 (= 3.57)

Callidus imposuit nuper mihi copo Rauennae:
    cum peterem mixtum, uendidit ille merum.

67 (= 6.72)

Fur notae nimium rapacitatis
compilare Cilix uolebat hortum,
ingenti sed erat, Fabulle, in horto
praeter marmoreum nihil Priapum.
dum non uult uacua manu redire,   5
ipsum surripuit Cilix Priapum.

68 (= 3.44)

Occurrit tibi nemo quod libenter,
quod, quacumque uenis, fuga est et ingens
circa te, Ligurine, solitudo,
quid sit, scire cupis? nimis poeta es.
hoc ualde uitium periculosum est.   5
non tigris catulis citata raptis,
non dipsas medio perusta sole,
nec sic scorpios improbus timetur.
nam tantos, rogo, quis ferat labores?
et stanti legis et legis sedenti,   10
currenti legis et legis cacanti.
in thermas fugio: sonas ad aurem.
piscinam peto: non licet natare.
ad cenam propero: tenes euntem.
ad lectum uenio: fugas edentem.   15
lassus dormio: suscitas iacentem.
uis, quantum facias mali, uidere?
uir iustus, probus, innocens timeris.

69 (= 7.95)

Bruma est et riget horridus December,
audes tu tamen osculo niuali

omnes obuius hinc et hinc tenere
et totam, Line, basiare Romam.
quid posses grauiusque saeuiusque   5
percussus facere atque uerberatus?
hoc me frigore basiet nec uxor
blandis filia nec rudis labellis,
sed tu dulcior elegantiorque,
cuius liuida naribus caninis   10
dependet glacies rigetque barba,
qualem forficibus metit supinis
tonsor Cinyphio Cilix marito.
centum occurrere malo cunnilingis
et Gallum timeo minus recentem.   15
quare si tibi sensus est pudorque,
hibernas, Line, basiationes
in mensem rogo differas Aprilem.

70 (= 3.8)

'Thaida Quintus amat.' 'quam Thaida?' 'Thaida luscam.'
'unum oculum Thais non habet, ille duos.'

71 (= 4.87)

Infantem secum semper tua Bassa, Fabulle,
    collocat et lusus deliciasque uocat,
et, quo mireris magis, infantaria non est.
    ergo quid in causa est? pedere Bassa solet.

72 (= 6.74)

Medio recumbit imus ille qui lecto,
caluam trifilem semitatus unguento,
foditque tonsis ora laxa lentiscis,
mentitur, Aefulane: non habet dentes.

73 (=7.39)

Discursus uarios uagumque mane
et fastus et aue potentiorum
cum perferre patique iam negaret,
coepit fingere Caelius podagram.
quam dum uult nimis approbare ueram   5
et sanas linit obligatque plantas
inceditque gradu laborioso,
– quantum cura potest et ars doloris! –
desît fingere Caelius podagram.

74 (=12.54)

Crine ruber, niger ore, breuis pede, lumine laesus,
  rem magnam praestas, Zoile, si bonus es.

75 (=3.34)

Digna tuo cur sis indignaque nomine, dicam.
  frigida es et nigra es: non es et es Chione.

76 (=3.78)

Minxisti currente semel, Pauline, carina.
  meiere uis iterum? iam Palinurus eris.

77 (=7.79)

Potaui modo consulare uinum.
quaeris quam uetus atque liberale?
ipso consule conditum: sed ipse
qui ponebat erat, Seuere, consul.

78 (= 2.80)

Hostem cum fugeret, se Fannius ipse peremit.
  hic, rogo, non furor est, ne moriare, mori?

79 (= 4.18)

Qua uicina pluit Vipsanis porta columnis
  et madet assiduo lubricus imbre lapis,
in iugulum pueri, qui roscida tecta subibat,
  decidit hiberno praegrauis unda gelu:
cumque peregisset miseri crudelia fata,   5
  tabuit in calido uulnere mucro tener.
quid non saeua sibi uoluit Fortuna licere?
  aut ubi non mors est, si iugulatis aquae?

80 (= 4.44)

Hic est pampineis uiridis modo Vesbius umbris,
  presserat hic madidos nobilis uua lacus:
haec iuga quam Nysae colles plus Bacchus amauit,
  hoc nuper Satyri monte dedere choros.
haec Veneris sedes, Lacedaemone gratior illi,   5
  hic locus Herculeo nomine clarus erat.
cuncta iacent flammis et tristi mersa fauilla:
  nec superi uellent hoc licuisse sibi.

81 (= 4.59)

Flentibus Heliadum ramis dum uipera repit,
  fluxit in obstantem sucina gutta feram:
quae dum miratur pingui se rore teneri,
  concreto riguit uincta repente gelu.
ne tibi regali placeas, Cleopatra, sepulchro,   5
  uipera si tumulo nobiliore iacet.

82 (= 7.37)

Nosti mortiferum quaestoris, Castrice, signum?
    est operae pretium discere theta nouum:
exprimeret quotiens rorantem frigore nasum,
    letalem iuguli iusserat esse notam.
turpis ab inuiso pendebat stiria naso,   5
    cum flaret madida fauce December atrox:
collegae tenuere manus: quid plura requiris?
    emungi misero, Castrice, non licuit.

83 (= 5.34)

Hanc tibi, Fronto pater, genetrix Flaccilla, puellam
    oscula commendo deliciasque meas,
paruula ne nigras horrescat Erotion umbras
    oraque Tartarei prodigiosa canis.
impletura fuit sextae modo frigora brumae,   5
    uixisset totidem ni minus illa dies.
inter tam ueteres ludat lasciua patronos
    et nomen blaeso garriat ore meum.
mollia non rigidus caespes tegat ossa, nec illi,
    terra, grauis fueris: non fuit illa tibi.   10

84 (= 9.29)

Saecula Nestoreae permensa, Philaeni, senectae
    rapta es ad infernas tam cito Ditis aquas?
Euboicae nondum numerabas longa Sibyllae
    tempora: maior erat mensibus illa tribus.
heu quae lingua silet! non illam mille catastae   5
    uincebant, nec quae turba Sarapin amat,
nec matutini cirrata caterua magistri,
    nec quae Strymonio de grege ripa sonat.
quae nunc Thessalico lunam deducere rhombo,
    quae sciet hos illos uendere lena toros?   10

sit tibi terra leuis mollique tegaris harena,
  ne tua non possint eruere ossa canes.

85 (= 10.63)

Marmora parua quidem sed non cessura, uiator,
  Mausoli saxis pyramidumque legis.
bis mea Romano spectata est uita Tarento
  et nihil extremos perdidit ante rogos:
quinque dedit pueros, totidem mihi Iuno puellas,   5
  cluserunt omnes lumina nostra manus.
contigit et thalami mihi gloria rara fuitque
  una pudicitiae mentula nota meae.

86 (= 10.67)

Pyrrhae filia, Nestoris nouerca,
quam uidit Niobe puella canam,
Laertes auiam senex uocauit,
nutricem Priamus, socrum Thyestes,
iam cornicibus omnibus superstes,   5
hoc tandem sita prurit in sepulchro
caluo Plutia cum Melanthione.

COMMENTARY

I (= 2.8)

'If these writings of mine, reader, appear in any way unclear or defective in style, the responsibility is not mine, but the copyist's, in his hurry to transcribe these verses for you. But if you think the fault *is* mine, then I shall have to conclude that you have no sense. "All the same they *are* bad." Of course they are: why deny the obvious? They are indeed bad – but you can do no better.'

This poem blends one of M.'s favourite themes – ironic depreciation of his artistic talents – with a second topic of which we hear much elsewhere, the incompetence and carelessness of scribal copyists. Cicero exclaimed in despair *de <libris> Latinis uero quo me uertam nescio; ita mendose scribuntur et ueneunt* (*Q. fr.* 3.5.6); cf. Strabo 609. Quintilian relied on the bookseller Tryphon to see to it that his team of scribes copied the original of his work as accurately as possible (*Inst. praef.* 3) – not an easy proposition, given that copying was done under dictation, rather than off a written text, thereby increasing the possibility of error, and that scribes were paid according to the number of lines copied, hence mistakes that arose from haste: see on 3–4.

Further reading: Kleberg (1992) 43–62 = (1967) 25–47

I   **chartis . . . in istis:** *charta* was strictly speaking the writing material which went to make up a papyrus roll (cf. Turner (1980) 4). The word is often used by M., always in the plural, in the sense of 'writings'. Cf. *OLD* s.v. 3b.

lector: addresses to the reader are numerous in M., but rare elsewhere in Latin poetry, except for Ovid, who uses them especially in the exile poems. Citroni on 1.1.4 suggests that the reason for their frequency is that M. was writing for a much larger public than usual.

2   **siue obscura nimis siue Latina parum:** the two phrases complement each other, since *Latinitas*, although its primary meaning is 'speaking or writing correct Latin' (Cic. *Opt. gen.* 4), also embraces the idea of clarity: cf. Cic. *De or.* 3.49 *Latine scilicet dicendo, uerbis usitatis ac proprie* ('without metaphor') *demonstrantibus ea quae significari et declarari uolemus*

73

sine ambiguo uerbo aut sermone. Ἑλληνισμός, of which *Latinitas* is a calque, similarly associates linguistic correctness and transparency of meaning: see Arist. *Rh.* 3.5, Desbordes (1991), M. C. Díaz y Diaz, *Emerita* 19 (1951) 39–56.

obscura nimis: a fault which M. elsewhere claims to avoid (2.86 and 10.21).

3   nocuit 'did the damage to'. An author could hardly examine person-ally every copy of his work: hence the value attached to special presentation copies corrected by his own hand: cf. 7.11 and 7.17.5–8.

librarius 'scribe', not 'bookseller' (Birt (1882) 207–8).

4   dum properat uersus annumerare tibi: in his hurry to 'tot up' the verses for the reader, the copyist introduced errors into the text. Scribes were paid by the number of lines copied, and would thus be tempted to speed up the rate of copying in order to increase their pay. Texts often show the results of such scribal haste, sometimes being corrupted to the point of unintelligibility (see K. Ohly, *Stichometrische Untersuchungen* (Berlin/Leipzig 1928) 39–41; cf. esp. his numbers xiv and xvi).

annumerare tibi: sc. *lectori. annumerare*, a financial term, has conno-tations of precision which are at odds with the sloppiness of the transcrip-tion: Cic. *Opt. gen.* 14 illustrates the point.

tibi: dative of advantage; a *captatio beneuolentiae* which will shortly be nullified by M.'s acknowledgment that the *lector* may not be well disposed.

5   quod si non illum sed me peccasse putabis: cf. Petr. 130.4 *non me sed instrumenta peccasse.*

peccasse: *peccare* is used of verbal, orthographic and artistic faults (*TLL* x 1.886.9–68), and thus applies with equal suitability to the transcrip-tional errors of the scribe and deficiencies in craftsmanship on M.'s part.

6   tunc ego te credam: the force of the future seems to be 'then I shall have no choice but to believe'.

cordis habere nihil 'have no sense'. The heart (*cor*) was regarded as the seat of wisdom or intelligence: cf. 7.78.4 *habes nec cor, Papyle, nec genium,* Cic. *Fin.* 2.24 *nec enim sequitur ut, cui cor sapiat, ei non sapiat palatus* with Reid. *credam cordis* sets up a neat alliterative balance with *peccasse putabis* 5.

7   'ista tamen mala sunt':   the *lector* objects: 'be that as it may (*tamen*), your verses are of poor quality'. For *mala* in this sense, cf. 7.81 *'triginta toto mala sunt epigrammata libro.' | si totidem bona sunt, Lause, bonus liber est.*

quasi nos manifesta negemus!:   having in 1–6 blamed any short-comings on the scribe, M. unexpectedly concedes, in response to the *lector*'s strictures, that his poems are worthless, thus attempting to deflect spiteful criticism by admitting its essential correctness (cf. 7.81, 7.90, 13.2). Professions of artistic inadequacy on the part of writers are conventional (Janson (1964) 124–33), and particularly characteristic of M.: see Kay's intro. to 11.1. The tone of mock modesty must be counterbalanced by M.'s assertions of his widespread popularity, e.g. 1.1, 4.49, 6.60, 7.88.

8   haec mala sunt, sed tu non meliora facis: M. likes to meet artistic censure with criticisms of his own, cf. **3**; 1.91, 1.110, 9.50.

sed tu non meliora facis 'the verses which you write are no better' (cf. **3**). M.'s admission of his shortcomings in 7 is amusingly undercut by the revelation that the criticisms which he seeks to defuse are the tendentious ones of a fellow poet.

2   (= 2.20)

'Paulus buys poems and recites his poems. They can certainly be called his: he purchased them.'

2 deals with the subject of literary theft by means of a play on *suus*. The poems which Paulus recites are certainly *sua*, seeing that he has purchased them (*emit . . . quod emas*): it is implied that, in reciting these, Paulus represents them as *sua* in another sense, i.e. as 'his own' creations. Similarly in 6.12 *iurat capillos esse, quos emit, suos | Fabulla.* † *numquid, Paule* (n.b.), *peierat* † ? Fabulla claims as her own hair a wig which she has bought.

Authors in antiquity were peculiarly exposed to the risk of plagiarism, there being no rules of copyright (cf. **5**.2n.). In book 1 M. often complains of individuals who attempt to pass off his compositions as their own (1.29, 38, 52, 66 and 72): several of these pointedly contrapose *meus* or *noster* (*my* creations) with *tuus* (*owned* by you), in a manner similar to the play on *suus* here. In protesting loudly about literary theft at this early stage in his publishing career, M. was indulging in self-advertisement: the clear implication is that his epigrams are considered worth stealing. Nevertheless the danger to which he adverts was real, and the potential gains to the plagiarist – gratification of his vanity and the patronage which attached to a successful author – not inconsiderable.

The appropriation of another's work was not difficult to carry off. The plagiarist simply substituted his own name on the *titulus* for the real author's,

and presented the work to the world as his own (Vitr. 7 *praef.* 10), a stratagem
which some writers sought to pre-empt by attaching at the beginning or
conclusion of their opus a *sphragis* ('seal of ownership') proclaiming their
authorship of the work: cf. Theognis 19–20 'let my seal of ownership be set
upon these verses, nor shall theft of them ever go unnoticed'. Notwithstanding such devices plagiarism was still widely practised or suspected (Vitr. 7
praef. 3, Plin. *Ep.* 2.10).

Further reading: Howell on 1.52.9, Speyer (1971) 29, Ziegler (1950)

1   Carmina Paulus . . . carmina Paulus: the pointed repetition
mimics sarcastically Paulus' insistence on his authorship.
     Paulus: a Paulus is attacked by M. in a number of poems, generally
as a stingy patron. More pertinent to the present epigram are 6.12 quoted
above and 4.17, where Paulus desires M. to write on his behalf verses which
will anger and embarrass Lycisca.

2   iure 'legitimately'; cf. 8.58 *cum tibi tam crassae sint, Artemidore, lacernae,*
| *possim te Sagarim iure uocare meo.*

3   (= 2.77)

'Cosconius, in criticising my epigrams on the grounds of length, you show
yourself a fool: by the same misguided criteria you would regard Nero's
colossal statue as excessively large, and Brutus' exquisite figurine of a young
child as excessively small. You are too ignorant to know that my predecessors
in the genre often composed epigrams two columns in length. But you,
Cosconius, make even distichs seem long.'

M. here defends himself against the charge of writing long epigrams by appealing to the precedent of his literary models Marsus and Pedo: in addition
he amusingly encloses his answer to Cosconius' criticisms between poems
of two lines apiece. Other epigrams on the theme include 6.65 (preceded
by a 32 line poem), where he invokes literary tradition to vindicate his
practice, and 1.110, in which, as here, he responds by turning the criticism
back on the attacker: *scribere me quereris, Velox, epigrammata longa.* | *ipse nil scribis:*
tu breuiora facis.

     3 reflects a lively debate about the proper length for an epigram. Plato,
Leg. 958e had insisted that funerary epigrams should not exceed four verses,
and Callimachus apparently favoured brevity in epigram as in other classes

of poetry. In the early years of the empire, Philip of Thessalonica, editor of the *Garland of Philip*, incorporated in his prefatory epigram a praise of ὀλιγοστιχίη, brevity (*AP* 4.2.10–11); cf. Parmenion, *AP* 9.342, from the same corpus. In the debate extreme positions were sometimes taken: cf. 8.29 *disticha qui scribit, puto, uult breuitate placere. | quid prodest breuitas, dic mihi, si liber est?* and *AP* 9.369 'the distich is an excellent epigram. But if you exceed three, you are rhapsodising (i.e. composing an epic), not reciting an epigram.' M. takes cognizance of such views by congratulating himself on the shortness of his epigrams (9.50, 10.1), and by penning numerous poems in distichs, of which books 13 and 14 represent the most conspicuous instances. But he also writes long epigrams such as **6**, 1.49, and 3.58, in this respect following his Latin predecessors (5–6n.) – hence the complaints of excessive length, whether real or fictitious.

Further reading: Joepgen (1967) 102–3, Lausberg (1982), Szelest (1980), Weinreich (1926) 3–7

1   Cosconi: the same Cosconius is criticised in 3.69 for writing epigrams that are free from obscenity and by implication boring.

longa 'too long', as in 3 and 7–8. Cf. Cic. *Brut.* 52, 2.1.11–12 *esse tibi tanta cautus breuitate uideris? | ei mihi, quam multis sic quoque longus eris!*

2   utilis unguendis axibus esse potes: Cosconius could be put to good use as *axungia*, axle-grease (Plin. *NH* 28.141), a colourful way of saying that Cosconius is *pinguis,* literally 'greasy/fatty', i.e. 'thick' or 'lacking in refined critical intelligence' (*OLD* s.v. 7).

3–4   hac tu credideris longum ratione... | ...dixeris esse breuem: i.e. 'the quality of a work has nothing to do with its size' or 'you have no idea of the proper proportions for an artefact of any kind'.

credideris 'you would believe': potential subjunctive.

3   hac...ratione 'by such [faulty] reasoning': cf. 6.17.4 *fur ista ratione diceris.*

longum 'too long': cf. 1 n.

Colosson: the colossal bronze statue of himself which Nero had intended to erect in the Domus Aurea. After his death, Vespasian converted it into a radiate statue of the Sun: cf. P. Howell, *Athenaeum* 46 (1968) 292–9. It was over 100 feet in height (Plin. *NH* 34.45, Suet. *Ner.* 31.1).

4   puerum Bruti: a fourth-century BC figurine of a child owned by M. Junius Brutus, who regarded it with such affection that it became known as *Bruti puer* (Plin. *NH* 34.82, K. Lehmann, *Hesperia* 14 (1945) 261). Cf. 9.50.5–6 *nos facimus Bruti puerum, nos Langona uiuum:* | *tu magnus luteum, Gaure, Giganta facis* where, as here, images from the plastic arts are used as a yardstick for measuring the length of a literary work.

breuem 'too short': cf. 14.151 (Zona) *longa satis nunc sum; dulci sed pondere uenter* | *si tumeat, fiam tunc tibi zona breuis,* Quint. *Inst.* 9.4.118.

5–6   A second line of defence: 'if I write long epigrams, I am merely following the example of my Latin predecessors'. Few Greek literary epigrams pre-dating M. were of any great length: cf. Szelest (1980).

5   Marsi doctique Pedonis: Domitius Marsus and Albinovanus Pedo are several times mentioned by M. as his models in epigram: cf. 1.*praef.* 11 and 5.5.6, **15**.24, 7.99.7, 10.20.10. The former wrote surviving epigrams on the deaths of Virgil and Tibullus, and his satiric *Cicuta* probably belonged to the same genre. See further on **15**.24. Little is known of Albinovanus Pedo, and nothing of his epigrams, except for what M. has to say.

doctique, which stands in pointed contrast to *ignoras*, imputes to both Marsus and Pedo a sensitivity to literary niceties which Cosconius conspicuously lacks: '*doctus* connoted most often for the Roman poets the culture, knowledge, literary erudition and technical expertise expected of writing' (A. L. Spisak, *TAPhA* 124 (1994) 298); cf. also A. Hus, *Docere* (Paris 1965) 239–43.

6   saepe duplex unum pagina tractat opus: *pagina* refers to the column of a papyrus roll rather than the page of a codex: the latter did not come into general use until the second century AD: cf. Birt (1882) 255. The figures for the number of lines in a column varied between 25 and 45 (Kenyon (1951) 55–7). If individual pieces by Marsus and Pedo ran to two *paginae* this would yield an epigram which was by any standards long.

duplex unum: pointed juxtaposition.

tractat 'deals with', 'handles' a topic in literature or oratory (*OLD* s.v. 9a). More usually it is the author who *tractat,* here, by transference, his *pagina.*

opus: *opus* in literary contexts normally refers either to a complete text such as Virgil's *Aeneid,* or to a single book of a larger *oeuvre.* In employing the noun, anomalously, of an individual epigram, M. pointedly alludes to the length of the pieces in question.

7–8 For the thought, cf. Philemon, fr. 99 K–A 'consider long-winded (μακρόν) the person who does not say even one of the things that are necessary – even if he speaks only two syllables. But do not think of as long-winded the person who speaks well, even if he says exceedingly many things and takes a long time in doing so. Treat Homer as proof of this principle. For he writes countless lines of hexameters, but no single person has called Homer long-winded,' Plin. *Ep.* 5.6.42–3, Lausberg (1982) 82.

8 sed tu, Cosconi, disticha longa facis: a neat oxymoron 'but you, Cosconius, compose distichs which are (too) long'. In contrast to M., whose longer epigrams by implication contain no superfluities (7), even distichs by Cosconius are long-winded and hence tedious.

4 (= 3.2)

'Whose gift do you wish to become, little book? Quickly get yourself a champion, lest you get recycled as wrapping paper for fish or be used as a cornet for incense or pepper. Do you flee into the bosom of Faustinus? Very wise. Now you can strut about anointed with cedar oil, and disport yourself as a deluxe volume. With him as your champion you needn't fear even Probus.'

The address to the book which shapes the poem goes back to Catullus (35.1–2) as does the opening quest for a suitable dedicatee (1 n.). In personifying the book as a slave (see below), in particular as a runaway, M. follows a Horatian precedent (*fugis* 6n.). M. is especially fond of the device, alluding to the book for example as a *uerna* (3.1.6; cf. 5.18.4; Kay's intro. to 11.1). Often, as here, the context is a prooemial epigram, the book being advised to seek some influential patron who will protect it against the malevolence of critics (e.g. 3.5, 4.86, 7.97, 8.72, 11.1).

In combining the apostrophe to the book with a detailed description of the papyrus book-roll (cf. Catull. 22.6–8), M. is inspired by the opening poem of Ovid's *Tristia*, where the poet addresses his book as a slave about to depart without his master for the City. As befits the mournful nature of its contents, the book will be *incultus*, and will lack the characteristic appearance of a luxury volume:

> nec te purpureo uelent uaccinia fuco –
> non est conueniens luctibus ille color –
> nec titulus minio, nec cedro charta notetur,
> candida nec nigra cornua fronte geras.
> . . . .
> nec fragili geminae poliantur pumice frontes,
> hirsutus sparsis ut uideare comis.
>
> (Ovid, *Tristia* 1.1.5–12)

Like Ovid, M. is sending his book to Rome from abroad, book 3 being written during a sojourn in Gaul. But whereas Ovid's book is appropriately decked in mourning rather than luxury garb, M.'s book, if it wins the favour of his patron Faustinus, will be published as a deluxe volume.

M. adds a new dimension to a traditional theme by building the epigram round an elaborate legal image. He had already done something similar in 1.52, where M.'s books, which are being recited by a *plagiarius*, a plagiarist, but literally a slave-stealer, are imagined as instigating a *causa liberalis*, a law suit in which a person claims that he is free. Since slaves could not speak in court, they had to find an *assertor* to plead on their behalf; in 1.52 this rôle is undertaken by the poet's patron Quintianus, who is to claim that the poems are not the slaves of the plagiarist, but freedmen, since their master (i.e. M.) has manumitted them by the act of publication. In **4**, the *causa liberalis* is also invoked. This time the book is depicted as a runaway slave who desires his freedom. He flees to the protection of Faustinus, who will act as his *assertor*; having won his freedom, he can walk proudly in luxurious garb like a wealthy freedman. Faustinus is referred to (2, 12) by the more general word *uindex* ('champion') rather than the technical term *assertor*, because his function is not only to plead for the slave's freedom but to defend him in the face of harsh critics.

The epigram serves to dedicate the published book to Faustinus (1 n.). Although it does not come at the very beginning – the usual position for dedications – it is closely linked to the first poem by the use in the latter of slave imagery (6 *uerna liber*), and follows up the statement there that the book was written in Gaul by revealing the person in Rome to whom it is sent. A discrepancy may be discerned, however, between the prooemial and dedicatory function of the poem and its internal logic. One might expect the published book to take the form of a luxury volume sent to Faustinus as dedicatee, yet the *libellus* that runs to Faustinus is a slave, and it is only after Faustinus takes up its cause that it assumes the luxurious garb of a freedman, i.e. is published (cf. 1.52.7 for the equation of manumission with publication). This might suggest that M.'s poems are being sent to Faustinus for his approval, as in 4.10, also sent to Faustinus, where it is specified (1–2) that the book has not yet had its edges smoothed with pumice and Faustinus is to emend it if necessary: it will then be published formally.

A way round the difficulty is offered by the suggestion of White (1974) 56 n.64 that **4** belongs to a group of epigrams of a dedicatory nature which show traces of having originally formed the prefaces of small collections, *libelli*, sent privately to individual patrons (*contra*, Citroni (1988) 36 n.61). In that case, **4** will have originally opened a *libellus* sent to Faustinus for his approval, but in the published work can stand as the dedicatory poem.

Further reading: Birt (1882), Buckland (1908) 652–75, Kenney, *CHCL* II 16 and 31 exc. 2, White (1974)

1   Cuius uis fieri, libelle, munus?:   in prefatory pieces the poet often asks himself who would be a suitable dedicatee: cf. Catull. 1.1–2 *cui dono lepidum nouum libellum | arida modo pumice expolitum?* and the opening epigram of Meleager's *Garland* (Meleager, *HE* 1–2 (= *AP* 4.1.1–2)).

munus: the book is frequently offered as a gift to the patron: cf. White (1974) 52, 56.

2   uindicem: the *assertor* in a *causa liberalis*: see intro. above. *uindex* is not used in this sense in legal texts; cf. however *uindicare in libertatem* (e.g. Liv. 3.48.5) and the use of *uindicta* of manumission via the *assertio libertatis* (Buckland (1908) 451).

3–5   The book is sure to be branded as worthless unless it finds a patron to argue its cause: a good example of M.'s characteristic mock-modesty.

3   nigram … culinam: cf. 10.66.3, 1.92.9 with Citroni. *culina* is an everyday term, in poetry restricted to satire and epigram. *nigram* = 'black with smoke' also suggests the infernal darkness to which the doomed book will be consigned (foll. n.).

cito raptus: without a *uindex*, the book/slave will remain a slave and will be rapidly hurried off to servitude in the kitchen. The expression also suggests the premature 'death' of the book (cf. **84**.2n.), death being equated with the absence of a readership: cf. Catull. 95.7–8 cited next n.

4   cordylas . . . tegas papyro: papyrus rolls containing bad poems are often depicted as being recycled in the form of wrapping paper for fish; cf. Catull. 95.7–8 *at Volusi annales Paduam morientur ad ipsam | et laxas scombris saepe dabunt tunicas,* Pers. 1.43, 4.86.9 *nec scombris tunicas dabis molestas,* 13.1.1–3. The topos has traditionally been interpreted as a reference to the wrapping of fish for transportation home from market, but baskets were apparently used for this purpose (e.g. Apul. *Met.* 1.24) and M.'s allusion (4.86.9) to the *tunica molesta*, the inflammable coat in which criminals were burnt, suggests the cooking of fish in a papyrus wrapping. See D. F. S. Thomson, *Phoenix* 18 (1964) 30–6.

cordylas: young tunny-fish: cf. Plin. *NH* 9.47 *cordyla appellatur partus, qui fetas redeuntes in mare autumno comitatur; . . . cum annuum excessere tempus, thynni (uocantur).* Thompson (1947) s.v., however, takes the word as equivalent to the *scombri* of Catull. 95.8 etc. (prev. n.).

madida: the precise allusion is difficult to determine. Thomson (n. on *cordylas . . . tegas papyro*) invokes a Greek cooking method whereby fish to be barbecued are parcelled in fig leaves, which, being naturally moist, protect the fish from burning and conserve the juices. He suggested that papyrus was so employed, but needed to be 'soaked' (*madida*) before use. But a Roman recipe which Thomson compares (Apic. 9.10.1), in which stuffed *sardae* are seasoned with oil, wine and fish sauce and wrapped in papyrus, makes no mention of pre-soaking, and the cooking method involves steaming the fish in a covered vessel. If M. does have such a recipe in mind, the papyrus will be *madida* through the steam, or through the marinade (cf. M. Salanitro, *InvLuc* 7–8 (1985–6) 131–2). It is dubious however whether Apicius' gourmet recipes are relevant in this everyday context.

5   turis piperisue: cf. Hor. *Ep.* 2.1.269–70 *tus et odores | et piper et quidquid chartis amicitur ineptis,* Pers. 1.43.

cucullus, a hood like a monk's cowl, is used metaphorically of a container, presumably in the same shape, in which spices were kept (N. Lewis, *Papyrus in classical antiquity* (Oxford 1974) 95). The choice of the term – a *cucullus* is a humble, everyday garment (Col. 1.8.9) – effectively underscores the contrast between the book's dandified appearance under the protection of Faustinus, and the humble fate which it might otherwise suffer.

6   Faustini: one of M.'s most frequently addressed patrons, especially prominent in this book. Extremely wealthy, he may have tried his hand at poetry himself: cf. Howell and Citroni on 1.25.

fugis: cf. 1.3.12 *i fuge* and Hor. *Ep.* 1.20.5 *fuge quo descendere gestis*, where books are likewise depicted as runaway slaves.

in sinum: cf. 3.5.7–8 *est illi coniunx, quae te* [sc. *librum*] *manibusque sinuque | excipiet.* The *sinus* is regularly the place where asylum and protection are received, e.g. Plin. *Pan.* 6.3.5.

sapisti 'you've made a wise decision'. Cf. 11.106.4 *transis hos quoque quattuor? sapisti.*

7   cedro . . . perunctus: to protect a papyrus roll from moths and decay, the back was smeared with cedar oil: cf. Plin. *NH* 16.197, Turner (1980) 3. Cedar thus became a symbol of good poetry, which was deemed worthy of preserving: cf. Pers. 1.42, Ausonius, I 5.13–14 Green *huius in arbitrio est, seu te iuuenescere cedro | seu iubeat duris uermibus esse cibum.*

ambules: suggests the upstart freedman who struts proudly through the city displaying his newly acquired wealth: cf. Hor. *Epod.* 4.5. *licet superbus ambules pecunia.*

8   frontis gemino decens honore 'handsome with your two edges decorated'. The top and bottom edges of the roll (*frontes*) were smoothed with pumice and stained: cf. Ov. *Tr.* 1.1.8, 11 cited intro., D. M. Possanza, *CQ* 44 (1994) 282 n.6.

9   pictis . . . umbilicis: painted knobs attached to the ends of the rod around which the papyrus was rolled, and projecting outside the roll. Cf. 5.6.15 *nigris . . . umbilicis*, W. Schubart, *Das Buch bei den Griechen und Römern* (2nd ed., Berlin 1921) 106–7.

10   te purpura delicata uelet: the roll was wrapped for protection and ornamentation in a membrane or parchment envelope, which, in the case of expensive editions, was often dyed purple: cf. Ov. *Tr.* 1.1.5 cited intro., 11.1.2 with Kay, Birt (1882) 64–5.

delicata 'luxurious'. Purple was associated with luxury (**54**.3n.).

11   et cocco rubeat superbus index: the index was an identifying tag of papyrus or parchment, attached to the back of the roll so as to hang outwards when the book was stored. In this case the tag is dyed red, a luxury colour (**54**.2n.); cf. Ov. *Tr.* 1.1.7 cited intro. See E. G. Turner, *Greek manuscripts of the ancient world* (2nd. ed., ed. P. J. Parsons, London 1987) 34 and plates 6–8.

superbus: see on *ambules* 7.

12   The approval and support of the book's dedicatee will remove fear of even the harshest criticism. Cf. Gallus, *FLP* 8–9 *non ego, Visce* | ... *Kato, iudice te* [i.e. with you (Lycoris) judging my poetry favourably] *uereor*, Nisbet (1979) 144–7: see Anderson et al. (1979).

illo uindice 'with him (Faustinus) as your champion'. Defending poetry in the face of criticism was a major rôle of patrons.

nec 'not even': *OLD* s.v. *neque* 2b.

Probum: Valerius Probus, the famous grammarian, who flourished under the Flavians. He collected manuscripts of earlier poets on which he performed literary as well as textual criticism (Suet. *Gram.* 24.2 with Kaster): he therefore stands for the harshest critic whom M.'s book is likely to encounter.

5   (= 4.72)

'You ask me to make you a gift of my books of epigrams, Quintus. I do not have a copy, but Tryphon the bookseller has. "Do you seriously expect me to pay money for such trifling stuff? I am not such a fool." Neither am I.'

The situation is much as in 1.117, where Lupercus desires to get from the poet a book of his epigrams for nothing, and is instead directed to Tryphon the bookseller, from whom he can purchase a deluxe copy. Lupercus replies that M. is not worth the expense, and, as here, the poet unexpectedly agrees.

The circulation of books in classical antiquity was primarily a private affair: an author sent copies of his work to friends (cf. 4.10) who, it was hoped, would pass them on to other friends, so that texts moved outwards in concentric circles. An ancillary to this – by the first century AD an increasingly important ancillary – was the book trade. One visited a bookseller when the author of the work required was not among one's circle of friends, or when no acquaintance had a copy: this was, for instance, the case with the old fashioned writings of various literary hacks whom Catullus as a joke threatens to buy up and send to Helvius Cinna (14.17–20). It follows from the above that one of the satiric points which M. is making against Quintus by refusing him a free copy is that the latter is presuming upon a friendship which the poet does not acknowledge.

Further reading: Dziatzko (1894) 559–76, id. *RE* III 981–4 s.v. *Buchhandel*, Starr (1987), Van der Valk (1957)

1   Exigis ut donem nostros tibi, Quinte, libellos: similarly Symmachus, *Ep.* 1.14 complains that he has not been given a copy of Ausonius' *Mosella*.

Exigis ut donem: *exigis* is forcible, 'demand', *donem* equally pointed, 'give for free'.

Quinte: probably a fictitious addressee of a satiric attack, as in 3.62. The context rules out identification with M.'s friend Quintus Ovidius, or the Quintus Pollius Valerianus of 1.113.5, described as unreasonably devoted to M.'s *iuuenilia*.

libellos: *libelli*, the deliberately unpretentious term employed by M. to describe his work, refers here to the books of epigrams published up to this point.

2   non habeo sed habet bibliopola Tryphon: not an improbable claim. M. may have given away all his copies to friends, or to the *bibliopola* for production of copies for sale, retaining only the archetype.

bibliopola Tryphon: booksellers were often of Greek extraction like Tryphon – a reflection perhaps of the importance of the book trade in Athens (Dziatzko, *RE* III 981–4). They procured from an author a copy of his work (whether for payment or not is unclear) and set a team of scribes to making copies for retail, thereby earning a profit for themselves, but not for the author (cf. 13.3). There were no royalties nor rules of copyright in antiquity, which is why M. can complain that, despite his popularity, his works earn him no money (5.16, 11.3): see Dziatzko (1894), Howell intro. to 1.2. Any profit made by a successful author came indirectly from the lucrative patronage which he attracted. It is unsurprising, therefore, that M. declines to give Quintus, who is merely posing as a friend for purely self-interested motives, a free copy of his epigrams. It would actually cost the poet money to do so: cf. on 4 below.

Tryphon: one of a number of booksellers who handled M.'s work. Tryphon is also known to us from the preface to Quintilian's *De institutione oratoria*.

3   aes dabo pro nugis: Quintus, having been denied a free copy of the *libelli*, is now shown to be too mean to pay for them, a refusal which he justifies by alleging their lack of worth. Our evidence for the price of books is partly based on expensive luxury editions (1.117.16–17, Stat. *Silu.* 4.9.7–9), but the purchase of any book would have involved some outlay: see Dziatzko, *RE* III 981–4.

nugis: a common term for light poetry, often used self-depreciatingly by M. of his work following the precedent of Catullus (Swann (1994) 47–55). 8.3 offers a good definition of what M. had in mind.

sanus: sc. *dummodo sanus sim* : cf. Cic. *Mur.* 13 *nemo . . . fere saltat sobrius*. For the use of an adjective to replace a clause, or in situations where Greek would use ὤν, see K–S II 1.239.

4 **nec ego** 'I won't either' be so mad as to spend money on trifles, i.e. incur expense by making a copy for you. It cost an author money to produce a book or a copy (1.66, Stat. *Silu.* 4.9.6–9): the outlay comprised the purchase of writing materials (2.1.4, Cic.*Att.* 13.25.3) and the hire of a scribe to do the copying (2.1.5–6, **1.**4n.).

6 (= 6.64)

'Although you do not spring from old-fashioned, morally upright stock, but are the effeminate offspring of libertine parents, you dare to criticise my poems – poems which are valued by the leading lights of the city, by men of impeccable literary judgment, by the emperor himself. But of course you alone have the critical acumen to judge their true worth. Damned if you don't have even less intelligence than the carcase of a slaughtered animal hauled by a butcher through the streets of Rome. Moreover, you have the effrontery to pen verses against me – verses that no one will read. But if the heat of my anger brands you with infamy, the mark will be indelible. Therefore forbear to provoke me: I am like a tame bear, gentle, but savage if roused. Your canine tendencies would be better exercised in chewing a fleshless hide.'

All self-respecting ancient poets have critics or rivals who attack their work. The pattern is as old as Homer or Pindar, but is especially associated with the Hellenistic poet Callimachus. If detractors do not exist, they can always be invented (Lefkowitz (1981)), for to attract criticism is to be revealed as someone who is felt worth the trouble of criticising, and it is but a short step from this to assert that such criticisms are motivated by jealousy of the target's artistic success: cf. 1.40, 4.27, 6.60, 9.97, 10.9.4, 11.94.1–2, Kay on 11.20.1. M. is no exception to the pattern. He constantly portrays himself as obliged to answer the strictures of persons who carp at his work. The two aspects most frequently singled out for stricture are the allegedly poor or uneven quality of M.'s work (cf. **1,** 2.71, 7.81, 11.90, 13.2) and his obscenity of language and content (*praef.* 1.10–25, 1.35, 11.2, 16.1–2, 20, Sullivan (1991) 64–72). The latter must be the subject of attack here. For in protesting that his antagonist censures his epigrams, despite being unconnected with the Fabiii or Curius, M. is accusing him of hypocritically arrogating to himself the austere and censorious morality of these ancient worthies, who elsewhere in M. represent old-fashioned standards which are affronted by the explicit sexuality of the poet's writings (7.68, 11.2, 16.6: cf. 11.104.1–2).

6 is unusual among the epigrams both for its length (see on **3**) and for its metre, the hexameter, which M. uses in only three other poems (1.53, 2.73, 7.98). Neither anomaly is adverted to in **6**, but both are criticised in the next, brief piece by a certain Tucca, to whom M. replies that each is sanctioned by epigrammatic usage: cf. Sullivan (1991) 63, Szelest (1980). Similarly the thirty-three-line **56** is followed immediately by a distich complaining that M.'s epigrams are too long.

1–3   Exemplars of old-fashioned virtue which could have given M.'s opponent, had he been born of such, the moral authority to criticise him. The Fabii, an old patrician family, often sustain this rôle; cf. Dio Cass. 61.17.4, M. 7.58.7 *aliquem Curios semper Fabiosque loquentem*. Their best known representatives were Q. Fabius Maximus Rullianus, hero of the Samnite wars and Q. Fabius Maximus Cunctator. The Curius of 2–3 is M' Curius Dentatus, famed for alternating personal labour in the fields with the highest offices of state (Courtney on Juv. 11.89). Historical *exempla uirtutis* were a stock rhetorical device of M. as of other Roman writers: cf. Litchfield (1914), Nordh (1954).

1   **Cum sis:** M. often commences an epigram with concessive *cum* in order to point a contrast (which here comes in 6–7), e.g. 3.93, **41**.

   rigida: often used of the 'unbending' morality of olden days: cf. 10.20.21 *rigidi . . . Catones*, Hor. *Ep.* 2.1.25 *rigidis . . . Sabinis*.

   creatus 'sprung from' is almost exclusive to poetry. The ironically dignified term fits the archaic context: cf. *CLE* 958 *uirtutes generis mieis moribus accumulaui, | progeniem genui, facta patris petiei, | maiorum optenui laudem, ut sibei me esse creatum | laetentur.*

2–3   **dum prandia portat . . . | . . . peperit . . . coniunx:** preparation of food was one of the main tasks of women in the country. Usually done by slaves, it fell to wives in humbler establishments: cf. Hor. *Epod.* 2.43–8. In keeping with the satiric context, M. exaggerates the exemplary

character of the rustic lifestyle, making Curius' wife work right up to the
moment of delivery, a practice foreign to Italy but admired by Greek and
Roman writers: cf. Var. *R.* 2.10.8–9, W. Scheidel, *G&R* 43 (1996) 7.

2   qualem: short for *nec talis sis qualem* i.e. it isn't as if you were like
the offspring of Curius and his wife, who would inherit their exemplary
morality.

    aranti: Curius (1–3n.) embodied the archaic Roman ideal of the
small peasant-cultivator, for which cf. Cato, *Agr.* 1 *praef.* 2–4, Col. 1. *praef.*
13–14.

3   hirsuto: Ker's emendation for the *hirsuta* of the MSS, which, although defensible (Virg. *G.* 3. 231 *frondibus hirsutis*), adds little to the sense.
hirsuto suits the context perfectly, since the long hair of the early Romans –
barbers were not introduced until *c.* 300 BC – came to symbolise their
archaic virtue: cf. Hor. *Carm.* 1.12.41, M. 7.58.7–8.

    deprensa 'caught short by birth-pangs'. The alternative reading *rubi-
cunda* 'sunburned' suits the context, as adverting to the idea that the old-style
farmer's wife was swarthy from working in the fields (**41**.3–4n.), but was
probably imported from a marginal gloss citing Ov. *Med.* 11–13 *forsitan an-
tiquae Tatio sub rege Sabinae* | *maluerint quam se rura paterna coli,* | *cum matrona
premens altum rubicunda sedile.* Cf. Housman, *CPh* 1103, J. D. Duff, *CR* 17
(1903) 222.

    coniunx: mock-elevated; the term for wife in epic, rarer in M. than
uxor and often found in more dignified contexts e.g. 5.7.8 and 6.47.3, 2.41.14
coniunx Priami.

4–5 repeat from a different angle the idea implicit in 1–3, that a child's
character is inherited from his parents, in the case of M.'s enemy, a pathic
and a prostitute.

4   sed patris ad speculum tonsi: excessive attention to coiffure
and prettifying oneself in front of a mirror were the mark of the effeminate
male. Cf. Juv. 2.99, Scipio *ap.* Gell. 6.12.5 *qui cotidie unguentatus aduersum
speculum ornetur . . . eumne quisquam dubitet quin idem fecerit, quod cinaedi facere solent?*

    matrisque togatae: unexpected. Instead of being *stolata*, garbed
like a respectable *matrona*, the critic's mother wore the toga, the mark of
a prostitute or convicted adulteress: cf. 2.39, 10.52, Sebesta and Bonfante
(1994) 50–1, 140–1, 144 n.44, McGinn (1998) 156–71.

5   **et possit sponsam te sponsa uocare:**   the enemy is as wom-
anish as his bride-to-be, having inherited his father's pathic proclivities.
The language is indebted to accounts of homosexual marriages, in which
the submissive male took the part of the 'bride': cf. Courtney on Juv. 2.117.

6   **emendare** 'to correct' M.'s work (cf. 7.11.1–2 *cogis me calamo manuque*
nostra | emendare meos, Pudens, libellos), on moral grounds.

   meos, quos nouit fama, libellos: the books which you presume
to criticise enjoy wide approval. M. often boasts of his popularity, e.g. 1.1.2
toto notus in orbe Martialis, 3.95.7–8. For the personification *nouit fama* cf.
1.39.2, 1.93.6; *quos nullus nouerit* (22) applies the opposite idea to the critic's
writings.

7   **tibi permittis** 'you presume'.
   felices 'felicitous, successful', a second reason why criticisms are out of
order.
   carpere: elsewhere in M. of maliciously 'criticising' his literary pro-
ductions, e.g. 1.91.1–2 *cum tua non edas, carpis mea carmina, Laeli. | carpere uel*
noli nostra uel ede tua.
   nugas: 5.3n.

8   **has, inquam, nugas:**   the emphatic use of the verb, often, as
here, to reinforce a demonstrative adjective or key word in anaphora: cf.
Ov. *Met.* 13.284 *his umeris, his inquam umeris.*
   aurem aduertere totam 'to lend a fully attentive ear', an auditory
variation on *animum aduertere*: cf. Prop. 1.1.37 *quod si quis monitis tardas aduerterit*
aures.

9   **non aspernantur:**   litotes. *aspernari* normally takes the acc. case:
cf. 5.30.5–6. For the infin., cf. Stat. *Theb.* 12.530, *Silu.* 1.2.105, Tac. *Ann.*
4.46.
   proceres: an elevated poeticism (cf. Bömer on Ov. *Met.* 3.530) suited
to 'the leading lights of the city and forum' who value M. as a poet. The
enthusiasm of these for M.'s work adds a third reason why the addressee
shows faulty judgment in criticising his epigrams.

10–15   Instances of favourably disposed *proceres urbisque forique*, culminating with the Emperor Domitian.

10   Silius Italicus, author of the epic *Punica*, mentioned here not just as
a famous literary man (*perpetui* n.) whose judgment in giving M.'s poems

house-room commands respect, but also as a distinguished consular and
advocate (cf. *proceres urbisque forique*, 7.63.6, *RE* II 3.79). M. often mentions
the influential Silius in flattering terms: cf. D. W. T. C. Vessey, *Hermes* 102
(1974) 109–16.

perpetui: i.e. who has gained immortality through his poetry; cf.
7.63.1 *perpetui numquam moritura uolumina Sili*. The younger Pliny is less
enthusiastic: cf. *Ep.* 3.7.5.

dignantur scrinia: *scrinia* were cylindrical cases in which papyrus
rolls were kept: cf. Th. Birt, *Die Buchrolle in der Kunst* (Leipzig 1907) 248–55,
Kenyon (1951) 62. According to Plin. *Ep.* 3.7.8 Silius had *multum . . . librorum*
in his several Campanian villas, but since he was also accused of *emacitas*
(ibid.), M.'s being thought worthy of admission to his *scrinia* need imply no
special distinction.

11   et repetit totiens facundo Regulus ore: usually explained
'and Regulus so often reads with his eloquent tongue' (silent reading was
relatively rare in antiquity: cf. B. M. W. Knox, *GRBS* 9 (1968) 421–35).
Equally possible, however, is 'and the eloquent-tongued Regulus (abl. of
description) so often returns to', in appreciation of their quality; cf. 15 *non
dedignatur bis terque reuoluere Caesar*, 9. *praef.* 8–9. M. Aquilius Regulus was a
leading advocate, and according to Pliny, a notorious *delator*/legacy-hunter.
He appears several times as a patron of M., though the tone is formal rather
than intimate. In the present context M. represents him as an orator of the
first order (cf. 4.16.6, 5.28.6). For an entirely different (and perhaps equally
biased) assessment of Regulus' forensic talents, cf. Plin. *Ep.* 4.7.

12   quique uidet propius magni certamina Circi: the Circus
Maximus lay in the valley between the Palatine and Aventine, where Sura
lived (next n.).

13   Auentinae uicinus Sura Dianae: i.e. Sura had a house on the
Aventine (a fashionable residential area under the empire) near the temple
of Diana. Although this passage is the sole evidence for Sura's house, we
know of baths, the *Thermae Surae*, near Diana's temple: cf. Richardson
395–6.

Auentinae . . . Dianae: the oldest shrine of Diana in Rome was on
this hill (*colle Dianae* 7.73.1). Cf. Richardson 108–9.

Sura: L. Licinius Sura, a fellow-Spaniard, mentioned by M. as a
patron at 1.49.40 and 7.47. He was erudite and politically important, especially under Trajan, but may have held the first of his three consulates

in 86 or earlier (T. D. Barnes, *Phoenix* 30 (1976) 76–9; cf. C. P. Jones, *JRS* 60 (1970) 98–104, Howell on 1.49.40).

14–15 If even Domitian, burdened as he is with affairs of state, can find time to read and enjoy me, who are you to criticise my poems? M. likes to boast that the emperor is one of his readers: cf. 1.101.2, **9a**.3–4, 4.27.1, 7.12.1–2, 7.99.3–4, Howell on 5.1.9.

14   dominus: 10.4n.
    sub pondere rerum: the metaphorical 'burden' of imperial responsibility, cf. Hor. *Ep.* 2.1.1, Ov. *Met.*15.1 with Bömer, Luc. 9.951.

15   bis terque 'several times over' (Brink on Hor. *Ars* 358), a sign of Domitian's appreciation.
    reuoluere: unroll the papyrus in order to read it.

16–17 'But you have more intelligence, and, with Minerva refining your wits to make them sharper, subtle Athens shaped your intellect', i.e. 'but you of course have far keener critical acumen than they'. For the sarcasm, cf. 3.26.4 *et cor solus habes, solus et ingenium.*

16   cor: the heart was generally regarded as the seat of intelligence: cf. **1**.6n.
    limante: *limare*, literally 'to file down', is used in a transferred sense of 'honing' or 'refining' literary style or intellect: cf. Plin. *Ep.* 1.20.22 *limatioris . . . ingenii, OLD* s.v. *limo* 2a, R. F. Thomas, *CQ* 33 (1983) 97 n.36. The metaphor of filing or polishing sits rather oddly with the physiological connotations of *cor*, perhaps in an effect of deliberate grotesquerie.
    Minerua: as the goddess who presided over intellectual pursuits, best qualified to sharpen the antagonist's critical acumen. The noun occupies the same locus as the *Caesar* of the previous line, in order to suggest the well-known connexion between Domitian and the deity (cf. Suet. *Dom.* 15.3).

17   acrius: proleptic.
    tenues finxerunt pectus Athenae: an ironic fiction suggesting that the critic did *not* enjoy the benefit of 'tertiary' study in Athens, where well-to-do Romans had traditionally gone to round off their education. *tenuis* (λεπτός) is used in its familiar sense of intellectually subtle or discriminating.

18–21 You have even less sense than a slaughtered animal carted by a butcher through the streets. The idea is developed from Plaut. *Mil.* 586–7 *sat edepol certo scio | occisam saepe sapere plus multo suem.* The debunking effect is heightened by the conspicuously unwholesome terms used to describe the carcase (*panticibus laxis, cum pede grandi, rubro pulmone, uetus nasisque timendum*).

18 ne ualeam, si: one of a number of self-imprecations used in popular speech to lend force to an asseveration: cf. 4.31.3–4 *ne ualeam, si non res est gratissima nobis | et uolo te chartis inseruisse meis,* Citroni on 1.39.8.

sapit 'has sense', but with a concomitant pun on the meaning 'tastes', as in 7.25.8, 11.90.8 and Cic. *Fin.* 2.24 (**1.**6n.)

altius: of 'higher' or 'loftier' understanding: cf. Val. Max. 9.13. ext. 1 *[Xerxes] opum magnitudine quam altiore animi sensu felicior.*

illud: the circumstantiality of detail argues a reference to the whole animal: cf. G. P. Shipp, *Antichthon* 4 (1970) 27.

19–21 quod . . . | . . . | omnia . . . lanius per compita portat: animals were slaughtered on his premises by the butcher, who either sold the flesh direct, or, as here, transported the carcasses through the streets for sale in the meat markets. Cf. J. M. Frayn, *Markets and fairs in Roman Italy* (Oxford 1993) 70.

19 panticibus: a coarse word for 'guts', generally of people, here, anomalously, of animals.

laxis: refers either to the pendulous belly of the animal or to its innards spilling out.

cum pede grandi: the type of animal in 18–21 is not specified, but the detail would suit an ox: if so, M. insultingly compares his enemy to a creature notorious for stupidity (14.219 *cor bubulum,* Cic. *Off.* 2.11 *expertes rationis . . . boues*).

20 nasisque timendum: i.e. malodorous. Carcasses which were not fresh (*uetus*) would quickly smell high in the Mediterranean climate.

21 crudelis: because of his 'butchery' of animals with his knife; cf. Petr. 62.12.

lanius: not only is the image of the slaughtered beast vividly disgusting, but the effect is enhanced by the disreputable character of the butcher's trade (7.61.9, Joshel (1992) 114–15).

22–3 audes praeterea, quos nullus nouerit, in me | scribere uersiculos: not content with criticising my work, you have the effrontery to pen epigrams against me: but no one is likely to read them. Cf. 3.9

uersiculos in me narratur scribere Cinna. | *non scribit, cuius carmina nemo legit.* The reason for the failure to gain a readership is in each case the miserable quality of the *uersiculi* (23n.). There is an implied contrast with M.'s success in attracting readers (9–15 and 6n.).

22   nullus: because of an original restriction to nom., acc. and dat. sing., *nemo* tends to be supplanted by a substantive *nullus*, especially in popular speech and in post-classical literature: cf. 3.27.2, LHS 204–5.

23   uersiculos: a deflationary diminutive suggesting M.'s opinion of the verses in question.

miseras et perdere chartas: the papyrus is alike 'wretched' and 'wasted' because of the poor quality of the verses set thereon: cf. **7**.7n., 2.1.3–4 *at nunc succincti quae sint bona disce libelli.* | *hoc primum est, breuior quod mihi charta perit,* Juv. 1.18.

chartas: the individual sheets which go to make up a papyrus roll (*charta*): cf. Catull. 22.6 *cartae regiae, noui libri,* **1**.1 n.

24–6 Should his opponent's verbal assaults incite M. to respond in kind, the result will be an unwanted (and indelible) notoriety, the price commonly paid for provoking an iambic or satiric poet to anger: cf. Catull. 40 and 116 with C. W. Macleod, *Collected papers* (Oxford 1983) 184. M. threatens to suspend his usual practice (1 *praef.* etc.) of not naming his enemies: cf. Ov. *Ib.* 53–64.

24   at si quid nostrae tibi bilis inusserit ardor: *bilis* is properly the fluid secreted by the liver and then by extension the 'anger' of which the liver was considered the seat: cf. Hagen (1961) 41–6. The language may be indebted to Hor. *Epod.* 11.15–16 *quodsi meis inaestuet praecordiis* | *libera bilis,* but the idea of the liver's being heated (*ardor*) by anger is very trite: cf. Hor. *Carm.* 1.13.3–4 *uae meum* | *feruens difficili bile tumet iecur.*

quid: any mark of infamy.

inusserit: the heat of M.'s anger will imprint a metaphorical brand of infamy upon his enemy, a strikingly novel collocation. *stigma* (cf. *stigmata* 26) generally refers to tattooing rather than branding (Jones (1987)), but *ardor* and *inusserit* suggest the latter: cf. Val. Max. 6.8.7 *inexpiabilique litterarum nota per summam oris contumeliam inustus.* The purpose of tattooing/branding was punishment and humiliation.

25   uiuet: because *uictura meis mandantur nomina chartis* (7.44.7).

haerebit: announces the motif of indelibility which the following verse will develop: cf. Suet. cited on 26.

totoque legetur in orbe: since, he claims, M. enjoys a worldwide readership (6n.), the infamy attached to the enemy by his ripostes will extend to the furthest confines of the globe: cf. 5.60.4–5. Earlier poets merely prognosticated that their attackers would become a *fabula per urbem* (Archil. fr. 172 W, Catull. 40, Hor. *S.* 2.1.45–6).

26 stigmata nec uafra delebit Cinnamus arte: not even Cinnamus' skill will avail to delete the imprint of verbal infamy. Cinnamus must be a doctor, like the Eros of 10.56.6, who specialises in removing scars; cf. Jones (1987) 143–4.

stigmata: for *stigmata* in a transferred sense, cf. Suet. *Iul.* 73 *Catullum, a quo sibi uersiculis de Mamurra perpetua stigmata imposita non dissimulauerat.* The production of metaphorical *stigmata* by retributive epigrams is probably suggested by the practice, in punitive branding/tattooing, of inscribing a form of words, sometimes referred to as an *epigramma,* upon the person so punished (Petr. 103.5).

nec: 4.12n.

27–31 'For your own sake, desist from your attacks. I am like a tame bear, gentle for the most part but savage if roused.' The use of a beast-analogy to characterise the dangerous irascibility of a satirist reflects a tradition extending back to Archilochus. Various creatures are employed, above all dogs (31–2n.); the bear simile is apparently M.'s invention.

27–8 nec ... | ... temptaueris: in second-person negative commands the perfect subjunctive often replaces the present, to which it is equivalent in sense.

nec ... | fumantem nasum uiui temptaueris ursi: for the bear as an emblem of dangerous ferocity cf. 3.19, Isoc. *Antid.* 213–14, Ov. *Met.* 10.540. Bears were indigenous to Italy, where they preyed upon flocks: cf. Toynbee (1973) 93–100.

27 rabido: in describing his enemy as 'demented' for provoking him, M. echoes Archil. fr. 172 W and Catull. 40.

perditus: a strongly pejorative term conveying the idea of destructive madness: cf. Cic. 1 *Verr.* 1.15 *iste homo amens ac perditus.*

ore: by continuing to compose verses against me.

28   **fumantem nasum:**   the nose is traditionally a seat of anger (Gow on Theoc. 1.18).

    uiui: in contrast to the *tacita caro* of 32.

29   A reference to the phenomenon of bear-taming: cf. Isoc. *Antid.* 213–14. Hand licking is a sign of tameness in animals (**10**.4 n.).

30   **dolor:**   the first of three synonyms in the line for 'anger'.

31   **ursus erit:**   he will behave as you would expect a bear to behave, reverting to its innate ferocity; cf. Gal. 5.40 K 'if you train a bear to be tame it will not maintain this disposition', Ael. *NA* 4.45.

31–2   **uacua dentes in pelle fatiges | ... rodere, carnem:**   in a further animal image, M. characterises his enemy as a dog, a common metaphor for aggressive individuals, including satirists or writers of malicious verses: cf. Hor. *Epod.* 6, M. 5.60, F. Muecke, '*Cave canem*: the satirist's image' in P. Petr, D. Roberts and P. Thompson, *Comic relations* (Frankfurt 1985) 113–22. The particular reference is to the canine habit of chewing hides (*pelle*), sometimes in combination with flesh (*carnem*): cf. Williams (1959). In advising his enemy to 'work on an empty hide and chew meat that cannot speak', M. is warning him to steer clear of attacks on one such as he who is perfectly capable of penning retaliatory epigrams; cf. Lucian, *Pseudol.* 1.

7   (= 10.4)

'You who read of Oedipus, Thyestes and other trite mythological subjects, what do you read of but monstrosities? What good will you derive from the fate of Hylas, Parthenopaeus and so on? What use to you is such vapid rubbish? Better to read literature that has some connexion with reality, that is to say my epigrams, which smack of real life and contain no fabulous monsters. But you don't want, Mamurra, to recognise your evil ways, or know what you are like. All right, read the *Aetia* of Callimachus.'

One of several pieces in which M. exalts the importance of his genre by attacking elevated poems on hackneyed mythological topics. According to M., his epigrams – in contrast to 'higher' poetry, the themes of which are divorced from reality – serve a useful social function because they enable the reader to acquire self-knowledge through recognition therein of his (or her) own faults. The usual generic hierarchy is reversed, as in 4.49: it is the higher genres rather than the lower which are mere trifles (n. on *ludibria*); Juvenal 1 expounds the same idea. In attacking mythological poetry, M. appropriates its idiom: most of the poem is in mock high style. The tone is set in the opening line, which contains two Greek accusatives, the poetic *caligantem*, and the elevated *Oedipodes*. The structure is highly artistic, with ring composition, *qui legis* being taken up in the last line by *legas*, and anaphoric *quid* introducing a series of questions (3–7). The *exempla* are carefully balanced: a pair of wicked men is followed by a pair of wicked women, all of whom have committed sins to do with family relationships, then three beautiful boys are named in one line, followed by three more allotted one line apiece. The list of boys is framed by monsters, human and literal. The mention of beautiful boys suggests a characteristic topic of Hellenistic poetry (cf. Phanocles' Ἔρωτες ἢ Καλοί, 'Loves or Handsome boys', Theoc. 13); most of the examples listed here appeared in Hellenistic or neoteric poems. The theme is thus an appropriate lead-in to the mention in 12 of Callimachus' *Aetia*, a key Hellenistic poetic text, here exemplifying the kind of verse which has no connexion with real life.

Although the epigram may be read as an attack on the higher poetic genres *per se*, M. may well be thinking in particular of his contemporary Statius, with whom he seems to have been on hostile terms (Heuvel (1937) 307), perhaps as a consequence of their rivalry for patronage (Henriksén (1998) 82). This possibility is supported by linguistic and other evidence within the poem: see on 1, 3, and 5.

Further reading: Citroni (1968), Henriksén (1998), Heuvel (1937) 299–330, Preston (1920), Sullivan (1991) 72–4

1   Oedipoden: *Oedipodes*, employed first in extant Latin poetry by Seneca, is an alternative for the more usual *Oedipus*. There may be a hit at Statius who, in his *Thebaid*, not only shows a conspicuous predilection for the word, but is the first to use it in the Greek accusative form.

caligantem . . . Thyesten: *caligantem* = either 'seeing dimly' (cf. Quint. *Inst.* 1.2.19) or 'in the dark'. The sun turned back from the sky at the sight of Thyestes feasting upon his own children – a topic which often symbolises the trite mythological themes of the 'higher' poetic genres: cf. 4.49.3–4 quoted on 7. *caligans* is another pointed allusion to Statius; the word is rare in epic apart from the *Thebaid*.

2   Colchidas et Scyllas 'women like the Colchian [Medea] and Scylla': further examples of trite mythological themes; cf. 5.53.1 and 10.35.5. Latin often uses a generalising plural where one specific exemplar is intended: cf. Hor. *Ep.* 1.1.64 *et maribus Curiis et decantata Camillis*. Scylla is presumably the daughter of Nisus, who killed her father by removing his purple lock, rather than the sea-monster of the same name: all four *exempla* in 1–2 are then *monstra* who committed crimes against members of their immediate family.

3   Hylas: the boy-love of Hercules carried off by water nymphs, another tired theme: cf. Virg. *G.* 3.6 *cui non dictus Hylas puer?*

Parthenopaeus: one of the Seven against Thebes. A clear reference to Statius: not only is unusual prominence afforded to this character in the *Thebaid*, but his boyish good looks – which fit him for inclusion in M.'s list of handsome youths – are especially stressed by Statius. See also Stat. *Silu.* 2.6.40–3 with Van Dam.

Attis: a beautiful youth who castrated himself to become a devotee of the Mother Goddess Cybele: cf. Catull. 63.

4   dormitor ... Endymion: the sleep of Endymion, a fair boy loved by the Moon goddess, was proverbial (cf. Suidas, 2.275 Adler 'you sleep as did Endymion', Otto, *Sprichw.* s.v.). First mentioned in this connexion by Sappho (fr. 199 L–P), he belongs mainly to Hellenistic and Latin poetry.

dormitor: an original coinage (cf. **19**.5). Words in -*tor* are widespread in moralising or satiric contexts, from Pompeian graffiti to Ciceronian speeches. They mark a person as given to a particular vice or habit (here, sleeping): cf. Virgil's ironic *latrator Anubis* (*A.* 8.698).

5   exutusue puer pinnis labentibus 'the boy stripped of his falling wings': a debunking periphrasis for Icarus comparable to Juvenal's *mare percussum puero* (1.54), where Icarus likewise stands for a hackneyed mythological theme. *labens* and *exutus* are both common in Statius, the latter used eight times in the *Thebaid*, as against three in the *Aeneid* and one in Ov. *Met.* *exutus* with a concrete rather than an abstract noun is unusual: cf. Stat. *Ach.* 1.427 *exuti [arboribus] uiderunt aëra montes*.

pinnis labentibus: in order to escape from Crete, Icarus was fitted by his father Daedalus with wings consisting of feathers held together by wax. Disobeying his father's orders, he flew too close to the sun, the wax melted, his wings 'fell off' and he plunged to his death: cf. Ov. *Fast.* 4.283 *lapsas ubi perdidit alas.*

6   amatrices: the nymph Salmacis attempted to rape Hermaphrod-itus while he was swimming in her pool (Ov. *Met.* 4. 285–388): hence her waters can be described as 'amorous'. *amatrix*, elsewhere a noun, is abusive and carries the connotation 'hussy' (S. Lilja, *Terms of abuse in Roman Comedy* (Helsinki 1965) 13). The oxymoronic juxtaposition of *odit* and *amatrices* might be a parody of Catullus' *odi et amo.*

7   quid . . . iuuant 'what use to you are . . . ?'

uana . . . miserae ludibria chartae: the emptiness (*uana*) of the subject-matter makes a mockery (*ludibrium*) of the unhappy paper upon which such stuff is inscribed; *chartae* is objective genitive: cf. Liv. 45.3.3 *Rhodios . . . uelut ad ludibrium stolidae superbiae in senatum uocatos esse.* Since *ludib-rium* can also mean a jest, there is an implication that it is elevated poetry which is frivolous rather than the humble genre of epigram. For the inver-sion, cf. 4.49.1–4 *nescit . . . quid sint epigrammata . . . | qui tantum lusus illa iocosque uocat. | ille magis ludit qui scribit prandia saeui | Tereos aut cenam, crude Thyesta, tuam.*

8   hoc lege, quod possit dicere uita 'meum est':   satirists and epigrammatists routinely claim that they represent life as it really is; cf. 8.3.19–20 *at tu Romano lepidos sale tinge libellos: | agnoscat mores uita legatque suos,* Juv. 1.85–6 *quidquid agunt homines, uotum, timor, ira, uoluptas, | gaudia, discursus, nostri farrago libelli est.*

quod possit dicere uita 'meum est' 'of which life could say "it is mine" ': a vivid personification. The thought is 'quod possit dicere uita suum esse', the acc. and inf. being converted into direct speech but with acc. *quod* retained instead of the expected *de quo;* cf. Shackleton Bailey (1989) 142.

9   Centauros . . . Gorgonas Harpyiasque: all semi-human mo-nsters (the Centaurs were half horse, the Gorgons maidens with snaky hair, and the Harpies had a woman's head and a bird's body): the fantastic character of the trio affords an apt contrast with *hominem* in the next line.

10   hominem pagina nostra sapit 'my poetry smacks of human beings'. 9–10 amplify the thought of 7–8, that epigram has real life as its subject, in contrast to the unreal themes of the higher genres.

11   Mamurra: the name recalls the henchman of Julius Caesar attacked by Catullus as a corrupt and debauched individual. Such a person would benefit from reading M.'s epigrams.

cognoscere: cf. 8.3.20, cited on 8.

mores = *malos mores*: cf. Plaut. *Trin.* 284 *noui ego hoc saeculum moribus quibu' siet*; Cic. *Cat.* 1.2 *o tempora, o mores!*

12   te scire: cf. the proverbial γνῶθι σεαυτόν ('know yourself'): self-knowledge is the first step to self-improvement.

Aetia Callimachi: the most famous work of the third-century BC Hellenistic poet and scholar Callimachus, dealing with the 'Origins' (*Aetia*) of various civic and cultic usages. The work normally symbolises the 'slender' style of poetry as opposed to the trite and inflated genus of epic but here is associated, as in the preface to Persius' *Satires*, with the unreal themes of elevated poetry. It is certainly true that the abstruse subject-matter of the *Aetia* has little connexion with real life. Cf. Citroni (1968) 280–2.

8   (= 10.5)

'Let whoever contemptuously writes scurrilous verses against the leading men and women of the State suffer homelessness, beggary, starvation and prolonged cold. May a pauper's death be preferable to the life which he must endure, and when his last hour finally comes, let him sense scavenging birds and dogs gathering about him. Let not his sufferings terminate with death, but let him undergo the torments of the eternally damned in Hades, and, when constrained by the Fury to acknowledge his guilt, let him confess his authorship of the offending poems.'

It is unclear whether the unidentified miscreant denounced in this epigram pens anonymous lampoons, or whether he composes pseudonymous ones which he passes off as M.'s. The latter possibility is more likely: not only does M. make an identical complaint elsewhere (7.12, 7.72, 10.33), but an instance occurs just two poems earlier, in 10.3, which is also in the same metre as **8**, choliambics, suggesting that the two poems are on the same topic. Furthermore, in curse-poetry (see below), the imprecations invariably arise from an offence offered by an enemy to the author of the curses.

A comparable scenario to the present epigram is found in Sidon. Apoll. *Ep.* 1.11, describing the circulation of anonymous satires which were falsely ascribed to a given poet or poets: the motives were presumably the same as here – to disguise the identity of the author for fear of reprisals while at the same time achieving greater currency for the satires by capitalising on the reputation of a successful author.

If someone was foisting upon M. pseudonymous lampoons against the nobility, this was a serious matter: Domitian took a dim view of abusive writings against leading individuals (Suet. *Dom.* 8.3). Of particular relevance to the situation here is Ulpian, *Dig.* 47.10.5.9–10, who states that under the praetor's edict *si quis librum ad infamiam alicuius pertinentem scripserit, composuerit, ediderit doloue malo fecerit, quo quid eorum fieret, etiamsi alterius nomine ediderit uel sine nomine, ut de ea re agere liceret, et si condemnatus sit qui id fecit, intestabilis ex lege esse iubetur;* cf. Suet. *Aug.* 55.

It is possible however that the situation depicted in 10.5 is a literary fiction. The punishments which M. wishes upon the offending party are grossly disproportionate to his crime: such overkill places M.'s epigram squarely in the tradition of Greco-Roman curse-poetry, where the penalties invoked upon the (often invented) target of the maledictions are frequently of a severity which is at odds with the relevant offence: see Watson (1991) 133–9 *et passim.* A striking instance of imprecational overkill is seen in Ovid's *Ibis,* the main surviving Latin representative of ancient curse-poetry. This text served as a major inspiration for the present epigram: see below.

Further reading: Rudd (1986) 62–81, Smith (1951), Watson (1991), Williams (1996)

1–2   For attacks on leading individuals of both sexes, cf. Tac. *Ann.* 1.72.12 *primus Augustus cognitionem de famosis libellis specie eius legis tractauit, commotus Cassii Seueri libidine, qua uiros feminasque illustres procacibus scriptis diffamauerat.*

1   Quisquis: the target of a curse-poem is often either anonymous or unidentified: cf. Euphorion's *Curses or the cup-stealer* (fr. 8 Powell), against 'whoever on his own stole my Alubeian cup', Watson (1991) 129–32.

stolaeue: the *stola,* the garb of respectably married Roman women, is used by metonymy for upper-class females: cf. Plin. *NH* 33.40 *etiamne pedibus induetur [aurum] atque inter stolam plebemque hunc medium feminarum equestrem ordinem faciet?,* L. M. Wilson, *The clothing of the ancient Romans* (Baltimore 1938) 152–61.

purpuraeue: i.e. the higher magistrates, who wore the red-bordered *toga praetexta;* cf. 8.8.4 *purpura te felix, te colat omnis honos, OLD* s.v. 3.

contemptor: the suffix *-tor* (**7**.4n.) suggests that the lampoonist makes a practice of such behaviour.

2   laesit impio uersu: for *laedo* of verbal assaults, cf. Hor. *S.* 2.1.65–8.

   impio: showing no reverence for those *quos colere debet.*

3   erret per urbem pontis exul et cliui: a localised variation on the common imprecatory motif of exile: cf. Ael. *VH* 3.29 '(Diogenes Cynicus) used to say...that he endured...the curses from tragedy, for he was "without a city, without a home, deprived of his native land, a wandering beggar"', Watson (1991) 35. M.'s enemy is to suffer exile, not as usual from his own city, but from its bridges and slopes, the traditional haunts of the beggars whose ranks he is to join: cf. **64**.10 and 25, Juv. 4.116 with Courtney. He will thus be unable to eke out an impoverished existence.

   erret per urbem: *urbs* = Rome (*OLD* s.v. 2). M. perhaps has in mind Homer's Irus, 'who used to go begging all over the city of Ithaca' (*Od.* 18.1–2).

   pontis exul et cliui: for the genitive, cf. Hor. *Carm.* 2.16.19–20 *patriae quis exul | se quoque fugit?*

4   interque raucos ultimus rogatores further develops the idea that the slanderer will become the meanest of beggars. Mendicancy is one of the commonest curse-motifs (Watson (1991) 36 n.161).

   raucos: hoarse with begging.

   rogatores: the *contemptor* of 1 has become the *rogator* of 4. The noun, perhaps a calque on Gk προσαιτεῖν, 'ask for alms', is found in the present sense elsewhere only at **10**.13.

5   oret caninas panis improbi buccas: the slanderer will be forced to beg for scraps of inferior bread, the staple diet of dogs in antiquity (Var. *R.* 2.9.10, [Theoc.] 21.44–5 with Gow), often flung to them in the form of so-called 'dog-bites' (κυνάδες); cf. Ath. 409d, Ar. *Eq.* 413–16.

   caninas...buccas: *buccas* = 'mouthfuls', *buccellas*. The scraps of bread fed to dogs were meagre: cf. Philostr. *VA* 1.19, Gell. 13.31.16, where *prandium caninum* stands for an abstemious meal.

   improbi = *uilis*, of poor quality: cf. Plaut. *Mil.* 728–9 *quae probast mers, pretium ei statuit, pro uirtute ut ueneat. | quae improbast, pro mercis uitio dominum pretio pauperat.* Roman bread fell into three categories, the poorest sort containing more bran than meal: cf. Blümner, *Technologie* I 77–80. Since it was on this last type that dogs fed (cf. Phaedr. 4.19.1–5, Juv. 5.10–11 with Courtney), the eating of it became synonymous with destitution: cf. Plaut. *Asin.* 139–42, Artem. *Oneir.* 1.49, J. Voigt, *RhM* 31 (1876) 123.

6–7　　illi December longus... | ... frigus extendat: in M., December is often synonymous with the chilliest time of the year (**82**.6n.). For another curse involving cold, cf. Hippon. fr. 115.9–12 W 'rigid with cold... and may his teeth rattle, as he lies like a dog helpless and face-downward'.

6　　longus: refers to what appears long: *OLD* s.v. 9c. To the homeless man, lacking shelter (*clusus... fornix*), the cold and rain of December seem to drag on for ever.

7　　clusus ... fornix: lit. 'a closed arch'. *fornix* refers either to an arched doorway (cf. Liv. 36.23.3 *fornices quoque in muro erant apti ad excurrendum, CIL* ii 1087), or to an arched ground-floor room (*cella*) where humble craftsmen conducted their businesses, the poor were housed, and prostitutes plied their trade. Such *cellae* could be closed up: cf. 11.61.3–4. On *fornix*, see G. Mansuelli in Autori vari, *Studi sull'arco onorario Romano* (Rome 1979) 15–17.

triste frigus 'savage cold': cf. Liv. 5.13.4 *tristem hiemem ... grauis pestilensque... aestas excepit, OLD* s.v. 7.

**8–9　　**'Let him often proclaim happy those who have died a pauper's death', an elegant particularisation of a common type of curse, invoking the prolongation of life in circumstances where death would be preferable: cf. Ov. *Ib.* 123–4 *causaque non desit, desit tibi copia mortis* | *optatam fugiat uita coacta necem,* Hor. *Epod.* 17.62–4, Watson (1991) 59 and 35 n.158.

8　　uocet beatos: there is a neat irony in the enemy's calling 'blessed' those who are carried to a pauper's grave, given the other common meaning of *beatus*, 'rich'.

clamitet: the frequentative is significant: there will be numerous occasions on which he will have cause to wish himself dead.

felices: for the dead ironically as 'blessed', cf. Hor. *S.* 1.9.28 '*omnes composui*'. *felices! nunc ego resto.*

9　　Orciniana... sponda 'Orcus' litter', named after Orcus the god of the dead, refers to the *sandapila,* a cheap bier upon which the poor were carried to cremation or burial: cf. 2.81, Suet. *Dom.* 17.3, Toynbee (1971) 45.

Orciniana: an emendation for the *Orciuiana* of the MSS (unintelligible, unless, as with the Australian undertakers Wood Coffill, Orcivius was a maker of biers whose name bore an inadvertent relationship to his profession).

10 **at cum supremae fila uenerint horae:** when his last hour comes. The length of the threads, *fila*, spun for each individual by the Fates determined the duration of his or her life.

11 **diesque tardus:** *dies* is a common euphemism for the day of death: cf. Virg. *A.* 10.467 *stat sua cuique dies*. Normally one would wish this day to be *tardus*; here however its tardiness forms part of the slanderer's punishment: cf. *CLE* 1299.3 *morte tardata uiuas aeger inops*.

sentiat canum litem: inspired by Ov. *Ib.* 171–2 *deque tuo fiet – licet hac sis laude superbus – | insatiabilibus corpore rixa lupis*, with the refinement that the quarrelling over the enemy's remains begins even before he is dead. The threat that one's body will be preyed upon by dogs and birds (cf. 12) is common in curses: cf. Watson (1991) 36 and 54. Such threats are not mere literary convention; Scobie (1986) 418–19 demonstrates that pariah dogs often battened upon corpses in Rome and its environs.

12 Let him move his rags in an attempt to shoo away the carrion birds which are assembling about him: cf. Hom. *Od.* 11.578–9 'and two vultures sitting on either side of him [Tityos] tore at his liver, penetrating into his intestines: and he kept on trying to ward them off with his hands, but could not'.

noxias aues 'birds of prey' i.e. vultures, which were notorious for gathering about the bodies of the dying: cf. Ael. *NA* 2.46, Sen. *Ep.* 95.43 *uultur est: cadauer expectat*. Two large vultures are indigenous to Italy: cf. Keller (1913) 31–2, Skutsch on Enn. *Ann.* 89.

panno 'rags', τὰ ῥάκη, the symbol of beggary *par excellence*: cf. Ar. *Ach.* 412–34, Plaut. *Asin.* 142 (5n.), U. W. Scholz, *Glotta* 43 (1965) 119–32.

13 **nec finiantur morte simplici poenae:** the wish for prolongation of suffering after death is another common imprecatory motif: cf. Tert. *De anim.* 4.5 *terram grauem imprecaris et cineri penes inferos tormentum*, *CIG* 3915.48–9, Watson (1991) 36, 254.

simplici 'by a straightforward death', SB's emendation of the transmitted *supplicis*: cf. Liv. 40.24.8 *cum in eo ne simplici quidem genere mortis contenti* *inimici fuissent.* Since the victim is not envisaged as begging for pardon, *supplicis* has to mean, improbably, *eius, qui supplicium patitur.*

14 sed modo seueri sectus Aeaci loris: in Latin literature Aeacus is the judge of the dead *par excellence* (Roscher I 112–13); he might therefore be administering torture in the manner of a *iudex quaestionis* to extract a confession: cf. *Culex* 376–7 *ergo iam causam mortis, iam dicere uitae | uerberibus saeuae cogunt sub iudice Poenae,* Juv. 1.9–10 with Mayor. But this would pre-empt the action of the Furies in the concluding verses. It is better to suppose that Aeacus is punishing the guilty new arrivals by means of flogging: cf. Ov. *Ib.* 187–8 *noxia mille modis lacerabitur umbra, tuasque | Aeacus in poenas ingeniosus erit.*

seueri 'inflexible', 'inexorable'.

15–17 In verse-imprecations the wished-for continuation of the enemy's sufferings after death often means assuming the torments of the eternally damned: cf. Ov. *Ib.* 189–90, Watson (1991) 101. For the replication of Sisyphus' punishment (15), cf. Ov. *Ib.* 191 *Sisyphe, cui tradas reuolubile pondus, habebis,* Sen. *Phaedr.* 1231: for Tantalus', cf. Ov. *Ib.* 193, Sen. *Phaedr.* 1232, Watson (1991) 228.

15 nunc inquieti monte Sisyphi pressus: as *pressus,* 'weighed down', shows, M. has in mind the account of Sisyphus' punishment in which he must carry a rock up an infernal hillside, rather than the better known one which makes him push the rock up the hill: for the former, cf. Sen. *Phaedr.* 1229–31 *ceruicilus his his repositum degrauet fessas manus | saxum, seni perennis Aeolio labor,* Sen. *HF* 751 with Fitch. The alternatives go back to Homer, who describes Sisyphus as both 'pushing' and 'lifting' a stone (*Od.* 11.592–600).

inquieti . . . Sisyphi: Sisyphus is 'restless': contrast 5.80.10–11 *nec inquieta | lassi marmora Sisyphi uidebit,* where the adjective refers to Homer's 'pitiless stone' which bounded down again as soon as Sisyphus had pushed it to the brow of the hill.

monte: a hyperbolic description of Sisyphus' rock, which was large (Sen. *HF*751 *ceruice saxum grande Sisyphia sedet*) but also a tangential allusion to the site of his labours: cf. Lucr. 3.1000–1 *aduerso nixantem trudere monte | saxum.*

16 inter undas . . . siccus: Tantalus was punished by being placed in an infernal pool, the waters of which drained away whenever he stooped to drink, making him paradoxically 'parched though surrounded by waves': cf. Hom. *Od.* 11.582–92.

garruli: refers to the version of Tantalus' offence which saw him 'speak out of turn': cf. Apollod. *Epit.* 2.1 'he blabbed the secrets of the gods to mankind', C. W. Willink, *CQ* 33 (1983) 31–3.

senis: Hom. ibid. 585 and 591 describes Tantalus as an 'old man'.

17   delasset omnes fabulas poetarum 'let him wear out all the tales of the poets' i.e. after exhausting all the punishments described by the poets, there will be more to come. The compendious curse reshapes Ov. *Ib.* 189–90 (15–17n.).

fabulas ironically injects a Lucretian note of doubt as to whether there is any substance to the myths.

18   et cum fateri Furia iusserit uerum: the brief of the Furies in the Underworld was primarily to punish sinners after judgment had been passed upon them, but it could extend to extorting confessions: cf. Ov. *Ib.* 183–4 *hic tibi de Furiis scindet latus una flagello,* | *ut sceleris numeros confiteare tui.* The idea arises from their function as assistants to the three infernal judges: torture was employed in the Roman courts to extract confessions: cf. Crook (1967) 274–5.

fateri . . . iusserit uerum: for such forced confessions of guilt in the Underworld, cf. Virg. *A.* 6.567 *subigitque fateri,* [Pl.] *Ax.* 371 c, which states that in infernal courtrooms telling lies was impossible.

Furia: Tisiphone, the Fury who in Roman poetry takes primacy in exacting retribution from wrongdoers.

19   prodente clamet conscientia: the promptings of conscience are not unconnected with the presence of the Furies, these being often rationalised as the pangs of a guilty conscience: cf. Cic. *Leg.* 1.40, *Pis.* 47.

'scripsi': the miscreant confesses that the scurrilous verse which he has passed off as M.'s were in fact his (see intro.). As often in M., the real point of the epigram is only revealed at the end.

9a and 9b (= 2.91 and 2.92)

The poems form a pair, the first taking the form of a petition to Domitian for the *ius trium liberorum*, the second celebrating the granting of the request. M. had already been awarded the privilege by Titus: cf. 3.95.5–6 *praemia laudato tribuit mihi Caesar uterque* | *natorumque dedit iura paterna trium*; he is asking

Domitian to reconfirm it, since *beneficia* granted by an emperor lapsed on that emperor's death.

Under the still operative Augustan marriage laws, possession of legitimate children conferred privileges (e.g. speedier progression through the *cursus honorum* for men, freedom from *tutela* for freeborn women with three children), while childlessness involved penalties, especially in the sphere of inheritance; for example, bachelors could not accept legacies left to them by non-family members, while those who were married without offspring could only accept half, and, except in special circumstances, partners in a childless marriage could only inherit one tenth of each other's estate. Persons with children were said to possess the *ius liberorum*, and this right, with its attendant privileges, could be granted by a legal fiction to childless persons. The *ius liberorum* was a highly sought after honour, granted sparingly by the Senate or, in the Flavian era, by the emperor.

Further reading: Daube (1976), McGinn (1998) 76–7, Treggiari (1991) 66–80, Watson (2003).

9a

'Caesar, whose safety gives us proof of the gods' existence, if my hastily-put-together poems have engaged your attention, allow me to seem what misfortune has denied me, the father of three children. This will be a consolation if my epigrams have not pleased you, a reward, if they have.'

Persons applying for the *ius trium liberorum* normally offered a written request to the emperor in person (**49**.2–3n.). Since Domitian ratified en bloc the *beneficia* bestowed by his brother Titus (Dio Cass. 67.2.1), it is unclear whether M. would have needed to make a separate petition.

Even if M. did make a personal application for *ius*, the epigram cannot constitute the actual petition, which would have been in prose and would have mentioned the previous granting of the *ius* by Titus. Rather it is a poetic version, reflecting elements of a real petition (see esp. 5n.) but adapted to the epigrammatic context by a concluding witticism. By omitting mention of Titus' grant, M. represents Domitian's putative gift of the *ius*, not as the routine renewing of a *beneficium*, but as a special favour which the emperor bestowed on him because he had personally read and approved of M.'s poetry. In short the epigram, along with its companion piece, both advertises

M.'s favoured position vis-à-vis the emperor and eulogises Domitian for his beneficence.

1   Rerum certa salus: cf. 5.1.7 *o rerum felix tutela salusque.*

2   sospite quo magnos credimus esse deos: the great gods give proof of their existence by keeping Domitian safe. Cf. 5.1.8, 7.60.1–2 *Tarpeiae uenerande rector aulae, | quem saluo duce credimus Tonantem.*

3–4   M. gives the reason why he deserves the *ius*, namely his epigrams. Among private recipients of imperial *beneficia*, poets, along with orators and doctors, were prevalent (Millar (1977) 491–506).

3   festinatis ... libellis: smaller poetic collections hastily put together and circulated to individual patrons before the official publication of the epigrams in book form. M. would certainly have included the emperor among the recipients of such offerings; the plural *libelli* suggests that he sent more than one collection to Domitian prior to book 2's publication. See White (1974) 46 and (1996) 402–3.
     totiens tibi lecta: cf. 1.101, 4.27.1 *saepe meos laudare soles, Auguste, libellos.*

4   detinuere oculos ... tuos 'have held your attention'.

5   quod fortuna uetat fieri: the *ius trium liberorum* was normally granted to those who, *through no fault of their own,* had been unable to comply with the spirit of the Augustan marriage legislation. In applying for the *ius* it was therefore appropriate to stress that the petitioner's lack of offspring was due to misfortune rather than choice: cf. Pliny's request for the *ius* on behalf of Suetonius (*Ep.* 10.94: next n.). It therefore follows that whether married or not at this stage (see below on *ualebis uxor*), M. must have had unproductive marriages in the past (cf. intro. 3).
     fortuna: cf. Plin. *Ep.* 10.94.2 *parum felix matrimonium expertus est, impetrandumque a bonitate tua per nos habet quod illi fortunae malignitas denegauit, Laudatio Turiae* Col. II 26–7, I. Kajanto, *ANRW* II 17.1.502–58.

6   natorum genitor ... trium: for the *ius trium liberorum*, see intro. Three children were granted so that the recipient could take full advantage of the rewards under the Augustan laws, though in many areas, such as the capacity to accept legacies, only one child, real or fictional, was sufficient.
     credar ut esse: the *ius trium liberorum* involved a legal fiction.

7   haec, si displicui, fuerint solacia nobis: included for the
sake of balance with 8, the line is notable for wit rather than logic: if
Domitian disliked M.'s poetry, he would hardly give him the *ius* as a consolation.

fuerint: 'will surely prove'; future perfect used forcibly to express the
certainty of a predicted result: cf. 9.58.6, Cic. *Tusc.* 1.30 *tolle hanc opinionem,
luctum sustuleris.*

9b

'When I requested the *ius trium liberorum*, he who alone could grant it gave
me the right as a reward for my poems. Farewell wife; my lord's beneficence
must not go to waste.'

2   Musarum . . . mearum 'my poetry': cf. 9.99.1 *Marcus amat nos-
tras . . . Musas.*

pretium 'reward' is synonymous with *praemia* in **9a**.8.

3   solus qui poterat: exemptions from laws such as the Augustan
marriage legislation, originally granted to individuals by the Senate, were
from the Flavian period the emperor's prerogative.

ualebis, uxor: future tense for present imperative, 'farewell, wife', a
mock formula of divorce: cf. Plaut. *Am.* 928 *ualeas, tibi habeas res tuas, reddas
meas.* The phrase has been taken in the sense 'farewell future wife', 'farewell
to ideas of marriage'. But this usage is unparalleled, whereas future with
imperative force is common in valedictions, e.g. Cic. *Att.* 6.5.4 *ualebis igitur et
puellae salutem Atticulae dices nostraeque Piliae*, M. 6.78.5. The meaning 'farewell
wife' does not preclude M.'s being unmarried at the time of writing: the
'divorce' would be grossly insulting, even in jest, to a real wife, and she is
best regarded as a literary construct invented for the sake of the joke.

4   non debet domini perire munus: I must not waste Domitian's
act of generosity by having a wife. If taken seriously, this is close to subversive:
the *ius* was granted to compensate worthy individuals for lack of children,
not as an excuse to get rid of a wife who had become redundant! M. is
however simply making an 'anti-wife' joke of the kind found in Comedy
and elsewhere in M. e.g. 4.24 *omnes quas habuit, Fabiane, Lycoris amicas | extulit:
uxori fiat amica meae.*

10   (= 4.30)

'Fisherman, stay far away from the emperor's fishpond at Baiae. These waters are swum by sacred fish which lick the hand of Domitian himself and come to him when summoned by name. An impious Libyan once fished these waters and, punished with blindness, now begs for alms at Baiae. Fisherman, withdraw before committing a similar sacrilege.'

The epigram exhibits a carefully articulated rhetorical structure: 1–2: injunction against fishing the imperial *piscina* at Baiae; 3: the reason for this: the fish are sacred, responding (4–7) to their imperial master Domitian as if to a god; 8–12: an admonitory *exemplum* reinforcing the prohibition of 1–2; 14–16: reiteration and expansion of the original warning. *innocens recede* (14) picks up *nocens recedas* (2) in a striking example of ring composition. The key terms *nocens, impius* (8) and *innocens* all occur in the same position in the verse, underlining the centrality of the idea that it is sacrilege to catch fish from the emperor's ponds at Baiae.

The poem establishes by implication the godhead of Domitian – whom flatterers were accustomed to style *dominus et deus* – by demonstrating that retribution of a kind associated with acts of impiety overtakes anyone attempting to harm the emperor's pet fish. In keeping with the subject-matter, the language of the poem has a solemn and sacral colour (cf. *procul, monemus, nocens, sacris, impius, sacrilegos, at, innocens, uenerare*), though it is not without touches of humour: 4n.

Weinreich (1928) 153–5 suggested that the speaker of the poem is the master of the imperial *piscina*. This is possible, but it is simpler to suppose that the epigram is placed in M.'s own mouth.

Further reading: Appel (1909), Toynbee (1973) 209–12, Weinreich (1928) 143–55

1–2   **procul...** | **...fuge** has a religious ring, in keeping with the idea that the fish are sacred to the 'god' Domitian; cf. Virg. *A.* 6.258 *procul, o procul este, profani*, Calp. Sic. 2.55. The use of *fuge*, in place of the usual *ite* or *este*, imparts a tone of urgency to the admonition.

1   **Baiano...lacu:**   the imperial 'fishpond' at Baiae. For *lacus* in this sense, cf. Col. 8.17.9. Salt-water *piscinae* fronting seaside villas were especially popular in the first centuries BC and AD (*RE* XX 1783–4); they seem to have been accessible to the public (D'Arms (1970) 135), which explains how a *piscator* (2) and the *Libys impius* (8) could poach from the imperial ponds.

monemus: *moneo* is often used parenthetically, particularly in sacral contexts, to convey solemn warnings and advice: cf. Sen. *Ag.* 732, 6.73.9 *uicini, moneo, sanctum celebrate Priapum*, Appel (1909) 187.

2   nocens: here in the specialised sense 'guilty of *nefas*'; cf. Stat. *Silu.* 3.3.13–14 *procul hinc, procul ite nocentes,* | *si cui corde nefas tacitum.*

3   sacris piscibus: *sacris* is emphatic, 'these are sacred fish which swim here', implying that their owner Domitian is a god. Tame fish were often associated with religious sanctuaries (see Ael. *NA* 12.30 for various instances); it was believed that, as here, harm would come to anyone who caught and/or ate such fish: cf. Keller (1913) 343.

natantur undae: the transitive use of *nato* is poetic: cf. Ov. *Ars* 1.48 *quae multo pisce natentur aquae.*

4–5   manumque ...| illam, qua nihil est in orbe maius: *maius* has a dual reference, to the authority wielded by Domitian and to the physical size of his hand, which is represented as larger than normal in consequence of his godhead (cf. 4.8.10 *ingentique tenet pocula parca manu*). For the two ideas, cf. Stat. *Silu.* 3.4.61–3 *ingentem totiens contingere dextram* | *electus quam nosse Getae, quam tangere Persae* | *Armeniique Indique petunt*!

4   norunt dominum: an allusion to Domitian's title *dominus et deus* (next n.) possibly inspired by Catull. 3.6–7 *suamque norat* | *ipsam tam bene quam puella matrem.* For the idea that fish can recognise their master, cf. Ael. *NA* 8.4 (Crassus' pet fish recognised his voice and came at his call).

dominum: a form of address favoured by Domitian and frequently employed by M. Although *dominus* did not become the official title of the emperor till Severan times (Sherwin-White on Plin. *Ep.* 10.1.2), Domitian insisted on its use at least in procuratorial documents (Suet. *Dom.* 13.2). Cf. Dominik (1994) 158–60, Sauter (1934) 31–6.

lambunt: often used of fawning animals (cf. Plin. *NH* 8.56 *cum ... uestigia* [*leo*] *lamberet adulanti similis*). Here it also represents an act of homage to the *numen* of Domitian: cf. 14.107 *ebria tigris* | *perfusos domini* [*Bacchi*] *lambere docta pedes*, Hor. *Carm.* 2.19.29–32 with N–H. Since tongues of fish are stuck to the palate (Plin. *NH* 11.171), they would not in reality be able to lick a hand, though we do hear of pet fish eating out of the hand (e.g. Plin. *NH* 32.16, Ath. 331E). For the blending of humour with imperial panegyric, see intro. 11–12.

6   quid quod: a rhetorical formula of transition, used to introduce an idea which develops a previous point, in this case, that the fish recognise their imperial master (3–4).

6–7   nomen habent et ad magistri | uocem quisque sui uenit citatus: cf. 10.30.21–4, Lucian, *Syr. d.* 45 'these [sacred fish] also have names and come when summoned'. Weinreich (1928) 144 refers *magister* to the keeper of the *piscina*, but the noun rather means 'their lord': cf. Cic. *Rep.* 3.33 *unus ... communis quasi magister et imperator omnium deus.* This is in conformity with the connective function of *quid quod*: see previous n.

8–11   An *exemplum* illustrating the consequences of disobeying the injunction of 1–2.

8   hoc ... profundo 'from this deep pool'. *profundum* is a grandiose word to use of a *piscina*, which would be no more than nine feet deep (Col. 8.17.3–4).

quondam: a typical feature of the paradigmatic style (Fraenkel on Aesch. *Ag.* 1040).

Libys impius: the Libyan offends against Domitian's *numen* by fishing his *piscina*. For injunctions against catching or eating sacred fish, cf. Ditt. *Syll.* 997 'one must not harm the fish or damage any of the vessels belonging to the goddess, or remove them by theft from the shrine'. Presumably the identification of the wrongdoer as a Libyan is meant to suggest that the incident actually occurred.

9   calamo tremente: a fishing rod; cf. Ov. *Met.* 8.217 *tremula dum captat harundine pisces.*

10   raptis luminibus ... caecus: the nature of the punishment is a manifestation of Domitian's divinity. Blindness is often visited retributively upon those who have offended the gods: cf. Teiresias (Callim. *Hymn* 5), Phineus (Apollod. *Bibl.* 1.9.21), Stesichorus, *PMG* 192 Page and L. Caecilius Metellus (Sen. *Contr.* 4.2), Vlahogiannis (1998) 29–32.

luminibus 'vision': *OLD* s.v. 9c.

repente: the suddenness emphasises the miraculous nature of the event.

13   Baianos sedet ad lacus rogator: having lost his livelihood, the fisherman is reduced to beggary. M may have in mind the Syrian penitents who break their country's taboo on eating fish: 'they put on sackcloth, then sit themselves down in the road on dung, and propitiate the goddess by growing terribly thin' (Men. fr. 544 Kock *CAF* iii 164).

14   at tu: *at* is used to introduce solemn injunctions with a religious flavour; cf. Liv. 1.12.5 *at tu, pater deum hominumque, hinc saltem arce hostes*, Prop. 2.5.17–18.

15   simplicibus cibis 'free from guile' (cf. Ov. *Met.* 15.120–1 *boues, animal sine fraude dolisque | innocuum, simplex*). The fisherman would have brought food to bait his hooks: he is advised to throw this harmlessly into the water.

16   uenerare: i.e. respect the sanctity of the fish by refraining from catching them.

    delicatos 'pet': cf. 10.30.22 *natat ad magistrum delicata murena.*

11   (= 9.18)

'I own, Caesar, a tiny estate in the country, and a small house in town. But whereas the former receives its water pumped from the nearby valley, my townhouse has no water laid on, although the Marcian aqueduct is close by. If you permit me to connect my townhouse to the aqueduct, the water will be as it were a fountain of the Muses or rain from Jupiter.'

In M.'s day, water for private use was obtained by Roman residents either through *fistulae* (lead pipes) leading from one of the eight aqueducts to individual houses, or, more commonly, from public fountains supplied by the aqueducts. Notwithstanding Strabo's claim (235) that most houses in Rome had their own water supply, the evidence of the *fistulae*, on which are inscribed the names of the recipients, suggests that this was a special privilege, afforded primarily to senatorial families and to a few *equites*, which did not pass to the new owner if a house changed hands (Evans (1994) 9, Bruun (1991) 58–60, 63–71). This privilege could be granted only by the emperor on petition (cf. Frontin. *Aq.* 3.2, 69.6) – hence M.'s request to Domitian here. Cf. also Millar (1977) 193.

    The epigram, like many addressed to the emperor, is stylistically elevated: for details see below. Since there is no corresponding epigram thanking Domitian for granting the request, many have assumed that M.'s petition was unsuccessful. This may be so, but it is equally possible that the request was granted and that a poem of thanks was included in the first edition of book 10 but subsequently suppressed when this was revamped after Domitian's death.

Further reading: Bruun (1991), Evans (1994), Hodge (1992)

1   Est mihi – sitque precor: cf. 1.108.1 *est tibi – sitque precor* with Citroni.

sit...precor longum te praeside: lit. 'I pray that it may be [mine] for a long time under your rule'. The line blends flattery of the emperor with a dash of self-interest. The wish that the incumbent monarch enjoy a long reign goes back to Hellenistic ruler-cult and enters Latin poetry via Hor. *Carm.* 1.2.45–50 (see N–H ad loc.); cf. 5.65.15–16 *pro meritis caelum tantis, Auguste, dederunt | Alcidae cito di, sed tibi sero dabunt.*

praeside: the word *praeses*, originally used of protecting deities, was applied under the republic to magistrates and Senate and thereafter to the emperors; cf. Ov. *Met.* 15.758 *quo [Augusto] praeside rerum.* M. employs the term of Domitian (6.2.5, 8.80.5), Nerva (11.2.6) and Titus (*Spect.* 2.11).

Caesar: M.'s normal form of address to Domitian.

2   rus minimum: M.'s Nomentan farm; cf. **14** intro. Like Horace with his Sabine farm (*parua rura Carm.* 2.16.37), M. routinely exaggerates the humbleness of his property, e.g. **20**.1–2, 1.55.3 *nec magni ruris arator.*

parui...in urbe lares: cf. 9.97.8 *paruaque in urbe domus.* This is the first certain reference to M.'s house in Rome; previously he had occupied a third-floor flat (1.117.7, 108.3). Although mention of the *domus* is attended by M.'s customary protestations of limited means, residence in a house, as opposed to an apartment in a tenement block, suggests a significant degree of prosperity. Cf. Frier (1977) 27.

lares: poetic for *domus.*

3   ualle breui: reinforces the idea that M.'s property is modest in scale.

quas det: relative clause of purpose.

sitientibus: cf. **20**.1 *sicci parua rura Nomenti.* For the personification, commonly used of dry soil in poetry and post-Augustan prose, cf. Ov. *Pont.* 1.8.60 *sitiens quas bibat hortus aquas.*

hortis: balancing *domus* 5, *horti* means not M.'s orchards but his 'country estate', including house and adjacent farmlands: cf. 5.62.1 *iure tuo nostris maneas licet hospes in hortis.*

4   laboratas 'laboriously raised', lit. 'worked at': cf. *OLD* s.v. 8.

antlia: some sort of water-lifting device, it has been identified as either a shaduf or a compartmented wheel which was rotated by treading (J. P. Oleson, *Greek and Roman mechanical water-lifting devices* (Toronto 1984) 59–60). The latter is more probable in view of *curua* and *laboratas* and the application of *antlia* to the treadmill to which slaves were condemned (Suet. *Tib.* 51). Water wheels were sometimes employed for irrigation (Vitr. 10.2, Strabo 807), but because of the expense, were not normally associated with small holdings (White (1970) 156 and (1975) 46, Hodge (1992) 248). If M. is referring to a water wheel, his farm accordingly cannot have been as modest as he suggests.

5   sicca domus queritur nullo se rore foueri: a highly poetic line, featuring *ros* as an elevated synonym for *aqua*, and the striking and slightly humorous personification *domus queritur*.

foueri 'is refreshed'.

6   Marcia: the Aqua Marcia, third oldest of the Roman aqueducts, built in 144 BC by the urban praetor Q. Marcius Rex, was used primarily to supply private houses and drinking fountains: see Evans (1994) 83–93, T. Ashby, *The aqueducts of ancient Rome* (Oxford 1935) 88–158. Although the Quirinal, where M.'s townhouse was located, was served by two other aqueducts, the Julia and the Anio Vetus, he evidently wanted a connexion to the Marcia because of its proximity (cf. *uicino*), and also on account of the purity and coolness of its water (cf. Frontin. *Aq.* 91.5, Plin. *NH* 31.41, 8.16.1).

sonet: a stream of water (*fons*) was fed from the aqueducts into street fountains (*salientes*), which consisted of a spout permanently discharging into a trough. The sound of the water constantly running nearby must have been tantalising.

7   quam dederis ... undam: i.e. *undam si dederis.*
undam: poetical for *aquam*.

8   Castalis: water from the Aqua Marcia will be as water from the fountain of Castalia, on Mt Parnassus, sacred to the Muses, and a source of poetic inspiration, cf. Ov. *Am.* 1.15.35–6 *mihi flauus Apollo | pocula Castalia plena ministret aqua,* Bömer on Ov. *Met.* 3.414. M. means that the gift of a water supply will inspire him to versified celebration of the imperial donor.

Iouis imber compliments Domitian by identifying him with Jupiter: see **12**.10n.

12 (= 12.15)

'The riches which used to gleam in Domitian's palace have been placed on public view in the temples. Jupiter looks with wonder and amazement at the expensive luxuries of that haughty monarch. These are goblets worthy of Jupiter and Ganymede. All the people, along with Jupiter, are enriched by them. But recently – for shame! – both we and Jupiter's shrines were impoverished.'

Treasures which Domitian had selfishly kept hidden from public view in his residence on the Palatine (*Parrhasia . . . aula*) have been placed by a successor, probably Trajan, in temples, including that of Jupiter, where they can be enjoyed both by the people and by the god, as is fitting for such opulence.

M. had previously composed extravagant praises of Domitian's palace (7.56, 8.36; cf. Stat. *Silu.* 4.2.18–31). It was long fashionable to accuse the epigrammatist of hypocrisy for flattering Domitian during his lifetime, but subsequently attacking his memory (cf. 10.72, 12.6.4 *longi terga dedere metus* and 11 *sub principe duro*). But such criticisms are misconceived: see intro. 9–10. The sentiments here expressed by M. must be read in the context of panegyric, where one means of eulogising a new emperor was to compare him favourably with his predecessor; this could involve heavy criticism of the deceased. For the general strategy, cf. Plin. *Pan.* 53.6 *meminerint . . . sic maxime laudari incolumem imperatorem, si priores secus meriti reprehendantur*, S. Braund in K. Cameron, ed., *Humour and history* (Oxford 1993) 56–69 at 61. It is instructive to compare the epigrams written by M. on Domitian after his assassination with Pliny's strictures upon the late emperor in his *Panegyric* of Trajan: measured by that yardstick, M.'s poems of dispraise may seem relatively restrained. Cf. for example *Pan.* 48.3 *nec salutationes tuas fuga et uastitas sequitur: remoramur resistimus ut in communi domo, quam nuper illa immanissima belua plurimo terrore munierat.*

1   **Quidquid . . . nitebat:** all the treasures which Domitian had accumulated in the imperial palace and which were passed down to the next emperor: cf. Millar (1977) 144–53.

Parrhasia . . . aula ('in the Arcadian hall': cf. 7.99.3, 8.36.3 and 9.11.8), a strikingly original description of the imperial residence on the

Palatine based on Virgil's *Parrhasius* (Arcadian) *Evander*, the first regal occupant of the *mons Palatinus* (*A.* 11.31). Completed in 92, Domitian's palace
consisted of the *Domus Flauia*, where state banquets and imperial *salutationes*
were held, and the *Domus Augustana*, the emperor's family residence. The
treasures later transferred to the temples no doubt came from both public
and private domains. On Domitian's palace, see further Richardson 114–
17, F. Coarelli, *Roma* (*Guide archeologiche Laterza* series, 3rd. ed., Roma–Bari
1985) 138–44.

nitebat: the verb has associations with regal splendour; cf. Sen. *Thy.*
414–15, *Ag.* 877 *ostro lectus Iliaco nitet.*

2   donatum est: probably by Trajan rather than Nerva. Whereas
the latter sold off many valuables from the palace to raise money (Dio Cass.
68.2), his successor, according to Plin. *Pan.* 34.3, restored property to the
public. There were precedents for this: Tiberius dedicated in the temple
of Augustus a painting by Nicias which Augustus had brought back from
Alexandria (Plin. *NH* 35.131), while much of the art collection in Vespasian's
Templum Pacis came from Nero's *Domus aurea.*

oculis deisque nostris: the valuable works of art regularly dedicated by private individuals and state leaders to the gods were open to public
view, so that temples served a secondary function as art galleries/museums.
Cf. Stambaugh (1978) 556–71, 586–87.

deis: i.e. the treasures were placed in more than one temple;
M. focuses on Jupiter's (4, 6–7) because of his special associations with
both Domitian and Trajan.

3–4   Scythicas uirentis auri | flammas lit. 'Scythian fires of green
gold' i.e. golden cups which took on a green hue from the flashing Scythian
emeralds which were embedded therein: cf. 14.109 *gemmatum Scythicis ut
luceat ignibus aurum | aspice,* Plin. *NH* 33.5. Jewelled cups were a symbol of
luxury, often associated with monarchs: cf. Cic. *Verr.* 2.4.62, Juv. 10.26–7
with Mayor.

3   Scythicas: Scythian emeralds were the finest of all; cf. Plin. *NH*
37.65.

4   flammas: for the gleam of emeralds so described, cf. Stat. *Theb.*
2.276 *arcano florentes igne zmaragdos,* M. 14.109 cited above.

Iuppiter: probably a reference to the Capitoline temple of Iuppiter
Optimus Maximus. Trajan appears as Jupiter's chosen vice-regent on coins

and in iconography (Fears (1981) 80–5). It was appropriate, then, that he dedicate the most precious of the Palace treasures to this god.

4–5   superbi | regis: both words are highly insulting. *rex*, a term with largely negative connotations for the Romans, replaces the more neutral *princeps*, while *superbia* was regarded as a vice characteristic of kings (Haffter (1956)). For the view that Domitian was less a *princeps* than a tyrant, cf. 10.72.8, contrasting Trajan with Domitian, *non est hic dominus, sed imperator.* For his alleged *superbia*, cf. Plin. *Pan.* 49 and 114. The indignant tone of *superbi regis* is underscored by the profusion of sibilants in 4–5.

5   regis ... luxus: *pace* E. Merli, *Maia* 47 (1995) 288, *luxus* (cf. SB) is preferable to the *lusus* of the MSS: like *luxuria* and its Greek synonym τρυφή, *luxus* carries negative connotations and is frequently associated with monarchical excess: cf. Sen. *Ep.* 83.25 *inter apparatissimas epulas luxusque regales.* The reader might be reminded of another luxurious regal palace, decorated with gold and gems, which had once stood on the site of the Domitianic edifice, Nero's *Domus aurea*: cf. Suet. *Nero.* 31, Tac. *Ann.* 15.42.1.

delicias: combines the meanings 'luxury' (cf. 1.59.1–2 *dat Baiana mihi quadrantes sportula centum. | inter delicias quid facit ista fames?*) and 'playthings', here unusually applied to inanimate objects: cf. 7.88.1–2 *fertur habere meos ... libellos | inter delicias pulchra Vienna suas.*

graues: both literally heavy (cf. Virg. *A.* 1.728–9 *grauem gemmis auroque ... pateram*) and metaphorically 'oppressive', to characterise Domitian's régime or indicate the strain which his luxury placed on state finances.

6   haec: deictic; M., as it were, points out to his readers the cups which are now disclosed to public view: cf. on **33**.6 and **80**.1.

pocula quae decent Tonantem: with the implication that such magnificent cups did *not* befit their previous possessor.

Tonantem: a regular epithet of Jupiter, used frequently by M.

7   haec sunt quae Phrygium decent ministrum: the Trojan (*Phrygius*) prince Ganymede was carried off to Olympus by Jupiter's eagle to serve as the god's cup-bearer and paramour. The magnificent cups befit both his new and his quondam regal status.

8   omnes cum Ioue nunc sumus beati: *beati*, rich, in contrast to *pauperes* (10), 'because the palatial wealth is in a manner made public property by being placed in the temples' (Paley and Stone).

9   pudet, ah pudet fateri: cf. 2.18.1, **22**.7, 6.10.4, 14.101.2.

10   omnes cum Ioue pauperes eramus: a somewhat disingenuous verdict in view of the special importance given by Domitian to Jupiter:
cf. Fears (1981) 74–80, Sauter (1934) 54–78, Darwall-Smith (1996) 113–15.
Domitian rebuilt the temple of Jupiter on the Capitol, destroyed by fire in
80 (Suet. *Dom.* 5); it probably contained at least a golden statue of the god
and may have been lavishly restored: cf. 11.4.3 with Kay.

13   (= 6.21)

'When Venus was uniting Ianthis in marriage to the poet Stella, she said
in the lady's presence: "I could not give you more"; but she whispered in
Stella's ear something more naughty: "Make sure you don't misbehave, you
breaker of hearts. I often beat Mars in anger when he strayed before we
were properly married, but since our union, he has never betrayed me: Juno
would like to have so faithful a husband." She spoke, and struck Stella's
breast with unseen whip. The blow is effective: but you, goddess, strike both
of them.'

The epigram celebrates the wedding of M.'s patron Stella (1 n.), an elegiac
poet (*uati* 1), to the widow Violentilla, here called Ianthis (1 n.). Venus is
represented as presiding over the ceremony, while simultaneously advising
the groom not to be unfaithful to his bride. As an example of husbandly
fidelity, Venus invokes her consort Mars, who, inclined to stray before their
marriage, became a model husband afterwards. The implied suggestion
that Stella should follow Mars's example is reinforced by Venus with a
blow of her whip, which will ensure that Stella's passion for his wife will be
such as to preclude any infidelity. The final line contains a surprise twist:
to ensure the success of the marriage, Venus should strike bride as well as
bridegroom (*caede duos*).

The epigram must be read in conjunction with the Statian epithalamium written for the same occasion (*Silu.* 1.2). If, as seems most likely, the
latter was written first (Watson (1999) 351), this would explain the prominence given by M. to Venus, who in *Silu.* 1.2 both accompanies the bride
in the wedding procession and plays a major rôle in bringing about the
marriage.

The epithalamium also helps clarify the real-life background. Stella had
written love elegies addressed to a mistress under the pseudonym Asteris
(*Silu.* 1.2.197–8): gossip was rife that Asteris was Violentilla, and that there

had been a love affair between Stella and this respectable widow (*Silu.* 1.2.28–30). Statius goes to great lengths to whitewash both his patron and Violentilla, portraying the latter as a chaste and reluctant bride, as well as focusing on those elements in Stella's poetry – the *exclusus amator* theme, for instance – which suggest that his love was unconsummated.

M., by contrast, implies via the Mars/Venus parallel that a sexual relationship had taken place before the marriage, and also hints that both Stella and Violentilla had been unfaithful to each other in the past and might continue to be so in the future. Such a suggestion, even in the jocular context of epigram, seems tactless and potentially offensive. The difficulty is solved if M. is referring, not to the real-life relationship of the couple, but to their literary *personae* as depicted in Stella's poetry. His elegies, in accordance with the genre, would have depicted a love affair during the course of which the lover was occasionally faithless and the *domina* fickle. Viewed in this light, the epigram is not a slur on the reputation of the bride and groom but rather a witty and graceful compliment to M.'s patron as a skilled love poet.

Further reading: Watson (1999)

1   Perpetuam: used adverbially, 'for ever'. Perpetuity of the marriage bond was a Roman ideal: cf. *coniugi perpetuae* on a wife's tombstone (*CLE* 1571.3), Williams (1958) 25. The prominent location of *perpetuam* points a contrast with the irregular nature of the relationship between Stella and Ianthis/Violentilla prior to their marriage.

Stellae: L. Arruntius Stella, a rich and cultured individual, suffect consul in 101 or 102, one of M.'s most important patrons, with whom he enjoyed a genuine friendship.

iungit 'unites in marriage', a moment enacted symbolically in the wedding ceremony by the *pronuba*'s joining of the right hands of the bride and groom. In literature and art, Juno often performs this function (Virg. *A.* 4.166 with Pease, S. Treggiari, *EMC* 13 (1994) 314–16). Venus' usurpation of the rôle of divine *pronuba* perhaps reflects her prominence in the Statian epithalamium (see intro.).

Ianthida: Ianthis (Greek acc. *Ianthida*) is a transparent pseudonym for Violentilla, ἴανθος or ἴον being Greek for violet (Latin *uiola*). The third-declension form Ianthis, in place of the common Ianthe, seems to echo that of Asteris, Stella's pseudonym for Violentilla in his love elegies (cf. Stat. *Silu.* 1.2.197–8).

uati as often, 'poet'. The emphatic position of the word reflects the centrality to the epigram of Stella's poetic *persona* (see intro.).

2   plus dare non potui: union with Violentilla was the greatest gift Venus could bestow upon Stella – a pretty compliment to the bride, praise of whom is standard in marriage songs. Cf. D. A. Russell, *PCPhS* 25 (1979) 104–17.

3   domina evokes the conceit of *seruitium amoris*, whereby the lover is represented as the slave of an exacting mistress (Copley (1947), Lyne (1979), Murgatroyd (1981)). The characterisation of Violentilla as *domina* presumably reflects her literary *persona* in the love elegies of Stella.

  in aurem: implies secrecy; contrast *coram domina*. Cf. 1.89.1–2 *garris in aurem semper omnibus, Cinna,* | *garrire et illud teste quod licet turba*.

4   quid: internal accusative with *peccare*; cf. Tib. 1.6.71 *si quid peccasse putet*, Ov. *Ars* 2.365.

  pecces: often applied to violations of amatory or conjugal fidelity, usually by the woman, less commonly by the man, e.g. Ov. *Ars* 2.408.

  exitiose: an unusual word in an amatory context, which has occasioned critical discomfort (see Grewing). If the text is sound, it appears to be used prospectively: should Stella stray, he will be 'destructive' either of the marriage or of Violentilla's peace of mind (cf. Tib. 1.5.48 *uenit in exitium callida lena meum*).

5   lasciuum: unrestrained in sexual matters, usually with reference to extra-marital amours: cf. Ov. *Ars* 3.27, **41**.8 *quem lasciuo strauit amica uiro*.

  furibunda cecidi: Venus is cast in the rôle of the jealous mistress of Roman elegy, who reacts with violence to her lover's real or suspected infidelity: cf. Ov. *Ars* 2.451 *ille ego sim, cuius laniet furiosa capillos*, Prop. 4.8.52–62, where Cynthia is also described as *furibunda*.

6   legitimos ... ante toros: Mars and Venus are best known as lovers apprehended in bed by Venus' husband Hephaestus (Hom. *Od.* 8.266–366, Ov. *Ars* 2.563–590), but sometimes appear as a couple in a stable relationship (e.g. Hesiod, *Theog.* 933–7; Augustan propaganda similarly presented the two as parents of the Roman race, glossing over the irregular nature of their union in myth). M.'s version, in which the deities are represented as having a love affair prior to a legitimate marriage, conflates these two separate traditions, a combination first found in Statius' epithalamium for Stella and Violentilla (52–3, 59–60).

uagus: of sexual inconstancy: cf. Col. 12.1, 12.96.8 *ne uagus a thalamis coniugis erret amor.*

7   postquam meus est: *postquam* with present indicative characterises an action commencing in the past but continuing in force until the present; cf. Cic. *Att.* 2.11.1.

nulla me paelice laesit: cf. Ov. *Ars* 3.739 *ante diem morior, sed nulla paelice laesa. paelex* describes the 'other woman' from the point of view of a female who is in a marital or quasi-marital relationship (Adams (1983a) 355). *laedere* is frequently used of the wrong done to a partner by infidelity.

8   frugi: here of sexual continence: cf. *CIL* x 4327 *Saluiae ... frugi castae probae,* Hor. *S.* 2.5.77. Mostly applied to females, the adjective in this sense can also be used of men: cf. [Quint.] *Decl. min.* 309.5 *me* [a convicted rapist] *antea frugi et innocentem.*

uellet 'would like'; *uellem, mallem, nollem* and *cuperem* are used with reference to the present in wishes which are considered impossible of fulfilment (K–S 1 180), such as Juno's here: Jupiter was an inveterate philanderer.

9   arcano ... loro 'with her secret whip'. In *Iliad* 14, Aphrodite possesses a desire-inducing girdle, variously described by Homer as a κεστός or ἱμάς (lit. 'thong'). Later writers seem to have understood this as a whip capable of producing sexual passion in the person whom it struck (*plaga* 10): cf. Pind. *Pyth.* 4.218–20, Hor. *Carm.* 3.26.11–12 *regina, sublimi flagello* | *tange Chloen semel arrogantem,* Faraone (1990) 219–29. The effect of the whip is unseen (*arcano*), like that of Cupid's arrows.

10   plaga: see on 9. Venus is described in the semi-literate *CIL* IV 1410 as *plagiaria,* an adjective which has sometimes there been associated with *plaga.* See A. Maiuri, *PP* 3 (1948) 162–4.

iuuat 'helps, is efficacious'. Since the working of the *lorum* is *arcanum,* this rules out the translation 'pleases him'.

caede duos: i.e. Violentilla as well as Stella. Housman (*CPh* 718–19), followed by SB, objected to this reading on the grounds that Violentilla would have been displeased by a broad hint that 'nothing but divine interposition would prevent her from committing adultery'. He therefore revived the suggestion of Heinsius [*sed tu iam dea*] *parce tuo,* i.e. Venus is asked to refrain from smiting Stella a second time. The tactlessness which Housman discerned need not, however, be present, if M. is referring to Violentilla's literary *persona*: see intro.

14   (= 7.36)

'Stella, when the roof of my humble country abode was letting in rain,
you sent me a gift of tiles to quell the leaks. Now that the chill winds of
December are blowing, can you neglect to offer the proprietor the same
protection as his property?'

The poem, one of several addressed to M.'s friend and patron Stella, thanks
him for his generous gift of tiles to reroof M.'s villa. In the concluding
verse the poet jestingly expostulates with Stella for covering his roof but
not providing him with a winter cloak: *tegis uillam, non tegis agricolam?* As
a literary man, Stella would not have taken this seriously: the request of
the impoverished and shivering poet for a cloak is a traditional one, going
back to Hipponax (fr. 32, 34 W; cf. Juv. 7.73, Ar. *Au.* 928–30, 939–45
with Dunbar), and it is more likely to have had its genesis in the verbal
opportunism of line 6 than in any genuine need on M.'s part for a new
outer garment.

   M. often refers to his estate at Nomentum, which he likes to represent as
modest (cf. **11**.2n.). Like most country properties, it comprised residential
buildings and adjoining farmlands and functioned both as an escape from
the city (cf. 2.38, 6.43, **20**), and as a source of income: cf. J. Percival in I.
M. Barton, ed., *Roman domestic buildings* (Exeter 1996) 65–90, N. Purcell in
T. J. Cornell and K. Lomas, edd., *Urban society in Roman Italy* (London 1995)
151–79.

Further reading: Barry (1996), Wikander (1988)

1–2   The grandiosity of the language, with *madidus Iuppiter* used of pouring rain, and bold personification of the villa (*perferre negaret* n.) is amusingly
at odds with the banality of the subject matter, a leaky roof.

1   **madidum ... Iouem:**   Jupiter was in origin the god of the sky,
and in poetry often stands for weather of one kind or another: cf. Hor.
Epod. 13.1–2 *imbres | niuesque deducunt Iouem*, Cook (1904).

      perferre negaret 'refused to withstand'. *nego* + infin. normally has
a personal subject. For the personification, cf. Sil. 16.548 *cineres ... simul
iacuisse negarunt*, Virg. *G.* 2.343.

2   **rudis** 'gimcrack', 'in bad repair', a description in keeping with
M.'s habitually exaggerated portrayal of his estate as humble: cf. 1.12.5

rudis...porticus with Citroni and Howell, P. T. Eden, *Mnemosyne* 43 (1990) 160–1.

   hibernis . . . aquis 'winter rains'. After autumn, winter was the time of greatest rainfall in central Italy: cf. Virg. *G.* 4.474 *ubi...hibernus agit de montibus imber*, **82**.6, Nissen I 391.

   uilla nataret aquis: M. hyperbolically suggests that when the rains came his villa 'was awash'. Although tiled roofs were normally quite waterproof (n. on *tegula* 4), flooding was likely if the roof was poorly maintained. Tiles, resting on the low pitched roof without any fastening, could easily be dislodged by storms, and since they were placed on the rafters without any form of protective sheathing (Wikander (1988) 206), missing or broken tiles would allow rain water to enter the house directly: cf. Vitr. 2.8.18 *cum...in tecto tegulae fuerint fractae aut a uentis deiectae, qua possint ex imbribus aquae perpluere*, Plaut. *Most.* 108–13.

   nataret: poetical in the sense 'be flooded', cf. Virg. *G.* 1.371–2 *omnia plenis | rura natant fossis*, Sen. *Ag.* 44.

3–4   **plurima . . . | . . . tegula** 'an abundance of tiles': a generous gift, as roof tiles were relatively expensive: cf. Barry (1996) 60, Wikander (1988) 206–7. Singular *plurima*, 'many a', is poetic: cf. Virg. *G.* 1.187–8 *cum se nux plurima siluis | induet in florem.*

3   **subitos . . . nimbos:** a cloudburst, with which the leaky roof cannot cope, whereas it might withstand steady rain.

   effundere 'pour off'; cf. Col. 6.23.1 *stabula deuexa sint, ut umorem effundant. effundere nimbos* is intended to sound paradoxical: one thinks more readily of *nimbi* 'pouring forth' water.

4   **muneribus . . . missa tuis** 'sent by you as a gift', modal ablative, cf. Catull. 65.19 *missum sponsi furtiuo munere malum* with Kroll, 101.8 *tradita sunt tristi munere*. The plural *muneribus*, unparalleled in this construction, is presumably used to stress the large quantity of tiles.

   tegula: three types were used in combination (1) flat pan tiles with upturned edges, laid side by side and fitted into the tiles in the row below (2) capping tiles, used to cover the gaps between upturned edges of adjacent pan tiles (3) ridge tiles, covering the gap between the top tiles on either side of the pitched roof. See Barry (1996) 56–7, Wikander (1988).

5   **horridus, ecce, sonat Boreae stridore December:** a line of pronounced stylistic elevation, deflated by the witty and bathetic 6. *horridus,*

Boreas, and *stridor* are most commonly found in poetic texts, the verse is elegantly framed by a noun-adjective pair, and the alliteration of *p* and *s* vividly marries sound to sense.

horridus: active, 'that makes one shiver'; cf. Virg. *G.* 3.441–3 *ubi frigidus imber* | *altius ad uiuum persedit et horrida cano* | *bruma gelu*, **69**.1 cited below.

Boreae: the north wind, which prevails in December, January and February, is regularly associated with winter cold: cf. Nissen I 384–5.

December probably stands for winter in general: cf. **69**.1 *bruma est et riget horridus December*. But there could be a more specific reference to the Saturnalia of late December, when a gift would be expected: see on **24**.

6 **tegis uillam, non tegis agricolam?** plays on two senses of *tego*: (1) cover a building with a roof (cf. Caes. *BG* 5.43.1 *quae [casae] more Gallorum stramentis erant tectae*) (2) cover/protect with a garment (cf. 4.19.11 *ridebis uentos hoc munere tectus et imbres*). It appears from the stress in 5 on the cold weather that M. is asking for a protective outer garment, a traditional request: cf. 6.82.12, 7.92.7 and intro.

agricolam: as the owner of a working farm, albeit averse to hard labour (**25**.4n.), M. could technically refer to himself as an *agricola* (cf. 12.72.6, Cic. *Deiot.* 27). The homoeoteleutic jingle *agricolam . . . uillam* lends point to the antithesis *tegis . . . non tegis*.

15   (= 8.55)

'Since the present age surpasses previous epochs and Rome's greatness has grown under Domitian, you are surprised, Flaccus, that there is no correspondingly great poetic genius. If there were to be patrons like Maecenas, there will also be men of equivalent talent to Virgil. To illustrate: Virgil was lamenting, in the *Eclogues*, the loss of his property, when Maecenas dispelled his poverty, thereby enabling him to become the greatest of poets. Moreover, he made him a gift of his slave boy Alexis, who was waiting at table. Overwhelmed by his beauty, Virgil immediately forgot about the *Eclogues* and was inspired to compose the *Georgics* and the *Aeneid*, although he had shortly before been a rough beginner. I could also mention innumerable other Augustan poets who benefited financially from patronage. Now, if you were to bestow on me gifts such as Virgil received from Maecenas, will I be a Virgil? No, a Marsus.'

Post-Augustan writers frequently lament the demise of the literary patronage of past times, in particular Maecenas' generous patronage of Virgil:
cf. *Laus Pisonis* 230–5, Plin. *Ep.* 3.21.3, Juv. 7.94–5. M. treats the theme
in a characteristically witty fashion, which depends on a reading of the
Eclogues as a quasi-autobiographical text. The identification of Tityrus in
Ecl. 1 with Virgil (8n.) had been promoted, in the context of a request for
patronage, by the Neronian poet Calpurnius Siculus, 4.160–4. But whereas
Calpurnius' reading is relatively faithful to the original text (Tityrus jour-
neys to Rome where a *deus* frees him from the threat of dispossession), in
M.'s account Tityrus'/Virgil's poverty is cursorily dismissed by the intercession of Maecenas, smiling enigmatically in the manner of a god (9–11): M.
would evidently like to be the beneficiary of a comparable piece of patronal
largesse. Moreover, Virgil is identified by M. with the Corydon of *Eclogue* 2,
hopelessly enamoured of the *puer* Alexis, but instead of being constrained,
like the original, to bewail the futility of his passion, he receives him as a
sexual bribe from Maecenas and is forthwith inspired to write the *Georgics*
and the *Aeneid*.

The central section of the epigram is noteworthy for its amusing and
sophisticated exploitation of literary motifs. The Maecenas of these lines has
affinities with the god who intervenes, in the so-called *recusatio*, to orientate
the poet's efforts in a new direction. M.'s language is pointedly reminiscent
of such scenes, especially Ovid's parodic *recusationes* in the *Amores*. *risit* recalls
Am. 1.1.1–4 *arma graui numero uiolentaque bella parabam* | *edere . . .* | *par erat inferior
uersus; risisse Cupido* | *dicitur atque unum surripuisse pedem*; cf. *Am.* 2.18.13–16.
For *accipe* (11) cf. *Am.* 1.1.23–4 *[Amor] lunauitque genu sinuosum fortiter arcum
| 'quod'que 'canas, uates, accipe' dixit 'opus'*. Finally, the idea that the sight of
Alexis acts as poetic inspiration, causing the poet both to forget (*excidit* 17)
his previous love and to change course poetically, recalls *Am.* 2.1.15–18 *in
manibus nimbos et cum Ioue fulmen habebam,* | *. . .* | *claudit amica fores: ego cum Ioue
fulmen omisi;* | *excidit ingenio Iuppiter ipse meo*. But whereas in the *Amores*, as in
other *recusationes*, the poet is directed away from serious composition to a
less elevated genre, M. humorously represents Maecenas' intercession as
influencing Virgil to turn from lower to higher genres (19–20). Moreover, in
contrast to the tradition of a beautiful boy or woman inspiring love poetry
(e.g. Prop. 2.1.3–4 *non haec Calliope, non haec mihi cantat Apollo,* | *ingenium nobis
ipsa puella facit*), here Alexis is amusingly and illogically presented as inspiring
Virgil to write the *Georgics* and the *Aeneid*.

The generically paradoxical character of the poetry which Alexis inspires is cleverly brought out by the use of words with epic resonances: Alexis is *pulcherrimus* (13), the epic term for 'beautiful', instead of *formosus*, as in *Ecl.* 2, and he serves *carchesia* (15) instead of the lexically humbler *pocula*. In addition, the beauty of Alexis is amusingly placed in tension with the unattractiveness of fat Galatea (17n.) and sunburnt Thestylis (18n.) whose unappealing appearance is made to symbolise the literary and generic rusticity which Virgil, under the inspiration of the *puer*, is abandoning: M. thus puts a wittily disingenuous construction on this most sophisticated text.

Two final aspects of humour in the epigram are the tendentious equation of enrichment by a patron with the simultaneous acquisition of poetic genius (12) and the surprise ending, in which M. reveals that, were he to receive gifts such as Maecenas bestowed on Virgil, he would become, not a second Virgil, but a second Marsus. The epigram began with the premise that the present dearth of poetic talent is directly related to the decline in patronage; the logical conclusion would be that if M. were the beneficiary of comparable support, he too could write fine epic poetry: cf. 1.107.4–6, 11.3.7–10.

Further reading: André (1967), Saller (1983), White (1982)

1–2 The claim that under the stewardship of the reigning emperor the present age is superior to earlier times is common from the Augustan period: cf. Hor. *Carm.* 4.15, Calp. Sic. 4, 5.19.1–2, Sauter (1934) 19–24.

2 **duce:** Domitian is often so referred to by M., perhaps in allusion to his favourite appellation *dominus et dux*.

3–4 In denying the existence of great epic poets in his day, M. ignores Silius Italicus, author of the *Punica*, whom he elsewhere compares favourably with Virgil: cf. 11.50.4. But mention of Silius, a wealthy exconsul having no need of the financial support of a patron, would be out of place here.

3 **ingenium** 'poetic genius'.
   sacri: poets are inspired by the Muses or Apollo; cf. Hor. *Carm.* 4.9.28 *uate sacro*, Ov. *Ars* 3.403. The epithet is especially appropriate to Virgil, for his tomb was virtually an object of worship: cf. 11.48.1, Plin. *Ep.* 3.7.8 *monimentum eius* [sc. *Vergili*] *adire ut templum solebat*.

Maronis: M.'s preferred name for Virgil. As the paradigm of an epic poet, he encapsulates poetic *ingenium*: cf. N. Horsfall, ed., *A companion to the study of Virgil* (Leiden 1992) 249–55.

4   bella sonare tuba: an elevated metaphor for the writing of epic poetry: cf. 11.3.8 *quantaque Pieria proelia flare tuba*, Ov. *Am.* 1.1.1–2 cited in intro. In view of the implied comparison in 1–4 with the Augustan era, *bella* may allude to Domitian's military successes, which deserve to be celebrated just as Virgil celebrated Augustus' achievements.

     sonare: cf. *Laus Pisonis* 230–1 *ipse per Ausonias Aeneia carmina gentes | qui sonat.*

5–6   sint ... non deerunt ... | ... dabunt: *sint = si sint.* The mixture of moods suggests that, should the contingency expressed hypothetically in the protasis eventuate, then the fulfilment of the apodosis will most certainly follow: cf. Hor. *Carm.* 3.3.7–8, M. 2.24.1–4.

5   Maecenates ... Marones: generalising plural, men like Maecenas and Virgil: cf. *Varios Marsosque* 21, **6**.1.

     Flacce: for M.'s friend Flaccus, see **53**.1 n. The choice of addressee may have been influenced by the context, *Flacce mi* being Maecenas' appellation for Horace (*FLP Maec.* fr. 2), after Virgil the best-known recipient of Maecenas' generosity.

6   Vergilium ... uel tua rura dabunt: even a remote country region like Flaccus' homeland could produce a Virgil, if there were a Maecenas to support him. Flaccus came from Patavium (1.61.3–4), a place regarded as a provincial backwater and famous for the *Patauinitas* said to have marred Livy's style: cf. Quint. *Inst.* 1.5.56, Ramage (1973) 106–10.

     uel tua rura echoes Virg. *Ecl.* 1.46 *fortunate senex, ergo tua rura manebunt.*

**7–10   ** reflect the story, based on an autobiographical reading of *Eclogues* 1 and 9, that Virgil, having lost his farm during the confiscations after Philippi, travelled to Rome where he recovered his land from Octavian through the aid of his patrons.

7   iugera perdiderat miserae uicina Cremonae: an allusion to *Ecl.* 9.28 *Mantua uae miserae nimium uicina Cremonae*, bewailing triumviral expropriations of agrarian land in Virgil's Mantuan homeland, and often thought to allude to losses suffered by the poet himself.

8   Tityrus: i.e. Virgil. The equation, which began early, was fostered both by autobiographical readings of *Eclogue* 1 (cf. Serv. on *Ecl.* 1.1 *et hoc loco Tityri sub persona Vergilium debemus accipere*) and by Apollo's addressing Virgil as Tityrus at *Ecl.* 6.4.

aeger 'sick at heart'; cf. Virg. *Ecl.* 1.12–13 *en, ipse capellas | protinus aeger ago* (spoken by Meliboeus, not Tityrus).

oues: for Tityrus' sheep cf. *Ecl.* 1.8 *saepe tener nostris ab ouilibus imbuet agnus*, Calp. Sic. 4.162–3 *'spreto' dixit 'ouili, | Tityre, rura prius, sed post cantabimus arma'*.

9–10 M. telescopes two different events: the restoration of Virgil's land through patronal intercession, and the enrichment of the poet by Maecenas. According to Donatus (*Vit. Verg.* 19) and Probus (*Vit. Verg.* 6–8), Virgil recovered his land through the good offices of his early patrons Pollio, Gallus, and Alfenus Varus. M. however follows an alternative version (cf. Servius, *Vit. Verg.* 22–3), that Maecenas, along with Pollio, was instrumental in recovering Virgil's farm: cf. P. White, *Promised verse* (Cambridge, Mass./London 1993) 45, 259.

9   risit: Maecenas laughs because Virgil's problems are easily dispelled. There is also a hint of the godly laughter which connotes effortless superiority to mortal concerns (Sapph. fr. 1.14 L–P, Theoc. 1.95–6), this fits the quasi-divine rôle played by Maecenas in 9–12 (cf. intro.).

Tuscus eques: apparently M.'s own coinage: cf. Prop. 3.9.1 *Maecenas, eques Etrusco de sanguine regum*.

paupertatem...malignam: a *iunctura* unique to M. *malignus* = 'grudging, giving little'. Poets are traditionally poor (**20**.4n.), but the theme is here keyed to the impoverishment of Virgil following the confiscation of his paternal farm (7–8).

10   celeri...fuga: cf. Virg. *A.* 3.243 *celerique fuga sub sidera lapsae*.

11   accipe: cf. Ov. *Am.* 1.1.24 (cited intro.).

diuitias: Virgil left nearly 10 million sesterces which he had received *ex liberalitatibus amicorum*, including Maecenas. Amusingly, M. makes the money secondary in importance to the gift of Alexis.

uatum: the choice of the word for inspired poet, *uates*, forges a tendentious connexion between the acquisition of wealth and the production of great literature. See J. K. Newman, *The concept of vates in Augustan poetry* (Brussels 1967).

esto: the sort of language which a divinity might use: cf. Virg. *A.* 4.237 *hic nostri nuntius esto* (Jupiter to Mercury), Ov. *Fast.* 6.127, *Met.* 1.461.

12   tu licet et nostrum ... Alexin ames':   in *Ecl.* 2 the handsome Alexis – a traditional catamite's name – is the *deliciae* of Iollas, whose slave Corydon is in love with the boy. Here and elsewhere, M. makes Virgil, who was identified with Corydon, the beneficiary of a piece of largesse on Maecenas' part which is elsewhere attributed to Asinius Pollio: cf. Donatus, *Vit. Verg.* 9, Grewing on 6.68.6. Biographies of ancient writers commonly impute homoerotic tastes to those who treat fictionally of such matters (J. A. Fairweather, *AncSoc* 5 (1974) 263–4).

14   marmorea ... manu: Alexis' skin is white, like marble. The epithet is often applied by poets to their beloved's complexion: cf. André (1949) 41, **44.**13n.

nigra: of a full-bodied red wine; cf. Plin. *NH* 14.80 *colores uinis quattuor: albus, fuluus, sanguineus, niger.* M. often applies it to Falernian: cf. 11.8.7 with Kay. *nigra* additionally effects a colour contrast with *marmorea*: cf. 8.77.5, 9.22.8, 9.90.5.

15   libata ... roseis ... labris 'which he had first touched (lit. tasted) with his rosy lips', a sexually provocative gesture (cf. 16) presumably aimed at his master, but also having an effect on Virgil. Lovers typically wish to drink from a cup immediately after it has been sipped by the desired person's lips: cf. 11.26.4 with Kay.

dabat 'served': cf. **35.**1.

roseis ... labris: a characteristic of boys which appealed to M., e.g. 4.42.10 *Paestanis rubeant aemula labra rosis.* The combination of rosy and white (14) flesh tones was much admired in *pueri delicati* (N–H on Hor. *Carm.* 1.13.2).

carchesia: a Greek word for a drinking cup, an elevated term common in Latin poetry but found only here in M.

16   quae poterant ipsum sollicitare Iouem 'which could have excited to passion Jupiter himself', alludes to Ganymede, Zeus's boy love and cup-bearer, with whom attractive boys are frequently compared or identified (cf. **35.**8n.). *sollicitare* also hints at the obscene sense 'cause an erection'.

17–18   excidit ... Galatea ... | Thestylis et: falling in love with Alexis caused Virgil to forget his girlfriends Galatea and Thestylis – an inference based on *Ecl.* 1.30–5, where Galatea is the former lover of Tityrus/Virgil and *Ecl.* 2.43–4, where Corydon/Virgil refers to Thestylis as his girlfriend, supplanted in his affections by Alexis.

17   excidit (sc. *mente*) 'vanished from his thoughts': cf. Ov. *Ep.* 2.105, Sen. *Med.* 561–2.

attonito 'thunderstruck' by the boy's beauty (cf. Ov. *Ars* 2.296 *attonitum forma fac putet* [*puella*] *esse sua*), but with a suggestion also of the sense 'inspired', by Alexis' looks: cf. Hor. *Carm.* 3.19.14–15 *ternos ter cyathos attonitus petet* | *uates*.

pinguis 'fat', not 'buxom' (SB): the logic demands that Galatea appear less attractive than her replacement Alexis.

18   rubras messibus usta genas: lit. 'burned by harvest suns in regard to her ruddy cheeks', acc. of respect. M. has in mind *Ecl.* 2.10–11 *Thestylis et rapido fessis messoribus aestu* | *alia serpyllumque herbas contundit olentes.*

usta 'tanned'; cf. Tib. 1.9.15 *uretur facies, urentur sole capilli.* Acceptable enough in rustic contexts (**41**.3–4n.), Thestylis' sunburnt cheeks become a blemish when compared with the 'peaches and cream' appearance of the urban slave Alexis. For dispraise of a swarthy complexion in females, cf. Brown on Lucr. 4.1160, A. Cameron, *GRBS* 31 (1990) 287–91.

19   protinus: for the immediacy of the effect of love on generic orientation, an idea here spoofed, cf. Ov. *Am.* 1.1.25–30.

ITALIAM concepit et ARMA VIRVMQVE: the gift of Alexis is viewed, amusingly, as Virgil's immediate source of inspiration for the *Georgics* and *Aeneid*.

ITALIAM: the *Georgics*, so named for the 'Laudes Italiae' of 2.136–76.

ARMA VIRVMQVE: the opening words of the *Aeneid*, as often, stand for the poem as a whole: cf. R. G. Austin, *CQ* 18 (1968) 108.

20   qui...Culicem fleuerat ore rudi: the *Culex*, included among the minor poems attributed to Virgil in the *Appendix Vergiliana*, was generally regarded in antiquity as an authentic early work (cf. 14.185.1 *facundi Culicem...Maronis*), an opinion nowadays largely discounted; cf. D. O. Ross, *HSCP* 79 (1975) 235–63.

fleuerat 'had sung in tearful strains of', alluding to the mock-pathetic subject matter of the *Culex*.

rudi: *rudis*, combining the ideas of youth/inexperience (cf. Cic. *Nat. d.* 3.7), and lack of artistic virtuosity (cf. Ov. *Tr.* 2.424), suggests that the inspiration provided by Maecenas' gift was so potent as to convert Virgil overnight (cf. *modo*) from a rough beginner (cf. *uix*) to the most sophisticated Latin poet.

21   **quid . . . loquar** 'why should I speak of'? A rhetorical way of drawing attention to a topic which one affects to omit (*praeteritio*).

Varios Marsosque: for the plurals, see 5n. Varius Rufus and Domitius Marsus were among the poets in Maecenas' circle who benefited financially (*ditata*) from his patronage. Cf. *Laus Pisonis* 238–9, 7.29.7–8, Bardon (1956) II 28–33, André (1967) 114–23.

ditata: a transferred epithet going effectively with *uatum*. For the verb in connexion with Maecenas' enrichment of a poetic protegé, cf. Hor. *Epod.* 1.31–2.

22   **magnus erit . . . numerare labor** 'it would be an enormous task to enumerate', an anomalous use of the future for the common *labor est* + infin.

23–4   If given gifts such as Maecenas bestowed on Virgil, M. would be inspired to write – not great epic, but great epigram.

23   **munera** refers both to money (cf. *ditata* 21, *diuitias* 11), and to the boy Alexis. For the idea that the gift of a beloved would turn M. into a great poet, cf. 8.73.4–6, 9–10 *non me Paeligni nec spernet Mantua uatem, | si qua Corinna mihi, si quis Alexis erit.*

24   **Vergilius . . . Marsus:**   symbols of epic and epigram respectively; cf. 5.5.6–8.

Marsus: for the epigrammatist Domitius Marsus, see intro. 36. He is chosen to represent epigram here because he had the patronage of Maecenas (n. on 21).

Vergilius non ero, Marsus ero: a surprise ending. In view of the emphasis throughout on the former, one expects M. to say that he will be a second Virgil.

16   (= 10.64)

'Polla, I ask you, as my patroness, to receive my epigrams in an uncensorious spirit. After all, your husband Lucan, though a great epic poet, was not ashamed to compose the occasional obscene piece.'

This brief poem is neatly constructed. 1–2 deal with epigram and its risqué character, 3–4 with Lucan's epic *Pharsalia*, 5–6 with both genres, showing that the author of the latter was not averse to forays into the former.

Apologies for the indecency of epigram often cite examples of notable Romans who did not consider it inconsistent with their *dignitas* to dabble in the genre. The outstanding instance in M. is 11.20, where an obscene epigram by Augustus is quoted in full. In similarly apologist spirit Pliny (*Ep.* 5.3) appeals to various precedents, including Cicero, Asinius Pollio, Marcus Brutus, Seneca and several emperors, as well as Virgil and Ennius. Some MSS of Pliny add the name of Lucan after Seneca, which would be independent evidence for the epic poet's composing obscene *uersiculi*, but it is possible that the addition was an extrapolation from the present poem. That Lucan had a risqué sense of humour is suggested by an anecdote in the Suetonian *Life*: *adeo ut quondam in latrinis publicis clariore cum crepitu uentris emisso hemistichium Neronis magna consessorum fuga pronuntiarit 'sub terris tonuisse putes'* (Suet. *Poet.* 47.16–20).

In addition to Polla (1 n.), who was also a patron of Statius, M. mentions a number of females who played this rôle, including Mummia Nigrina (4.75, 9.30), Claudia Rufina (11.53), Sabina (10.93), Sempronia (12.52) and above all Marcella (cf. **17**).

Further reading: Nisbet (1978), P. White (1975) 280–6

1   Contigeris, regina, meos si . . . libellos: the apologetic tone is reminiscent of several epigrams addressed to Domitian (cf. 1.4.4 *contigeris nostros, Caesar, si forte libellos*), P. White (1975).

   regina: the female equivalent of *rex* in its sense of *patronus*. It is the formal term of address used by a client wishing to ingratiate himself with a patron with whom he is not on intimate terms (cf. 1.112 *cum te non nossem, dominum regemque uocabam:* | *nunc bene te noui: iam mihi Priscus eris*).

   Polla: Argentaria Polla, the widow of Lucan. In the early 90s AD she had celebrated her deceased husband's birthday in elaborate fashion, commissioning poems for the occasion from both M. (7.21–3) and Statius (*Silu.* 2.7). P. White (1975) argues, from the somewhat tentative and formal tone of 1–2, that despite these offerings, M. had not succeeded in gaining the intimate friendship of his patroness. Cf. Nisbet (1978).

2   non tetrica nostros excipe fronte iocos: receive in a spirit of tolerance poems which are meant only in jest, a request which M. makes when addressing persons who might take offence at the licence of epigram, e.g. Domitian, in his rôle as ruler and censor (1.4); cf. 4.82 and 4.14. There are two reasons why Polla might react unfavourably to M.'s epigrams: she is a respectable woman and she is the widow of a serious epic poet.

tetrica: the adjective here refers to old-fashioned disapproval of risqué poetry: cf. 4.82.4 *non tetrica nugas exigat aure meas*; 11.2.7 *lectores tetrici*, 1.62.1–2 with Citroni.

fronte: the brow was an indicator of moral judgment, cf. 1.4.5, 4.14.11 *nec torua lege fronte, sed remissa.*

iocos: often used in apologetic contexts to suggest that M.'s poems are not to be taken seriously, and so should not cause offence, e.g. 1 *Praef.* 8 *absit a iocorum nostrorum simplicitate malignus interpres*, 1.35.10–14 *lex haec carminibus data est iocosis,* | *ne possint, nisi pruriant, iuuare.* | *quare... | parcas lusibus et iocis rogamus,* | *nec castrare uelis meos libellos.*

3   ille tuus uates: in this honorific context, M. naturally uses the dignified term for poet.

Heliconis gloria nostri 'pride of Roman poetry'; cf. Ov. *Ars* 1.290 *candidus, armenti gloria, taurus erat.* Mount Helicon, the Muses' seat and source of inspiration for both Latin and Greek versifiers, here stands for poetry itself: cf. Ov. *Tr.* 4.10.23–4 *toto... Helicone relicto* | *scribere temptabam uerba soluta modis*, Prop. 3.5.19. M. elsewhere praises Lucan's poetic genius (1.61.7–8, 7.23.1–2), although he also admits in 14.194 that not all regard him so highly.

4   Pieria 'belonging to the Muses'; cf. 11.3.8 *quantaque Pieria proelia flare tuba*. The Muses' original home was Pieria, a district near Mount Olympus (Hes. *Theog.* 52–3); their father was the Macedonian king Pierus, hence the patronymic Pierides.

caneret cum fera bella tuba: a conventional expression (**15**.4n.) for the composition of epic poetry on martial subjects; in Lucan's case the Civil War between Caesar and Pompey. *caneret cum* 'when he was singing', implies that Lucan composed obscene verse (5–6) at the same time he was writing his epic Pharsalia.

5   non... erubuit 'was not embarrassed to'.

lasciuo: refers to the obscenity of epigram, as often in M., e.g. 11.20.1, 1.4.8 *lasciua est nobis pagina, uita proba.*

6   si nec pedicor, Cotta, quid hic facio? a pentameter; Lucan's epigram must have been a distich or a longer poem in elegiacs. By itself, the line appears to mean 'if I'm not even being sodomized (implying he would like to be), what am I doing here?' The form *pedicor* is surprising: Roman males do not elsewhere represent themselves as taking a passive rôle in sexual activity, even in jest (Edwards (1993) 70–1). Men *qui pedicantur* are routinely attacked as *cinaedi*, e.g. 3.95.13, 7.62.5–6, likewise the inflicting of *paedicatio* is a humiliating punishment: cf. Catull. 16.1, M. 11.63.5 *pedicant, Philomuse, curiosos, Priap.* 35.1. In the light of the above, two solutions are possible: (1) Lucan expressed sentiments which were unparalleled: perhaps for this reason the epigram cited by M. was notorious. (2) Lucan's poem might have gone something like: if I don't fellate, if I don't even get sodomized, what am I doing here? i.e. not being a *cinaedus*, I have no business here. On this view, M. would be citing the pentameter out of context in order to obscure the original meaning and effect a surprise ending, intended both to shock and amuse.

nec 'not even': **4**.12n.

pedicor: the obscenity (Adams, *LSV* 123) might seem inconsistent with M's insistence elsewhere that such language is unsuitable for the ears of a respectable women (cf. **85**.8n.); his addressee, however, is not an ordinary *matrona*, but a sophisticated patroness of literature. If, as Nisbet (1978) suggests, she was the granddaughter of the epigrammatist Argentarius who was noted for his ingenious crudity, then she may have had a special appreciation for her husband's efforts in the genre.

17   (= 12.31)

'This *uilla rustica* with its woodland, meadows, streams, shade, kitchen garden, fish and fowl was Marcella's gift to me. I would not exchange it even for the fabulous orchard of Alcinous.'

The epigram thanks Marcella, M.'s patroness (*dominae*), for the gift of the pleasant villa at Bilbilis to which the poet retired after thirty-five years in Rome (*post septima lustra reuerso*). The idyllic description of his new country home is pointedly juxtaposed with a lurid account of the horrors of the metropolitan rental market in the following epigram. Like Horace's description of his Sabine farm (*S.* 2.6.1–3), which M. almost certainly had in mind, its form is that of the rhetorical ἔκφρασις τόπου, 'set-piece description of a place' (see Spengel, *Rhet. Graec.* II 118): as the commentary demonstrates, the epigram bears a notable thematic and structural relationship to the ekphrastic, pseudo-epistolary and much more elaborate descriptions of country establishments in Sen. *Ep.* 55 and 86, Stat. *Silu.* 1.3 and 2.2, and, most famously, in the Younger Pliny's account of his much more grandiose *uillae* in *Ep.* 2.7 and 5.6.

Like most *uillae rusticae*, M.'s villa was certainly a working, rather than a merely ornamental, establishment (cf. **14** intro.). At the same time, M.'s description contains many elements of the idyllic literary landscape (*locus amoenus*) which takes its inspiration from the famous garden of Alcinous in Hom. *Od.* 7.112–32 – a wood, streams, shade, ever-flowing water, meadows, remarkable fertility allied to a benign climate, and birdsong. This overlap between the functional and the ideal is by no means surprising, because, as Purcell (1987) 201 has pointed out, 'the Roman view of landscape is a very literary and traditional one' and this view actually determined patterns of villa-construction in some cases, so that literary ideas about the *nemus* and the *locus amoenus* may well have influenced not only descriptions but also the physical constitution of such establishments.

Further reading: Curtius (1953), Dolç (1953) 94–6, 163–7, Schönbeck (1962), Schulten (1955)

1–2   haec textilis umbra supini | palmitis: shade is a characteristic of the *locus amoenus*, e.g. Theoc. 7.136–9; it is here provided by a canopy of vines trained on a trellis, *pergula*, in which arrangement the tendrils not only grew up vertical props but also across horizontal cross-beams, where they intersected (*textilis*): see White (1970) pl. 53. Vines so trained produced extensive shade (Plin. *NH* 14.11, White (1970) 233), whence the popularity of the *pergula* in lands such as the Iberian peninsula where summer temperatures were very high. It is probable that M.'s *pergula* had been built out from under the eaves of the house, so as to form as it were a continuation of the roof, an arrangement still visible in modern-day Italy: cf. Plin. *Ep.* 5.6.38 *laetissima uitis per omne tectum in culmen nititur et ascendit. non secus ibi quam in nemore iaceas, imbrem tantum tamquam in nemore non sentias.*

1   Hoc nemus, hi fontes, haec textilis umbra supini: the ἔκφρασις τόπου is characterised by anaphora of demonstratives: cf. **80**, 8.65, Stat. *Silu.* 2.2.50–4 *haec pelagi clamore fremunt, haec tecta sonoros | ignorant fluctus terraeque silentia malunt. | his fauit natura locis, hic uicta colenti | cessit* etc.

nemus: the wood or grove was an essential element of the *locus amoenus* (cf. Hor. *Ep.* 1.10.6–7, Schönbeck (1962) 49–56), but also a constitutive feature of villa-complexes: cf. 10.51.7, 10.58.4, Plin. *NH* 31.6, Stat. *Silu.* 1.3.17–18.

fontes: a *sine qua non* of the literary pleasance as well as sacro-idyllic landscapes (Theoc. 1.1–2, Vitr. 7.5.2, Schönbeck (1962) 19–33), but also a desideratum on a country estate: cf. Var. *R.* 1.11.2 *uilla aedificanda potissimum ut intra saepta uillae habeat aquam, si non, quam proxime: primum quae ibi sit nata, secundum quae influat perennis*, Plin. *Ep.* 2.17.25, 5.6.20.

textilis: vine shoots have a tendency to intertwine with each other: cf. K. D. White (1975) pl. 3c.

supini: the leaves of the vine shoots growing over the horizontal cross-bars of the trellis appear 'flat on their back' from the point of view of a person positioned below them.

2   palmitis: properly a vine-shoot, here collective singular for whole vines: cf. Stat. *Silu.* 3.1.147 *et Icario nemorosus palmite Gaurus*.

hoc riguae ductile flumen aquae: an irrigation channel serving M.'s farm. Such rural conduits formed the great bulk of Roman agricultural irrigation: see C. Knapp, *CW* 12 (1919) 73–4, 81–2, Hodge (1992) 249. The need for such channels was great in non-coastal Spain, with its very high summer temperatures and low rainfall (White (1970) 155), and access to a convenient source of water something to be prized (cf. Strab. 137, App. *Iber.* 88).

riguae: active; cf. Virg. *G.* 2.485 *rura mihi et rigui placeant in uallibus amnes*.

ductile 'that is led along a course': a rare word, deriving from the use of *duco* in connexion with irrigation; cf. Virg. *G.* 1.106, *Anth. Lat.* 635.9–10 *aquae strepentis uitreus lambit liquor | sulcoque ductus irrigat riuus sata*.

3   prata: a feature again both prominent in idyllic landscapes (Lucian, *Ver. hist.* 2.5, Curtius (1953) 195) and characteristic of country estates: cf. 1.114.2, Plin. *Ep.* 2.17.3, 5.6.10–11,18.

nec bifero cessura rosaria Paesto: the rosebeds on M.'s estate are the equal of the famous rosebeds of Paestum, a coastal town some 90 km south of Naples: cf. Virg. *G.* 4.119, Prop. 4.5.61–2, Ov. *Met.* 15.708 *tepidique rosaria Paesti*. Despite recognition of their commercial potential (cf. Cat. *Agr.* 8, Var. *R.* 1.16.3), flower gardens did not bulk large in ancient agriculture. Even if by M.'s time attitudes were changing (cf. Col. 10 *praef.* 1), in the quasi-idyllic ambience of M's estate their aesthetic appeal is to the fore.

nec ... cessura 'that would not yield even': in encomiastic contexts the thing being eulogised is often said to be superior/equivalent to some more famous instance of the same phenomenon. This device was particularly common in Statius, whose favourite term for such 'outdoing' was *ceda(n)t*: cf. *Silu.* 1.1.84 etc. Cf. Curtius (1953) 162–6, P. Focke, *Hermes* 58 (1923) 335–9.

bifero ... Paesto: repeated from Virg. *G.* 4.119, where Mynors comments 'some roses do bloom twice, but *biferi* is probably a poetic expression for an unusually long season, like *bis grauidae pecudes* 2.150, ultimately inspired by the gardens of Alcinous in Hom. *Od.* 7.117–21'.

4 **quodque uiret Iani mense nec alget holus:** M.'s gardens are so well situated that even in midwinter greens flourish, untouched by frost. This claim may owe more to literature than to life. Ideal landscapes characteristically escape extremes of heat and cold (cf. Hom. *Od.* 4.563–8, Virg. *G.* 2.149, Davies (1987), enjoying a vernal climate which promotes preternatural fertility in plants (Hom. *Od.* 7.117–21, Hor. *Epod.* 16.43–6, Schönbeck (1962) 39–41). On the other hand, most of Spain endures severe cold in winter: cf. Strabo, *Iber.* 47 and 78, 1.49.19–20 (winter in Bilbilis), Schulten (1955) 155–60, 427–31.

quodque uiret Iani mense ... holus: in ideal landscapes the earth yields produce even in the winter season.

holus: collective singular for *holera*, green vegetables (cf. 3.58.50, 7.31.5), simple country fare: cf. Hor. *S.* 2.2.117, 2.6.64, Juv. 11.78–9.

5 **quaeque natat clusis anguilla domestica lymphis:** an eel or eels kept as pets in a fishpond, which was a feature of villas from the late republic onwards (Balsdon (1969) 207–8). We hear much about tame eels: cf. Ael. *NA* 8.4, 12.30, Plut. *De sol. an.* 976a, Ath. 331e, Plin. *NH* 32.16, Thompson (1947) 58–61.

clusis ... lymphis: a poetic periphrasis for *piscina*, which cannot have been 'closed off' to the extent of lacking an inlet for water. Eels being sensitive to dirt, their pools required a constant inflow and outflow (Arist. *HA* 592a).

domestica 'tame': cf. Sen. *Ep.* 85.8, Col. 8.14.3 *genus uarium* [sc. *anserum*] *quod a fero mitigatum domesticum factum est.*

6 **quaeque gerit similes candida turris aues:** dovecotes (*turres, turriculae*) were erected by pigeon-fanciers on the roofs of villas: cf. Plin. *NH*

10.110 [*columbarum*]*amore insaniunt multi; super tecta exaedificant turres his*, Var.
R. 3.7.1. Birdsong, including that of doves, is another characteristic of the
locus amoenus: cf. Virg. *Ecl.* 1.57–8 *nec tamen interea raucae, tua cura, palumbes,* |
nec gemere aeria cessabit turtur ab ulmo.

similes: *concolores*: cf. 6.77.8 *quaeque uehit similem belua nigra Libyn.*

candida: cf. Col. 8.8.3 *totus autem locus et ipsae columbarum cellae poliri
debent albo tectorio, quoniam eo colore praecipue delectatur hoc genus auium.*

7   munera sunt dominae: *munera* summarises what has gone before and signals the transition to the concluding thank you.

dominae: the poet's 'patroness' Marcella (8n.). Cf. Plin. *Ep.* 7.24.7 *per
adulationis officium in theatrum cursitabant... ac deinde singulos gestus dominae cum
canticis reddebant.* The term, like its commoner male equivalent, is honorific
and respectful: see Mayor on Juv. 8.161, J. Svennung, *Anredeformen* (Uppsala
1958) 340–6.

post septima lustra reuerso: years may be reckoned by quin-
quennia; cf. Hor. *Carm.* 4.1.4–7. M. returned to Spain after living in Rome
for 34 years (10.103.7–8).

reuerso 'having returned home'; cf. 12.59.2 *post annos modo quindecim
reuerso*, Ter. *HT* 68, Tac. *Hist.* 2.92.

8   Marcella: lavishly eulogised in 12.21, according to which no one
could guess that she was Spanish rather than Roman by birth (on Iberians
bearing Roman names, see J. Richardson, *The Romans in Spain* (Oxford 1996)
176–7). She was probably a powerful widow (Dolç (1953) 94–6). Poems in
praise of living women are rare in M. and are invariably for patronesses
(4.75, 9.30, 11.53).

regna: a place where one is master: cf. Virg. *G.* 3.476–7 *desertaque
regna* | *pastorum. parua* creates a mild oxymoron, *regna* generally having con-
notations of sumptuousness: cf. 4.40.3, **36**.16, **20**.19. The metaphor anticipates the mention in 9–10 of a king in the shape of Alcinous, ruler of the
Phaeacians.

9–10   si mihi Nausicaa patrios concederet hortos, | **Alcinoo
possem dicere 'malo meos'.**   This couplet, an elegant way of praising
Marcella's gift, is inspired by Hom. *Od.* 7.313–15, where Alcinous offers
Odysseus his daughter Nausicaa's hand, a house and an estate, an offer
which will likewise not be taken up. Here the proposal is transferred to
Nausicaa, in order to effect a parallel with Marcella.

si ... concederet ... | ... possem 'if [Nausicaa] were to offer ... I could [say]'. The imperfect subjunctive is sometimes used in conditional clauses where one would expect a present subjunctive of hypothetical futurity: cf. Cic. *Diu. Caec.* 19 *Sicilia tota si una uoce loqueretur, hoc diceret.* In such cases the emphasis is on the unlikelihood of the contingency, rather than its potentiality.

Nausicaa: the final 'a' of Nausicaa is always long, as here.

patrios ... hortos: the fabulous gardens of Alcinous (Hom. *Od.* 7.112–32), at once a functioning orchard and *locus amoenus* of preternatural beauty and fertility.

10   **'malo meos':** in preferring his own gardens to those of Alcinous, M. continues the flattering *synkrisis* already exploited in line 3.

18 (= 10.47)

'These, Martialis, are the ingredients of happiness: inherited property, fertile land, a hearth always lit, freedom from stresses, physical health, easy social intercourse, a simple dinner, a night not drunken but pleasantly tipsy, a faithful but not prudish sexual partnership, deep sleep: wish to be as you are and have no higher ambitions, don't be afraid of death but don't desire it either.'

This is one of M.'s most famous compositions, notable not so much for profundity of thought as for 'a consistent moral philosophy given a pithy and cultivated expression' (Sullivan (1991) 217). It represents M.'s answer to the familiar philosophical debate on the constituent elements of happiness. The ethic is essentially Epicurean (nn. on *salubre corpus* 6, *amici* 7, *non ebria* 9, *somnus* 11, line 13), but with the important difference that peace of mind is attained, according to M., not by scientific knowledge, as in Epicurean teaching, but by adopting a lifestyle designed to avoid worries of any kind.

As often in philosophically coloured texts (Vischer (1965) 154–5, Kier (1933) *passim*), the ideal existence is associated with the country, where a healthy lifestyle can be pursued and the anxiety-producing activities characteristic of the urban existence can be avoided. M.'s poem shares many themes with stock poetic discourses on the advantages of country over city life, such as Virg. *G.* 2.458–540, Hor. *Epod.* 2 and Tib. 1.1: for instance, a hearth fire, peaceful sleep, a plain diet, *pudicitia*. In these passages, however, the ideal life is that of the farmer and includes hard labour (e.g. Virg. *G.* 2.472, 513–22, Hor. *Epod.* 2, Tib. 1.1.7–8, 29–32, Kier (1933) 67–75). M., by contrast, writes from the viewpoint of the comfortably off urban dweller for whom country life represents an escape from the inconveniences of the city and involves only leisure activities. In this respect he is closer to the ideal described by Horace in *S.* 2.6, where a rustic, 'Epicurean' lifestyle features simple fare and relaxed conversation on philosophical topics. M.'s pleasures, however, are of a decidely less cerebral nature than Horace's.

In one particular respect the epigram is characteristically Martialian, namely in the emphasis on the patron/client relationship, or rather the absence thereof, as a vital element in the ideal existence (5, 7nn.). He represents it as a major factor in his decision to retire from the city, and the present epigram must be read with this circumstance in mind, for the happy life here depicted is the one which the poet hoped soon to achieve in Bilbilis.

Further reading: Adamik (1975), Kier (1933), Sullivan (1991) 215–17, Vischer (1965)

1   Vitam . . . beatiorem: since M. deals with the ingredients of the happy life, not with what makes life happier, the comparative expression is not materially different in sense from *uita beata*, the standard Latin term for 'happiness', the goal of all ancient philosophies, especially the Epicurean; cf. Hor. *S.* 2.4.95 *uitae praecepta beatae*, Epicurus, *Ep. Men.* 128–9 'pleasure is the beginning and end of the happy life', Sen. *Dial.* 7.1.1.

2   iucundissime: a common form of address to a close friend: cf. Catull. 14.2 *iucundissime Calue*, Cic. *Fam.* 9.9.3 *mi iucundissime Cicero.*

Martialis: Julius Martialis, M.'s oldest and closest friend in Rome (12.34.1–2), addressed in every book except the second and the eighth, and the dedicatee of the sixth. To judge by M.'s other poems to him he had a preference for the moralising type of epigram. A further reason for the choice of addressee is the emphasis laid by the Epicurean school on the value of friendship: cf. on *amici* 7.

3   res non parta labore sed relicta: wealth acquired by inheritance without the necessity of engaging in hard work.

non parta labore: the manner of expression may reflect the Epicurean tendency to see pleasure in negative terms (absence of pain): cf. *lis numquam, toga rara* 5, *non ebria, sed soluta . . . | non tristis . . . et tamen* 9–10.

4   non ingratus ager: land which expresses gratitude for the labour expended on it in the form of good yields. Cf. [Quint.] *Decl. mai.* 12.4, Plin. *Pan.* 31.1 *fertiles annos gratasque terras precor.*

focus perennis: a topos of the simple country life: cf. Tib. 1.1.6 *dum meus assiduo luceat igne focus,* **19**.19n.

5   lis numquam: cf. 2.90.10 *sit sine lite dies. lis* refers to law suits, in which client and patron lent each other mutual support; it was one of the major nuisances of life in the city. Cf. **25**.3n.

toga rara: wearing the toga was synonymous with the client's burdensome lifestyle in the city, its absence symbolic of the relaxed life in the country: cf. **19**.17n.

mens quieta evokes Epicurean ἀταραξία 'freedom from anxiety', which is also associated with the country life and release from the troublesome duties of the urban client, e.g. Virg. *G.* 2.467 *at secura quies*; conversely the urban *cliens* Juvenal is *inquietus* (**19**.1).

6   uires ingenuae: a modest amount of strength such as befits a freeborn man; M.'s viewpoint is that of the comfortably situated urbanite whose time in the country is devoted to undemanding, gentlemanly pursuits, while slaves do the real work. For this use of *ingenuus,* cf. Ov. *Tr.* 1.5.71–2 *illi* [sc. *Vlixi*] *corpus erat durum patiensque laborum: | inualidae uires ingenuaeque mihi,* M. 3.46.5–6.

salubre corpus: in Roman writers good health is commonly associated with country life: see Kier (1933) 58–63. Bodily health was also one of Epicurus' ingredients of happiness (Epic. *Ep. Men.* 128, 131).

7   prudens simplicitas 'frankness tempered with discretion'. A feature of friendship in Epicurean and other writers is that the friend, unlike the flatterer, can speak his mind freely, while judiciously mixing criticism with praise: e.g. Philodemus, *On frankness* fr. 36, 48, Plutarch, *De adulatore et amico* 70–2, Konstan (1997) 103–5, 112–13, 141–2.

pares 'well matched' suggests real friends of one's own class, as opposed to the client/patron relationship which was based on inequality of social standing. Cf. Ov. *Tr.* 3.4.44 (discouraging cultivation of great men) *amicitias et tibi iunge pares.*

amici: friendship is of especial importance in Epicurean philosophy: cf. Epicurus, Κύριαι Δόξαι 27 'of all the accessories that wisdom procures for the happiness of the well-rounded life, the greatest is the treasure of friendship', Cic. *Fin.* 1.65–70, P. Mitsis, *Epicurus' ethical theory* (Ithaca 1988) 98–128, Rist (1980).

8   conuictus facilis 'easy social intercourse', in contrast to dinner parties in the city where one could not always choose congenial company. Such comfortable and relaxed dining was characteristic of the Epicurean/country lifestyle; cf. Hor. *S.* 2.2.118–20, 2.6.59–76 with Muecke.

sine arte mensa refers to the plain fare commonly associated with the rustic lifestyle, and has Epicurean resonances: cf. Epicurus, *Ep.* 3, Hor. *S.* 1.6.114–15, 2.2.70–1, 2.6.63–5, Kier (1933) 5–20, Vischer (1965) 22–9.

9–10   nox non ebria ... | non tristis torus et tamen pudicus: the language might reflect ripostes to the criticism of Epicureans as being excessively given to sensual pleasure e.g. Cic. *Fin.* 1.37 *nunc autem explicabo uoluptas ipsa quae qualisque sit, ut tollatur error omnis imperitorum intellegaturque ea quae uoluptaria, delicata, mollis habeatur disciplina quam grauis, quam continens, quam seuera sit.*

9   nox non ebria sed soluta curis: drinking enough to become pleasantly relaxed but not intoxicated is a poetic commonplace; cf. Gerber (1988).

non ebria: drunkenness was condemned by Epicurus: cf. Epic. *Ep. Men.* 132.

sed soluta curis: the language suggests both the relaxing power of wine (cf. Dionysus' epithet Λυαῖος, the 'Loosener') and Epicurean ἀταραξία, the latter, however, attained by philosophical reflection rather than bibulous means: cf. Lucr. 2.45–6 *mortisque timores | tum uacuum pectus linquunt curaque solutum.*

10   non tristis torus et tamen pudicus 'a marriage bed not prudish but nevertheless virtuous'. Although the ideal *matrona* was conventionally expected to maintain her *dignitas* even within the privacy of the bedroom (**41.**7n.), such a woman would in M.'s view have made a boring sexual companion. Cf. 11.104.15–16 where Penelope, faithful but sexually responsive, is held up as an ideal, and the advice, adapted from Herodotus, that a wife should 'doff her modesty along with her clothes' (Diog. Laert. 8.43).

et tamen pudicus: sexual fidelity was routinely expected of Roman wives: **43.**2n. *pudicitia* is often associated in particular with the idealised country life e.g. Hor. *Epod.* 2.39–40 *quodsi pudica mulier in partem iuuet | domum atque dulces liberos*, Virg. *G.* 2.524, Kier (1933) 75–82.

11   somnus qui faciat breues tenebras 'sleep of such a type as makes the darkness short', i.e. free from anxious wakefulness which makes the night seem endless. Untroubled sleep is a feature of the Epicurean lifestyle and of the *uita rustica*: cf. Epictet. 3.24.39 'what other do they [Epicureans] want than to sleep without hindrance?', Hor. *S.* 2.6.61, Tib. 1.10.9–10 *somnumque petebat | securus uarias dux gregis inter oues*, Virg. *G.* 2.470. M. is drawing an implied contrast with the difficulty of getting adequate sleep in the city: cf. **19**.14n., **20**.2n.

12–13   uelis ... malis | ... metuas ... optes: the final requirements for a happy life are expressed protreptically as subjunctives, varying the nouns of 3–11.

13   summum nec metuas diem nec optes: one should neither be afraid of death nor long for it. Both ideas are in keeping with Epicurean dogma. For the first, cf. Epicurus, *Ep. Men.* 126, Lucr. 3.830–1094. The second is in line with the Epicurean prohibition on suicide: see Diog. Laert. 10.119, Van Hooff (1990) 185.

19   (= 12.18)

'While you wearily traipse around the city attending on powerful patrons, Juvenal, I have been welcomed home after many years by my native Bilbilis and have become a country dweller. I live a life of idleness, and make up for all the sleep I lost during those 30 years in Rome. I can dress informally and when I rise – late – I am greeted by a well-stocked fireplace and home cooking. There is an attractive huntsman and a young bailiff. This is how I want to live and die.'

This epigram, addressed to M.'s friend Juvenal in Rome, is a variation on the rhetorical commonplace of the superiority of country to city living. Here the pleasures of rural idleness, often praised as a temporary escape from life in the city, gain added piquancy from the fact of M.'s permanent retirement from Rome to live in his provincial hometown after a lapse of 34 years.

The epigram is not, however, a straightforward description of M.'s life in retirement. The poet plays throughout with the conventions of the city v. country theme, recalling pieces such as Tib. 1.1, Hor. *Epod.* 2 and Virg. *G.* 2. Whereas words connoting plenty and luxury are applied pejoratively in these texts to aspects of city life, M. employs such language of his (relatively) impoverished rural circumstances, implying that true riches consist not in the appurtenances of urban luxury, but in a simple rural existence which provides him with all the bounty that he could wish for. A similar technique is used in 10.96, esp. 5–6 *in qua res parua beatum | me facit et tenues luxuriantur opes*; in the present epigram however there is more extensive allusion than in 10.96 to poetic predecessors.

Thus *superbus* (9, 19), *ingens* (13), *improbus* (13) and *cultus* (20), which normally suggest various forms of excess associated with the city (cf. Virg. *G.* 2.461–2, Hor. *Epod.* 2.7–8), are here applied by a process of inversion to M.'s rural retreat. Similarly *multa uilica quem coronat olla* 21 bathetically recontextualises Virgil's *intenditque locum sertis et fronde coronat* (*A.* 4.506), part of an elaborate description of Dido's pyre.

This playing with convention suggests that the poem is not a wholly realistic and serious portrayal of M.'s life in retirement. There are other hints to the same effect. For instance, M.'s description of himself as *rusticus* (8) along with the apology for his homeland's *nomina crassiora*, suggests the urbanite who can gently mock his 'rustic' existence. In addition, several details have an air of unreality. *uestis* (18) may be entirely literary in its inspiration (n. *ad loc.*). Broken furniture too (18) does not comport either with the suggestion of abundance in 19–20 or with M.'s equestrian census: the detail is redolent of genre scenes depicting dire poverty (cf. **64**.11 n.). Finally, there is the sexual fantasy with which the poem concludes, in particular, M.'s possession of a *uilicus* who is young and sexually attractive: hardly the sort of person who would in reality be chosen for such a job (25n.).

It is a reasonable assumption that the epigram was written shortly after M.'s return to Spain before the harsh realities of life in a small town, and his resultant nostalgia for Rome, began to make themselves felt (contrast e.g. **25**). But, as implied above, even in this poem M. displays a rueful awareness that his country existence is an idyllic dream owing more to literary fantasy than to practical reality.

Further reading: Cairns (1975), Dolç (1953) 129–33, Howell (1998)

1   Dum tu . . . erras: the client's irksome trekking from one house to another to attend his patrons' *salutationes* symbolises the rigours of life in the city; cf. **73**.1 n. For *erro* in this context, cf. 6.50.2 *errabat gelida sordidus in togula*.

inquietus 'restless', of what is in constant motion: cf. 5.80.10–11. Also suggested is the sense 'lacking sleep' (cf. Hor. *Epod.* 5.95, Sen. *HO* 1526): see 14n. Bilbilis posed no such problems (13–16).

2   clamosa: the densely populated Subura, with its numerous artisans' workshops and brothels, was especially noisy. Cf. Juv. 11.51 *feruenti... Subura*, Richardson s.v. *Subura*.

Iuuenalis: almost certainly the Satirist; he also features in 7.24 and 91. In all three the joking tone suggests that the two men were close friends. The no doubt exaggerated description of Juvenal as a client may have some basis in fact, since the Satirist depicts himself as such, e.g. 1.99–101. On Juvenal's life, see Courtney (1980) 1–10, and cf. 22n.

Subura: the notoriety of this area as a 'red-light' district does not warrant the assumption that the client is merely passing through it en route to the houses of the rich. Wealthy Romans sometimes lived there, e.g. Stella (12.3.9–10).

3   collem...Dianae: the Aventine; cf. **6**.13n.

teris 'you wear out' (i.e. you tread repeatedly) often refers in M. to the perambulations of clients, e.g. 2.11.2, 10.10.2 *mane salutator limina mille teras*.

4   limina...potentiorum: cf. Hor. *Epod.* 2.7–8 *forumque uitat et superba ciuium | potentiorum limina*. The client, after waiting in the *uestibulum* outside the door, was admitted into the *atrium* to greet his patron, crossing the 'threshold' to do so.

5   sudatrix either 'which makes one sweat' (cf. 10.48.10 *ructatrix mentha* 'mint which causes belching', 7.27.10), or 'habitually sweating', the epithet being transferred from the wearer of the *toga* to the garment itself: in favour of the latter are 14.135.2 *algentes... togas* and 12.36.2 *algentem... togam*, and the common use of the suffix *-tor/-trix* to describe a reiterated activity: cf. Salemme (1976) 119–20.

toga: the garment, made of thick wool, caused the wearer to perspire. See further 17n.

uentilat: ironically, the waving toga 'fans' its wearer while being responsible for his overheated state.

uagum 'always on the move' (cf. Fordyce on Catull. 64.271); used elsewhere by M. of the client's peregrinations, e.g. 4.78.3 *discurris tota uagus urbe*, **73**.1 n.

6   maior Caelius et minor: the Caelian hill proper and the lobe
known as Caeliolus (Var. *L.* 5.46) or Caeliculus (Cic. *Har. resp.* 32). The
latter was a favoured spot for the residences of the wealthy.

7   me (balancing *tu* 1) introduces the second section of the poem, con-
trasting the speaker's relaxed country lifestyle with Juvenal's wearisome
existence in Rome.

multos ... post Decembres: December, marking the end of the
calendar year, stands by metonymy for the year itself: cf. 3.36.7–8 *hoc per
triginta merui, Fabiane, Decembres,* | *ut sim tiro tuae semper amicitiae?*

8   accepit suggests a warm welcome (cf. Virg. *A.* 6.692–3 *quas ego te
terras et quanta per aequora uectum* | *accipio*), in contrast to the formal greeting
received at the houses of the rich patrons.

rusticum ... fecit 'has made me a country-dweller'. Cf. Tib. 1.1.7–8
ipse seram teneras maturo tempore uites | *rusticus et facili grandia poma manu.*

9   auro ... et superba ferro: the Tagus, whose tributary the Tag-
onius (Tajuna) was close to Bilbilis, was famous for its alluvial gold; cf.
1.49.15 *aureo ... Tago,* 12.2.3. Bilbilis was also known for iron and the manu-
facture of swords: cf. 4.55.11 *saeuo Bilbilin optimam metallo,* Plin. *NH* 34.144.
The iron was tempered in the water of the river Salo (Jalón) which was
particularly cold: cf. 14.33.1–2. See Dolç (1953) 129–33, Howell on 1.49.4.

Bilbilis: M.'s birth-place, a Celtiberian town of some importance in
north-east Spain, 4 km from the modern Calatayud in the province of
Aragón. Cf. Howell on 1.49.3, Sullivan (1991) 172–83, Dolç (1953) 107–67.

10   pigri colimus labore dulci: 'a kind of double oxymoron, since
"cultivation" is contradictory with "idleness", and "hard work" is not usually considered "pleasant"' (Howell (1998) 177). The language reflects M.'s
novel definition of a *rusticus*: not a hard-working farmer who cultivates his
fields, but one unenergetically 'cultivating', i.e. frequenting pleasant spots
(n. on *colimus*).

pigri: pursuing a lifestyle free from tiring physical exertions, in con-
trast to that of 1–6: cf. 10.104.13–15 *iucundos mihi nec laboriosos* | *secessus* (sc.
in Spain) *pretio paret salubri,* | *qui pigrum faciant tuum parentem,* **25**.4.

colimus 'I frequent', 'visit'. There is an implied contrast with Juvenal
who frequents the halls of the rich in Rome (cf. 3.38.11 *atria magna colam*).

11   Boterdum: Boterdus is known only from here and 1.49.7, where
the *delicati dulce Boterdi nemus* should perhaps be identified with the orchards

of Campiel on the bank of the Ribota below Bilbilis: see Dolç (1953) 189–92, Sullivan (1991) 182.

Plateamque: a town near Bilbilis on the river Salo: cf. 4.55.13–15 *ferro Plateam suo sonantem | quam fluctu . . . | armorum Salo temperator ambit*; see Dolç (1953) 210–14.

12   nomina crassiora: Spanish names apparently sounded harsh to Greek and Roman ears, cf. 4.55.9 *nostrae nomina duriora terrae*, Strabo 155, cf. also Auson. 17.4.3–4 Green *Bissula, nomen tenerae rusticulum puellae, | horridulum non solitis sed domino uenustum.*

13   improbo . . . somno 'an outrageous amount of sleep'. *improbus* usually has a pejorative force, and is often used in contexts where city luxury is contrasted with rustic simplicity, e.g. Hor. *Carm.* 3.24.62. Enjoyment of sleep is a stock feature of rural bliss; cf. Virg. *G.* 2.470–1 *mollesque sub arbore somni | non absunt*, Hor. *Epod.* 2.28, M.1.49.36. It is especially welcome to a retired *cliens* suffering from chronic sleep deprivation (next n.).

14   quem nec tertia saepe rumpit hora: sleep extending well into the daylight hours, implicitly contrasted with the urban *cliens'* obligatory pre-dawn rise (**73**.1 n.) and arrival at his patron's house by the first hour of the day: cf. 4.8.1, 10.82.2, Juv. 3.127, Marquardt-Mau 259.

nec 'not even': **4**.12n.

rumpit: cf. Juv. 5.19–20 *propter quod rumpere somnum | [cliens] debeat.*

15   mihi . . . repono 'I repay to myself', a technical term for making good a debt, in this case all the sleep forfeited (*quidquid uigilaueram*) during M.'s years as a *cliens* in Rome: cf. Sil. 5.533–4 *cessata reponere auebant | tempora* 'they were eager to make up for lost time'.

16   ter denos . . . annos: an approximation: M. lived in Rome for 34 years before retiring; cf. 10.103.7–9.

uigilaueram: the pluperfect stresses that sleep deprivation is a thing of the past.

17   ignota est toga: absence of the toga is a feature of the relaxed country lifestyle: cf. 1.49.31 *nusquam toga*, Plin. *Ep.* 5.6.45 *nulla necessitas togae* [sc. on his Tuscan estate], Juv. 3.171–2. It symbolises relief in particular from the duties of the urban *cliens*, for whom the wearing of the toga was mandatory. This elaborately-arranged woollen garment, containing at least ten metres of material, was time-consuming to put on and incommodious to wear, especially in summer (*sudatrix* 5); by M.'s time its use was confined

to holidays and ceremonial occasions, in particular the daily *salutatio*. See
S. Stone in Sebesta and Bonfante (1994) 13–45, Vout (1996).

17–18   datur petenti | rupta proxima uestis a cathedra: on
waking up, M. does not don the toga, as he would in the city, but asks his
slave to hand him something to put on, and is given the nearest piece of
clothing (or cloth) to hand from a broken chair.

18   rupta . . . cathedra: broken furniture was a traditional symbol
of poverty (cf. **64**.11). The *cathedra* was properly an easy chair, commonly
used by women, and often associated with luxury (cf. G. M. A. Richter,
The furniture of the Greeks, Etruscans and Romans (London 1966) 101 –2); here it
appears to be simply a generic term for chair.

   uestis: two meanings are possible: (1) a garment, probably the *tunica*,
the everyday dress for indoors. The *tunica* has been casually left lying on
a chair rather than being carefully stored, like the toga, in a cupboard or
clothes press – a further indication of rustic informality; (2) a chair cover:
these were draped on the chair, rather than being permanently attached
(Plaut. *Stich.* 94, Juv. 9.52, Blümner (1911) 123). Since the chair is broken
and thus useless, the cover left on it can be recycled to serve as a garment.
Cf. Callim. fr. 241 Pf. where Theseus, caught in a storm, throws off his wet
clothes and is given by Hecale a cheap piece of cloth from the couch.

19   surgentem sc. *me*.
   focus: blazing hearths often feature in idealised descriptions of the
country, where firewood was readily available (cf. *uicini*) and large open
fires were less of a hazard than in the city (**65** intro.): cf. Theoc. 11.51, Tib.
2.1.21–4, Hor. *Epod.* 2.43 *sacrum uetustis exstruat lignis focum*, 1.49.27 with
Howell.
   superba: used in its literal sense of 'lofty', 'high' (**30**.6n.).

20   uicini strue cultus iliceti 'adorned with a huge pile of wood
from a nearby holm oak forest'. Striking hyperbole: *strues* is elsewhere used
of a great pile of wood in an engineering operation (Liv. 21.37.2), or of a
funeral pyre e.g. Luc. 6.824–6.
   uicini: cf. 1.49.27 *uicina in ipsum silua descendet focum*, Plin. *Ep.* 2.17.26.
   iliceti: botanical fact: M. mentions an oak grove at Burado, to the
north of Bilbilis (4.55.23) and ilex trees still grow near the site of Bilbilis
(Sullivan (1991) 181).

21   multa ... olla 'with many a pot', a poetic use of the singular *multus*.

uilica: a female slave or freedwoman who played the rôle of *materfamilias* on the country estate. Her duties included cooking for the household (cf. *olla*). Usually, but not always, she would be the wife of the *uilicus*: she certainly cannot be in this case (n. on *leuis* 25). Cf. J. Carlsen, 'The uilica and Roman estate management', in H. Sancisi-Weerdenburg et al., *Re agricultura: in memoriam P. W. de Neeve* (Amsterdam 1993) 197–205.

coronat 'rings': cf. Prop. 4.4.7–8 *uallo praecingit acerno | fidaque suggesta castra coronat humo*. There may be a deliberate effect of parody here: cf. intro.

22   uenator sequitur 'next a hunter arrives': as at 1.49.29, where a huntsman (in both cases a slave or freedman) is invited to dinner, M. associates with humble folk. The absence of companions other than the *uilica*, *uenator* and *uilicus* emphasises M.'s release from the social obligations incumbent on the *cliens* in Rome.

ille quem tu | ... cupias habere 'a person such as you would desire to have [sex with]'. *tu cupias* is sometimes taken as generalising, but the second person generalising subjunctive is not normally reinforced by *tu* (see Fordyce on Catull. 22.9), and metrical considerations suggest that *tu* is emphatic (next n.), referring to the addressee. The innuendo that Juvenal is given to pederasty is a joke between two close friends and might even be an allusion to erotic *nugae* written by Juvenal.

tu: emphatic: M. normally ends a hendecasyllabic line with a monosyllable only if the word is closely linked grammatically to the preceding and thus bears no special emphasis, e.g. *factum est* or *non uult* (Sáez (1998) 242).

23   secreta ... silua: in the country, *amor* can be carried out in remote and hidden places; cf. [Tib.] 3.19.9 *sic ego secretis possum bene uiuere siluis*, Kier (1933) 82–3.

habere: euphemistic for 'to have intercourse with' (Adams, *LSV* 187–8), meaning in this case *pedicare*.

24   dispensat 'distributes rations'. On a large estate, a *dispensator* would manage the household expenses, while the *uilicus* would oversee the agricultural side of things (cf. Cic. *Rep.* 5.5 *uilicus naturam agri nouit, dispensator litteras scit*); in M.'s humble establishment the *uilicus* combines the two jobs.

24–5   rogatque longos | ... ponere ... capillos 'asks permission to cut his long hair'; cf. 5.48.1–3 *secuit nolente capillos | Encolpos domino, non* *prohibente tamen.* | *permisit.* Long hair was associated with slave *delicati*, and the ceremonial cutting of their hair marked not only their arrival at manhood but also the end of their pederastic rôle: see Howell on 1.31; Kay on 11.78.4. Since M. here describes his ideal lifestyle, one would not expect his *uilicus* to be anxious to put an end to his rôle as *delicatus*, but the phrase is probably an oblique way of stating that he is of an optimum age for a sexual relationship with his master, still without a beard (*leuis*) but old enough to want to be a man (i.e. engage in heterosexual activity): cf. 2.48.5–6 *grandem puerum diuque leuem* | *et caram puero meo puellam.* Several have argued for a different interpretation, 'asks [the boys] to cut their long hair' (cf. H. Tränkle, *WS* 109 (1996) 143–4). Since *serui tonsi* often symbolise moral rectitude (cf. 11.11.2–3 *pocula . . .* | *. . . tonso pura ministro* with Kay), a phenomenon traditionally associated with the country, whereas long-haired *pueri delicati* are symbolic of urban sophistication and luxury, such an action on the part of the *uilicus* would be in keeping with a poem which exploits the topos of the idealised country life. But if M. were foregrounding the idea of sexual rectitude, why is the *uilicus* himself described as *leuis*, which suggests that he is a catamite?

rogat . . . | **. . . ponere:** for *rogare* + infin., cf. Catull. 35.8–10 *quamuis . . . puella* | *euntem . . .* | *. . . roget morari*, 1.109.13 *rogat leuari* with Citroni.

25   leuis 'smooth-cheeked', i.e. having not yet grown a beard: cf. 2.48.5, 11.63.3. According to Col. 11.1.3, 14, the ideal age for a *uilicus* is 36–65 years; he should also be *uenereis amoribus auersus*. In the romanticised atmosphere of the epigram, however, the *uilicus* is made young and sexually attractive.

26   uiuere: the epigram shows the theoretical *uita beatior* (**18**) put into practice.

perire: M.'s statement that he wishes to end his days in this fashion, concludes the poem on a slightly sombre note, in recognition of the fact (cf. 16), that he is now quite elderly (**25**.4n.).

20   (= 12.57)

'You ask, Sparsus, why I so often retreat to my little country place at Nomentum. I do so because a poor man can neither think nor sleep in the city. There one's life is ruined by a multiplicity of sounds which go on all day and night, so that sleep becomes a near impossibility. You, Sparsus, are insulated from the tumult and bustle of Rome, perched up high in your sumptuous *uilla urbana* overlooking the metropolis but enjoying all the amenities of the country: but the noise of Rome invades my very bedchamber. Whenever it becomes too much for me and I want some sleep, I go to my estate.'

The present poem deals in M's favourite catalogue-form with a topic which is better known from Juvenal's briefer account in *Sat.* 3, the impossibility of getting sleep in Rome unless one is extremely rich and housed accordingly: *plurimus hic aeger moritur uigilando* ... | ... | ... *nam quae meritoria somnum* | *admittunt? magnis opibus dormitur in urbe.* | *inde caput morbi. raedarum transitus arto* | *uicorum in flexu et stantis conuicia mandrae* | *eripient somnum Druso uitulisque marinis* (232–8). In contrast to Juvenal, M. draws a detailed comparison between the plight of the sleep-starved poor man (3–17, 26–8) and the wealthy individual who is unaffected by city noise (18–25). The metre is choliambic, in keeping with the mildly satirical tone of the piece.

1–2   Cur ... | ... quaeris: for this opening formulation, cf. 6.67 and 10.22. For the sentiment, cf. Plin. *Ep.* 2.17.1 *miraris cur me Laurentinum ... tanto opere delectet.*

1   sicci: M.'s estate (next n.) relied on pumped water (**11**.3–4).

   parua rura Nomenti: M.'s farm situated in pleasantly hilly country at Nomentum, some 15 miles NE of Rome, upon whose unpretentiousness he likes to insist: cf. **11**.2n.

2   laremque uillae sordidum 'and the farm's humble abode', reinforcing the suggestion that the property is modest. *sordidus* refers literally to the dirt associated with straitened circumstances, but comes by extension to mean 'poor' or 'humble': cf. Yavetz (1965). *Lar* refers by a common metonymy to the house attached to M.'s estate (cf. Hor. *Carm.* 1.12.44 *cum lare fundus*, with N–H): its modest character is also mentioned at 6.43.3–4 *me Nomentani confirmant otia ruris* | *et casa iugeribus non onerosa suis.*

   petam: for the Nomentan farm as retreat, cf. 2.38, 6.43.

3–4   nec cogitandi ... | in urbe locus est pauperi: the familiar complaint of the literary man that he cannot think creatively amidst the noise of the city: cf. Hor. *Ep.* 2.2.77–80 *scriptorum chorus omnis amat nemus et fugit urbem* | ... | *tu me inter strepitus nocturnos atque diurnos* | *uis canere et contracta sequi uestigia uatum?*, Sen. *Ep.* 56.1–5. Here, unusually, the idea is restricted to the poor man: the wealthy individual, who can afford luxury accommodation (20n.), will not be so troubled.

nec quiescendi | ... pauperi: Rome was noisy, making sleep difficult in the crowded tenements where the majority of the population lived: cf. Juv. 3.234–5 cited intro., Hor. *Ep.* 1.17.6–8, Stat. *Silu.* 3.5.85–8.

3   Sparse: as the name Sparsus is very rare, this must refer to either Sextus Julius Sparsus, suffect consul in AD 88, or his son. Syme, *RP* IV 108 opts for the former because of the opulence of the addressee's estate, Pitcher (1984) 454–6 for the latter. Cf. Plin. *Ep.* 4.5 with S-W.

4   pauperi 'of modest means': cf. Sen. *Ep.* 87.40 *ego non uideo quid aliud sit paupertas quam parui possessio.* M.'s self-categorisation calls for serious qualification. Not only is his *paupertas* relative to Sparsus' enormous wealth (18–25), but poets are traditionally impoverished and the term is besides exceedingly flexible: M., like Horace before him (*Carm.* 2.18.10–11), can call himself *pauper* (2.90.3, 4.77.3, 5.13.1) despite his equestrian status and his possession of a town house and a country estate. Cf. Kay on 11.32, E. Scamuzzi, *Riv St Class* 14 (1966) 188–200.

uitam '(good) quality of life', a common usage in M.: cf. 6.70.15, Howell on 1.15.4.

5–15   Practitioners of mostly banausic occupations who by their noisiness disturb M. round the clock.

5   ludi magistri mane: elementary teachers, whose schools began before daylight. There are frequent complaints about the noise which they made in controlling their pupils: cf. 9.68.1 –4 *quid tibi nobiscum est, ludi scelerate magister,* | *inuisum pueris uirginibusque caput?* | *nondum cristati rupere silentia galli:* | *murmure iam saeuo uerberibusque tonas*; A. D. Booth, *EMC* 17 (1973) 107–14. The poorer sort taught in the open air (Hor. *Ep.* 1.20.17–18), increasing the potential for disturbing the neighbourhood. Cf. Bonner (1977) 115–18, Harris (1989) 236–7.

nocte pistores: cf. Ps.-Manetho *Apotel.* 1.80 Koechly 'bakers who work during the darkness'. The nocturnal din for which they are responsible may also encompass their pre-dawn hawking of their produce: cf. 14.223.

6   aerariorum marculi: the *aerarius*, a worker in bronze or other metal, hammered thin sheets of metal to fashion a variety of implements or to produce relief-work (Blümner, *Technologie* IV 227–53). The *marculus* or *martulus* was a hammer of the smaller type used for delicate work, as opposed to the heavier *malleus*: cf. L. Deroy, *AC* 28 (1959) 5–31.

die toto: neatly balancing *mane* and *nocte.*

7–8   The *nummularius*, state-appointed banker, one of whose tasks was to receive obsolete coins and replace them with a current issue, makes his table rattle by dropping Nero's coins on it. He may be testing to see if the coins are counterfeit, in which case they would not be acceptable for exchange. Cf. Schol. Pers. 5.105 *ut aes obuolutum auro percutiendo intelligas*, Epictet. *Arr.* 1.20.8 'throwing down the *denarius* he pays attention to its sound'. Alternatively, he may throw down genuine Neronian coins on the table to express his contempt for the coinage of Nero, under whom a major devaluation involving reduction of weight and alloys took place. See further H. Mattingly, *Roman coins* (London 1960) 123–4, 130–1, R. Herzog, *Aus der Geschichte des Bankwesens im Altertum. Tesserae Nummulariae* (Giessen 1919) 13.

7   **otiosus:**   presumably so described because he sits at his table all day, listlessly repeating the same activity.

sordidam: discoloured by the dirt or rust which amasses on the coinage.

quatit 'strikes repeatedly'; cf. Hor. *Carm.* 1.25.1–2, Stat. *Ach.* 2.157–8.

mensam: sc. *nummulariam*, the technical term for the counter or table of the *argentarius*.

8   **Neroniana . . . massa** 'Neronian metal', a sarcastic circumlocution for Nero's debased currency. *massa* is properly speaking the metal in coins: cf. Serv. *Aen.* 6.861, *TLL* VIII 429.45–50.

9–10   *balux* is a Spanish word apparently denoting a tiny nugget of gold: cf. Plin. *NH* 33.77 *inueniuntur item [auri] massae, nec non in puteis, et denas excedentes libras; palagas, alii palacurnas, iidem quod minutum est balucem uocant*, Holder (1896) 338–9. 'The process of beating out gold-leaf appears to be described. The grains of gold were laid on a smooth flat stone and hammered with a mallet of hard wood' (Paley and Stone). D–S I fig. 659 illustrates the procedure.

9   **malleator:**   rare; elsewhere only in inscriptions and late texts.

Hispanae: in the first centuries BC and AD the Iberian peninsula was Rome's main source of gold, the deposits being primarily concentrated in the NW: cf. O. Davies, *Roman mines in Europe* (Oxford 1935) 94–116.

10   **tritum:**   that the *saxum* is *tritum* from constant use directs attention to the unremitting nature of the noise.

nitenti: with the gold-dust that adheres to it.

fuste: an apparently unique use of *fustis* for *malleus*, developed from its original sense of a cudgel used to beat delinquent soldiers (M. Leumann, *Hermes* 55 (1920) 107–11 = *Kl. Schr.* (Zürich 1959) 35–8).

11   nec ... Bellonae: the ministers of Bellona, a Sabine goddess who was conflated with the Cappadocian deity Ma, and whose cult involved noise, ecstasy and self-mutilation: cf. D. Fishwick, *JRS* 57 (1967) 142–60. Bellona's prominence under the empire owed much to an association with the longer established and more important cult of Cybele.

entheata: the adjective, found only here (= *entheus*), refers to the ecstatic condition in which Bellona's devotees, *fanatici*, danced and prophesied: cf. Luc. 1.565–7, Juv. 4.123–4 *sed ut fanaticus oestro | percussus, Bellona, tuo diuinat.*

12   The shipwrecked notoriously held forth (*loquax*) in public about the dangers which they had survived (cf. Juv. 12.81–2). This might be a means of begging (Lucian, *Merc. cond.* 1), but M.'s *naufragus* additionally sports 'a bandaged body', in an attempt to elicit alms in sympathy for injuries really or allegedly sustained in the wreck. The commoner tactic was to display a painting of the shipwreck and hence the reason for the solicitant's destitution (Juv. 14.301–2 with Mayor).

13   A second type of noisy beggar, the mendicant Jew, a well-known satirical type (Juv. 3.11–16, 6.542–7, L. Feldman, *Jew and gentile in the ancient world* (Princeton 1993) 171–2). The Jewish population of Rome, which by the late first century AD was considerable, was not affluent, to judge *inter alia* from the humble character of its graves. Nevertheless, the depiction of Jews as professional beggars (*a matre ... doctus rogare*) may owe less to actual indigence than to the Jewish tradition of charity towards the destitute, which ensured that there were always numerous beggars in their midst. Another factor may have been the traditional teaching that one should make every effort not to become a public charge, which could have led Roman Jews to take up occupations which might have seemed to non-Jews mere beggary. Cf. H. J. Leon, *The Jews of ancient Rome* (Philadelphia 1960) 234–47, D. S. Barrett, *LCM* 9.3 (1984) 42–6.

14   sulphuratae lippus institor mercis: a hawker of sulphur matches; cf. 10.3.3 *quae sulphurato nolit ... ramento*, Sen. *Q. nat.* 1.1.8, G. W. M. Harrison, *CQ* 37 (1987) 203–7.

lippus: probably from the sulphur fumes, but *lippitudo* is also a characteristic in scoptic contexts of low-class or disreputable types, to which
category *institores* belong: cf. 12.59.9, R. MacMullen, *Roman social relations*
(Yale 1974) 139 s.v. κάπηλος.

15–17   One could as soon tally the hours of sleep lost in Rome as count
the number of hands that beat bronze in an attempt to inhibit an eclipse of
the moon. This is the climax of the catalogue, in the shape of a rhetorical
ἀδύνατον, 'figure from impossibility', of the type that involves incalculably
large numbers: cf. 6.34.2–6, H. V. Canter, *AJPh* 51 (1930) 32–41. Normally
in the ἀδύνατον the two clauses are joined syntactically, but this is not
invariably so: there is accordingly no reason to abandon the better attested
quis (with a period after 15) in favour of the *qui* of the *deteriores* (placing a
comma after 15).

15   **pigri:**   active, sleep which makes one sluggish: cf. Catull. 63.37.

16–17   Bronze implements were clashed during an eclipse of the moon
in an attempt to drive off the malign influences thought responsible for
this: cf. Plut. *De fac.* 944b, Gow on Theoc. 2.36. The reason for the choice
of bronze was probably its sonorousness rather than any special magical
virtue which attached to the metal: cf. Tupet (1976) 39–43.

17   The description of the eclipse, which was conventionally attributed
to witches drawing down the moon from the sky, is anomalous in several
respects: (1) the drawing down is effected by a *rhombus* rather than, as is
normal, by magical utterances. The only other references to the use of
the rhombus for this purpose are *PGM* IV 2296 and **84**.9 *quae nunc [sciel]
Thessalico lunam deducere rhombo?* (2) *uapulat*, 'is beaten', is an unusual word
for the procedure (cf. C. Mugler, *REA* 61 (1959) 48–9). (3) the sense of *secta*
is unclear and the detail unparalleled in other accounts of the *deductio lunae*.
The meaning is probably that the moon appears 'cut in two', when the
eclipse is under way but not yet complete, at which point the bronze would
be clashed in the hope of halting the process: cf. Tac. *Ann.* 1.28. Another
suggestion is that *secta* refers to the action of clouds in obscuring the moon
during the *deductio* (Hill (1973) 224).

18–25   The reason for Sparsus' initial question: his own circumstances
are such that he cannot understand the problem which afflicts M.

19   Petilianis: houses might retain the name of once famous owners: cf. Nep. *Att.* 13.2, Suet. *Aug.* 72.1, Pl. *Phaedr.* 227b. Friedländer thinks of Q. Petillius (*sic*) Rufus, cos. AD 83 or Q. Petillius Cerealis, cos. suff. in AD 70 and 74.

   delicatus: pampered, living in luxury.

   regnis: poetic plural, 'realm', the grandiose dwelling of the super-rich: cf. 4.40.3.

20   There was a fad among wealthy Romans for building on hill slopes whence one's property looked down from a commanding height upon adjacent localities: cf. 4.64.9–13, Tac. *Ann.* 14.9.1, Fehling (1974) 48–9, 54–5.

   plana … domus: the house was apparently built on an artificially levelled terrace, so as to provide an unimpeded view; such reshaping of the landscape was a prominent feature of Roman villa construction (Purcell (1987) 193–4). Other suggestions: 'ground floor' (but villas were usually single storeyed), 'having a flat roof'.

   despicit: for the verb of a view from a villa, cf. Plin. *Ep.* 5.6.38.

21   rus in urbe: cf. 4.64.25 *hoc rus, seu potius domus* (townhouse) *uocanda est* (a property on the Janiculum). The Romans did not share the modern taste for remote, unurbanised landscapes, but preferred villas where the amenities associated with city living were combined with an artificially created rural ambience: cf. Plin. *Ep.* 5.6.35 *et in opere urbanissimo subita uelut inlati ruris imitatio*, Purcell (1987).

   uinitorque Romanus: a second paradox. Roman villas were working farms and there is nothing surprising about the presence of vineyards (10.48.19, 13.119, Plin. *Ep.* 5.6.9, 29–30), but the vine-dresser, an archetypal symbol of the countryside (Virg. *Ecl.* 10.36), would not normally be found in Rome.

22   Another surprise: the 'yield' (*OLD s.v. autumnus* 2) from Sparsus' vines is not inferior to that of a vineyard in the *ager Falernus*, the region of Italy from which came the best wines (though quantity does not necessarily equate to quality of vintage).

   nec: 4.12n.

23   intraque limen latus essedo cursus: Roman villa gardens often featured a hippodrome (cf. Plin. *Ep.* 5.6.32–3), which in some cases was a purely ornamental structure named for its resemblance to a racecourse, but in others was genuinely used for riding: cf. 12.50.5 *pu-luereumque fugax hippodromon ungula plaudit*, K. Lehmann-Hartleben, *Plinio il Giovane. Lettere scelte con commento archeologico* (Florence 1936) 54. *intraque limen* adds a touch of paradox; *latus* once more suggests the luxuriousness of the appointments.

essedo: a two-wheeled Gallic military chariot adapted by the Romans as a fashionable mode of transport.

24–5 M. leaves till last what he sees as the most advantageous feature of the villa, the possibility of undisturbed sleep. Pliny's Laurentine villa boasted a similarly restful bedchamber (*Ep.* 2.17.22).

24 in profundo: slumber 'down in the depths' SB, an unusual variation on *somnus profundus*.

25 dies 'daylight'; cf. Plin. *Ep.* 2.17.22 *cubiculum . . . ne diem quidem sentit, nisi fenestris apertis.*

26–8 My bedroom is so close to the street that sleep deprivation is inevitable; whenever I can stand this no longer, I head for my villa.

26 nisus: the 'thrusting' of the crowd (Heinsius) is preferable to the inept *risus* of the MSS. W. S. Watt, *AC* 63 (1994) 277 objects that this does not provide the requisite level of noise and proposes *gressus*, the 'tramp' of the passers-by, but pushing forward through the streets could be accompanied by a good deal of sound, whereas footfalls are hardly obstreperous.

27 taedio: used of something that wears one out: cf. Liv. 38.19.3 *taedio se fatigaturos hostem censebant.* The combination with *fessus* is regular, e.g. Liv. 21.35.6, Tac. *Ann.* 12.39.15.
   fessis: sc. *nobis*.

28 quotiens libuit: the perfect is standard in frequentative clauses when the main clause is in the present, in order to stress the temporal priority of the subordinate clause.

21 (= 2.14)

'Selius leaves no possibility untried, whenever he sees that he must dine at home. In the hope of picking up an invitation, he hurries to one landmark after another in Rome, not just its civic structures and temples, but even its

less-salubrious private baths. In desperation, he even bathes three times in
the public *thermae*. Having tried all this without success, he runs back to his
starting point, the Portico of Europa with its mural of a bovine Jupiter, in
the hope of encountering a friend who is out late. Divine bull, I beg you,
ask Selius to dinner.'

This is part of a cycle of three poems in book 2 on the inveterate diner-
out Selius (cf. 2.11 and 27), and depicts Selius' frantic attempts to secure
a free dinner. In his obsessive desire to avoid eating at home, in his frequenting of public places in the hope of an invitation, and in his shameless
importuning of potential hosts, Selius resembles the professional parasite of
Comedy, particularly the Greek exemplars, who opportunistically accept
an invitation to dinner wherever it is offered (Damon (1997) 28–9). In the
context of M.'s poems, however, Selius is simply the greedy *cliens* carried
to an extreme, or alternatively the *cliens* seen from the patron's point of
view.

  Selius is one of M.'s most amusing and felicitous creations. The
anaphora of the opening line, *nil intemptatum . . . nil . . . inausum* immediately
establishes the *cenipeta*'s desperation as he faces the unwelcome fact (2) that
he must dine *chez* Selius. *currit* 3 reaffirms the motif of frantic desperation
while emphasising Selius' loss of dignity: to run, except for purposes of exercise (4), was servile behaviour (3n.). 5–6 *si nil Europa fecit . . . si quid Phillyrides
praestet et Aesonides* introduce via personification an idea of importance in the
poem: that in Selius' mind Rome's imposing public structures are equated
with the possibility of picking up a dinner invite there. Lines 7–8 ironically
apply to the protagonist language appropriate to worshippers (nn. *ad loc.*):
Selius' presence in Isis' temple is not for devotional, but dinner-hunting
purposes. Next, becoming increasingly desperate, Selius visits unappealing
private baths which, it is implied, the more discriminating would shun.
The mention of four establishments in two lines and of three in the next
couplet, signal the frantic redoubling of Selius' efforts. But when all these
come to nothing (*omnia cum fecit, sed renuente deo*), Selius is forced, absurdly,
to revert to his starting point, the Portico of Europa, the idea of return
being reinforced by the replication in 16 of the syntactical pattern already
employed of Selius' initial efforts (6). Finally, unable to stand the sight of
Selius any longer, the poet breaks in with an irritated apostrophe to the
Zeus-bull pictured in the Portico – he should invite Selius to dinner: clearly
no human is going to do so.

A feature of the epigram is the prominence of animal themes. First sounded in the shape of Europa, who was carried across the sea by a bovine Jupiter, it reappears with the mention of the centaur Chiron (*Phillyrides* 6), who was half man half horse, with the apostrophe to the *maesta iuuenca* (8) and with the individuals after whom the baths of 12 are named, Gryllus (Gk γρύλλος, 'pig') and Lupus (lit. 'Wolf'). All this lays the motivic groundwork for the concluding, and absurd, appeal to the divine bull.

Further reading: Damon (1997), Prior (1996), Ribbeck (1883), Sposi (1997)

1   Nil intemptatum . . . nil linquit inausum: the repetition of *nil* and the alliteration of *i* stress Selius' desperation. The rare *inausum* elsewhere has connotations of criminal excess (cf. Virg. *A.* 8.205–6 *ne quid inausum | aut intractatum scelerisue doliue fuisset*), and thus humorously suggests the extremes to which Selius goes to secure an invitation.

2   cenandum . . . esse domi: the worst fate which can overtake a parasite or a *cliens* soliciting a dinner; cf. 12.77.4–6 *ipse diuom | offensus genitor trinoctiali | affecit domicenio clientem,* Lucian, *Parasit.* 12.

  quotiens implies that this contingency arises too often for Selius' liking.

  iam uidet 'sees at last', i.e. the unwelcome fact can no longer be resisted.

3   currit (cf. *recurrit* 15) suggests undignified haste. Running is more the mark of a slave than a free man, but persons such as Selius have rendered themselves servile by their occupation: cf. 2.53.3 *liber eris, cenare foris si, Maxime, nolis,* Juv. 5.161–73, Damon (1997) 32–3.

  Europen: a Portico in the Campus Martius, apparently so called because it contained a mural depicting the rape of Europa by Jupiter in the form of a bull. Its precise location is unclear: see Richardson s.v. *porticus Europae,* Kay on 11.1.11; Prior (1996) 124–6 argues that the Portico of Europa was a popular name for the *Porticus Vipsania* (**79**.1 n.).

4   laudat Achilleos . . . pedes: in attempting to cadge a meal, *clientes* and parasites resorted to gross flattery: cf. 2.27.1 *laudantem Selium,* 12.82.13–14, Ter. *Eun.* 248–53, Plin. *Ep.* 2.14.5 (*laudiceni*). Selius flatters Paulinus by comparing him to Achilles, who in the *Iliad* is often described as 'swift-footed'. The Portico of Europe was a haunt of runners (7.32.11–12).

  sine fine 'endlessly', suggesting the persistence of the professional *captator cenae.*

5   si nihil Europe fecit 'if Europa has yielded nothing'. The personification of Europa foreshadows the address to the bull /Jupiter in the last
line.

Saepta: the *Saepta* or *Saepta Iulia* was a large rectangular enclosure
east of the future Pantheon and west of the temple of Isis. Along two of its
sides were colonnades. According to the generally accepted view of Gatti
(contested by B. G. Ackroyd, *Athenaeum* (1996) 591–7), one of these was the
Porticus Argonautarum (cf. *Aesonides* 6). Dedicated by Agrippa in 26 BC, and
restored after a fire (AD 80) by Domitian, the *Saepta* was a popular place to
take a stroll: cf. Sen. *Dial.* 4.8.1.

6   si quid Phillyrides praestet 'to see if Philyra's son may come up
with something'. *si* is used with the subjunctive in contexts where the idea
of expectation or hope is present in the verb: cf. *OLD* s.v. 11.

Phillyrides: Chiron, son of the nymph Philyra. The matronymic
is spelt with a double *l*, as elsewhere in poetry, to make the first syllable
long and avoid a metrically intractable tribrach. Among the statues in the
Saepta was a group of Chiron and Achilles (Plin. *NH* 36.29).

Aesonides 'son of Aeson', i.e. Jason. The reference is probably to one
of a group of statues depicting the Argonauts in the *Porticus Argonautarum*
(the remains of the west wall of this Portico, next to the Pantheon, have
large niches suitable for the display of sculpture: see Richardson s.v. *Saepta
Iulia*).

7   deceptus 'cheated of his expectations'. For this use of the verb,
more common in the form *spe decipere*, cf. Stat. *Silu.* 2.3.35 *quid faceret subito
deceptus praedo?*

Memphitica templa: Memphitica = Egyptian. The reference is to
the temple of Isis in the Campus Martius next to the Saepta. It would be
a good place to look out for an *amicus* who might issue a dinner invitation:
the goddess's cult enjoyed special popularity under the Flavians. See R.
E. Witt, *Isis in the Graeco-Roman world* (London 1971) 233–4. The phrase
Memphitica templa echoes and refashions the context of Ovid, *Ars* 1.77, who
recommends this and the Portico of Pompey (10n.) as places to pick up girls.

frequentat 'haunts': cf. 10.58.11–12 *qui nocte dieque frequentat | limina*,
Ov. *Met.* 10.169–70. The verb has a sacral flavour (cf. Apul. *Apol.* 56 *nullum
templum frequentauit*, Bömer on Ov. *Met.* 3.691), and is hence amusingly ironic:
Selius 'hangs about' Isis' temple – but not out of religious devotion.

8   **assidet** 'sits beside'. The choice of verb may have been influenced by *maesta*, since *assideo* is often used of sitting beside a person who is mourning, e.g. Petr. 111.4 *assidebat aegrae fidissima ancilla, simulque et lacrimas commodabat lugenti.*

cathedris: seats in the temple of Isis (cf. *tuis*). Unusually for an ancient religion, the worshippers of Isis remained seated: cf. Tib. 1.3.29–30, Stambaugh (1978). Since *cathedrae* were associated with women (3.63.7 *femineas... cathedras*), Selius may be angling for an invitation from a female worshipper, but Isis attracted devotees of both sexes, including Domitian: cf. S. K. Heyob, *The cult of Isis among women in the Graeco-Roman world* (Leiden 1975) 81–110.

maesta iuuenca: Isis, who in Hellenistic Egypt absorbed the attributes of the cow-headed goddess Hathor and was subsequently identified in Latin poetry with Io (see below). *maesta* suggests two ideas: (1) the mourning of the goddess for her consort Osiris, in which context especially she was represented in cow form (Plutarch, *De Is. et Os.* 366E; cf. Hdt. 2.132, Apul. *Met.* 11.11 with Griffiths); (2) the sufferings of Io, who was turned into a cow by Jupiter to hide her from Juno and persecuted by the goddess in this form: cf. esp. [Aesch.] *PV.*

9   **centum pendentia tecta columnis:**   the Hecatostylon, a portico of 100 columns on the north side of the Portico of Pompey. It consisted of a double colonnade, the inner aisle being raised a step above the outer and having more columns.

pendentia 'poised/suspended on': cf. SHA *Alex. Seu.* 26.7 *Basilicam Alexandrinam instituerat... ita ut tota columnis penderet.*

10   **Pompei dona:**   the Portico of Pompey which adjoined his theatre. Consisting of a colonnade surrounding a large rectangular area with shady walks, fountains and works of art, it was one of the most popular strolling areas in Rome (Platner-Ashby s.v. *Porticus Pompei*).

nemusque duplex: plane trees planted on both sides of the portico: cf. Ov. *Ars* 1.67 *tu modo Pompeia lentus spatiare sub umbra*, 3.19.1–2.

11–12   The reference is to private bathing establishments, which were named after their owners or else the original founders (C. Bruun in J. De Laine and D. E. Johnston, edd., *Roman baths and bathing* (Portsmouth, Rhode Island 1999) 75–85 at 75).

11   nec ... spernit: suggesting that these were places which most people *would* spurn. For speculation as to their location, see E. Rodríguez-Almeida, *MEFRA* 101 (1989) 243–49. Such establishments are unlikely to be frequented by the well-to-do: the implication is that Selius is not fussy about the class of host with whom he dines.

12   Grylli tenebras Aeoliamque Lupi: the baths of Gryllus and Lupus also stand for inferior bathing establishments at 1.59.3, where those of Gryllus are characterised as *tenebrosa*.

tenebras: in contrast to the public baths (*thermae* 13), which were erected in open spaces and had numerous windows, many privately run establishments were dark, being built on any available block and often hemmed in by other buildings on the sides, as well as having shops in front (R. Meiggs, *Roman Ostia* (2nd ed., Oxford 1973) 416–17). Cf. Fagan (1999) 20–1.

Aeoliam ... Lupi: M. humorously nicknames the baths of Lupus *Aeolia*, no doubt because they were draughty. Aeolia was the home of Aeolus, ruler of the winds: cf. Virg. *A.* 1.52–4 *Aeoliam uenit. hic uasto rex Aeolus antro | luctantes uentos . . . | imperio premit.*

13   nam 'moreover' effects a transition to a new subject: see *OLD* s.v. 4.

thermis: the large public baths. In M.'s day there were three of these, the Baths of Agrippa, Nero and Titus. Given that all the other landmarks referred to in the epigram are concentrated in a small area in the Campus Martius (see N. G. L. Hammond ed., *Atlas of the Greek and Roman world in antiquity* (New Jersey 1981) map 19*b*), whereas the Baths of Titus were roughly a mile away near the Colosseum, M. must be thinking of the first two *thermae* only, both of which were situated in the Campus Martius.

iterumque iterumque iterumque: a comically hyperbolic version of the more common *iterumque iterumque*, 'again and again', e.g. Virg. *A.* 2.770 *iterumque iterumque uocaui*. Selius commutes back and forth between the public baths (following n.), taking one bath after another, in the forlorn hope of meeting someone there who might ask him to dinner, bathing establishments being a possible source of last-minute invites (cf. 12.82). Editors often follow Gilbert in emending to 'nam thermis *iterum ternis* iterumque lauatur', but it is unlikely that all three *thermae* are meant: see previous n.

14   renuente deo: cf. Tib. 1.5.19–20 *at mihi felicem uitam, si salua fuisses, | fingebam demens, et renuente deo*. The anonymous *deus* stands, as often, for *fortuna* or τύχη, but the word is also chosen to look ahead to the closing plea to Jupiter (17–18).

15   lotus: middle, 'after bathing', an ironic understatement after 13.

Europes (Gk gen. sing.) probably refers, as in 3, to the portico rather than the piece of art after which it was named.

tepidae 'warmed up' by the afternoon sun: cf. 3.20.12–14 *an delicatae sole rursus Europae | inter tepentes post meridie buxos | sedet?.*

buxeta: plantations of box trees, located in the portico to provide shade; the tree, which grows to a height of five metres, is evergreen and is noted for its thick foliage (cf. Ov. *Ars* 3.691 *densum foliis buxum*; O. Polunin, *Trees and bushes of Europe* (London 1978) 132).

recurrit: normally one proceeded directly to dinner after bathing, but, in default of an invitation, Selius hurries back to his starting point.

16   si: see 6n.

serum: most people would be at dinner by now: the usual afternoon routine consisted of exercise, followed by the baths (eighth–ninth hours), and after that dinner (ninth hour). Selius is by this stage so desperate that he goes back to the spot where he began his cenatorial captation, in the hope that someone is out later than usual; cf. 2.11.2 *quod ambulator porticum [Selius] terit seram.*

amicus: here = *patronus*. The word is a courteous term for both patron and client: cf. Saller (1982) 7–15.

17   per te perque tuam, uector lasciue, puellam: the bull in the painting (3n.), i.e. Jupiter, is amusingly addressed in prayer form as if it were the god himself; alliteration and the appeal to a god by *per* are a feature of the sacral style. The address prepares for the punchline in which the statue is asked to issue a dinner invitation to Selius.

uector: cf. Sen. *HO* 553 *taurus puellae uector Assyriae.*

18   ad cenam Selium tu, rogo, taure, uoca: there being no humans left in the Portico, the bull is asked to invite Selius, to put him out of his misery. The concluding joke has seemed weak to many, and various more subtle explanations have been offered, none entirely satisfactory: (1) Selius should be thrown to a bull in the arena (cf. *Spect.* 16b.1–2 *uexerat Europen fraterna per aequora taurus: | at nunc Alciden* (i.e. a *bestiarius* representing Hercules) *taurus in astra tulit.* (2) Jupiter should invite him to dine in heaven i.e. remove him from the world. (3) the bull will give him a meal suitable for cattle (SB *ut herbis pascatur amaris*).

22   (= 4.67)

'Gaurus requested his longstanding patron, a praetor, to give him 100,000 sesterces to bring him up to the equestrian census of 400,000. The praetor refused, on the excuse that he had to give far larger donations to the chari-oteers Scorpus and Thallus. What ingratitude, what misuse of wealth! Are you prepared, praetor, to expend on a horse what you will not expend on a horseman [i.e. potential equestrian]?'

The epigram satirises the adulation and monetary rewards showered on popular charioteers and the ingratitude of patrons who fail to grant re-quests for remuneration from clients of long standing. M. uses a similar combination of themes in 5.25, where patrons are reproached for being prepared to pay the equivalent of the knights' census for an equestrian statue of Scorpus, while neglecting the interests of their clients.

Successful charioteers could accumulate considerable wealth in the form of prize money and of gifts from appreciative admirers: cf. SHA *Aur.* 15.4. A certain Diocles earned nearly 36 million sesterces in a career which spanned AD 122–36 (*ILS* 5287); cf. also Juv. 7.114 with Courtney. M. elsewhere voices resentment, from the viewpoint of the *pauper cliens*, at the vastly greater earnings of Scorpus (10.74.2–6).

Substantial gifts of money from patrons, such as Gaurus requests, are attested. Pliny the Younger gave large sums as dowries for friends' daughters and he helped a client to qualify for equestrian status (*Ep.* 1.19; cf. Sen. *Ben.* 3.9.2); cf. also *ILS* 1949, H. Hill, *The Roman middle class* (Oxford 1952) 215. It is unclear, however, to what extent such patronal generosity was unusual: cf. Saller (1982) 123. M. frequently complains about the reluctance of contemporary patrons to grant such favours, e.g. 5.19.9–10; cf. 14.122.1 *ante frequens sed nunc rarus nos* [sc. the knight's gold ring] *donat amicus.*

Further reading: Balsdon (1969) 314–24, Saller (1982)

1   Praetorem pauper: the juxtaposition underscores the differing financial status of the praetor and his would-be beneficiary.

pauper: a relative term (**20.**4n.), here describing a person whose capital is below that of the senatorial class and in M. often referring to the client who regards himself as 'poor' in comparison with his wealthy patron, e.g. 5.18.9–10 *quotiens amico diuiti nihil donat, | o Quintiliane, liberalis est pauper.*

Gaurus: this comparatively rare name, used several times by M. in various contexts, may here have an ironic resonance, since γαυριᾶν, 'bear oneself proudly, prance' is properly applied to horses, the proximate cause of Gaurus' financial discomfiture. On M.'s Gaurus see Garthwaite (1998) 168–9.

2   cana notus amicitia: well known to the praetor because of their longstanding 'friendship' (a courteous term for the patron-client relationship: Saller (1982) 11–15). The phrase explains why Gaurus might feel justified in making such a request.

cana: literally 'grey-haired', sc. 'old, longstanding', is strikingly applied to an abstract term: cf. 1.15.2 *si quid longa fides canaque iura ualent,* Catull. 95.6, 8.80.2.

3   suis haec tantum deesse trecentis: Gaurus is 100,000 short of the equestrian property qualification: cf. Hor. *Ep.* 1.1.58–9 *sed quadringentis sex septem milia desunt: | plebs eris.* Romatius Firmatus received 300,000 from his patron Pliny the Younger to make his estate up to the equestrian census (*Ep.* 1.19).

4   ut posset domino plaudere iustus eques: i.e. so that he could legally sit in the fourteen rows reserved in the theatre for the *equites* by the *Lex Roscia theatralis,* a provision reaffirmed by Domitian (*domino*): cf. **55** intro. and n. on *iustus.* The patriotic motive advanced for Gaurus' wish to sit in these seats makes his request seem all the more reasonable.

domino plaudere: cf. 6.34.5–6 *quaeque sonant pleno uocesque manusque theatro, | cum populus subiti Caesaris* [Domitian] *ora uidet.* The theatre was a major venue for the crowd to demonstrate publicly their approval of the emperor: cf. Millar (1977) 379, Z. Yavetz, *Plebs and princeps* (Oxford 1969) 18–24.

iustus, 'legitimate', alludes to the widespread abuse of Otho's theatre edict – the subject of several epigrams in book 5 – which led Domitian to reinforce it in his capacity as censor.

5   Scorpo: Flavius Scorpus, the most famous charioteer of M.'s day (**28** intro.). Given the size of his earnings (intro.) the praetor's donation to him at Gaurus' expense is particularly offensive.

Thalloque: mentioned only here by M. and presumably also a prominent contemporary charioteer. An *auriga* named Thallus is attested on an inscription of AD 90 (*ILS* 3532; cf. *ILS* 5287.14).

6   utinam centum milia sola darem implies that his donation is much larger than this. Although the praetor affects to complain about the amount he has to spend, such a gesture would be a guaranteed means of winning him popularity, especially since equestrian statues, for which it appears the money will be used (8n.), were often erected in race courses, providing a constant reminder to the public of the donor's generosity.

7–8   M. complains of the praetor's selfish use of his money for his own benefit (prev. n.), rather than in repaying the services of his client (see on *ingratae*). There is an element of snobbery in M.'s outrage that such a sum should be spent on a charioteer, who would have been of slave or freedman status, rather than on a potential member of the equestrian class.

7   ah pudet ingratae, pudet ah male diuitis arcae: cf. Ov. *Met.* 9.531, **12**.9 *at nuper – pudet, ah pudet fateri.*
      pudet 'shame on'.
      ingratae: refers to failure on a patron's part to reciprocate his client's services. 'Nothing was baser than an *ingratus amicus*' (Saller (1982) 14).
      male diuitis: the praetor's money chest (*arca*) is used for what is in M.'s eyes a bad purpose. For a comparable sentiment in a similar context, cf. 5.25.11 *o frustra locuples.*

8   A neatly balanced line, the word-play emphasised by positioning *equiti* and *equo* at the end of each half of the pentameter.
      equiti 'would-be *eques*'; cf. Hor. *Epod.* 6.13 *qualis Lycambae spretus infido gener* '(intended) son-in-law'.
      equo probably refers to commemorative equestrian statues of the two charioteers; cf. 8.44.6–7 *ante equos omnes | aedemque Martis et colosson Augusti.* That Scorpus was the subject of at least one such statue is confirmed by the presence of his name on a surviving statue base (*CIL* VI 10052); cf. 5.25.9–10 *quam non sensuro dare quadringenta caballo, | aureus ut Scorpi nasus ubique micet?*

23   (= 6.88)

'This morning at your *salutatio*, I accidentally called you by your name instead of addressing you as master, Caecilianus. How much, you ask, did such a great liberty cost me? It robbed me of 100 farthings.'

Clients greeting their patrons were expected to use the formal title *dominus et rex*: failure to do so was regarded as insolent. Cf. 2.68.1–3 *quod te nomine iam tuo saluto, | quem regem et dominum prius uocabam, | ne me dixeris esse contumacem*; Suetonius (*Vesp.* 15) remarks that Helvidius Priscus' greeting of Vespasian by his private name was overlooked by the emperor, which suggests that such a lapse of formality was normally viewed as reprehensible. In the present epigram, M. has made a similar *faux pas* in addressing his patron Caecilianus. As a result, he has not received his *sportula*, 100 farthings, but such a paltry sum is hardly a great loss.

The epigram is primarily a satire against a stingy patron (cf. **24**). Caecilianus gives his clients only the minimum *sportula* of 100 quadrantes, or 6.25 sesterces, an amount which M. regards as ungenerous: cf. 9.100, expressing dissatisfaction with a *sportula* of 3 denarii (12 sesterces). It may also be implied that Caecilianus provides nothing else in the way of 'extras' such as gifts or dinner invitations.

SB interprets the final line 'the dinner which went with it (the *centum quadrantes*) . . . would not have been worth eating' but this assumes that the *sportula* was made up of money *and* a dinner. The *sportula*, literally 'a small basket', originally consisted of edibles, but a handout of money had for a long time taken the place of the food. The money *sportula* might on occasion be supplemented with a dinner (cf. 4.68, 9.100 and 12.29); it would, however, have been impractical as well as tedious for patrons to invite their clients to dinner every time they received their dole – the reason, no doubt, why the experiment of replacing the money dole with a dinner, mentioned in the third book (7, 14, 30), quickly lapsed.

The epigram is cast in the common form of *Erwartung* and *Aufschluss*. The latter is often led into by a question: see intro. 15–20. Here the question (3) is phrased in such a way as to suggest that the poet's blunder is serious, causing the reader to expect an equally grave punishment, but it turns out that M. has only lost 100 *quadrantes*.

Further reading: Mohler (1931)

1   Mane salutaui: refers to the greeting of the patron by the client at the morning *salutatio*, usually in the form *aue* (or *salue*) *domine et rex* (cf. Sen. *Ben.* 6.34.3, M. 1.55.6, 1.108.10).

uero . . . nomine: when addressing a person of higher rank by name in a formal situation, the expected form was *praenomen* + *cognomen* (J. N. Adams, *CQ* 28 (1978) 165). Perhaps M. is to be imagined as using the most intimate form of address, the *praenomen* only, which would be even more offensive; cf. 1.112 *cum te non nossem, dominum regemque uocabam:* | *nunc bene te noui: iam mihi Priscus eris.*

casu 'accidentally'.

2　　**dominum:**　*regemque* is to be understood: cf. 4.83.5 *dominum regemque salutas,* 10.10.5, 2.68.1–2 cited above, Juv. 8.161 *dominum regemque salutat. dominus* here suggests that the client stands in the position of a slave vis à vis the master/patron: cf. on *libertas* 3.

Caeciliane:　the name, used elsewhere by M. of a stingy person (1.20, 2.78), is applied by him to a variety of fictitious characters.

3　　**libertas:**　i.e. speaking more freely than is allowed. The word also suggests the common assimilation of the client to a slave who is not at liberty to act as he pleases: cf. 2.68 cited above, where M., greeting a former patron by his name instead of by the title *rex et dominus,* likens himself to a manumitted slave.

4　　**centum quadrantes:**　the standard amount of the *sportula,* the money hand-out given to clients for their services: cf. 1.59.1, 3.7.1, Juv. 1.120. The sum is the basic minimum, but more was expected: see intro.

24　(= 7.53)

'You passed on to me at the Saturnalia, Umber, all the gifts which you had received from your clients during that festival. These were numerous enough – eight large Syrian slaves were employed to convey them – and their worth minimal. How much more convenient it would have been to send a single slave with five pounds of silver!'

Because the Saturnalia was a major occasion on which clients could expect rewards for their services, the value of gifts given at that time was of special concern. Clients must often have been discontented, and epigrams such as the present one are a reflexion – satirically exaggerated – of this. It was in keeping with the licence of the Saturnalia to voice one's complaints, though in a jocular manner; Stat. *Silu.* 4.9, for example, humorously remonstrates with a patron for sending the poet a worthless book. In M. such complaints are always addressed to fictitious persons (see on Umber 1).

In this and similar contexts, the catalogue form is often used. Stat. loc. cit. 23–45 lists cheap gifts which would have been worth more than the wretched one received: several are paralleled in the present epigram.

In 4.88 M. details modest presents that an addressee might have sent in return for his own small offering. Other catalogues in a Saturnalian context include 4.46, 5.18.2–3 and 7.72; Stat. *Silu.* 1.6 tabulates food items scattered at a Saturnalian show given by Domitian.

Further reading: Damon (1992), Nilsson, *RE* II 2.201–11 s.v. 'Saturnalia', Oliver (1977)

1   misisti: Saturnalian gifts were either delivered to the recipient's home, as here, or distributed as *apophoreta* at a dinner party.

Saturnalibus: originally an agricultural festival held on 17 December in honour of Saturnus, the Saturnalia was later extended to several days of festivities, the main features of which were *licentia* (e.g. drinking, gambling, reversal of slave/master rôles) and the exchange of gifts. This second aspect of the festival is closely linked in M. to the patronage system (Sullivan (1991) 13–14); it offered the client the chance to receive something more for his services than the usual *sportula*.

Vmber: likewise at 12.81 the name of a patron who is stingy with Saturnalian gifts. The name, which suggests a 'shadowy' individual, is fictitious, as are those of other mean patrons, e.g. 5.84, 8.33, 10.29, 10.57, 11.105: M. could not risk jeopardising a potential source of support by explicit criticism (cf. Damon (1992) 301–3).

2   contulerant quae tibi quinque dies: Umber passes on all the items which he himself has received as Saturnalian gifts. For the practice, cf. 4.88.4 and 5.19.11.

quinque dies: the Saturnalia comprised at least five days in M.'s time (cf. 14.79, 141, 4.88.2 *et iam Saturni quinque fuere dies*) and may have unofficially extended over seven days: cf. 14.72.2, Lucian, *Sat.* 2.

3   bis senos ... septem: the transparent disingenuousness of Umber's 'generosity' is underlined by having him send a large number of the same cheap gifts. The multiple *triplices* and toothpicks are presumably duplicated gifts, each received separately, which Umber gathers together and passes on, hoping that quantity will compensate for quality.

triplices: a set of three wax-coated wooden tablets bound together with thongs threaded through holes in the sides and used for writing notes or letters; cf. 7.72.2, 10.87.6, Cic. *Att.* 13.8 with SB, Fordyce on Catull. 42.5. We also hear of *duplices* (Ov. *Rem.* 667) and *quinquiplices* (14.4). They exemplify cheap Saturnalian gifts: cf. 7.72.1–2 *gratus sic tibi, Paule, sit December | nec uani triplices breuesque mappae <ueniant>*, 10.87.5–7.

dentiscalpia: toothpicks, presumably the cheaper kind made of quills: cf. 14.22 *lentiscum melius: sed si tibi frondea cuspis | defuerit, dentes pinna leuare potest* and *AP* 6. 229.5–6, where a quill toothpick is described as a 'poor present'.

4   his comes accessit: the elegant personification is in ironic tension with the minimal value of the items to which it refers.

spongia: given as an *apophoretum* at 14.144; cf. Suet. *Aug.* 75. Sponges were used, *inter alia*, for erasing writing from a papyrus (4.10.6), at the baths, and for wiping the dining table clean: cf. **36**.7, 14.144.1, D–S IV 1.1442–5. The following *mappa* and *calix* suggest that M. has the last in mind.

mappa: a dinner napkin (**32**.8n.). They feature among Saturnalian presents at 5.18.1. *breues mappae* (cf. on *triplices*) and *luridae mappae* (Stat. *Silu.* 4.9.25) are typical of cheap gifts given at that season.

calix: an unpretentious vessel, in M. sometimes associated with poverty: cf. 1.92.6–7 and 11.32.4. The word is avoided in epic but used in the less elevated poetic genres.

5   semodius...fabae: 1/6 amphora or 8 *sextarii*, about 4.5 litres. At 4.46.6 a *semimodius fabae* similarly features in a list of cheap Saturnalian presents.

fabae, collective singular, regular with names of legumes and other foodstuffs: cf. Hor. *Ep.* 1.16.55, 10.15.5 *quando fabae nobis modium farrisue dedisti?* The *faba*, broad bean, was humble fare: cf. Hor. *S.* 2.6.63, M. 5.78.10, 10.48.16.

cum uimine Picenarum: Picene olives, though well regarded (1.43.8, Plin. *NH* 15.16), were inexpensive (5.78.19–20, 11.52.11) and, in Saturnalian contexts, typify a cheap gift: cf. 4.88.7, where a humble present is *rugosarum uimen breue Picenarum*. Olives could be eaten fresh or preserved in oil and stored in jars; the mention of a *uimen* (wicker basket) suggests the former. Pallad. 12.22 emphasises that olives for immediate consumption should be picked in November and eaten within eight days. The olives received by M. at the Saturnalia are therefore well past their best, or else late picked, and hence inferior, like those at 11.52.11 which have 'felt the frost'.

6   Laietanae: the best of various emendations for the MSS *Laletanae* (cf. 1.26.9 with Howell and 1.49.22 with Citroni).

Laietanae . . . sapae: *sapa* is strictly speaking boiled-down *mustum*, unfermented wine, used for medicinal purposes (Plin. *NH* 23.62), for preserving grapes (Cato, *Agr.* 7.2) and for fattening snails in jars (Var. *R.* 3.14.5). Here it is simply a colourful term for bad wine: cf. **56**.23 *uel cocta fumis musta Massilitanis.* Laietanian wine, produced near Barcelona, was known for its inferior quality: cf. 1.26.9.

nigra lagona: the jar is blackened with smoke, a description which would normally indicate that it contained a vintage draught, wine being aged in an upper room to which smoke had access; cf. Tib. 2.1.27–8 *nunc mihi fumosos ueteris proferte Falernos | consulis,* M. 1.26.8. M. may be suggesting that Umber has attempted to hide the poor quality of the wine by storing it in an old, recycled jar. Alternatively, Laietanian wine, like Massilian, may have been excessively smoked: cf. **56**.23n.

7   **parua . . . cottana:**   a small species of fig grown in Syria: cf. Plin. *NH* 13.51. They appear among modest Saturnalian gifts at 4.88.6 and Stat. *Silu.* 4.9.28. The epithet *parua* is both an authentic description of this type of fig and reaffirms their worthlessness.

canis . . . prunis: *canus,* used in its transferred sense of 'old' (**22**.2n.), effects a colour contrast with *prunis,* which are dark purple in hue. Elsewhere in M. (5.18.3, 13.29.1 *pruna peregrinae carie rugosa senectae*) prunes are described as 'old' on account of their wrinkled appearance.

8   **et Libycae fici pondere testa grauis:**   another modest gift: cf. 4.46.10 *et ficus Libyca gelata testa.*

Libycae fici 'African figs'; for the singular, see on *fabae* 5.

grauis: the *testa* is so described because the figs were preserved in a dense congealed mass: cf. 4.46.10 cited above, Col. 12.15.5 *cum calore solis emollitae sunt, colligunt, et . . . inter se compositas comprimunt in figuram stellarum flosculorumque, uel in formam panis redigentes: tum rursus in sole assiccant, et ita in uasis recondunt.*

9   **uix . . . triginta nummorum:**   genitive of value, 'worth barely 30 sesterces' (*nummus = nummus sestertius*). A similar obsession with the low monetary value of gifts is seen in 5.19.11, 10.57, 11.105 and Stat. *Silu.* 4.9.

10   **quae grandes octo tulere Syri:**   both the large physique and the number of the slave-porters represent a further attempt on Umber's part to mislead as to the value of the gifts.

octo suggests the *octophoron*, a litter borne by eight slaves and employed as a luxurious means of travel: cf. Cic. *Verr.* 2.5.27 *ut mos fuit Bithyniae regibus, lectica octophoro ferebatur*, 9.2.11–12, Blümner (1911) 447. If M. means us to understand that the gifts are conveyed in an *octophoron*, the mode of transportation belies the cheapness of the gifts carried therein, and also implies that Umber's stinginess is unwarranted if he is wealthy enough to own such a litter.

Syri: Syria was the provenance *par excellence* of slaves: cf. Cic. *Prou. cons.* 10, Liv. 36.17.5 *Syri et Asiatici Graeci . . . uilissima genera hominum et seruituti nata*, H. Solin, *ANRW* II 19.2.772. Syrians were often used as litter-bearers, cf. 9.22.9–10, Juv. 6.351 *quae longorum uehitur ceruice Syrorum*.

11   commodius: a double entendre, 'with less trouble' and 'more advantageously' sc. to me.

12   argenti . . . pondera quinque: silver plate weighing five Roman pounds (1,637 grams): this might come in a number of forms (Strong (1966) 128–55). Silver objects had their weight inscribed on them, so that they could be redeemed at need for cash at the price per lb of silver (cf. Oliver (1977) 13). 5lbs of silver plate would have been a far more generous gift than those listed in 3–8, worth at most 30 sesterces: assuming a rate of between 3 and 3.26 grams of silver to the denarius (see D. R. Walker, *The metrology of the Roman silver coinage*, 1 (Oxford 1976) 120–1), 5lbs would have had a redeemable value of just over 2,000 sesterces.

pondera: (pound) weights; the more usual expression was *pondo* (by weight), e.g. Cic. *Cluent.* 179 *auri quinque pondo* [sc. *libras*] *abstulit*.

puer 'slave', as often, but the word carries a further suggestion of physical immaturity, in contrast to the *grandes . . . Syri* of 10.

25   (= 12.68)

'Client, paying me an early morning call – I left Rome precisely to avoid this – you should seek advocacy from some wealthy patron. I'm not trained in law, but an elderly retired poet, anxious to enjoy the leisure and sleep which I couldn't get in the city. If I can't sleep even here in Bilbilis, I'm going back to Rome.'

The poem, written after M.'s return to Spain, offers a counterbalance to **19**, where the poet's life in retirement is portrayed idealistically, emphasising the opportunity at Bilbilis to lie in late, making up for the years of lost sleep in Rome (13–16). The situation described in **25** would appear to be closer to reality (cf. M.'s complaints about Bilbilis in the preface to book 12, and see further intro. 4–5 for M.'s retirement).

A major nuisance of the patronage system in Rome, often complained of by M. in his persona of impoverished *cliens*, was the necessity of rising before dawn in order to attend the *salutatio* of his patron or patrons (**19**.14n.). In the present epigram we are reminded that the patron, too, is obliged to curtail his sleep to greet his early morning visitors – here, a client in need of legal assistance.

It is relatively unusual for M. to adopt the persona of a *patronus*. The most common context for so doing is the dinner party where M. plays the rôle of the host (cf. 5.44, 5.50, 8.67 and 9.35). In portraying himself here as a harassed *patronus*, M. constructs an eminently plausible scenario. Although the poet's comparatively simple lifestyle in Bilbilis might have relieved him of the need to cultivate wealthy patrons, he must have soon discovered that, as a local person returning to his homeland after a successful career in Rome, he could not escape the attentions of clients hoping for his support. In 1.49 33–6 M. had promised his friend Licinianus, about to retire to Spain, *procul [erit] . . . querulus cliens | . . . non rumpet altum pallidus somnum reus, | sed mane totum dormies.* M. perhaps meant the reader familar with his work to enjoy the irony.

Further reading: Saller (1982)

1   Matutine: often used by M. in association with the *salutatio*, e.g. 1.55.6 *matutinum portat ineptus haue*, 12.29.7. The application to persons who carry out activities early in the day is poetic: cf. Virg. *A.* 8.465 *Aeneas se matutinus agebat.*

cliens: a less than courteous form of address, vividly expressing M.'s view of the morning caller as a pest. The technical term for a 'person who sought his fortune by attendance on another' (White (1978) 79–81), *cliens* was normally avoided in favour of the more polite *amicus* (cf. Saller (1982) 9). In M. the word commonly refers pejoratively to a client from the patron's viewpoint, e.g. 1.49.33 cited intro., 4.88.4 *a querulo . . . cliente*, 7.62.4.

urbis mihi causa relictae 'the reason for my leaving the city'. M. elsewhere gives the impression that he retired from Rome to escape the duties of the client (e.g. 10.74, 10.96, cf. **19**), but the present remark need not be entirely disingenuous: M. had clients of his own in Rome, albeit mentioned only rarely (e.g. 8.42).

2   atria . . . colas: since clients were received in the *atrium* at the morning *salutatio* (cf. Hor. *Ep.* 1.5.31 *atria seruantem . . . clientem*, **19**.4n.), *atria colere* stands for courting a patron: cf. 3.38.11–12 *'atria magna colam'. uix tres aut quattuor ista | res aluit, pallet cetera turba fame.*

atria . . . ambitiosa: i.e. *atria ambitiosorum*. The client would do better to seek out patrons wanting to cut a public figure who would appreciate the attendance which a *cliens* would bestow in return for legal assistance (3n.).

si sapias . . . colas 'you would be wise to pay court to'; cf. Plaut. *Per.* 797 *iurgium hinc auferas, si sapias.*

3   non sum ego causidicus: the reason for the client's visit is to request assistance with a legal case, a regular duty of patrons towards their clients: cf. 2.32, Saller (1982) 29, 130. Such requests were often made at the *salutatio*, cf. Stat. *Silu.* 4.4.41–2 *nec iam tibi turba reorum | uestibulo querulique rogant exire clientes.* M. tries to deter his client by protesting that he is not a professional lawyer.

sum: elided, as at 11.104.2 *non sum ego nec Curius nec Numa nec Tatius*; cf. 10.9.5, 13.76.1, L. Müller, *De re metrica* (2nd edn, Petropoli et Lipsiae 1894) 339–40.

causidicus: a professional advocate who, unlike a patron, charged a fee: cf. Quint. *Inst.* 12.7.8–12. The word has contemptuous associations (Cic. *De orat.* 1.202, Juv. 7.106 with Courtney, Quint. *Inst.* 12.1.25 with Austin) which well convey M.'s distaste for getting involved in legal matters. See further Howell 1.17 intro.

amaris litibus: the pejorative tone further reveals M.'s attitude to law suits, made distasteful by the attendant acrimony: cf. Virg. *G.* 2.501–2, 5.20.5–7 *nec nos atria nec domos potentum | nec lites tetricas . . . nossemus.*

4   sed piger et senior Pieridumque comes: three reasons why M. would make an unsuitable advocate. He is not given to energetic pursuits, he is getting on in years and he is a poet by profession.

piger: 19.10n.

senior: as often, equivalent to *senex*; cf. 7.88.3 *me legit omnis ibi senior iuuenisque puerque.* At the time of writing M. was around 60.

Pieridum comes 'a devotee of the Muses' (cf. Stat. *Theb.* 8.549 *comes Musis*), a high-flown expression for the avocation of poet. The pompous tone is suitable for a patron dismissing an annoying client.

Pieridum: see **16**.4n.

5   otia: the leisure enjoyed in the country, where one was free from the obligations of the client; cf. 1.55.3–6, 4.25.8, 6.43.3. Such *otium* was especially sought after by poets: see Kier (1933) 63–7, J.-M. André, *L'otium dans la vie morale et intellectuelle romaine* (Paris 1966).

somnus: cf. **19**.13n., where, as here, the luxury of sleeping past the early hours symbolises release from the burdens of the patronage system.

6   redeo, si uigilatur et hic 'if sleep is impossible even here, I'm going back [to Rome]'.

redeo: a colloquial use of the present for the future, particularly frequent with *eo* and its compounds; see C. E. Bennett, *Syntax of early Latin* I (Boston 1910) 18–19.

hic: one of only three pentameters in M. which end in an accented monosyllable, the unusual metre throwing strong emphasis on the word (G. A. Wilkinson, *CQ* 42 (1948) 71).

26   (= 5.24)

'Hermes, delight of your age, skilled in all the gladiators' weapons, at once combatant and trainer, feared by and conqueror of your most notable rivals, expert at defeating your opponent without killing him, your own substitute, enricher of the seat-contractors, darling of the gladiators' women, fearsome with spear, trident, or crested helmet, excelling in every kind of combat, Hermes, all things at once and greatest of all.'

This epigram, eulogising a gladiator, Hermes, takes the form of a mock hymn which praises its addressee in hyperbolic terms, in some cases so extreme as to belong to the realm of fantasy (cf. 2n.). As hymnal parodies typically do, the poem contains many features of genuine hymns: the anaphora of the god's name (cf. *Anth. Lat.* 389.38–60, an invocation to Sol), the list of his characteristic attributes and accomplishments (ἀρεταί), the use of relative clauses to celebrate his virtues (5–6), the insistence on his uniqueness (ibid.), and the problematical *omnia solus et ter unus* in the final verse. Mock hymns are often for persons of humble status, e.g. Ovid's address to the slave doorkeeper in *Am.* 1.6. The present piece is a case in point: most gladiators were of servile origin.

The hyperbolic character of the praise lavished on Hermes has led to the conclusion that he is a fiction (Versnel (1974) 403), in which case the gladiator's name was chosen to facilitate the hymnal parody. It is, however, possible that M. had in mind a real gladiator, whose theophoric name suggested the idea of casting the poem in the form of a hymn to a god. Inscriptions confirm that the name Hermes was often adopted by gladiators, but there is no independent evidence for the existence in M.'s day of a famous one of this name.

Although Hermes' prowess is clearly exaggerated, and the majority of gladiators did not survive past the fourth year, it was possible for an outstanding one to enjoy both fame and the reasonably long career which M.'s celebration of Hermes imputes to him. There are funeral inscriptions for comparatively long-lived gladiators, e.g. *ILS* 5098 for one who died at 35 after 20 victories. Cf. Köhne and Ewigleben (2000) 69–70.

Further reading: Köhne and Ewigleben (2000), Robert (1940), Versnel (1974), Ville (1981)

1   Hermes: gladiators usually took a 'stage' name (Ville 1981) 308–10); Hermes was a popular choice. The name might have been thought a good omen. Hermes/Mercury conducted the souls of the dead to Hades; in the same way, a gladiator named Hermes might despatch dead men to Hades.

Martia saeculi uoluptas 'delight of the age in matters to do with Mars' i.e. as a gladiator. As god of war, Mars was honoured by gladiators whose armour and weapons resembled those of soldiers: cf. Kyle (1998) 80–1.

saeculi uoluptas echoes parodically the opening of Lucretius' hymn to Venus, *Aeneadum genetrix, hominum diuumque uoluptas*.

2   omnibus eruditus armis: an expert in all the various weapons and armour used by gladiators: in M.'s day there were 13 classes of gladiator, distinguished largely by their equipment (Köhne and Ewigleben (2000) 45–64). The statement is hyperbolic: gladiators normally specialised in one type of combat, or at most two (Ville (1981) 307–8). On the level of hymnal parody, the phrase suggests the omnipotence of gods (Versnel (1974) 379).

3   et gladiator et magister: trainers (*magistri*) were often former gladiators, but the two occupations were not usually pursued simultaneously. It was, however, common in hymns to ascribe to a god two qualities which normally exclude each other (Versnel (1974) 380 n.66).

4   turba sui tremorque ludi: he fills the other members of his school with confusion and dread. Members of the same school fought against each other: cf. Quint. *Inst.* 2.17.33. Cf. the Libyan gladiator 'whom all who were matched with him in the stadium feared' (Robert (1940) 303 no.106). Alliteration is a feature of the hymn-style.

5–6   unum | . . . uni: μόνος, *solus*, and *unus* are used in hymns to indicate the sphere in which a god has no rival (L. Watson, *Mnemosyne* 35 (1982) 96): even the finest gladiators are no match for Hermes. Invincibility is a theme both of aretalogies and gladiatorial epitaphs: for the latter, cf. Robert (1940) no. 30 'no one gained a victory over me'.

5   Helius is a gladiator's name (Robert (1940) 298 n.5). Helius, like Aduolans (6), is presumably a star of the day. There may be a touch of parody here: Helius, who in religion is the highest of the gods (e.g. *Corpus Hermeticum* 5.3 'the Sun is the mightiest of the gods in heaven, to whom all the heavenly gods submit') nonetheless yields to Hermes.

6   cadit 'falls to the ground' (in defeat, not necessarily in death: cf. 7).
   Aduolans: gladiators frequently bore names suggestive of physical or moral qualities e.g. Celer, Pugnax, Ferox: cf. Ville (1981) 309.

7   uincere nec ferire doctus: *ferire* = 'strike dead': cf. Luc. 5.363–4 *tiro rudis, specta poenas et disce ferire, | disce mori.* Hermes has the skill to win fights without killing his opponent outright. A victory was gained not only by striking a fatal blow but also by forcing one's opponent to admit defeat by dropping his shield and raising a finger of the left hand: the presiding magistrate then consulted the spectators as to whether the vanquished gladiator should be spared or killed. This procedure explains why the ability to defeat without killing was valued: it endeared the victor to the spectators by affording them the opportunity to influence the outcome of the contest.

8   suppositicius sibi ipse 'himself his own substitute'. *suppositicii*, substitutes (cf. *CIL* IV 1179), were reserve fighters who took the place of a fallen gladiator in cases where the victor was called on to fight a second bout. The phrase apparently means that, because Hermes invariably wins, he has no need of a substitute. The illogical notion of acting as substitute for oneself may parody the idea of a god taking his own place, which is not unusual in various theologies (Versnel (1974) 403–5).

9   diuitiae locariorum 'source of wealth to the seat-contractors'. *locarius*, found only here and possibly *CIL* XIII 8183, must refer to entrepreneurs who bought seats in bulk and resold them at a profit. Names of prominent fighters who were scheduled to appear were advertised in advance. A star like Hermes would guarantee good ticket sales, bringing prosperity to the seat contractors.

10   cura laborque ludiarum 'darling and heart-throb of the gladiators' women'. Gladiators were notorious for their sexual attractiveness, not only to *ludiae* (see n. below) but to women in general: cf. Petr. 126.6, *CIL* IV 4342 *suspirium puellarum* | *Tr.* | *Celadus*, 4356 *Tr.* | *Celadus, reti.* | *Crescens* | *puparru domnus*. According to Juv. 6.82–113 a senator's wife, Eppia, was so enamoured of a gladiator as to elope with him.

cura laborque: best taken in an erotic sense (previous n.). *cura* = 'an object of love': cf. Ov. *Am.* 1.3.16 *tu mihi, si qua fides, cura perennis eris*; *labores* is used of the pangs of love (Hor. *Carm.* 1.17.19–20 with N–H, [Tib.] 3.6.7: *ite procul durum curae genus, labores*). Some explain that Hermes is 'a source of worry and trouble to the gladiators' women' because his gladiatorial skill threatens the lives of their partners. But while *labor* can mean 'a cause of distress' (cf. Sil. 3.75), *cura* + genitive invariably refers to someone who is the object of another's care or concern.

ludiarum: not, as often supposed, 'women attracted to gladiators', but women attached to the gladiatorial schools who provided for the gladiators' sexual needs: cf. L. and P. Watson (1996) 588–91.

11   belligera ... hasta: two types of gladiator carried a lance: the *hoplomachus* (**61**.1 n.) and the *eques. superbus* may suggest that M. has in mind the latter: the *equites*, who fought against each other, were the first pairs to compete: their entrance on white horses like Roman cavalrymen, wielding a lance and carrying the equestrian shield, must have been imposing. Cf. Köhne and Ewigleben (2000) 37, 48.

12   aequoreo ... tridente: i.e. with fisherman's trident. The *retiarius*, armed like a fisherman with trident, net and dagger, was matched with the *secutor*, whose smooth rounded helmet with its small eye-holes and fin-like crest resembled a fish. Cf. Köhne and Ewigleben (2000) 61.

13   casside languida timendus: probably refers to the imposing helmet with central crest to which was attached a plume of horse-hair or feathers, worn by the *murmillo*, *Thraex*, and *hoplomachus* (cf. Köhne and Ewigleben (2000) 37–8, 45, 49, figs. 21, 49). The crest curved forward, so that both helmet and plume had a drooping appearance. M. may have in mind a Homeric formula: cf. Hom. *Il.* 6.468–70 '(Astyanax) distraught at the sight of his dear father, afraid of the bronze and the horse-hair plume, when he saw it nodding terribly from the top of his helmet', D. Page, *Sappho and Alcaeus* (Oxford 1955) 210–13, Virg. *A.* 8.620 *terribilem cristis galeam.*

14   gloria Martis uniuersi: having focused on Hermes' prowess in three types of bout, the poet now reiterates his claim that Hermes is *omnibus eruditus armis.* As in 1, Mars refers to gladiatorial combat.

15   omnia solus 'alone all things'. The phrase, which reflects the *solus–omnia* polarity in ancient religion (cf. *CIL* x 3800 *te tibi una quae es omnia dea Isis*, Versnel (1974) *passim*) refers parodically to Hermes' total mastery of the gladiatorial art.

   ter unus 'thrice (i.e. very) unique'. A difficult expression, which works best as a parody of *Trismegistos* 'thrice (very) greatest', under which title Hermes was worshipped when synthesised with the Egyptian Thoth. Hermes Trismegistos was omniscient and a teacher of all things (G. Fowden, *The Egyptian Hermes* (Cambridge 1986) 32): this fits well with the nonpareil Hermes of the epigram. On chronological grounds, an allusion to the Christian Trinity is excluded. An attempt to see a reference to Hermes as embodying three things in his one person (e.g. the three types of combat mentioned in 11–13) would be intolerably bathetic after *gloria Martis uniuersi* and *omnia solus.*

27   (= 8.53)

'A roaring as loud as when countless lions give voice in the wilds of Africa was recently heard in the Roman amphitheatre. The sound came from a single lion – but it was a prince among the breed. How imposing his shape and how noble his death! How did Africa come to rear such a magnificent specimen? Was it one of the lions that draw Cybele's chariot? Or was it the Nemean lion sent down from heaven?'

The epigram centres on the death of a particularly imposing lion in a wild beast show (*uenatio*) given by Domitian in 93 as part of the celebrations marking his successful conclusion of the Pannonian campaign (cf. 8.26, 30, Jennison (1937) 75–9). Such shows, in which large numbers of exotic animals appeared, had long been mounted by Roman leaders as a means of self-aggrandisement and of winning favour with the public. M. often employs epigrams on *uenationes* to eulogise the presiding emperor, notably in the *De spectaculis*, on the games staged by Titus for the opening of the Colosseum in AD 80. Other examples include the 'lion and hare' cycle in book 1 and 5.65, probably on the *ludi* which formed part of Domitian's double triumph in 89.

Lions featured in *uenationes* from the early second century BC (Jennison (1937) 60–75); here, however, M.'s decision to focus on a lion rather than some other exotic beast has especial significance. The lion had markedly regal associations (E. R. Goodenough, *Jewish symbols in the Greco-Roman period* (New York 1958) VII 37–52) and, in the wild, lion hunts were the preserve of kings and emperors (D–S V 688–9 s.v. *uenatio*, Wiedemann (1992) 62–3). By drawing attention to these associations (7–8nn.), M. forges a parallel between the lion as king of the beasts and Domitian as ruler of mankind.

The lion is exploited in other ways to flatter the emperor. By postulating the identification of the amphitheatric lion with the Nemean lion slain by Hercules (15–16), M. draws a comparison between Hercules and Domitian, who, as presenter of the games, can be viewed as a modern-day incarnation of the hero: cf. 5.65. Moreover, the catasterisation of the Nemean lion as the constellation Leo provides an opportunity to remind us of Domitian's deified family and his *pietas* towards them (16n.).

In contrast to Statius' poem on the accidental death of a tame lion in the ampitheatre (*Silu.* 2.5), M.'s epigram is singularly devoid of sympathy for the lion. This difference illustrates the ambivalence of the Romans' attitude to wild animals. While they could value them as pets, or because they were tame, the slaughter of animals in an amphitheatric *uenatio* was, as in the epigram, viewed differently: the *uenatio* was a combat of man against beast and the killing of the beast represented the triumph of man over the violence of nature. Furthermore, the exotic character of a beast such as a lion both symbolised the extent of Rome's empire and reflected glory on the imperial giver of the show. But glory is enhanced if one's opponent is especially worthy or formidable; hence M.'s emphasis on the outstanding ferocity, beauty and bravery of the lion.

Further reading: Köhne and Ewigleben (2000) 70–4, Toynbee (1973) 17–21, 61–3, Wiedemann (1992) 55–67, Zaganiaris (1977)

1–4   The comparison with lions, which invokes a common epic device (cf. 2–3nn., Hom. *Il.* 11.548–55, 12.299–306), gives the opening of the epigram an elevated flavour.

1   **Massyla per auia:** *Massylus*, properly 'of the Massyli', an African tribe, stands for 'African'; in poetry the name of a people or place is used to identify a whole country. Africa was the main source of lions for the Roman arena (Toynbee (1973) 61), including the present specimen (13).

    murmur: the 'roaring' of a lion or tiger; cf. Luc. 1.209–10 *erexitque iubam et uasto graue murmur hiatu | infremuit.*

2   **innumero quotiens silua leone furit:** cf. Sen. *Phaed.* 348–50 *Poeni quatiunt colla leones | cum mouit Amor. | tum silua gemit murmure saeuo.* The collective singular is often used with reference to animals: cf. E. Löfstedt, *Syntactica* (Lund 1942) 1 13–14.

    silua: wooded, though not necessarily densely forested land grazed by animals (3–4): cf. Gaius, *Dig.* 50.16.30.5 *pascua silua est, quae pastui pecudum destinata est.* The detail of domesticated animals threatened by a lion as they pasture in woodland may derive from the lion simile of Hom. *Il.* 5.161–2.

    silua . . . furit 'the wood roars with': the *furor* of the lions is transferred to the *silua* as in Virg. *G.* 3.150 *furit mugitibus aether.* For *furo* of loud sounds cf. 9.68.7 *mitior in magno clamor furit amphitheatro*, Stat. *Theb.* 6.625–6.

3   **pallidus:** the herdsman shares his charges' fear. M. probably had in mind the simile of Hom. *Il.* 17.61–7 where 'pallid fear seizes' herdsmen in the face of a lion's attack.

    mapalia: a Punic word, explained as *casae Poenicae* by Fest. 133 L., perhaps a sort of 'mobile farmyard' erected by the nomadic North African *pastores.* Cf. Pease on Virg. *A.* 4.259.

4   **reuocat:** from the *silua* to the relative safety of the *mapalia.*

    sine mente pecus: *sine mente* corresponds to *attonitos*: the sheep (*pecus*) are 'out of their minds' with fear: cf. Ov. *Ars* 1.121–2 *nam timor unus erat, facies non una timoris: | pars laniat crines, pars sine mente sedet.*

5   Ausonia: by pointed contrast with the animal's North African homeland (13).

terror: by metonymy = a person or thing which causes terror; cf. 9.71.7 *terror Nemees.* φόβος is similarly used.

6   quis . . . non crederet 'who would not have believed?', imperfect subjunctive with past potential force (Woodcock §121).

gregem: used more frequently of domesticated than of wild animals. The allusion to a pride of lions is unparalleled.

7   cuius tremerent ipsi quoque iura leones 'before whose authority the lions themselves would tremble'; cf. Hor. *Carm.* 3.21.19–20 *neque iratos trementi | regum apices neque militum arma.*

tremerent: generic/consecutive subjunctive (Woodcock §156).

ipsi: even his fellow lions would yield to his sway, not to mention lesser animals, whose king the lion was accounted: cf. Opp. *Cyn.* 4.144 θῆρες ἄνακτες 'lordly beasts', Zaganiaris (1977).

iura: the word, not used elsewhere of animals, suggests a parallel between the lion as ruler of all creatures, and Domitian as emperor of all mankind. The connexion is fostered by the fact that lions were an emblem of royalty: see intro.

8   cui diadema daret . . . Nomas: even Numidia, famous for the ferocity of its lions (Ov. *Ars* 2.183), would have awarded this particular specimen the crown. *diadema* continues the regal metaphor; the *diadema* was a headband worn by Persian kings and came to symbolise royalty: see N–H on Hor. *Carm.* 2.2.21.

marmore picta: lit. 'variegated with marble', i.e. 'with its variously coloured marble', referring to the yellow marble with red veins known as 'Numidian' (**30.**12n.). There may be an implied compliment to Domitian, who employed it for the columns of the great peristyle of his *Domus Augustana* – the first large-scale public use of this marble since the time of Augustus. See J. Ward Perkins, *JRS* 41 (1951) 96.

Nomas used as a feminine noun = Numidia (cf. 9.75.8).

9–10   'O what adornment, what dignity did the golden shade of his curving mane, when it stood erect, spread upon his neck'.

9   decus alludes to the lion's mane – a development of the noun's use with reference to human hair; cf. Sen. *Dial.* 10.12.3. In view of the regal metaphor at 7–8 it is pertinent that *decus* is often applied to a diadem: cf. Quint. Curt. 5.8.13 *nec di siuerint ut hoc decus mei capitis . . . demere mihi* [*Dario*] *quisquam audeat.*

honorem: synonymous with *decus* (*OLD* s.v. 6b). Cf. Stat. *Theb.* 8.572–4 *leo Caspius . . .* | *. . . nullo . . . iubae flauentis honore* | *terribilis.*

10   aurea: cf. Agatharch. *Mar. rubr.* 69 '[the lions'] manes gleaming in such a way that from their necks shines a tawny hue akin to gold', Stat. *Theb.* previous n.

lunatae: a lion's mane, when the beast is viewed from the front, describes a crescent-like curve: see Toynbee (1973) pl. 18.

cum stetit: lions' manes are a sign of vigour, 'erect' when the animal is aroused (e.g. Virg. *A.* 10.724–6 *si forte . . .* | *conspexit* [sc. *leo*] *capream . . .* | *gaudet . . . comasque arrexit*).

umbra, properly what casts a shade upon or covers, extends, uniquely, to a lion's mane the noun's use with reference to hair; cf. Petr. 109.9.3 *nunc umbra nudata sua iam tempora maerent.*

11   grandia quam decuit latum uenabula pectus: the lion's imposingly broad breast seemed made for the hunting spears, with their wide blade (Virg. *A.* 4.131).

uenabula: by the middle of the first century AD, the standard weapon of wild beast fighters (*uenatores*) in the arena.

12   quantaque de magna gaudia morte tulit 'how much joy he derived from his great death'. The lion is supposed to have experienced satisfaction at its glorious death, so to speak, at the hands of Domitian, a quasi-Hercules (15 n.).

13   unde tuis, Libye, tam felix gloria siluis? 'whence, Libya, [came] such felicitous glory for your woodlands?' *unde*, often with ellipse of the verb, carries an implication of surprise at something beyond the bounds of normal experience: cf. Virg. *A.* 9.19–20 *unde haec tam clara repente* | *tempestas?*

Libye: Greek 1st decl. vocative of Libya, here = Africa.

felix gloria: cf. *Spect.* 18.2 *tigris, ab Hyrcano gloria rara iugo.*

14–16 answer the question posed in 13 by hypothesising two miraculous origins for the lion: did it come from Cybele's team? Or was it in fact the Nemean lion returned to earth?

14   a Cybeles ... iugo: the goddess Cybele rode in a chariot drawn by a team *(iugum)* of lions; cf. Lucr. 2.600–1 *hanc* [sc. *Cybelen*] *ueteres Graium docti cecinere poetae | sedibus in curru biiugos agitare leones.*

15   an magis 'or rather', implying that the second alternative is preferable.

Herculeo ... ab astro: the constellation Leo, commonly identified in Latin poetry with the Nemean lion slain by Hercules. M. hints that Domitian, by staging the death of a beast which could be confused with the Nemean lion, has matched the achievements of Hercules; cf. 5.65.15–16. This identification of Domitian with Hercules was later made explicit by the emperor himself, when he dedicated to the hero a temple containing a statue bearing his own features (cf. 9.64.1–2).

Germanice: Domitian, who adopted this title after his triumph over the Chatti in AD 83, is often so addressed by M., especially in the eighth book where his military successes are to the fore.

16   uel frater uel pater ipse: Domitian's two predecessors, his brother Titus and his father Vespasian. Speculation that they may have sent down the Nemean lion from heaven reminds the reader that Domitian had deified and enshrined them in the *templum Vespasiani et Titi.* Domitian is thus implicitly complimented for his *pietas,* as well as gaining reflected glory from his divine lineage; cf. Darwall-Smith (1996) 178.

ipse 'in person' *(OLD* s.v. 4) suggests the close interest which the deified Vespasian takes in his son's doings.

28   (= 10.50)

'Let Victory, Popular Favour, Honour and Glory adopt the gestures of mourning. Scorpus, you are dead, and have prematurely yoked your team in Hades. Why was the end of your life as close as the goal in the circus always was for you?'

A lament for the death of the famous charioteer Flavius Scorpus, whose passing is also recorded three poems later in the epitaphic 10.53. The epigram contains many features of the poetic epikedion (cf. below), but cannot properly be classed as such, since one of the main elements, consolation, is missing.

Whereas M. on other occasions voices resentment at the large sums of money showered on Scorpus and his kind (cf. on **22**), he here expresses, if not his own, at least the sentiments of the Roman people as a whole on the death of a popular hero. Charioteers were subject to widespread adulation: by way of illustration Cameron (1973) 244–52 cites Plin. *NH* 7.186 about one supporter of the Reds who threw himself on the funeral pyre of his favourite charioteer.

Unlike the possibly fictitious gladiator Hermes (**26**), Scorpus' existence is confirmed by inscriptional evidence. *CIL* vi 10048.19 records that he won 2,048 victories (cf. 10.53.4 *dum numerat palmas, credidit esse senem*); he is also depicted driving a chariot on the tomb of T. Flavius Abascantus (*CIL* vi 8628). He rode for the Green faction (*CIL* vi 10048.19; cf. 10.48.23), which would explain his popularity: the Greens were supported by the common people, the Blues by the aristocracy. Scorpus was honoured with at least one equestrian bronze statue (**22**.6n.), and in addition received large sums as prize money (cf. intro. to **22**). Since he is mentioned as alive at 11.1.15–16, his death must have occurred between December 96 (the publication date of book 11) and 98, when the second edition of book 10 was published. Although he had not yet reached his 27th birthday (10.53.3), there is no compelling evidence to show that he did not die of natural causes. Kay on 11.1.16 implies that Scorpus was the victim of a racing accident, and such incidents must certainly have been common, given that 'part of the tactics of driving was deliberately to foul an opponent' (Harris (1972) 205–7). Had Scorpus met such an end, however, it seems unlikely that M. would have failed to mention the fact: compare *CIL* vi 10049, a tombstone for two brothers which specifies that they were killed while racing.

Further reading: Cameron (1973), Estève-Forriol (1962), Harris (1972), Lattimore (1942), Syme (1977)

1–4   In the epikedion, appropriate persons or deities are typically invited to join in lamentation for the deceased (Estève-Forriol (1962) 126). Cf. Catull. 3.1, on Lesbia's *passer, lugete o Veneres Cupidinesque*, Stat. *Silu.* 5.3.89–90, where the mourners for Statius' father (a poet and orator), include *Pietas*, *Iustitia* and *Facundia*. The deities invoked may be either official objects of cult (e.g. *Venus, Pietas*) or personifications (e.g. *Facundia*): *Victoria* and *Honos* fall into the former category, *Fauor* and *Gloria* into the latter.

1   **Frangat ... palmas:**   as a sign of mourning, Victory is to break the symbol (*palmas* n.) with which she is associated. Cf. Ov. *Am.* 3.9.7–8, on the death of Tibullus, *ecce puer Veneris fert euersamque pharetram | et fractos arcus et sine luce facem.*

Idumaeas ... palmas: cf. Virg. *G.* 3.12 *primus Idumaeas referam tibi, Mantua, palmas.* Since palm trees grew in southern Italy (Hehn (1976) 204–11), such victory-palms could have been procured locally, but called by the poets 'Idumaean' because Idumaea (used loosely in poetry for Judaea or Palestine) was famous for them (Luc. 3.216, Plin. *NH* 13.26 *Iudaea ... incluta est uel magis palmis*).

Victoria: worshipped as a deity since the early third century BC (Latte, *RR* 235), and often depicted on statues, coins and reliefs holding a crown in her right hand (cf. *AP* 15.46–7, Cameron (1973) 17). The personi-fied Victory was prominent in the Circus, where her figure led the introduc-tory procession of deities (cf. Ov. *Am.* 3.2.44–5, *RE* II 8.2528 s.v. 'Victoria').

palmas: originally the winners of Circus races were presented with palms and crowns, in imitation of the Greek games (Liv. 10.47.3). In later times considerable sums of money were added, but the palm remained the symbol of victory *par excellence*: cf. Ov. *Am.* 3.2.82 *ille* [sc. *auriga*] *tenet palmam.* In circus inscriptions *palma* stands for 'a victory' e.g. *CIL* VI 10049; cf. Cameron (1973) 17.

2   plange ... pectora nuda: beating the breast – often bared as here – was a standard gesture of mourning: cf. Prop. 2.24.51–2, *CLE* 398.7 *maeret et ad cineres plangit sua pectora palmis*, Toynbee (1971) 45. The so-called 'poetic plural' is particularly common with parts of the body: see E. Löfstedt, *Syntactica* I (Lund 1942) 29, 47–50.

Fauor: Popular Support: cf. Ov. *Tr.* 2.506, Tac. *Dial.* 29.3 *peculiaria huius urbis uitia ... histrionalis fauor et gladiatorum equorumque studia. faueo* is a technical expression for 'being a fan of' a rider: cf. Ov. *Am.* 3.2.2, Plin. *NH* 7.186 *Felice russei auriga elato, in rogum eius unum e fauentibus iecisse se.*

saeua ... manu: the violence with which *Fauor* is to beat his breast characterises the depth of popular grief at Scorpus' passing.

3   mutet ... cultus: put on the dark garments of mourning; cf. Prop. 4.7.28, Ov. *Met.* 11.669, Tac. *Ann.* 3.2, Blümner (1911) 497.

Honor: for the word in a similar context, cf. Ov. *Pont.* 2.11.21 *ad palmae per se cursurus honores* [*equus*]. There was a cult of *Honos* (Latte, *RR* 235–7), though he is mainly associated with Virtus rather than the circus.

iniquis ... flammis: *iniquus* is frequently used, especially in *CLE*, of death, but its application to the *flammae* of the funerary pyre is apparently unique; closest is Stat. *Theb.* 4.673–4 *usque adeone parum cineri data mater iniquo | natalesque rogi?*

munera: the offering of a lock of hair to the deceased is attested first in Hom. *Il.* 23.141. It is questionable whether the practice is authentically Roman. A number of the allusions in Latin texts can be explained by their Greek setting or by their epic milieu which may reflect Homeric usage: cf. Petr. 111.9; Ov. *Fast.* 3.562–3 with Bömer, Ov. *Ep.* 11.116 with Knox. Prop. 1.17.19–21, however, seems to suggest that the custom *was* practised at Roman funerals.

4   coronatas: *Gloria,* which attends victory, wears on her head the emblem by which the latter was symbolised: for a crown given to victors, cf. *AP* 16.336, 340, [Ov.] *Hal.* 68 *seu septem spatiis Circo [equi] meruere coronam,* n. on *palmas* above.

Gloria: for the term in a racing context, cf. Virg. *G.* 3.102 *quae gloria palmae.*

5   heu facinus!: *heu,* an exclamation mainly confined to poetry, is particularly common in epikedeia and verse epitaphs. The 'crime' is that of the divine powers responsible for prematurely taking away a life: cf. 11.91.3, *CLE* 1225.3 *heu scelus, heu crudele nefas facinusque tremendum.* Such indignant protestations often occur in cases of *mors immatura:* cf. Lattimore (1942) 183–4, Kay on 11.91.3.

prima . . . iuuenta goes with both *fraudatus* and *occidis*; cf. *CLE* 1232.1 *hic puer octauo fraudatus clauditur anno.* The expression *prima iuuenta,* 'in early youth' is common in verse epitaphs, e.g. *CLE* 1260.1 *hic situs Amphion ereptus prima iuuenta.*

6   et nigros tam cito iungis equos: in the Underworld, Scorpus now drives black horses, an appropriate colour for an infernal *auriga:* cf. Ov. *Met.* 5.360 (Pluto's team). It was thought that the deceased person continued in the world below the activities which (s)he had pursued in life: see **83**.7n. The colour of Scorpus' horses is unknown, but while black horses were often employed in the Circus (e.g. *CIL* vi 10047, 10056), the point of line 6 – that the horses which Scorpus now drives are black – would be much diminished if that had also been the hue of his teams in life. There is also a nice irony in a frequently victorious charioteer driving black steeds, white horses being associated with victory (Sauvage (1975) 17–18).

nigros: by the first century AD *niger* had supplanted *ater* as the term for 'black' in funereal contexts: cf. André (1949) 56–9, 362–3.

tam cito: *cito* is common in verse epitaphs lamenting a premature death; e.g. *CLE* 1823.12, *CIL* ix 292.7–9 *iniqua | fata quae nos tam | cito disiunxerunt.*

7–8 'Why was that goal, always speedily gained by your chariot and in a brief compass, so near at hand for your life as well?'

7   curribus ... properata: *curribus* is dative of agent after *properata*. The transitive use of the verb is unusual; the normal construction is *ad metam properare*: cf. Ov. *Ars* 2.727. There is a pun on *properare* with reference to early death (cf. Ov. *Met.* 10.31 *Eurydices ... properata retexite fata, CLE* 1402.8 *quem mihi tam subito mors properata tulit*).

breuis: the turning point is described as 'short' because an expert charioteer reached it as quickly and directly as possible by seizing the inside position ahead of his rivals. The unique application of *breuis* to *meta* stems from a play on the adjective in its common meaning of a 'short' life: cf. Hor. *Carm.* 4.13.22–3 *sed Cinarae breues | annos fata dederunt, CIL* xi 3194.

8   meta: the turning posts (*metae*), at either end of the race-track, consisted of three tall cones crowned with egg-like objects set on a high platform: cf. Humphrey (1986) 255–7. The metaphor of the 'goal', i.e. end of life, is common: cf. Ov. *Tr.* 1.9.1 *uitae ... tangere metam*, Apul. *Met.* 4.20, *CLE* 740.5 *uitae metas.*

29   (= 3.87)

'Chione, it is rumoured that you have never been fucked and that nothing is purer than your cunt. Yet when you bathe, you don't cover up the right part: it is your face which should be modestly concealed.'

This is an attack on a prostitute with the ironic sobriquet Chione ('Snow White') who, though reputedly chaste, is in fact a *fellatrix*. M. treats the identical theme in 4.84: *non est in populo nec urbe tota | a se Thaida qui probet fututam, | cum multi cupiant rogentque multi. | tam casta est, rogo, Thais? immo fellat.* As often in M., the reader is initially drawn into an assumption (Chione's chastity) which will prove spurious. But, characteristically, there are also multiple hints that things are not as they seem. *rumor* (1) is keyed in M. to the idea of sexual perversion, and the presence of two primary obscenities suggests an attack on Chione, since M. reserves this class of language for invective. Furthermore, Chione in 3.34 (**75**) bore a name that was laughably inappropriate: the reader is led to suspect a comparable piece of inappropriateness here. Finally, the name Chione had been applied to a *fellatrix* only shortly before, at 3.83. In view of these considerations, the final revelation of Chione's sexual impurity is no great surprise. What is more striking is the vivid image employed to convey that information.

To reveal Chione's sexual proclivities, M. wittily suggests that when bathing she should wear her *subligar* on her face, thus modestly covering that part which is put to sexual use, her mouth. The *subligar* is casually mentioned as an item which she might be assumed to have on in the baths. Other evidence, however, suggests that Chione's wearing of a bathing costume – particularly given her profession – was anything but normal. By M.'s time mixed bathing had become common, and women who engaged in it – who would certainly have included *meretrices* like Chione – probably did so unclothed: cf. 3.51.2–3 *dicere, Galla, soles 'nuda placebo magis',* | *et semper uitas communia balnea nobis,* 3.72.4 *sulcos uteri prodere nuda times.*

If Chione's wearing of a bathing costume is anomalous, a further touch of humour is added: the amusing image of a prostitute who frequents the baths clad ostentatiously in a bikini. Such an unusual show of modesty might also explain how the rumour has arisen that Chione is a virgin. Presumably we are to imagine that Chione's behaviour is an attempt to conceal her true depravity.

Further reading: Fagan (1999) 24–9, Ward (1992)

1   rumor: often hints at perverse sexual practices, esp. oral sex, e.g. 3.80.2 *rumor ait linguae te tamen esse malae,* 3.73.5.

   Chione is used several times in M. for a prostitute. Roman prostitutes typically have Greek names: cf. M.'s Phyllis, Leda, etc., J. Griffin, *JRS* 66 (1976) 96–7.

   fututam: for this basic obscenity, cf. Adams, *LSV* 118–22.

2   cunno: the tone of this word varies (Adams, *LSV* 80–1). M., however, normally employs it abusively, especially in attacks on women e.g. 1.90.77 *inter se geminos audes committere cunnos,* 3.93.13.

   purius: here refers to virginity, but in M. normally means 'uncontaminated by oral sex' (cf. **47**.5n.). Its use here thus prepares for the revelation that Chione is a *fellatrix*.

4   si pudor est: generally used to reinforce an appeal to someone's sense of decency, e.g. Ov. *Am.* 3.2.23–4 *tu ... qui spectas post nos, tua contrahe*

crura, | *si pudor est.* Here it has a pointed sexual reference, implying a sense
of shame about sexual activity (cf. 1.34.7–8 *a Chione saltem uel ab Iade disce*
pudorem: | *abscondunt spurcas et monumenta lupas*) or associated bodily parts: cf.
Ov. *Ars* 2.618 *pars . . . sub iniecta ueste pudenda latet.*

subligar: a loincloth worn by workmen (Plin. *NH* 12.59) or actors
(Juv. 6.70); here it must refer to the bottom half of a two-piece bathing costume, like that worn by the famous 'bikini girls' from the Piazza Armerina,
though it is unclear whether these are bathers, athletes or stage perform-
ers (cf. N. Goldman in Sebesta and Bonfante (1994) 233, Yegül (1992) 34,
Nielsen (1990) 141).

faciem: the mouth was thought to be made impure by practising
oral sex (cf. **46**).

30   (= 6.42)

'Oppianus, if you don't experience the baths of Claudius Etruscus, you will
die unbathed. His baths outdo the most famous spas, are especially well
illuminated by natural light, and are notable for the beauty of the marble
used in their construction, and the purity of the water. You are not listening
and show signs of boredom. You will die unbathed, Oppianus.'

This epigram and another eulogy of Etruscus' baths by Statius (*Silu.* 1.5) are
the earliest examples of the bath encomium, which had become a standard
rhetorical theme by the second century AD: cf. Lucian's *Hippias* or *The*
Bath, Anth. Lat. 108–13, 201–5, 264–5, 345, 362, 372 SB, *AP* 9.606–40.
Such pieces typically praise the physical beauty of the baths, including the
quality of the light and the water, and the colourful marbles which were a
prominent feature. Cf. A. Hardie, *Statius and the Silvae* (Liverpool 1983) 132,
K. M. Dunbabin, *PBSR* 57 (1989) 6–46, Busch (1999).

It is unclear whether the baths of Etruscus were in his townhouse in
Rome or whether they were one of the many establishments under private
ownership open to the public. In favour of the former is the fact that Statius
apparently attended the baths at Etruscus' personal invitation (cf. White
(1974) 43). Similarly, whether or not 9.19 (*laudas balnea uersibus trecentis* |
cenantis bene Pontici, Sabelle. | *uis cenare, Sabelle, non lauari*) is, as often thought,
a dig at Statius, the epigram seems to have in view baths in the house
of a rich patron. On the other hand, whereas country villas and wealthy

homes in provincial towns usually included a bath complex (McKay (1975) 42, Yegül (1992) 50–5), baths in private houses within the city may have been much less common (Hodge (1992) 329). Moreover, M.'s exhortation to Oppianus to use the baths implies that the latter could choose to do so without a specific invitation from Etruscus. A possible explanation is that Etruscus' baths were a privately owned establishment open to the public, but catering to a select clientele, perhaps with a high admission price which could be waived in the case of clients or friends invited specially by the owner. For baths run by *equites* as a profitable source of investment, see Bruun (1991) 74.

Comparison of the epigram with *Silu.* 1.5 reveals an apparent discrepancy between the two accounts. Whereas the baths, according to M., featured Laconian marble (11), alabaster (14) and 'snakestone' (15), Statius specifies that Laconian is confined to a border (40–1), while alabaster and snakestone are excluded altogether (35). On the assumption that M.'s description in 8–15 refers, like Statius' account, to the *caldarium* (hot steam bath) it has been suggested that Statius knew M.'s poem and deliberately corrected a mistake by him; more probably, when he speaks of alabaster and snakestones in 14–15 M. is describing, not the *caldarium*, but the *sudatorium*: cf. on *siccos . . . aestus* 14.

Further reading: Dodge and Ward-Perkins (1992), Fagan (1999), Nielsen (1990), Yegül (1992), Busch (1999) 35–57

1   **Etrusci:**   Claudius Etruscus, a wealthy Knight, was the son of an imperial freedman whose administrative talents had led to his acquisition of equestrian status under Vespasian. When Etruscus' father was banished by Domitian, he accompanied him into exile and was responsible for his recall: see P. R. C. Weaver, *CQ* n.s. 15 (1965) 145–54. Etruscus reappears as patron of both M. and Statius in poems eulogising his filial *pietas* (6.83, 7.40, Stat. *Silu.* 3.3).

thermulis: *thermae* usually designates larger, luxurious baths, especially the imperial ones, in contrast to smaller establishments, usually known as *balnea*, to which category Etruscus' baths properly belong (cf. Stat. *Silu.* 1.5.13). M. may be attempting to elevate the status of Etruscus' baths by suggesting their luxuriousness (Fagan (1999) 16–17). The diminutive *thermulae* not only suggests the comparatively small size of the baths, but also carries affectionate connotations.

2   illotus morieris: i.e. you'll die without having ever experienced a real bath, perhaps a parody of Virg. *A.* 4.659 *moriemur inultae. lotus* is the normal word for 'having taken one's bath'.

3   tibi blandientur: not 'will charm you' (SB, Grewing) but 'will caress you': cf. Plin. *NH* 34.88 *matri interfectae infante miserabiliter blandiente. fouere* is similarly used of warm water.

4   fontes Aponi: a bath complex built at medicinal springs near Patavium (Padua) in Cisalpine Gaul, formerly the site of a cult of the Celtic healing god Aponus: cf. G. E. F. Chilver, *Cisalpine Gaul* (Oxford 1941) 188–9, C. Gasparotto, *Padova Romana* (Rome 1951) 44, 140.

   rudes puellis 'not familiar to women' i.e. open to men only. The dative after *rudis* is unparalleled. The reason why women did not frequent the spa is unclear. The Patavian women were famous for their conservative morals: cf. Plin. *Ep.* 1.14.6, M. 11.16.7–8 *tu quoque nequitias nostri . . . libelli | uda, puella, leges, sis Patauina licet.* It has therefore been suggested that their moral probity prevented these women from bathing publicly with men. Alternatively, the prohibition of women resulted from some ancient superstition (L. Lazzaro, *Fons Aponi* (Padova 1981) 52). It is also possible that the native cult of Aponus had excluded women, like that of the Venetic healer god Sainat(is) Trumusiat(is) at nearby Calalzo Làgole, which may have been open only to men (see L. Pauli, *The Alps: archaeology and early history* (rev. ed. transl. E. Peters, London 1984) 154–5), but the evidence is inconclusive.

5   mollis Sinuessa: a coastal town to the north of Cumae which was famous for the healing powers of its sulphur springs. *mollis* refers to the mildness of its climate: cf. Tac. *Ann.* 12.66 (Sinuessa's *mollitia caeli*), Kay on 11.7.12.

6   fluctus Passeris: the Aquae Passerianae in Etruria, 7 km north of Viterbo, now the Bagni Giasinelli.

   superbus Anxur 'lofty Anxur': Anxur is the old Volscian name (Plin. *NH* 3.59) for the town later known as Tarracina, on the coast of Latium. It was the site of mineral springs (cf. 5.1.6 *salutiferis candidus Anxur aquis*) and a holiday retreat (10.58.1). Horace's description of the town as *impositum saxis late candentibus* (*S.* 1.5.26) shows that *superbus*, derived from *super*, is used in its literal sense of 'elevated'. Cf. Virg. *A.* 7.630, Sen. *Tro.* 829–30 *Pelion regnum Prothoi superbum, | tertius caeli gradus.*

7   Phoebi uada: possibly the Aquae Apollinares in Etruria: see Grewing ad loc.

principesque Baiae: the 'leading' spa resort: see Howell on 1.59, D'Arms (1970) 139–40. *que* = 'or', as at Catull. 4.8 and often.

8–10   Great value was set on natural light in baths, which were built facing south to receive the maximum amount of afternoon sunlight: see Sen. *Ep.* 86.8, Plin. *Ep.* 1.3.1 *balineum illud quod plurimus sol implet et circumit,* Stat. *Silu.* 1.5.45, Yegül (1992) 39, 382. In the case of Etruscus' baths, the situation is as favourable as possible. The brightness of the high quality marble (11–15) will have contributed to the prolongation of the daylight.

8   uacat: the MSS offer *uacat* and *micat* ('gleams'), the latter unattractively redundant after *nitidum.* Commentators usually pass over *uacat* in silence, or else explain 'is clear of clouds' but the cloudlessness of the sky is in no way contingent on a physical structure like baths. The sense is probably 'is free of encumbrances', in the shape of surrounding buildings which might block out the sun: cf. on *tenebras* **21.**12.

serenum sc. *caelum.*

11   Taygeti uirent metalla refers to green Laconian 'marble' from Mt Taygetus in Laconia, in reality a type of green porphyry. It was dark sea green with large flecks of lighter green crystals, and was used for *opus sectile* or veneer. See Dodge and Ward-Perkins (1992) 158, pl. 1b. Statius specifies that in Etruscus' baths it was used as a border for the Synnadic marble (*Silu.* 1.5.40–1).

12   et certant uario decore saxa 'and the marbles contend [with each other] in their variegated beauty', a striking personification. *uario* refers to the rich patterning of the marble: see foll. n.

13   quae Phryx et Libys altius cecidit: Synnadic marble from Synnas in Phrygia and Numidian marble from Simitthus (in modern Tunisia). The former was dark purplish-brown with streaks of white, the latter (*giallo antico*) yellow with blood red veins: see Dodge and Ward-Perkins (1992) plate 1f, plate 2b.

altius: from the deeper beds and therefore of finer and more compact quality.

14   siccos ... aestus suggests the *sudatorium*, a heated chamber for taking an optional dry sweat bath between visiting the *tepidarium* (warm bath) and the *caldarium* (hot bath): cf. Sen. *Ep.* 51.6 *quid cum sudatoriis, in quae siccus uapor corpora exhausurus includitur?*, Yegül (1992) 38, Nielsen (1990) 159.

pinguis onyx: not the modern 'onyx' (a type of quartz mixed with agate) but alabaster, a true marble occurring as stalagmites in caves. It was white, yellowish or greenish with wavy bands of white, yellowy-brown or pink: see J. Ward-Perkins in *Enciclopedia dell'arte antica, classica e orientale* IV (Rome 1961) 864 and figs. 1, 6 facing 862. *pinguis* suggests both costly, and 'rich or oily, [which] admirably expresses the appearance and feel of this marble' (Stephenson).

15   flamma tenui calent: both walls and floor of the *sudatorium* were heated by hot air from the central furnace of the baths. According to Yegül (1992) 381, the surfaces of both floor and walls were not excessively hot to the touch, which is why the heat is *tenuis* 'subtle'. Cf. Stat. *Silu.* 1.5.59 *tenuem . . . uaporem.*

ophitae: a type of granite, speckled in green and white, so called from its resemblance to the skin of a snake (ὄφις). It was used for small columns: cf. Plin. *NH* 36.55 *neque ex ophite columnae nisi paruae admodum inueniuntur.* see Gnoli (1988) 154–7.

16   ritus . . . Laconum: a form of bathing originating in Sparta, whereby the hot steam bath in the *caldarium* was omitted, the bather confining himself to a dry sweat (*contentus . . . arido uapore* 17) followed by a cold water plunge (*mergi* 18). The dry sweat was worked up in the *sudatorium* (known in its earlier form as the *Laconicum*), which was centrally heated by the hypocaust system. Cf. Yegül (1992) 383–9, Nielsen (1990) 158–9.

18   cruda: fresh, in its natural state.

Virgine Marciaue: i.e. cold pools supplied from either the Aqua Virgo or the Aqua Marcia. Stat. *Silu.* 1.5.26–7 confirms that the baths were connected to both these aqueducts. Richardson s.v. *Balneum Claudii Etrusci* thinks this would locate the baths in the Campus Martius, but the Quirinal is preferred by Almeida in E. M. Steinby, ed. *Lexicon topographicum urbis Romanae* I (2nd ed. Rome 1993) s.v. *Balneum Claudii Etrusci.* Both aqueducts were renowned for the quality of their water. For the Aqua Marcia, see **11**.6n. For the Aqua Virgo, cf. Plin. *NH* 31.42 (famed as a source of water for bathing), 7.32.11, 11.47.6, Ov. *Ars* 3.385 (noted for coolness) and Cassiod. *Var.* 7.6 (its purity).

mergi 'plunge into': see 16n.

19–21   So clear, so pure and transparent is the water that it seems as if one is looking directly upon the gleaming Parian marble which lines the pool, rather than through a sheet of water.

19   **lucet** 'is transparent'. Statius, *Silu.* 1.5.52, 55 also remarks on the clarity of the water in which bathers took a cold dip: unlike M. he specifies its location outdoors (*extra* 51).

20   **undas:**   poetical for *aquas*.

21   **uacuam:**   as if the pool were empty: see on 19–21.
      lygdon refers to a pool lined with white Parian marble (λύγδος) which was noted for its gleaming whiteness (**44**.13n.).

22–3   To prepare for the concluding ring composition, M. apostrophises his addressee, accusing him of boredom with the theme, a typical touch of artistic self-depreciation.

22   **aure . . . supina:**   lit. 'with ear inclined backward', i.e. with languid, apathetic ear: an original turn of phrase, coined on the analogy of *auribus pronis*, lit. 'with ears inclined forwards', i.e. strained to attention.

24   **illotus morieris, Oppiane** echoes line 2, but the motive for the statement is different.

31   (= 3.12)

'You certainly gave your guests a good unguent yesterday, Fabullus, but you served no food. It's a nice thing to smell sweet and go hungry – much the same thing as being dead.'

This is a witty recasting of Catullus' tongue-in-cheek thirteenth poem *Cenabis bene*, in which Fabullus is invited to 'an enjoyable dinner' with Catullus – enjoyable as long as Fabullus provides all the necessities – food, wine and wit (*sal*): the sole contribution which the impoverished Catullus can make is a wondrous *unguentum* given to Lesbia by the *Veneres Cupidinesque*. In M.'s epigram Fabullus is no longer the invitee but the host, who, like Catullus, proffers nothing but a high-quality unguent (*bonum unguentum*). Whereas, however, Catullus' contribution was limited by his empty coffers, and the poem functions in part as a self-ironising satire on the poet's poverty (*nam tui Catulli | plenus sacculus est aranearum* 7–8), M. suggests that his Fabullus, by contrast, represents the *ne plus ultra* of a type frequently encountered in his epigrams, the stingy host: cf. the following epigram (3.13), also 1.20, 2.19, 3.94, 8.22, 9.85, 11.31, Szelest (1963) 28. Fabullus does not, however, like many such hosts, merely serve fare that is poor in quality or quantity, or inferior to that which he himself enjoys. Instead, like the Mancinus of 1.43, he serves nothing at all (*nihil scidisti*).

Further reading: Szelest (1963)

1–2   Vnguentum ... dedisti | conuiuis here: it was traditional to perfume oneself with unguents at banquets: cf. Xen. *Symp.* 2.3, Hor. *Carm.* 1.4.9 with N–H, Lucr. 4.1132 with Brown. These were normally provided by the host: cf. Ath. 129a and e, 686c, Petr. 60.4, **56**.27–8.

1   Vnguentum, fateor, bonum: the unguent was satisfactory, nothing else was. The paratactic use of *fateor* is colloquial: cf. Plaut. *Pseud.* 913 *fuit meum officium ut facerem, fateor*, Citroni on 1.90.5. *bonum* echoes *bonam atque magnam | cenam* Catull. 13.3–4.

2   here: whereas in Catullus Fabullus can look forward to a good dinner 'in a few days' time', M.'s poem is a retrospective on a bad one.

sed nihil scidisti: *scindo*, like *carpo*, is a technical term for carving meat (3.94.2, *OLD* s.v. 5d), but here stands for serving food to guests.

3   res salsa est bene olere et esurire: for the pronounced use of elision in this line, see intro. 28.

salsa in its transferred sense of 'witty' is a reminiscence of the *sal* which Fabullus is enjoined to bring in Catull. 13.5. In both poems the culinary setting plays on the literal meaning of *sal*.

et: adversative = *sed* or *tamen*; cf. *OLD* 14a.

esurire: Catullan language: cf. 21.1, 10, 23.14. Greek epigrams satirise hosts who serve 'famished' dishes': cf. *AP* 11.312.2–3, 313.4, 11.371 'do not invite me: I know all about your dishes which serve only hunger ... defrauding the wretched plates with starvation'.

4–5   qui non cenat et unguitur ... | hic mihi uere mortuus uidetur: dead bodies were anointed prior to burial or cremation to counteract the effects of putrescence: cf. Hom. *Il.* 18.350, Virg. *A.* 6.219 *corpusque lauant frigentis et unguunt*, Pers. 3.103–5. The reference in *non cenat* is to the funeral feast, at which the dead were present but could not partake, unlike the living: cf. Non. 48.4 M., Fest. 294a 18 M., Toynbee (1971) 50.

The situation of Fabullus' guests, anointed but deprived of food, is precisely (*uere*) similar: there is also a hyperbolic suggestion that they are liable to die of starvation.

4   Fabulle: Fabullus is the addressee of a number of M.'s epigrams, elsewhere too with thematic reminiscences of *cenabis bene*: see on **71**.

32   (= 7.20)

'There is no creature more wretched and gluttonous than Santra. When he's obtained an invitation to a formal dinner after angling for it for days he dashes off there and helps himself to large amounts of food and drink, which he takes home – only to sell these the following day.'

Santra, like Selius (**21**), is a dinner hunter (cf. 2–3); the epigram focuses not on the *cenipeta*'s attempts to gain an invitation, as in **21**, but on Santra's behaviour at the dinner itself and the surprise aftermath. After a series of deliberately misleading clues, which lead the reader to regard Santra as a typical gluttonous parasite who steals all the food he can in order to provide himself with a meal the following day, in the final word of the poem M. reveals the real motive for Santra's thefts of food and drink – financial gain.

The build-up begins in the first line, which attributes to Santra two typical traits of the parasite, impoverishment and gluttony (1 n.). The latter trait is seemingly demonstrated in 2–7, where Santra takes large quantities of luxurious foods, which, one assumes, he eats on the spot, like the glutton in Lucillius, *AP* 11.207, who devours as much as possible before handing the leftovers to his slave (cf. Lucian, *Symp.* 11). From line 8 the items taken are secreted in Santra's *mappa*, and later in the fold of his robe (14), for consumption, one expects, at home. Stealing food for subsequent use is a well-established characteristic of both the parasite (e.g. Alciphron, *Epist. parasit.* 20.2) and the gluttonous dinner-guest: cf. Lucillius, *AP* 11.205, M. 2.37, 3.23, and esp. Lucian, *Symp.* 11. The *Leitmotiv* of gluttony reappears at 18 (*gula*) and 22, where the juxtaposition of *gulosus* at the beginning of the verse and *uendidit* at its end underlines the surprise that this 'glutton' does not eat his stolen food but sells it.

A further question of interest is the order of the various dishes in the banquet. M. cannot be describing Santra's progress through them in chronological sequence, since some items are out of order. For instance oysters (7) should come first, as they form part of the *gustatio* (*hors d'oeuvre*), while the sow's womb (11) would be served with the main course, not after the dessert items of fruits and pastries. The progression is best regarded as a movement from the choicest to the least desirable items, as Santra becomes increasingly undiscriminating in his selection of food. He begins with the most luxurious foodstuffs on the menu, first the larger (3–5), then the smaller (6–7), followed by dessert items (8–10). Having gone through all the desirable foods, he turns, in an ascending triad of repulsiveness, to items which other diners disdain: delicacies which have lost their appeal (11–12), half-eaten table scraps (14–15) and finally leftovers lying on the floor (16–17).

The epigram is in scazons, often used by M in contexts of invective: see intro. 28–9. The unusual metrical pattern in lines 1 and 22 (see nn. ad loc.) gives the epigram an arresting opening and close.

Further reading: Damon (1997)

1   The unusual metrical pattern of this line, involving resolution in the first three feet (anapaest + tribrach + dactyl), is employed elsewhere by M. only at 10.100.4 *aquilisque similes facere noctuas quaeris*.

Nihil est miserius ... Santra: *nihil* + comparative neuter adj. with reference to a person is colloquial (Hofmann (1951) 90). The idiom is frequent in M.: cf. 2.71.1 *Candidius nihil est te, Caeciliane* where, as here, it introduces and characterises the subject of the poem.

miserius 'more wretched' i.e. a starveling: cf. 2.51.1–6 *unus saepe tibi tota denarius arca* | *cum sit ... infelix uenter ...* | *... semper miser ... esurit.* Santra is so poor, M. sarcastically implies, that he must rely on dinner invitations, like the typically impoverished parasite (Damon (1997) 28).

gulosius: *gulosus*, 'gluttonous', is an insulting term found in poetry only in M. and at Juv. 11.19. The trait is characteristic of the parasite: cf. Damon (1997) 25–6.

Santra: the name, apparently Etruscan (Schulze (1904) 343, 369), is used twice elsewhere by M. in different contexts (**44**.7, 11.2.7). The first element of the word may have associations with gluttony: cf. the glutton Sannos in Hipponax, fr. 118 W.

2   **rectam ... cenam:**   a formal banquet, on a grander scale than an everyday dinner party. Cf. 2.69.7, Marquardt-Mau 208–11.

cucurrit: Santra runs to dinner with undignified haste; cf. Lucillius, *AP* 11.208, **21**.3n. *cum* + perfect indicative ('whenever'), underlines that this is Santra's habitual behaviour.

3   tot diebus: the dinner invitation has taken considerable time and effort to obtain. Compare the efforts of Selius (**21**).

captauit: *capto* = 'angle for a dinner invitation'; cf. 2.18.1 *capto tuam, pudet heu, sed capto, Maxime, cenam.* The verb is commonly used of legacy-hunters, with which the *cenipeta* has much in common (Damon (1997) 118–19).

4   ter...quater: he asks not merely for 'seconds' but for a third and a fourth serving.

poscit: conveys a more forcible request than *petit*.

apri glandulas: **56**.20n.

lumbum: the loin was the choicest portion of the *aper*; cf. Plin. *NH* 8.210. Boar was an expensive luxury: cf. **36**.1 n., André (1981) 115.

5   utramque coxam leporis et duos armos: hares were a choice meat; cf. 13.92.2 *inter quadripedes mattea prima lepus.* They were sometimes quartered (Apic. 8.8.9.1), which would give two haunches (*coxae*) and two shoulders (*armi*). Santra greedily takes the whole animal rather than a single portion. Gourmets preferred the shoulder (Hor. *S.* 2.4.44, 2.8.89–90), but Santra is not so discriminating.

coxam '(human) hip' refers to the haunch (i.e. the loin together with the leg).

6   peierare de: in order to get more than his share of thrushes, Santra claims falsely that he has not yet had any, or else that he has received less than he really has. *peierare* is unusual in the sense 'to tell lies', and is not elsewhere followed by *de*.

turdo: thrush was a popular delicacy: cf. André (1981) 122, Hor. *S.* 2.2.74 with Muecke.

7   ostreorum...liuidos cirros 'oysters with blue beards'. *liuidos* describes the dark bluish-grey colour of oyster gills (cf. on *cirros*). The suggestion (Steier, *RE* xvi 77, A. C. Andrews, *CJ* 43 (1948) 301) that these are red-gilled oysters (cf. Pliny cited on *cirros*) which have gone 'off' – hence *liuidos* – is a red herring. The lit. translation 'the blue beards of oysters' is less likely, since it would imply that Santra takes the 'beards', which his fellow diners have discarded. But oysters, at least nowadays, are served whole or, less commonly, with the beards already removed by the cook: it would be difficult and messy to separate the gills at table.

ostreorum: oysters were a prime delicacy at Rome: Plin.*NH* 32.59, M. 3.45.5–6, 7.78.3–4.

rapere 'to snatch greedily'. Santra unblushingly (*nec erubescit*) grabs large quantities of oysters; the verb also implies theft.

cirros: lit. 'locks of hair', 'fringe', the gills of the oysters, or the 'beard' as they are popularly known. They are termed *cirri* because of their resemblance to a fringe of hair: similarly oysters with dark red gills, prized by gourmets, were known as *calliblephara*, 'with beautiful eyelashes' (cf. Plin. *NH* 32.61).

8   buccis placentae: the *placenta* was cooked in a giant slab and cut into small morsels (*buccae*) for serving; cf. Cato, *Agr.* 76, E. S. P. Ricotti, *L'Arte del convito nella Roma antica* (Rome 1983) 239. *buccis* lit. 'mouthfuls', is colloquial: cf. Petr. 44.2, Suet. *Aug.* 76.2 *duas buccas manducaui*, from an informal letter.

placentae: *placenta* (Greek πλακοῦς, acc. πλακόεντα) is usually translated as 'cake', but the ingredients given by Cato (*Agr.* 76), which include flour, groats, sheep's cheese and honey, show that it was a confection of layered pastry of the kind still popular in Greece and the Middle East. Cf. J. Solomon, *Hermes* 106 (1978) 539–56 at 555.

sordidam linit mappam 'he soils his napkin'. Given that *placenta* was coated with honey, making it sticky, it is best to take *sordidam* as proleptic, lit. 'he smears his napkin [with pieces of *placenta*], making it dirty'. *lino* is often used of smearing with cosmetics or dirty substances: cf. 3.42.2, **73**.6, 9.22.13, **41**.3.

mappam: a linen cloth which each guest brought with him (12.28), both for wiping the hands and as a receptacle for *apophoreta*: cf. Petr. 66.4. It could also be employed, as here, to conceal stolen items of food: cf. 2.37.7–8.

9   illic et 'in it also'; the *buccae placentae* are the first of a number of items secreted in the *mappa*.

uuae ... ollares: grapes were preserved in jars (*ollae*): cf. Col. 12.45.2–3, Coleman on Stat. *Silu.* 4.9.42.

10   Punicorum ... grana malorum: at Trimalchio's feast pomegranate seeds are part of the *gustatio* (Petr. 31.11). *malum punicum* ('Punic fruit') is the original name for the pomegranate (*malum granatum*), which first came to Rome from Carthage; later it was grown in Italy. See André (1981) 76.

11   excauatae pellis indecens uuluae: sows' wombs, *uuluae*, were a choice food (foll. n.), but the description of the skin as *indecens* 'unsightly', implies that it was normally discarded. The contents of the womb have been removed and eaten by another guest, leaving the skin, which Santra takes. Wombs were usually served whole, but could also be stuffed, like a haggis (cf. Apic. 2.3.1 *uuluulae isiciatae*): if M. has this in mind it would be the stuffing, rather than the flesh of the womb, which has been removed.

uuluae: a special delicacy: cf. Hor. *Ep.* 1.15.41 *nil uulua pulchrius ampla*; André (1981) 138.

12   lippa ficus: a characteristically bold use of language to refer to an opened fig with juice running from it, which might resemble the eye of someone suffering from *lippitudo* (**44**.11 n.). Figs gape when mature (cf. 11.18.15–16) and ripe, juicy figs were desirable (Ath. 79a, M. 13.23.1–2), but here the fig has been damaged and split, either in transit to, or at the table, so that the juice runs out.

debilis: a second personification, the epithet, 'crippled, disabled', normally referring to people. M. probably means that the mushroom has been damaged: cf. **33**.8.

boletus: a delicious type of edible fungus, highly regarded by gourmets (Sen. *Ep.* 95.25), and often preferred to ordinary kinds of mushroom: cf. 3.60.5 *sunt tibi boleti, fungos ego sumo suillos*, Juv. 5.146–7. The name may derive from the Spanish town of Boletum, modern Boltaña, which is still famous for its mushrooms (A. A. Imholz, *AJPh* 98 (1977) 71–6).

13   mille: indefinite, 'countless'.
rumpitur 'is full to bursting'; cf. Virg. *G.* 1.49 *immensae ruperunt horrea messes*.
furtis 'stolen objects'.

14   rosos 'nibbled at', of left-overs.
tepenti: warmed by his body heat; cf. Apul. *Met.* 2.29 *torum tepentem adultero mancipaui*.
spondylos 'vertebrae', i.e. joint-bones or spare-ribs. Cf. Alciphron, *Epist. parasit.* 15.3 where a parasite receives table scraps including knuckle-bones (ἀστράγαλοι). In a culinary context, *spondylus* normally refers to a kind of mussel (Thompson (1947) 250–1), but these would be swallowed whole rather than nibbled at.
sinu: the fold of the toga or the *synthesis* (dinner suit) used as a pocket. It was convenient for concealing objects: cf. Tib. 2.6.45–6 *furtim . . . tabellas | occulto portans . . . sinu*.

15 **deuorato capite ... truncum** 'bereft of its head which has been devoured' by one of the other guests, abl. of separation as at 2.83.3 *trunci naribus auribusque uultus*. The unappetising nature of this left-over is suggested by pejorative language: *deuorare* ('wolf down') is commonly used of animals rather than people (e.g. Phaedr. 1.8.4 *os deuoratum fauce cum haereret lupi*) and *truncus* suggests mutilation: cf. Sen. *HF* 1025–6 *corpori trunco caput | abest.*

capite: birds were consumed in their entirety: cf. Gellius, 15.8.2, remarking that fastidious gourmets eat only the lower part of most birds, which implies that the upper part was normally eaten also.

turturem: a delicacy: cf. Plaut. *Most.* 46, M. 3.60.7, André (1981) 121.

16 **longa** 'stretched at full length', a novel usage. Santra reaches under the table for scraps thrown on the floor.

dextra: the choice of hand is primarily dictated by convenience, since diners reclined on the left elbow and took food with the right hand. In view, however, of the common association of the left hand with stealing (e.g. Ov. *Met.* 13.111 *natae ... ad furta sinistrae*), M. may also be suggesting that by using his right, rather than his left, hand Santra attempts to conceal his thievish intentions.

17 **analecta:** the noun, found only here and 14.82.2, refers to a slave employed to 'pick up' (ἀναλέγειν) table scraps thrown on the floor by the diners; cf. Hor. *S.* 2.8.11–12. The practice is illustrated in the mosaic motif of the 'unswept room', depicting left-over food lying on the ground: cf. Plin. *NH* 36.184, W. Deonna and M. Renard, *Croyances et superstitions de table dans la Rome antique* (Brussels 1961) 113–37, pl. 15 fig. 19–20.

canes: table scraps were fed to dogs: cf. Petr. 64.6, **56**.19, Lucian, *Sat.* 35.

18 **esculenta ... praeda:** *esculentus* is commonly used when edible and potable items are juxtaposed: cf. Gell. 4.1.17.3 *quod esculentum aut posculentum est.*

gulae 'gluttony'; cf. 1.20.3 *quid dignum tanto tibi uentre gulaque precabor?*, Hor. *S.* 2.2.40 with Muecke.

19 **mixto ... uino** 'wines stolen from different glasses' (SB). *misceo* is normally used of mixing wine with water prior to drinking (e.g. Cato, *Agr.* 158.2, 3.49.1, **66**.2); M. humorously assigns a novel meaning to a commonplace term.

lagonam replet: a *lagona* held approx. 26 litres. The absurd hyperbole is underlined by *repleo* 'to fill full'.

ad pedes: with *lagonam*. Diners reclined with their feet angled towards the back of the couch, behind which attendant slaves were stationed (**56**.18n.). Santra passes back to his slave the half-finished wine cups, which the latter pours indiscriminately into the *lagona*. Usually it is left-over food which is handed to the *seruus*: cf. Lucillius, *AP* 11.207, M. 2.37.8, Lucian, *Symp.* 11.

20   per ducentas cum domum tulit scalas emphasises Santra's poverty: he lives at the top of a large apartment block, like Juvenal's Ucalegon (Juv. 3.199).

ducentas ... scalas: *ducentas*, used of a large number, is approximate rather than exact (cf. 8.20.1, Plaut. *Truc.* 341). Remains of staircases at Ostia have 27 steps per storey (Packer (1971) 28, 135), so that a flat reached by around 200 steps would be on the seventh floor, an obvious exaggeration, though not excessively so: *insulae* may have reached a height of six storeys. See A. Wotschitzky in R. Muth, ed., *Natalicium Jax* (Innsbruck 1955) 151–8.

scalas 'steps', an unusual sense. *scala* properly means a flight of stairs: cf. 1.117.7 *scalis habito tribus*.

21   obserata: double doors folding inwards, the norm in Roman dwellings, were fastened by a bar (*sera*) put across. See P. Howell, *Philologus* 112 (1968) 132–5.

anxius: Santra is worried about theft, ironically, in view of his thievish activities (*furtis* 13).

cella: a poor man's humble garret: cf. 3.30.3, Juv. 7.27–8.

22   A pure choliambic verse, rare in M. (Pelckmann (1908) 51, intro. 29).

gulosus ille: *gulosus*, in combination with the stress on Santra's poverty in 20–1, effects a neat ring composition, alluding back to *miserius and gulosius* in 1 and reinforcing our impression of Santra as an impoverished and gluttonous parasite in preparation for the final surprise twist.

uendit: the action marks Santra as miserly; both Simonides and Themistocles were accused of meanness for selling food received as a gift (Ath. 656c–d, Plut. *Them.* 5.1).

33   (= 8.6)

'Nothing is more boring than Euctus' "originals", when he harangues his guests at length on the alleged mythological pedigree of his silverware. And when you've admired the "ancient" embossed work, you're served new wine in old cups.'

Euctus, the target of this epigram, combines in his person several types: (1) individuals (cf. 4.39, 8.34) who falsely claim to possess authentic pieces of silver by famous fifth-century Greek silversmiths, such as did exist (cf. Plin. *NH* 33.154); Euctus goes further by claiming, absurdly, that his cups date from Homeric times; (2) the host who subjects his guests to a lengthy discourse before they are permitted to dine (e.g. 3.50); (3) the stingy host who offers his guests poor wine and/or food (cf. **56**); (4) the host who attempts to impress his guests by his literary knowledge, but succeeds only in displaying his ignorance (see below): cf. Petr. 52, where Trimalchio boasts of the engraving on his cups which depicts 'Daedalus shutting Niobe into the Trojan horse'.

Euctus' speech (5–14) is conspicuous for its elevated language: cf. the poetic plural *proelia* (7), the epithets *Pylius* (10) and *Phrygius* (14), and the Virgilian *Laomedonteus* (5), *longaeuus* (9), *Aeacides* (12) and *pulcherrima Dido* (13). This profusion of high-flown vocabulary, unusual in the satiric epigrams, serves to characterise Euctus as pompous and self-important, mirroring on a stylistic level the grandiosity of the claims which he makes for the antiquity of his artefacts. In tracing the alleged pedigree of his vessels, however, Euctus makes a number of faux-pas (nn. on 6, 7–8, 10, 11, 13). An important source of humour, then, is the incongruity between the pretentious style of Euctus' discourse and his ignorance in literary matters.

Further reading: Strong (1966), Watson (1998)

1   Archetypis: silver vessels engraved by skilled artisans, as opposed to the mass-produced copies from plaster casts which were popular in M.'s day. Euctus' cups are probably of the latter type. Cf. Reinhold (1971) 284 and n.44.

uetuli: a diminutive often used by M. with contemptuous force; cf. 1.41.13, 11.71.1, **39**.1.

odiosius 'more tedious'.

Eucti: preferable to the alternative *Aucti* (Watson (1998) 30–1). The Greek name Euctus suggests servile origins (cf. *CIL* vi 10899,13843,17314), which sits well with the Trimalchio-like boorishness and ignorance of its bearer.

2   ficta Saguntino...luto: pottery from Saguntum in Spain. It represents unpretentious table ware (4.46.14–16, 14.108), which M. prefers to Euctus' silver 'antiques'.

cymbia: used as a generic term for cups; cf. Isid. *Or.* 20.5.4.

3   fumosa...stemmata: *fumosa*, 'smoky', Lipsius' persuasive emendation for the *furiosa* of the MSS, is used by analogy with the wax images of ancestors which hung in the atrium of a Roman nobleman to advertise his lineage (*stemmata*) and imbibed the smoke from the hearth-fire (cf. Cic. *Pis.* 1 *commendatione fumosarum imaginum*, Juv. 8.8). There may be an additional connotation of worthlessness or vanity; cf. Pers. 5.19–20 *non equidem hoc studeo, bullatis ut mihi nugis | pagina turgescat dare pondus idonea fumo* with Kissel.

4   garrulus: the enjambement throws Euctus' loquacity into relief.

mucida: the wine lies so long unsealed during Euctus' narration that it 'spoils' before the guests can drink it. The adjective is properly used of mouldy comestibles; cf. Col. 12.39.1.

5   Laomedonteae: Laomedon was an early king of Troy during whose reign the walls of the city were built. The poetic adjective *Laomedonteus* suits the epic subject-matter, and also characterises Euctus as pretentious.

fuerant: pluperfect for perfect/imperfect is not uncommon in Latin poets, particularly Propertius and Ovid: cf. P. J. Enk, *Mnemosyne* 8 (1940) 318–20. Here it may also suggest remoteness of time and hence the antiquity of the cups.

haec: the first of a series of deictic *hic*'s at the beginning of successive couplets: Euctus points to the artefacts as he speaks.

6   ferret ut haec muros struxit Apollo lyra: Euctus gets his mythology wrong. In the usual version (e.g. Hom. *Il.* 7.452–3, Pind. *Ol.* 8.40, Hyg. *Fab.* 89) Apollo and Poseidon constructed the walls of Troy while working as hired labourers for Laomedon, not in order to get precious cups from the latter. Worse, *struxit...lyra* shows that Euctus is confusing the building of Troy's walls with the miraculous construction of the walls of Thebes by Amphion, who charmed the stones into place by the power of his lyre (Ap. Rhod. *Arg.* 1.735–41, Prop. 1.9.10, Hor. *Carm.* 3.11.2).

7–8 refer to the battle between the Lapiths and the Centaurs at the wedding of the Lapith Pirithous to Hippodame, provoked by the attempted rape of the bride by the Centaur Eurytus. In this couplet, confusion once more subtly undercuts Euctus' pretensions (7n.).

7   hoc cratere ... commisit proelia Rhoecus: in the best-known version of the myth (Ov. *Met.* 12.210–535), it was Theseus who 'initiated the battle' by hurling an *antiquus crater*. Euctus' mistake reflects the prominence of Rhoecus in Ovid's narrative. There may also be a garbled reminiscence of Virg. *G.* 2.455–6 *ille furentes | Centauros leto domuit, Rhoecumque Pholumque | et magno Hylaeum Lapithis cratere minantem.*

ferox: cf. Luc. 6.390 *Rhoece ferox.* The Centaurs, with the exception of Chiron, were known for their savagery.

8   pugna debile ... opus: an unusual personification: the *crater* was 'wounded', i.e. damaged, when employed as a weapon (7n.).

9   hi duo ... fundi: i.e. 'this cup with two *fundi*', an allusion to the famous cup of Nestor described in Hom. *Il.* 11. 632–4, 'a very beautiful cup studded with gold rivets ... and it had four handles, and two gold doves were feeding about each, and there were two πυθμένες underneath'. The meaning of 'two πυθμένες' was already disputed in antiquity. M.'s rendering *fundi* suggests that he took it to refer to two bottoms, one a double or false one, such as is seen in many Cretan pots. Other suggested explanations of πυθμένες are (1) 'supports' for the handles, as in the cup from the fourth shaft grave at Mycenae; (2) 'legs': cf. Hom. *Il.* 18.375.

censentur Nestore 'is valued because of its association with Nestor': cf. 1.61.3 *censetur Aponi Liuio suo tellus.*

10   pollice de Pylio trita 'rubbed by the Pylian thumb' i.e. by the thumb of the Homeric Nestor, king of Pylos: a deliberately precious expression serving to characterise Euctus. The thumb was the part of the hand most likely to 'rub' the handle where the doves were located (9n.), but *pollex* could also refer to the hand as a whole: cf. Ov. *Ep.* 17.266 with Kenney.

de replacing ablative of instrument, characteristic of elevated poetry (e.g. Ov. *Met.* 6.80 *percussam ... sua ... de cuspide terram*), though also found in the humbler genres (L. Callebat, *Sermo cottidianus dans les Métamorphoses d'Apulée* (Caen 1968) 201–3), is probably intended as a further piece of stylistic preciosity on Euctus' part.

trita ... nitet 'is shiny through being worn down' (cf. Hor. *S.* 1.3.90–1 *catillum | Euandri manibus tritum*) over many years (*longaeuo*), leaving the surface smoother and shinier than in its original state. Euctus may be attempting to prove the authenticity of his silver by pointing to its worn condition: cf. Plin. *NH* 33.157 [the art of engraving] *ita exoleuit, ut sola iam uetustate censeatur usuque attritis caelaturis si nec figura discerni possit auctoritas constet.*

columba: since Nestor's cup had two doves on each handle, the use of the singular may be another pointer to the non-authenticity of Euctus' cup.

11–12: based on Hom. *Il.* 9.204, where Achilles (*Aeacides*), greeting Odysseus and Ajax, tells Patroclus to 'set forth a larger mixing bowl (κρητῆρα)... and mix stronger wine (ζωρότερον), and prepare each a cup (δέπας), for these are my dearest friends'.

11   scyphus: another mistake on Euctus' part: the term normally denotes a drinking cup rather than a mixing bowl.

12   Aeacides: grandson of Aeacus, i.e. Achilles. A high-flown epic patronymic; cf. Virg. *A.* 1.99, Stat. *Ach.*1.1.

uiuidius 'livelier', i.e. stronger. Homer's ζωρότερον was generally understood in antiquity to mean 'purer', sc. with a lesser admixture of water (cf. M. L. West, *CR* 16 (1966) 135–6). Some, however, derived it from ζωτικός ('lively'): cf. M. R. Arundel, *CR* 12 (1962) 109–11. If Euctus' *uiuidius* alludes to this second tradition, it may be an attempt on his part to show off abstruse learning.

merum: poetic for *uinum*.

13–14 allude to the banquet at the end of *Aeneid* 1, where Dido, in honour of the guest-friendship between Trojans and Tyrians, passes round the drinking cup among her nobles, beginning with Bitias. The jarring juxtaposition of Virgilian diction (*pulcherrima Dido, patera, Phrygius*) with everyday language (cf. *propinauit, cena*), debunks Euctus' pomposity.

13   propinauit Bitiae: the verb suggests the custom at Greek and Roman banquets of drinking a toast to a lover or someone specially honoured, and immediately passing the cup to that person: cf. Theoc. 14.18, Cic. *Tusc.* 1.96, 2.15.1, **56**.31, Lucian, *Merc. con.* 16, W. Heraeus, *RhM* 70 (1915) 1–41. Euctus has misinterpreted Dido's action in passing the cup first to Bitias as a toast to him.

pulcherrima Dido: a quotation from *Aen.* 1.496 and 4.60.

14   patera: Virgil's term for the utensil in question (*A.* 1.729, 739, 4.60).

Phrygio . . . uiro 'the Trojan hero'. *Phrygius* is a poetic synonym for 'Trojan'.

cena: like *propinauit*, more suitable to a Roman dinner party than to Dido's feast (at *Aen.* 1.723 called by the epic term for 'banquet', *epulae*). See further 13–14n.

15–16 A surprise twist, introducing a new aspect of Euctus' boorish-ness. The 'antique' vessels are used to serve immature, and thus inferior, wine: cf. 10.49.3 *propinas modo conditum Sabinum.*

15   **miratus fueris cum** = *cum miratus eris* 'after (hypocritically) ad-miring'. On the usage see H. Blase, *ALLG* 10 (1898) 321–3.

16   **in Priami calathis Astyanacta bibes:** Priam stands for the era of the Trojan war from which the cups allegedly originate; Astyanax, infant grandson of Priam, is used by a bold personification for young wine.

calathis: *calathus*, properly a basket made from wicker-work, is some-times used in the sense 'cup'.

34   (= 8.23)

'Rusticus, you think I'm cruel and too fond of my stomach when I beat the cook on account of a poor dinner. If you think that a trivial reason for a whipping, for what reason *do* you want a cook to be beaten?'

This is one of three epigrams which centre on the beating of slave-cooks. In the others (3.13 and 3.94), M. castigates an owner for flogging his cook, a stance which might seem inconsistent with the present one. The satire in these cases is, however, directed less against the ill-treatment of a slave than a host who uses a cook's supposed incompetence as an excuse not to offer food to guests.

Corporal punishment of slaves was regarded in Rome as the prerogative of the owner, a means both of maintaining discipline in the household and of reinforcing the distinction between slave and free (Saller (1991) 151–60, Bradley (1994) 28–30). Opposition to the practice *per se* is occasionally voiced; cf. Tac.*Germ.* 25, M. Griffin, *Seneca* (Oxford 1976) 257–85. For the most part, however, objections were directed at maltreatment of slaves for no good reason.

The major factor in determining whether chastisement of a slave seemed justified was whether the punishment administered was warranted by the offence (cf. Gai. *Inst.* 1.53, Hor. *S.* 1.3.80–3, Sen. *Ep.* 47.3, Juv. 6.487–93). The issue in the present epigram is whether spoiling the dinner represents a valid reason for a whipping: M. argues that it does, Rusticus disagrees. Rusticus represents the stern moralist for whom an excessive concern with one's belly (*nimium gulosus* 1) is exemplified by a master's punishing a slave cook harshly for failing to perform to his satisfaction. Plutarch, *De coh. ir.* 457B, 461C, cites, as one example of people unreasonably prone to anger (cf. *saeuus* 1), the glutton who beats his cook for shortcomings in preparation and cooking of the food; he also recounts a similarly disreputable tale of Cato (*Cat. Mai.* 21.3).

Whether M.'s reader would sympathise with Rusticus' moralistic view-point is questionable; the name Rusticus, hinting at a lack of sophistication (2n.), suggests that he might not. In any case, the poem is hardly a serious discussion of the rights and wrongs of corporal punishment, but a joke using as its basis the traditional comic theme of slave-beating. For the motif specifically in connection with cooks, cf. Laberius, *Mimes* 134 *cocus, si lumbum adussit, caedetur flagris.*

Further reading: Bradley (1984/7) 113–37, Harcum (1914), Saller (1991)

1   saeuus: of excessive and unjustified cruelty towards slaves, some-thing frowned upon by the law.

nimium ... gulosus: attaching excessive importance to food; cf. 12.64.2.

2   Rustice: only here in M., but common in inscriptions (Kajanto 265, 310–11). The name suggests (1) that its bearer is boorish and unsophis-ticated; (2) that he shares country values, which espoused plain foodstuffs and deprecated urban culinary luxury (**18**.8n).

caedo 'I have him beaten':   although we hear of masters personally beating slaves (cf. Juv. 14.63), *caedo* is probably factitive (cf. M. McDonnell, *CQ* 46 (1996) 484–5); cf. Petr. 49 *despoliatur cocus atque inter duos tortores maestus consistit.*

caedo cocum: cooks were highly valued and expensive to buy (Harcum (1914), 51–7, 62–8, J. C. B. Lowe, *Cl Ant* 4 (1985) 80–3), but in a Roman household – in contrast to New Comedy – they were invariably slaves, and so liable to corporal punishment.

3   flagrorum: the *flagrum*, a cat-o'-nine tails of knotted cord, was the most savage of the implements used for beating slaves, which suggests that

M.'s reaction is excessive. Cf. Hor. *S.* 1.3.117–19, Blümner (1911) 293 n.6, Courtney on Juv. 6.479.

4   uis . . . uapulet: both the paratactic construction and the verb *uapulare* suggest the milieu of Comedy which underlies the epigram.

35   (= 9.25)

'Afer, you exhibit signs of jealousy whenever I gaze at your handsome young waiter. I am merely looking, as is natural: do you expect me to avert my gaze? If you are so jealous that you object even to this innocent behaviour, I suggest you invite only blind men to dinner.'

The physical attractiveness of young male slaves to the average Roman upper-class man is well documented; cf. **52** intro. Handsome young slaves with long hair were often employed as wine waiters (*dantem uina* 1): cf. **57**.6, N–H on Hor. *Carm.* 1.29.8, L. Malten, *Hermes* 53 (1918) 165–8. The choice of a good-looking slave to serve the wine was a means of enhancing the enjoyment of dinner guests (cf. 11.56.11–12 *dum Caecuba miscet, | conuiuas roseo torserat ore puer*). Here, however, the host Afer reacts with jealousy to every admiring glance directed by M. at his waiter Hyllus (for a similar theme, cf. 10.98.5, Strato, *AP* 12.175). The reason for his jealousy must be that Afer avails himself of Hyllus' services not only as waiter but as bed-mate, a practice of which Seneca complains (*Ep.* 47.7, 95.24 *puerorum infelicium greges quos post transacta conuiuia aliae cubiculi contumeliae exspectant*); cf. **52** intro. M. claims that his behaviour is innocent, but Afer's suspicions, one senses, are well founded: M.'s pleading throughout the poem carries an air of disingenuousness: see on 1, 3, 4, 7–8 and 9. Moreover, sexual interest in another's slave was a real possibility: guests sometimes made overtures to a host's slave without the latter's permission (cf. Lucian, *Epist. Sat.* 38, *Symp.* 15), and sexual relations with an *alienus seruus* were formally recognised in law, ranking as *stuprum*, and subject to legal sanctions at the owner's discretion: cf. A. Watson, *Roman slave law* (Baltimore 1987) 61–4.

Further reading: Verstraete (1980), Williams (1995) and (1999)

1   quotiens aspeximus 'whenever I look at'. In view of *auertam* 5, *aspeximus* is best taken as plural for singular, rather than as referring to the assembled guests. The verb is well chosen to suggest that Afer reads lustful feelings into M.'s gaze: cf. Quint. *Decl. min.* 291.2 *alienam matronam aliter, quam leges permittunt, aspexisti, OLD* s.v. 2a.

Hyllum: a common slave name (13 exx. in *CIL* vi), also employed of an attractive young catamite at 4.7. Its use here may have been suggested by a resemblance to Hylas, the boy favourite of Hercules (cf. 7). Slave names, both in M. and in real life, often had erotic associations: cf. Baumgart (1936) 55.

2   lumine ... turbidiore 'with a rather disturbed gaze'. *lumen* ('eye') foreshadows the importance of ocular motifs in the epigram. *turbidus*, a strong term used e.g. of the glance of the maddened Hercules (Sen. *HF* 954), here conveys intense feelings of sexual jealousy: cf. Stat. *Silu.* 3.4.14–15 [Ida] *dedit superis illum* [Ganymede] *quem turbida semper | Iuno uidet refugitque manum nectarque recusat.*

Afer: a name employed several times by M. in satiric contexts, but without any consistency of characterisation. Sometimes borne by men of senatorial rank (Kajanto 205), it is an appropriate sobriquet for a *patronus*, as at 4.37 and 9.6.

notas 'observe', but with a suggestion also of 'censure' or 'reprimand'.

3   quod, rogo, quod scelus est: the insistent form of the question (*quod, rogo, quod*), suggests that M. 'doth protest too much' that Afer's fears are groundless.

mollem: the term is commonly used of *pueri delicati* (e.g. Hor. *Epod.* 11.4, Petr. 97, M. 12.75.4); it suggests the youthful, effeminate appearance which was thought desirable in such slaves and might even be prolonged artificially: cf. Sen. *Ep.* 47.7, *RAC* iv 628 s.v. *effeminatus.*

spectare: cf. 9.59.3 *inspexit molles pueros oculisque comedit.*

**4   M. suggests that he looks on Hyllus with the same respectful admiration as when he looks on the sun etc.; but by mentioning sun and stars first, he deliberately undermines his case: these are common symbols of erotic attractiveness (N–H on Hor. *Carm.* 1.12.48).

**5–6   Is M. to avert his gaze from Hyllus as though from the Gorgon Medusa, a mythical being of such repulsiveness that all who looked on her were changed to stone? It was by turning his head away that Perseus avoided this fate when beheading the Gorgon: cf. Luc. 9.676 *Perseos auersi ... harpen, LIMC* vii 2 *Perseus* figs. 108, 113, 132a, K. Schauenburg, *Perseus in der Kunst des Altertums* (Bonn 1960) 77–82. The best known event involving the Gorgon took place at a banquet (Ov. *Met.* 5); this may have suggested M.'s analogy here.

6   oculos oraque . . . tegam: M. probably has in mind the icono-
graphical motif in which Perseus shows the Gorgon's head to a group of
Satyrs, who not only avert their faces but also shield their eyes with their
hands or arms: see *LIMC* VII 2 *Perseus* figs. 32, 33, 67, 68.

tegam: preferable to the alternative reading *petat*. It balances *auertam*,
and the emphasis is placed, appropriately, on the reaction of the guest.

7–8   In employing mythical *exempla* to reinforce his argument, M. draws
on rhetorical practice; but his use of otherwise unknown aspects of the myths
(see below) to make these relevant to a contemporary situation is especially
reminiscent of Ovid (P. Watson, *CPh* 78 (1983) 117–26). Ovidian too is the
way in which the *exempla* slyly undercut the poet's argument: in the myth
of Hylas, the sight of the boy by the Nymphs resulted in his rape, while
in 8 the pederastically inclined Hermes is obviously a risky playmate for
Jupiter's cup-bearer and boy-love Ganymede. The implication is that Afer's
suspicions may not, after all, be wide of the mark.

7   trux erat Alcides, et Hylan spectare licebat: despite his notoriously prickly temper, Hercules allowed others to look at his boy-love
without reacting as Afer does. *trux* is used of persons with a difficult or
violent disposition: cf. Stat. *Theb.* 11.46–7 *trux . . .* | *Amphitryoniades*, Ov. *Ars*
2.186. The detail is almost certainly invented by M. and clearly disingenuous, given Hercules' penchant for violence when his sexual desires were
thwarted.

Alcides 'grandson of Alceus', a common poetic appellation of Hercules.
et = *et tamen* (*OLD* 14a).
Hylan: a boy loved by Hercules, who was inconsolable when he was
carried off by the Nymphs: cf. Ap. Rhod. *Arg.* 1.1207–72, Theoc. 13, Prop.
1.20, Virg. *Ecl.* 6. 43–4.

8   ludere Mercurio cum Ganymede licet: *ludere* suggests the
well-known theme of Ganymede playing at knucklebones with the child
Eros: cf. Ap. Rhod. *Arg.* 3.115–18, with Hunter. Ganymede's innocuous
playmate is replaced by the potential sexual predator Mercury, known for
his ithyphallicism (cf. Callim. *Iamb.* 9) and depicted on an Attic vase in
pursuit of a boy, identified by Beazley as Ganymede (cf. *ARV* 530, 26).

Ganymede: mentioned because, like Hyllus, he combined the function of cup-bearer and boy-love: cf. **12.**7n., **57.**6n.

9   teneros spectet: the third occurrence of *spectare* in seven lines.
M. protests overmuch.

10   Phineas...Oedipodas 'men like Phineus and Oedipus' i.e. blind men. For the generalising plural, see **6**.1n. Oedipus, whose self-blinding formed the finale of Sophocles' *OT*, is an *exemplum* of a sightless man. Phineus was a Thracian prophet who was robbed of his eyesight by the gods for reasons which are variously reported. Similarly in *AP* 12.175, Strato sarcastically suggests to a host who likewise resents his guests looking admiringly at his pretty slave boys, that he should go drinking with the blind Teiresias.

inuites 'I suggest you invite': mock-polite subjunctive of exhortation.

36   (= 12.48)

'If you serve me expensive foodstuffs as though this were ordinary fare and without any expectation that these are what I fancy, well and good. But if you think you will be written in as my heir on account of a few Lucrine oysters, I no longer wish to accept your hospitality. The meals which you provide are sumptuous, I allow. But the pleasure which these afford is short-lived, with gastric upsets as their immediate consequences, and in time afflictions such as jaundice and gout. On these terms not even the most magnificent sacral dinners are worth it, and the finest of wines would taste like cheap plonk. Choose others to lure into testamentary dispositions with your magnificent repasts. I would rather have an impromptu and plain dinner with a friend, one such as I can afford to reciprocate.'

This poem combines, not altogether seamlessly, two themes, that of captation, and an attack on the ruinous consequences of luxurious dining. The *captator* had a number of schemes for enticing his prey (see on **58**). These included the provision of sumptuous dinners: cf. Petr. 125.2, Juv. 5.98–106, 6.38–40. Of particular note are Juvenal's ironic remarks at 4.18–21 concerning Crispinus' purchase of a gigantic mullet, *consilium laudo artificis, si munere tanto | praecipuam in tabulis ceram senis abstulit orbi. | est ratio ulterior, magnae si misit amicae, | quae uehitur clauso latis specularibus antro.* The old and childless Polystratus enjoyed at the hands of legacy-hunters 'wine with a fine bouquet and a table that surpassed even those of Sicily' (Lucian, *Dial. mort.* 19.2); cf. Plut. *De am. prol.* 497 c.

   The second main theme of the epigram, that of luxury foodstuffs, draws freely on dietetic theory as expounded in medical and philosophical texts as well as literary works coloured by philosophical thought. A key tenet of such writings, which underlies the whole epigram, is that luxury foodstuffs and gluttony are injurious to one's health: cf. Musonius 18a–b ('On food') *apud* C. E. Lutz, *YClS* 10 (1947) 112–21, *Epicurea* ed. Usener 465, Lucian, *Cyn.* 9, Plut. *Conu. sept. sap.* 160A, Sen. *Ep.* 95.25, Col. *praef.* 1.16–17. And not only was culinary self-indulgence considered injurious to the health over the long term, inflicting diseases such as gout and jaundice (9–10 nn.), but its pleasures were short-lived and intestinal retribution inevitable, an idea graphically expressed in lines 5–10: cf. Plut. *De san. tuend.* 125E, Crates preached eating plain food 'and in general not going beyond cress and olives to omelettes and fish, thereby putting the body at odds with itself from satiety and causing it derangements and diarrhoea', nn. on 5–10.

Further reading: Kier (1933), Vischer (1965)

1–2   Boletos et aprum si tamquam uilia ponis | et non esse putas haec mea uota 'if you serve these delicacies not *as* delicacies, but as your ordinary fare, and not because you fancy that these are what I particularly desire'.

1   Boletos: 32.12n.

aprum: wild boar, *animal propter conuiuia natum* (Juv. 1.141), was another delicacy, much favoured under the Empire (Plin. *NH* 8.210, Blümner (1911) 175–6); cf. **32.**4n.

tamquam uilia: the adjective is used of food that is 'cheap' and hence 'plain' or 'ordinary': cf. Hor. *S.* 2.2.15 *sperne cibum uilem*, 9.26.6 *appetitur posito uilis oliua lupo*, Vischer (1965) 27–9.

2   uota: things prayed i.e. wished for: cf. 1.55.1 *uota tui breuiter si uis cognoscere Marci*, Juv. 5.18.

uolo 'well and good' (SB). The verb additionally suggests the guest's response, *uolo*, to the host's invitation to avail himself of the food on offer, expressed in the form *uis?* or *uisne?* Cf. Juv. 5.135–6 *da Trebio! pone ad Trebium! uis frater ab ipsis | ilibus?*

3–4   si . . . heres | uis scribi propter quinque Lucrina: the real purpose behind the host's provision of sumptuous dinners.

heres | . . . scribi: the technical phrase for entering someone in one's will as heir was *aliquem heredem scribere*: cf. *Vocabularium iurisprudentiae Romanae, V* (Berlin 1939) 280–5, Hor. *S.* 2.5.48–9 *ut et scribare secundus* [substitute] | *heres*. In the absence of *sui heredes*, i.e. persons e.g. children whom he was expected to name as heirs in his will, the *testator* would appoint one or more *extranei heredes* from among his friends, clients, patrons and so on. Cf. Champlin (1991) 103–54.

3   si fortunatum me fieri me credis: usually translated 'but if you think I am becoming rich'. But the logic of the passage is better served by explaining 'but if you think I am made happy thereby' (and will therefore be more accommodating of your testamentary aspirations). Cf. *AP* 9.643.7–8 'do you gratify your mouth with foodstuffs, reckoning these to be good fortune (εὐτυχία)?', Lucian, *Conuiu.* 22.

4   propter quinque Lucrina: according to Diocletian's edict on prices (*CIL* III suppl. 5.6) oysters were sold by the hundred, and we read of persons devouring that number or even four times more at a single sitting (Juv. 8.85–6, SHA *Clod. Alb.* 11.4). So *quinque Lucrina* may carry the implication of 'a *mere* five oysters'.

Lucrina: oysters from the Lucrine Lake near Baiae, which were especially prized (Hor. *Epod.* 2.49, 6.11.5, 13.82, Plin. *NH* 9.168). For oysters as luxury food, cf. **32.**7 n.

5–10   A slightly awkward change of tack. Having in lines 1–2 tacitly conceded his interest in luxury foods, M. proceeds to condemn the pleasure which they give as ephemeral, and the foods as injurious to the health.

5–6   sed cras | nil erit, immo hodie, protinus immo nihil: an elegant example of *climax* (*gradatio*), which often involves three cola, but in poetic texts rarely more than one overlapping word: cf. however Prop. 2.1.47–8 *laus in amore mori; laus altera, si datur uno | posse frui. fruar o solus amore meo!* Cf. Wills (1996) 329–36.

5   lauta: often of sumptuous food and drink. Cf. Kay on 11.31.20 and Fest. 104.9 L *lautitia epularum magnificentia*.

fateor: for the paratactic use see **31.**1 n.

6   protinus . . . nihil: a gastric upset will be the immediate consequence of eating such rich (*lautissima*) foodstuffs. At the conclusion of Lucian's *Conuiuium* the guests, who have eaten and drunk too well, 'were led off to bed, most of them vomiting in the streets'. Cf. Sen. *Ep.* 108.15, (exotic foods such as oysters and *boleti* are *facile descensura, facile reditura*).

7–8 expands graphically on *protinus nihil*. The *lautissima cena* of 5 will shortly be excreted, vomited up or voided as urine.

7 quod sciat infelix damnatae spongia uirgae: the rich repast will provoke an attack of diarrhoea, necessitating the use of the *xylospongium* (see below). Attacks on the consequences of gluttony sometimes adopt an even more drastically scatological tone than this: cf. *AP* 9.642.1–6 (on a public toilet in Myrina) 'All the luxury of mortals and their expensive foodstuffs being here excreted has lost its previous charm. For the pheasants and the fish and . . . all those meretricious concoctions of food here become dung. And the bowels rid themselves of everything that a hungry gullet received,' Clem. Alex. *Paed.* 3.7. Defecation has contemptuous associations (Fehling (1974) 34) which M. exploits to the detriment of the *captator*-host.

quod sciat: cf. Catull. 29.18–9 *secunda praeda Pontica, inde tertia | Hibera, quam scit amnis aurifer Tagus.* The personification is reinforced by *infelix* and *damnatae.*

damnatae spongia uirgae: i.e. the *xylospongium*, a communal sponge attached to the end of a stick which was used to wipe oneself after defecation: cf. Sen. *Ep.* 70.20 *ibi lignum id quod ad emundanda obscena adhaerente spongia positum est, P. Mich.* 471.29, Ar. *Ran.* 479–90. It was presumably rinsed ready for the next user in the trough of running water which was attached to most public latrines. On ancient sanitary practices, see R. Neudecker, *Die Pracht der Latrine* (München 1994) 10, 17.

damnatae: mock-solemn, 'doomed' (SB).

8 quicumque canis 'any dog which happens along'. Schrevel correctly explained (*canes*) *qui ad uomitum accurrunt*: cf. OT *Proverbs* 26.11 'like a dog returning to his vomit is a stupid man who repeats his folly', Plin. *NH* 8.106 (of a hyena) *uomitionem hominis imitari ad sollicitandas canes quos inuadat.* Some think that the allusion is to dogs feeding on excrement (cf. 1.83, Phaedr. 1.27.11, and Scobie (1986) 407–22 for the filthy state of Rome's streets), but since M. specifies urine and excrement elsewhere in the couplet, vomit is the logical subject of reference here. Nausea and vomiting are often mentioned in the context of over-indulgence: cf. Plut. *De san. tuend.* 126e–127a, Cic. *Phil.* 2.63, Sen. *Ep.* 95.29, 6n.

iunctaque testa uiae: the wine imbibed at dinner will be voided into the large amphorae with a broken neck (*uasa curta*) which were placed in the public streets by fullers for use by passers-by: cf. Titin. *apud* Macrob. *Sat.* 3.16.5, 6.93.1–2. Fullers, whose job involved the cleaning of dirty clothing, made extensive use of urine, with its alkaline and cleansing properties: cf. Isid. *Orig.* 11.1.138, R. D. Brown, *HSCPh* 96 (1994) 195. For a clear account of the fullers' trade, see O. Jahn, *ASG* 12 (1862) 305–11.

9–10 These lines primarily indicate the consequences of gormandising on luxury foodstuffs, but also reflect the widespread belief that the consumption of flesh was especially injurious to the health: cf. Harcum, *CW* 12 (1918–19) 58–61 and 66–8, J. Haussleiter, *Der Vegetarismus in der Antike* (Berlin 1935) 140–4.

9 **mullorum:** red mullet. Thompson (1947) 264–8 distinguishes two types, of which the smaller, *mullus barbatus*, is the commoner form in the Mediterranean. Galen 6.715 Kühn (justifiably) describes it as 'superior to other fish in the pleasure which comes from eating it'. Mullet is often included by M. in lists of luxury foodstuffs; cf. 3.77.1, 7.78.3 *sumen, aprum, leporem, boletos, ostrea, mullos.*

leporum: on this delicacy, see **32**.5n.

suminis: sow's udder, another noted Roman delicacy: cf. Kay on 11.52.13. In this unwholesome context, M. may have intended his readers to think of the conspicuously unsanitary way in which the dish was procured (Plut. *De esu carn.* 997A).

exitus 'outcome' with a concomitant pun on the sense 'evacuation': cf. Cael. Aurel. *Cel. pass.* 2.24 *inuoluntario exitu stercorum siue urinae.*

10 **sulphureusque color:** not simply a reference to the sallow colour caused by over-indulgence (Hor. *S.* 2.2.21 with Muecke). The vivid and unusual *sulphureus* suggests that M. has in mind the yellow tinge of jaundice, a disease which was blamed on excessive eating and drinking: cf. Hippoc. *Morb. int.* 37 (7.258 Littré) 'jaundice . . . comes about particularly from surfeit of food and drunkenness, and chilly weather. Then the body immediately changes hue and becomes sallow', Sen. *Ep.* 95.15–16, D. Baumann, *Janus* 35 (1931) 153–68, 185–206.

carnificesque pedes 'feet which torture you', a striking expression for the agonies of gout, widely believed to be the consequence of gastronomic excess, and often referred to as excruciating (see **73**.7n.). The metaphor of torture is often applied to physical suffering: cf. Fantham (1972) 84, 101 and 128. *carnifices pedes* may however conceal a more specific image. One of the tasks of the *carnifex* was to oversee the driving of nails into the feet of persons who were being crucified: cf. Plaut. *Most.* 359–60 *ego dabo ei talentum primus qui in crucem excucurrerit:* | *sed ea lege ut offigantur bis pedes, bis bracchia,* M. Hengel, *Crucifixion* (London 1977) 31; J. Blinzler, *Der Prozess Jesu* (4th ed., Regensburg 1969) 377–9. The expression 'feet which torture you' may thus assimilate the pangs of gout to the pain experienced by those whose feet had been nailed to a cross by order of the *carnifices.*

11–12   Even the most sumptuous repasts imaginable would not be worth the costs to health detailed in the preceding lines.

11   Albana ... comissatio: Domitian's annual celebration of the *Quinquatria* or *Quinquatrus* at his Alban villa from 19 to 23 March in honour of Minerva (Suet. *Dom.* 4). *comissatio*, 'revel', suggests the idea of excess, and although the festival is nowhere else associated with luxurious feasting, both the lesser *Quinquatrus* (17 June) and Nero's celebration of the *Quinquatria* incorporated a *conuiuium* (Suet. *Ner.* 34.2, Tac. *Ann.* 14.4), while Varro's *Quinquatrus* (*Men.* 440–8) treats of feasting and digestion. Moreover, Domitian apparently celebrated the *Quinquatria* 'in grand style' (Dio. Cass. 67.1–2).

12   nec Capitolinae ... dapes: the *epulum Iouis in Capitolio* in honour of the Capitoline Triad Jupiter, Juno and Minerva, celebrated on 13 November and, in Imperial times, on 13 September in conjunction with the *Ludi Romani*. The whole senate participated in the banquet, which was sumptuous (Plaut. *Trin.* 468–73). Cf. Marquardt, *Staatsverwaltung* III 384–9, 498.

   pontificumque dapes: Roman pontifical feasts were notoriously lavish: cf. Hor. *Carm.* 2.14.28, 1.37.2 with N–H, Macrob. *Sat.* 3.13.13 *iam luxuria tunc accusaretur quando tot rebus farta fuit cena pontificum.*

13–14   To one suffering the effects of over-indulgence, even the finest fare brings no pleasure, a common idea: cf. Hor. *S.* 2.2.21–2, Plut. *De san. tuend.* 126D.

13   imputet ... fiet: *imputet = si imputet.* For the mixed conditional, see **15**.5–6n. *imputare* is properly 'to set down something to someone's account', but sometimes, as here, means little more than 'bestow': cf. 4.82.1–2 *hos quoque commenda Venuleio, Rufe, libellos | imputet et nobis otia parua roga.*

   deus: indefinite, 'a god', as at Hor. *Epod.* 14.6 *deus deus nam me uetat.*

   nectar: as the drink of the gods *ipso facto* delicious. Even this would be spoiled if the beneficiary were not in a condition to enjoy it.

   acetum: literally wine gone sour, is a disparaging term for a cheap and unpalatable vintage: cf. Hor. *S.* 2.3.115–17 *si positis intus Chii ueterisque Falerni | mille cadis ... acre | potet acetum*, Pers. 4.32.

14   et Vaticani perfida uappa cadi: Vatican wine is elsewhere mentioned by M. in unflattering terms: cf. 10.45.5 *Vaticana bibas, si delectaris aceto*, 1.18.2 with Howell. M. Johnston, *CW* 21 (1928) 128 quotes from the

New York Times the following: 'Leo XIII . . . was the last Pope to try to grow wine grapes on the slopes of the Vatican Gardens . . . The result was an acidulous vintage which the obsequious courtiers pronounced delicious, but they could hardly avoid making wry faces when drinking it.'

perfida: because its insipidity is not apparent until drunk.

uappa: flat and insipid wine: cf. Ps.-Acro on Hor. *S.* 1.2.12 *uappa proprie dicitur, quod nec uinum nec acetum*, C. Seltman, *Wine in the ancient world* (London 1957) 152.

15–18   'Select others to ensnare with your sumptuous dinners. I would rather have an unpretentious meal with a genuine friend.'

15   cenarum . . . magister: for the term, cf. *CIL* XIV 2112 cols. 2.8–9 and 14–16 *magistri cenarum ex ordine albi facti quo ordine homines quaterni ponere debeb[unt] uini boni amphoras singulas et panes . . . et sardas [numero] quattuor, strationem, caldam cum ministerio*. The expression is apparently adapted from the familiar *magister bibendi*, who determined the strength of the drinks at a *conuiuium*.

16   quos capiant: the legacy-hunter 'captures' or 'ensnares' his prey: cf. Hor. *Ep.* 1.1.77–9 *sunt qui | frustis et pomis uiduas uenentur auaras, | excipiantque senes quos in uiuaria mittant.*

mensae regna superba tuae 'the proud domain of your table', a sarcastic way of characterising the prandial sumptuousness of the *captator*'s repast. *regna* reflects usages like *rex mensae* (Macrob. *Sat.* 2.13), of the host, and βασιλεύς lit. 'king', of the symposiarch (Plut. *Q. conuiu.* 622A, Lucian, *Conuiu.* 4), *superba* the fact that *superbia* was a defining characteristic of *reges*: **12.**4n.

17   subitas 'impromptu, improvised'. Cf. Suet. *Claud.* 21.4 *ad subitam condictamque cenulam inuitare se populum.*

ofellas: according to K. M. Dunbabin, *CR* 49 (1935) 10, *ofellae =* (pork) cutlets, but the sense is much too restrictive here, and must rather be 'morsels' (*CGL* v 228.38 s.v.), or 'potluck': cf. Mayor on Juv. 11.142–4 *nec frustum capreae subducere nec latus Afrae | nouit auis noster, tirunculus ac rudis omni | tempore et exiguae furtis imbutus ofellae.*

18   haec mihi quam possum reddere cena placet: i.e. nothing fancy or expensive. *quam possum reddere* is a sly hint that the *captator*'s attempts to land M. are misconceived.

37 (= 1.102)

'The painter who painted your Venus, Lycoris, meant, I'm sure, to flatter Minerva.'

Commentators usually explain this epigram as a satire against an incompetent painter, comparing 5.40 *pinxisti Venerem, colis, Artemidore, Mineruam:* | *et miraris opus displicuisse tuum?* On this view, M. ironically affects to believe that an ugly picture of Venus was a deliberate attempt by the painter to gratify Minerva, who is flattered (*blanditus est Mineruae*) to find herself more beautiful than her successful rival in the Judgement of Paris. There is, however, a crucial difference between 5.40 and 1.102: the former is addressed to an artist, the latter to a *meretrix*, Lycoris, a name used elsewhere by M. in connexion with physical defects (3.39, 4.62.1, 7.13.2). Given this fact, and M.'s propensity to attack females, especially of this class, the present epigram is better read as an attack on Lycoris, who has served as the model for her portrait of Venus. But unlike two other notable courtesans, the famous beauty Phryne who was the model for the painter Apelles' celebrated *Aphrodite anadyomene* (Ath. 590f), and the homonymous Cytheris/Lycoris (1 n.), M.'s Lycoris is decidedly unattractive. Hence any representation of Venus based on her must seem, the poet sarcastically suggests, like a deliberate attempt on the painter's part to flatter Minerva by overturning the Judgement of Paris.

Further reading: Citroni on 1.102, Durand (1946), Gilbert (1882), L. and P. Watson (1996) 586–8

1   tuam: not only because the portrait of Venus belongs to Lycoris, but also because she was the patron deity of *meretrices*, who decorated their houses with representations of the goddess (Gilbert (1882) 364).

   Lycori: the unusual name is borrowed from Cornelius Gallus, who used it as the pseudonym for his mistress, the courtesan and freedwoman Volumnia-Cytheris: cf. Nisbet (1979) 148, 152–4. Her name thus establishes by implication Lycoris' profession. In contrast to M.'s addressee, the original Lycoris was a beauty: cf. Prop. 2.34.91–2, 8.73.6 *ingenium Galli pulchra Lycoris erat.*

2   blanditus ... est Mineruae: a painter might have flattered Minerva because she was the patroness of all artists (Ov. *Fast.* 3.831–4).

puto: used ironically: see *OLD* s.v. 8. The parenthesis lends emphasis to the word.

38   (= 3.76)

'Bassus, you are aroused by elderly females but disdain young ones. It is not the beautiful woman, but one on the threshold of death who attracts you. Is not this utter madness, to be able to do it with a Hecuba, but not an Andromache?'

This quatrain mocks the perverse sexual tastes of Bassus, which express themselves in a striking paradox: indifference to young beautiful women and lust for old ones, who were routinely asserted in classical antiquity to be *ipso facto* sexually unattractive. Examples include the scene of the *Ecclesiazusae* where three women, depicted by Aristophanes as hags, compete for the attentions of a young man in face of the more potent charms of a young girl (878–1111), the sneer directed to an elderly *hetaira* 'for I see that your desire outruns the realities of your age' (*AP* 6.47.6) and Horace's jeering *fis anus, et tamen | uis formosa uideri . . . et cantu tremulo pota Cupidinem | lentum sollicitas* (*Carm.* 4.13.2–6). M. often exploits the theme, e.g. 7.75 *uis futui gratis, cum sis deformis anusque. | res perridicula est,* 10.90.7–8.

In describing a woman as a *uetula*, M. is not using the same terms of reference as today: not only is considerable satiric exaggeration involved, but various factors contributed to a cultural perception of a woman as 'old' who would not be so described nowadays – the early age of marriage, poorer overall quality of health and a far lower life expectancy. In M., as elsewhere, the unattractiveness of ageing females is normally asserted in the context of attacks on lust-crazed old women. Here by contrast the sexual ageism merely provides the backcloth to the epigram, in which the emphasis falls on the perversity of Bassus' erotic preferences.

The poem is tightly structured, each line consisting of two antithetical phrases. In three out of four verses the antitheses are reaffirmed by internal rhyme of semantically opposed words (*uetulas . . . puellas, formosa . . . moritura, Hecaben . . . Andromachen*).

Further reading: Watson (1994)

1   Arrigis ad: the verb is frequent in M., generally as here with ellipse of *penem*. For the construction with *ad*, cf. 4.5.6 *nec potes algentes arrigere ad uetulas.*

fastidis: commonly used of sexual or amatory disdain: cf. Virg. *Ecl.* 2.73 *inuenies alium, si te hic fastidit, Alexin,* Petr. 127.1.

Basse: the target of a number of M.'s scoptic epigrams. It may not be irrelevant in an epigram on penile perversity that *basus* is a vulgar form of *uas,* 'phallus' (Adams, *LSV* 42–3).

2   moritura: in sexual invective older women are often described hyperbolically as close to death or even as already dead: cf. Nicharchus, *AP* 11.71.4 'now she should be seeking not a husband, but a tomb', Hor. *Carm.* 3.15.4 *maturo propior...funeri,* M. 3.93.23–8.

placet 'finds favour with you sexually', cf. 3.70.3 *cur aliena placet tibi, quae tua non placet, uxor?*

3   hic...haec: like other Latin poets, M. is given to anaphora of *hic:* cf. Ov. *Fast.* 2.774 *hic color, haec facies, hic decor oris erat,* 6.68.5–6, 10.66.3–4, R. Wöbbeking, 'De anaphorae apud poetas latinos usu' (Dissertation Marburg 1910) 24–30.

hic, rogo, non furor est?:   cf. **78**.2.

mentula demens: the penis is often treated as having an existence of its own: cf. Hor. *S.* 1.2.68–9, M. 9.37.9–10 *promittis sescenta tamen; sed mentula surda est,* | *et sis lusca licet, te tamen illa uidet,* 11.19.2, G. Giangrande, *MPhL* 1 (1975) 140, *QUCC* 21 (1976) 45 n.4. The expression *mentula demens* may have been suggested not only by the sound-play, but also by Greek θύμος, 'penis' (Hipponax, fr. 10 W) and θυμός 'mind'.

mentula: the archetypal obscenity, used some forty-nine times by M.: cf. Kay on 11.15.10, Adams, *LSV* 9–12.

4   cum possis: sc. *futuere.* Cf. 3.32.1–2 *'non possum uetulam?',* quaeris, *Matrinia: possum* | *et uetulam, sed tu mortua, non uetula es,* J. N. Adams, *Phoenix* 35 (1981) 122.

Hecaben: Hecuba, an archetype of extreme age, stands for the type of the elderly ugly female: cf. *AP* 11.408.5–6 'rouge and white lead will never make Hecuba into Helen', M. 3.32.3.

Andromachen: opposed to her mother-in-law Hecuba as an icon of youthful beauty (cf. Dares Phrygius 12, Roscher I 344). The opposition (cf. 10.90.6) may be original to M.: contrast between Hecuba and Helen is more common; cf. J. Mossman, *Wild justice. A study of Euripides' Hecuba* (Oxford 1995) 211–17.

39   (= 4.20)

'Caerellia pretends to be an old woman, although young, Gellia to be a young one, although old. Each is in her own way insufferable.'

This short symmetrical piece seems to have drawn its inspiration from an epigram of (?) Papinius *apud* Var. *L.* 7.28 *ridiculum est cum te cascam tua dicit amica,* | *fili Potoni, sesquisenex puerum.* | *dic rusum pusam: sic fiet 'mutua muli.'* | *nam uere pusus tu, tua amica senex,* in which the superannuated girlfriend of the boyish 'son of Potonius' is jeered at for trying to gloss over the disparity in their respective ages by calling her lover *casca*, 'old'. To even things up, the poet ironically suggests, the young man ought to call his elderly beloved *pusa*, 'a little girl'.

Each epigram deals with two parties whose respective ages are deliberately misrepresented, young becoming old and old young. In each the vehicle for the joke is a strikingly colloquial term, *pusus/a* in Papinius' case and *pupa* in M.'s. In addition, length and metre are the same, and there are verbal resemblances too (*ridiculus, dicit*). There are, however, major differences between M. and his model. In M. the two principals are female. Nor does he offer any motive for the ladies' inversion of their age, whereas in the earlier epigram the purpose of the misrepresentation can easily be inferred: to disguise the asymmetry in years between the two lovers, a phenomenon which attracted widespread disapprobation: cf. Watson (1994) 71–2.

Further reading: Ferraro (1988)

1   Dicit se uetulam, cum sit Caerellia pupa: Caerellia's claim seems unmotivated, so line 1 may function merely as a counterbalance to 2, where Gellia does have a plausible motive for misrepresenting her age (see *ad loc.*). If there is a reason for Caerellia's actions, it could be either that older women were considered less inhibited sexual partners because of their greater experience (*AP* 11.73, [Lucian], *Amores* 25, Ov. *Ars* 2.675–80), or that Caerellia, like the girl in Papinius' epigram, is attempting to cloak an embarrassing gap in years between herself and an older lover.

Dicit se uetulam: Caerellia absurdly applies to herself the term which is elsewhere used as an insulting designation for an ageing female.

Caerellia: the Caerellii were a plebeian family. The best known female member of the clan was a woman who was close to Cicero in his later years and, some said, his lover (*RE* III 1284).

pupa: lit. a female doll (*CGL* v 622.35), such as girls played with and dedicated to Venus prior to their marriage. From these associations *pupa* becomes a colloquial word for *puella*: cf. Auson. 17.4.2 Green, *CIL* iv 6842 *si quis non uidi(t) Venerem quam . . . pupa(m) mea(m) aspiciat*, R. Danese, *Stud Urb* B3 LIX (1986) 47–57, J. Kepartvocá, *LF* 106 (1983) 187–8.

2   pupam se dicit Gellia, cum sit anus: whereas it is highly anomalous for a young girl to masquerade as old, ageing women often, in satiric texts, attempt to pass themselves off as younger than their years, in order to appear still sexually attractive: cf. Brecht (1930) 62–3, Howell intro. to 1.19. M. was especially fond of the topic: e.g. 1.100 *mammas atque tatas habet Afra, sed ipsa tatarum | dici et mammarum maxima mamma potest.*

Gellia: the name appears a number of times in M., always in satiric contexts. 3.55, mocking a Gellia for excessive use of perfumes, suggests that here too Gellia represents an ageing belle striving to remain attractive: *uetulae* attempting to disguise their years often resorted to an over-liberal use of cosmetics (cf. Plaut. *Most.* 274–7).

3   ferre nec hanc possis, possis . . . nec illam 'one can't abide either one or the other', generalising second person subjunctive (Woodcock §119). Postponement of the second *nec* effects a chiasmus, a feature which normally extends, as in 1–2, over two or more verses (Wills (1996), index s.v.). For another exception cf. 2.3.1 *Sexte, nihil debes, nil debes, Sexte, fatemur.*

nec: originally less elevated than *neque* (LHS 451–2), the form is usual in post-Augustan poetry (Axelson (1945) 115–18).

Colline: the only other reference to him in M. is 4.54, where he is said to have been victorious in Domitian's Capitoline contest – probably in AD 86 (*RE* IV 481, *PIR* s.v.).

4   altera ridicula est, altera putidula: the first must be Caerellia, since *putidula* is more appropriately applied to the aged Gellia: see following n.

putidula: a belittling diminutive (cf. J. Hanssen, *Latin diminutives* (Bergen 1951) 136–49), apparently a Martialian coinage to balance *ridicula*: for a similar effect, cf. Catull. 12.16–17 *haec amem necesse est | ut Veraniolum meum et Fabullum.* The meaning is either 'disgusting' (cf. F. Skutsch, *Kleine Schriften* (Leipzig 1914/Hildesheim 1967) 393–6) or 'tiresome' (cf. Cic. *Att.* 1.14.1 *uereor ne putidum sit scribere . . . quam sim occupatus*). In either event, *putidula* also suggests that the elderly Gellia is 'disintegrating' with age: cf. Hor. *Epod.* 8.1 *rogare longo putidam te saeculo, Priap.* 57.2, Ussher on Ar. *Eccl.* 884.

40   (= 8.54)

'Catulla, most beautiful but also most worthless of all the women who have ever lived, if only you were less beautiful or more chaste!'

This epigram is one of several where M. pays homage to his predecessor Catullus. The piece is replete with Catullan reminiscences in its metre (1 n.), thought and language: indeed every word in the poem is used by Catullus (see below). Also Catullan is the pronounced chiasmus in line 4: cf. Paukstadt (1876) 31. The significantly named *amica* to whom the poem is addressed, at once beautiful and faithless, is modelled upon Catullus' Lesbia, who exhibited the same combination of qualities.

Further reading: Paukstadt (1876) 27, 31, Schulze (1887) 637

1   Formosissima quae fuere uel sunt recalls the opening of three Catullan poems, 21, 24 and esp. 49, which similarly begins with a superlative in the vocative: *disertissime Romuli nepotum, | quot sunt quotque fuere, Marce Tulli, | quotque post aliis erunt in annis.* All these pieces are, like the present epigram, in hendecasyllables, a favourite metre of Catullus and especially associated with him by M.

formosissima: a subjective word, frequent in erotic contexts, describing not just physical beauty but also sexual attractiveness: cf. Catull. 86.5–6 *Lesbia formosa est, quae cum pulcherrima tota est, | tum omnibus una omnis surripuit Veneres.* On *-osus* terminations, see P. E. Knox, *Glotta* 64 (1986) 90–101. Superlative adjectives are a Catullan mannerism: that *formosus* and *uilis*, common in M., appear only here in the superlative points to deliberate imitation of C.

quae = *earum quae*, the personal pronoun being omitted before a relative in a different case; cf. Nep. *Di.* 9.5 *miseranda uita [eorum] qui se metui quam amari malunt.*

sunt: the monosyllabic ending of this and the following verse is reminiscent of Catullus, who has 17 examples in his hendecasyllabics: such endings are rare in the epigrams of M. which use this metre: cf. Ferguson (1970) 175.

2   uilissima: *uilis* characterises the unfaithful Lesbia at Catull. 72.5–6.

3   o quam: *o* is very common in Catullus; for exclamatory *quam* cf. Catull. 31.4. *quam te libenter quamque laetus inuiso.*

fieri is also used by Catullus in the context of a change in character: cf. 73.1–2, 75.3–4 *ut iam nec bene uelle queat tibi, si optima fias,* | *nec desistere amare, omnia si facias.*

4 formosam minus aut magis pudicam: cf. Ov. *Am.* 3.11.41 *aut formosa fores minus aut minus improba uellem.* If the lady's beauty were diminished she would become less attractive to M., so that her failure to be faithful to one lover (*pudica*) would no longer be an issue for him.

minus ... magis: for the contrast cf. Catull. 72.8 *cogit amare magis, sed bene uelle minus.*

41 (= 10.68)

'Although your home is neither Ephesus nor Rhodes, nor Mitylene, but the very heart of Rome, although your parents are of good old Italian stock, you use Greek endearments on every occasion – you, a native-born Roman! Such language belongs to the bedroom – and the bedroom of whores at that. Overtly sexual movements could not be more arousing. Yet even if you master all the Greek erotic vocabulary, Laelia, you can never become a Lais.'

An attack on Laelia, a Roman *matrona*, for her affectation of Greek endearments. Such language, objects M., is more suited to a prostitute than to a well-bred Roman lady. Appropriate speech was one of the virtues of a woman (cf. *CIL* I 1211.7 *sermone lepido, tum autem incessu commodo, CLE* 1988.4). Certain categories of language were regarded as inappropriate for *matronae* because they were sexually titillating. The prohibition applied not only to basic Latin obscenities (**85**.8n.; cf. 5.2, 11.2, 15) but also to Greek terms of affection: cf. Juv. 6.196–7 *quod enim non excitet inguen* | *uox blanda et nequam? digitos habet,* an attack on a *matrona* who uses expressions like ζωὴ καὶ ψυχή. Conversely, Ovid recommends precisely such language to the *meretrices* whom he purports to advise in the *Ars*: cf. 3.795–6 *nec blandae uoces iucundaque murmura cessent* | *nec taceant mediis improba uerba iocis.*

1 Ephesos ... Rhodos ... Mitylene: mentioned because the cities of Eastern Greece, like Corinth (11 n.), were known for their loose lifestyle, and language such as Laelia employs would be more at home there. The use of the Greek, rather than the Latin, terminations of the three place-names prepares for the attack on Laelia's use of Greek vocabulary.

2   sed domus in uico . . . Patricio: the *uicus Patricius*, mentioned also at 7.73.2, lay between the Esquiline and Viminal hills. It derived its name from the patricians reputedly settled there by the early king Servius Tullius, and was one of the oldest and most important streets in the city. Laelia's residence there suggests that she is Roman through and through.

Laelia: chosen not only as a typical name for a Roman *matrona* (cf. 5.75), but also for the sake of the alliterative joke in the last line.

3–4   The provenance of Laelia's parents establishes her as of pure Italian stock. *cum tibi sit* must be supplied with both *mater* and *pater*.

3   coloratis . . . Etruscis: the Etruscans, suntanned through labour in the fields, symbolised the quintessential Italian qualities of hard work and impeccable virtue. Cf. Virg. *G.* 2.533 (on just such a lifestyle) *sic fortis Etruria creuit.*

numquam lita: middle, 'who never smeared herself' sc. with cosmetics; the detail complements *coloratis*. Cosmetics, used by sophisticated women to improve the complexion (Ov. *Med.* 97–8), were widely regarded as betokening an unhealthy interest in sex: cf. Sen. *Dial.* 12.16.4 *non faciem coloribus ac lenociniis polluisti*, B. Grillet, *Les femmes et les fards* (Lyon 1975) 97–106. Laelia's virtuous mother will have none of them.

4   durus: suggests a sturdy rustic (cf. Virg. *G.* 2.531 *corporaque agresti nudant praedura palaestra*), the male equivalent of the exemplary woman of 3: cf. Ov. *Ars* 3.109–10 *si fuit Andromache tunicas induta valentes, | quid mirum? duri militis uxor erat.*

Aricina de regione: Aricia, in the Alban hills, was a pre-Roman settlement named after the mother of Hippolytus' son Virbius, who appears among the followers of Turnus at Virg. *A.* 7.761–2. As an ancient provincial town, it could be used to symbolise old-fashioned morality: cf. Cic. *Phil.* 3.15 *Aricinum . . . uetustate antiquissimum . . . splendore municipum honestissimum.* Cf. **64**.10n.

5   κύριέ μου, μέλι μου, ψυχή μου 'my lord, my honey, my soul'. A common type of endearment (cf. Heliodor. 8.6.4 ζωὴν καὶ φῶς καὶ ψυχήν, Plaut. *Bacch.* 17–18 *cor meum, spes mea, | mel meum*); here in Greek, the language of love: cf. Juv. 6.195 ζωὴ καὶ ψυχή, Brown on Lucr. 4.1160–9, P. Boyancé, *REL* 34 (1956) 125–6.

congeris usque: Laelia heaps Greek forms of endearment upon all and sundry, instead of confining them to the bedroom: cf. Juv. 6.196, where a woman uses sexually charged Grecisms *in turba*.

6 pro pudor!: a common expression of disapproval: cf. Sen. *Dial.* 11.17.4 *pro pudor imperii.*

Hersiliae ciuis et Egeriae: as a 'fellow-citizen of Hersilia and Egeria', the wives of Romulus and Numa respectively, Laelia is as Roman as one could be. The two legendary women are implicitly contrasted with Laelia as paradigms of matronly excellence: cf. Ov. *Met.* 14.832–4 (Hersilia), Ov. *Met.* 15.547–51 (Egeria).

7 lectulus has uoces, nec lectulus audiat omnis: the diminutive suits the erotic context; cf. Prop. 2.15.1–2 *o me felicem! o nox mihi candida! et o tu | lectule deliciis facte beate meis,* 10.38.6–7. The bed was the appropriate place for sexually arousing language: cf. Ov. *Ars* 2.723–4, 3.796 (intro. n.), 11.104.11 (foll. n.).

nec lectulus . . . omnis: i.e. not the marriage bed. The modesty expected of a *matrona* extended even to the marital bedroom: cf. Plut. *Coniug. prae.* 139c, 140c, 144c, *Amat.* 752c, **86**.6n.; 11.104.11 *nec motu dignaris opus nec uoce iuuare,* holds such conventional standards up to scorn.

8 quem . . . strauit: *lectum sternere,* like λέχος στορέσαι, is euphemistic for 'prepare a bed for lovemaking'.

lasciuo uiro: a lover, as opposed to a husband. For *lasciuus* so used, cf. Ov. *Ep.* 17.77 (Helen to Paris), **21**.17.

amica: a *meretrix*; cf. Adams (1983a) 348–50. Such women made a feature of erotic language: cf. 11.29.3, 60.7 and the *Ars amatoria* passages cited on 7.

9 scire cupis quo casta modo matrona loquaris 'do you want to know how you, though a chaste matron, talk' (i.e. how you sound)?

10 numquid, quae crisat, blandior esse potest? 'surely one who moves seductively (i.e. a prostitute) could not have a more arousing effect'. This is SB's emendation of the MSS reading *numquid, cum crisas, blandior esse potes?* which would mean that Laelia's language is just as sexually arousing (*blandior*) as when she moves lubriciously (*cum crisas*) during intercourse. But a *casta matrona* like Laelia (9) should not *crisare*: cf. Lucr. 4.1270–7, where such movements, a form of contraception and a means of giving pleasure, are suitable for *meretrices* rather than wives; cf. also 11.104.11 cited on *nec lectulus . . . omnis.*

crisat: used of deliberately lubricious wiggling of her bottom by the female during intercourse in order to enhance erotic pleasure: cf. Priap.

10.4 *crisabit tibi fluctuante lumbo*; Adams, *LSV* 136, grossly understates the sense.

11–12   M. combines two ideas, (1) even if Laelia masters the Greek erotic vocabulary in its entirety, this will not make her a Lais (i.e. Greek courtesan) because she will always be essentially a Roman *matrona*, (2) Laelia's propensity for Greek endearments is a waste of time: no matter how wanton her speech, she will never be entirely (*omnino* 12) successful as a seductress, since she fails to possess the beauty of famed courtesans like Lais.

11   **totam . . . Corinthon:**   i.e. all the Greek erotic language in the prostitute's repertoire. Corinth was notorious for its sexual licence (cf. Hor. *Ep.* 1.17.36). As well as having large numbers of temple prostitutes in Aphrodite's shrine, the city was the home of several famous secular courtesans, including the elder Lais: see J. B. Salmon, *Wealthy Corinth* (Oxford 1984) 398–400.

12   **Laelia, Lais:**   the mockery of Laelia is enhanced by the soundplay.

     Lais: in view of the allusion to the city in 11, probably a reference to Lais of Corinth, the elder of two famous courtesans of that name, renowned for beauty: cf. Ath. 588–9, 587d, Ov. *Am.* 1.5.9–12. Alternatively, we might translate 'a Lais', Lais being a generic name for a (Greek) courtesan cf. 11.104.21–2 *si te delectat grauitas, Lucretia toto | sis licet usque die, Laida nocte uolo* with Kay.

42   (= 3.85)

'Who persuaded you to cut off the nose of your wife's lover? It is not in this part that he has offended you. Fool, your wife has lost nothing thereby. His prick is still intact.'

The two penalties for adultery mentioned in this epigram, facial mutilation (1–2) and emasculation (3–4), are based respectively on Greek myth and Roman usage. The revenge taken by the husband on his wife's paramour (1–2) reflects the punishment visited by Menelaus upon the Trojan Deiphobus (cf. 4), who took over Helen after Paris' death: cf. Virg. *A.* 6.494–7 *atque hic Priamiden . . . | Deiphobum uidit, lacerum crudeliter ora, | ora manusque ambas, populataque tempora raptis | auribus et truncas inhonesto uulnere nares.* Here only the cutting-off of the latter-day Deiphobus' nose receives mention, but in the

parallel epigram 2.83 ears also feature, as in Virgil. Conversely M.'s suggestion that the husband was a fool to leave the lover's *mentula* untouched (3–4)
reflects the impromptu sanctions meted out by Roman husbands to adul-
terers caught *in flagrante delicto* with their wives, the most drastic of which
was castration: cf. Hor. *S.* 1.2.44–6, Plaut. *Mil.* 862–3, Val. Max. 6.1.13
*eos quoque, qui in uindicanda pudicitia dolore suo pro publica lege usi sunt... Carbo
Attienus a Vibieno, item Pontius a P. Cerennio deprehensi castrati sunt,* M. 2.60.3,
Adams (1983b) 313, Treggiari (1991) 264–75, McGinn (1998) 206.

1   **Quis tibi persuasit:**   i.e. you were foolish to listen to him.

   nares abscidere: the specific model is Deiphobus (4), but such punishments are frequently encountered in other Greek contexts: cf. Hesych.
s.v. τόμια, Hom. *Od.* 22. 474–5 'they... cut off [Melanthius'] nose and
ears with the pitiless bronze', G. L. Kittredge, *AJPh* 6 (1885) 151–69,
E. Rohde, *Psyche* (London 1925) 582–6. The essential Greekness of the
procedure underlines its irrelevance to the situation in hand.

   nares: in keeping with the epic flavour of the punishment, *nares* is
preferred to its less elevated synonym *nasus*: cf. Grassmann (1966) 73.

2   **non hac peccatum est parte, marite:**   M. alludes wryly to
the belief, enshrined in the so-called *lex talionis*, that retribution should be
visited upon the part of the body which had sinned: on this principle, the
adulterer ought to have been castrated (4). Cf. Galen v 584 Kühn, R. Hirzel,
Die Talion, Philologus Supptbd. 11 (1910) 407–82, Watson (1991) 42–6.

   tibi: dative of disadvantage.

3   **nihil hic tua perdidit uxor** particularises *stulte, quid egisti?* Un-
castrated, the adulterer can continue his activities exactly as before. The
implication that the wife might wish to maintain her relationship with her
grossly mutilated paramour is highly insulting.

4   **cum sit salua... mentula:**   the husband has neglected to remove the very part which should have been lopped. *mentula* was a primary
obscenity: cf. **38**.3n.

   tui... Deiphobi 'of that D. of yours' i.e. that latter-day D. who has
come your way. *tui* is superior to the *sui* of the *Itali*, which focuses attention
on the cuckold's wife rather than on the retributive measures which he
should have taken.

43   (= 6.7)

'It is at most a month, Faustinus, since Domitian's revival of the Augustan adultery law, and already Telesilla is wedding her tenth husband. Anyone who marries so often doesn't marry, but is simply an adulteress in legal guise. I would be less offended by a woman who openly commits adultery.'

This is one of several poems written on the occasion of Domitian's revival of the Augustan *lex Iulia de adulteriis coercendis*, which made adultery an offence punishable by law. It has been argued, in particular by Garthwaite (1990), that M. is not merely satirising an habitual adulteress, but belittling the law itself by demonstrating its failure to stop the determinedly promiscuous and by suggesting that the law encourages even worse behaviour than it punishes. Such an interpretation is unnecessary: rather than mocking the law and by implication the lawgiver, M. is using the marital legislation as a springboard for a witty attack on an individual who responds to the new order of things by engaging in a highly dubious form of serial monogamy – surely a subtle way of reaffirming the marital values so outrageously flouted by Telesilla. There is no reason to suppose that Domitian would not have relished the joke as harmless: cf. 1.4.7 *innocuos censura potest permittere lusus*.

Like 6.22 and 6.45, the present epigram satirises what was in all likelihood a real-life phenomenon: the adulteress who marries her lover to avoid prosecution under the revived legislation. Telesilla however carries this procedure to ridiculous extremes, marrying ten husbands in the course of a month: previously, one assumes, she would have taken ten lovers in the comparable period. The case of Telesilla is palpable satiric hyperbole, but the existence in actuality of such marital leapfrog is suggested by attacks elsewhere on Roman women who contract multiple marriages within a brief space of time: cf. Sen. *Ben.* 3.16.2–3 *quaedam . . . nobiles feminae non consulum numero, sed maritorum annos suos comput<a>nt et exeunt matrimonii causa, nubunt repudii,* Juv. 6.224–30.

Further reading: McGinn (1998) 106–20, Treggiari (1991) 277–98, 278 n.84, Holzberg (2002) 70–1

1   **Iulia lex:**   the *lex Iulia de adulteriis coercendis*, passed by Augustus in 18 BC, was revived (*renata est*) by Domitian around 89–90.

   populis: i.e. the various peoples of the Roman Empire. Cf. Grewing on 6.2.3.

Faustine: 4.6n.

renata est: at 6.4.3 the verb is used of *templa* restored by Domitian. Rebirth was a common theme of imperial propaganda: cf. L. Bösing, *MH* 25 (1968) 145–78.

2   Pudicitia: a personification (cf. *intrare ... iussa*) of the most important female virtue, referring in particular to sexual fidelity on the part of a wife: cf. Treggiari (1991) 218–20, 232–7, Williams (1958) 16–29. A shrine to Pudicitia plebeia had been established in the early third century BC (Liv. 10.23.6–10), and there may have been a parallel shrine to Pudicitia patricia: cf. Liv. 10.23.3, Courtney on Juv. 6.308, Richardson s.v., R. E. A. Palmer, *RSA* 4 (1974) 113–59.

3   tricesima lux: i.e. one month. Telesilla acquires a new husband approximately every three days. It is anomalous for thirty to stand, as here, for a small amount: the reverse is usually the case; cf. 7.81.1, 11.24.13, 12.86, Fordyce on Catull. 9.2.

    lux: a common poetic metonymy for 'day'.

4   et nubit decimo iam Telesilla uiro: a pun. *nubere*, like Greek γαμεῖν, means both 'marry' and 'have intercourse with'. Legally speaking Telesilla *nubit* in the first sense, but in practical terms she does so in the second, a situation captured in the witty paradox *adultera lege est*.

    decimo ... uiro: ten is often used by M. as a hyperbolically large number; cf. 4.46.19, 66.4, 5.7.2, **85**.5, 11.29.4. As with *nubit*, *uiro* plays on two meanings, 'husband' and 'lover'.

    Telesilla: a diminutive formed from Greek τέλος ('fulfilment'); Telesilla is a real, if rare appellation: cf. *CIL* vi 27141 and Nisbet (1998) 79 n.2 for an Argive Telesilla who was a paradigm of virtue, making M.'s choice of name highly ironic. The name, which reappears at 11.97, could also suggest the lady's proclivities: Greek τελεῖν can be employed as shorthand for the common expression τελεῖν γάμον 'to be married': cf. LSJ s.v. Grewing suggests a different possibility, that the name signifies, as at 11.97, 'little fulfilment', which is the lot of Telesilla's various husbands.

5   quae nubit totiens, non nubit: the purpose of the Augustan marriage legislation was to promote matrimony as a vehicle for the rearing of legitimate children. Telesilla's 'marriages' flagrantly flout this intention, their frequency disclosing motives of lust, not procreation.

    adultera lege est: Telesilla is an adulteress whose conduct is given a patina of legitimacy by repeated nuptials.

6   offendor moecha simpliciore minus: in M.'s eyes Telesilla's
behaviour is even worse than straightforward (*simpliciore*) adultery, because
it involves blatant hypocrisy. For the ablative of agent without *a/ab*, cf. Hor.
Carm. 1.6.1–2 *Scriberis Vario fortis et hostium | uictor Maeonii carminis alite.*

   moecha 'adulteress'. *moecha* has a more pejorative colour than the legal
term *adultera*, as shown by its alternative sense of 'whore': cf. Catull. 42.11
moecha putida, redde codicillos, 3.93.15 *inter bustuarias moechas,* Adams (1983a)
350–3. Its effect is to emphasise the sluttishness of Telesilla's behaviour.

44   (= 6.39)

'Cinna, you have become by Marulla the "father" of seven offspring – not
seven free-born children. For none of them is yours, not even the son of
a friend or neighbour, but the product of your wife's amours with various
of the household slaves, as their heads and faces clearly show. If Coresus
and Dindymus had not been eunuchs, you would by now have a troop of
children as large as Niobe's.'

One of a number of epigrams in book 6 on the subject of unchastity (**43**
intro.), this poem presents in graphic detail the results of adultery on the
part of a *matrona*: her husband is raising seven children, each of whom bears
a striking physical resemblance to one of his slaves. The aristocratic names
Marulla and Cinna (1 n.), along with the presence in their household of
a number of luxury slaves (9–10, 17, 19), suggest that the couple are well-
to-do and of high social position. The epigram is (1) an attack on the
propensity of upper-class women to commit adultery with low-born or
servile lovers: cf. 1.81, Petr. 126 *quaedam enim feminae* [sc. *matronae*] *sordibus
calent, nec libidinem concitant, nisi aut seruos uiderint aut statores altius cinctos*; (2) a
satire against husbands who not only fail to control their wife's amorous
tendencies, but allow the results thereof to be raised as their own children,
thus parading before the world their wife's infidelities and laying themselves
open to ridicule; cf. Lucillius, *AP* 11.215 'the painter Eutychus begot twenty
sons, and not one of his children bears any resemblance to him'. In a
case such as the present the husband would be particularly compromised,
since the offspring introduce not only extraneous, but servile blood into
the family, a circumstance particularly feared: cf. Garrido-Hory (1981a)
307–11, and 3n.

   The situation depicted in the epigram is of course grotesque exaggeration. Since the decision on whether or not to raise a child lay at Rome with

the father, husbands could get rid of any unwanted progeny, let alone seven bastards. What point, then, is M. making by presenting us with a father who tolerates this state of affairs? Is it implied that Cinna has raised the children because he wishes to have sons, but is unable to produce his own, whether through impotence, or because his wife prefers other lovers, or because Cinna is interested sexually in males, rather than females (cf. *concubino* 13)? Is he satirised for his naiveté in thinking he can pass off as his own children who are patently not his? Is he so besotted with Marulla that he simply refuses to believe the evidence of his eyes?

In order to emphasise that Cinna's 'children' are the offspring of slaves, they are made as un-Roman as possible. Their alleged fathers are given foreign and/or slave names; the children proclaim their paternity by exhibiting physical traits, such as curly hair, which mark them as non-Roman (cf. Thompson (1989) 31–6). One, possibly two, of Marulla's offspring are black (6–9nn.): for the theme, cf. Juv. 6.599–601 with Courtney, Calp. Flacc. *Decl.* 2. Given the connexion of physical defects with ethical shortcomings (cf. **74**), the 'deformity' of the children also perhaps symbolises the moral turpitude responsible for their conception, *adulterium* between a *matrona* and a lover of low status.

The poem is in choliambics (intro. 28–9). Since the metre was allegedly invented by Hipponax as a distorted form of iambics which paralleled the distortion/perversion of his subjects, its use is especially appropriate in this epigram.

Further reading: Edwards (1993), Gleason (1990), Thompson (1989)

1   Marulla: an aristocratic name (several Marulli are listed in *PIR* v 221), underlining the social gap between the adulteress and her paramours.
     Cinna: an equally upper-class name: cf. 6.17.
     septem: often used by M. to represent a large number (e.g. **62**, **50**.9–10), but here also anticipating the reference to *Niobidarum grex* 20.

2   non liberorum 'non-children': a surprise; after *pater . . . factus es*, one expects *liberorum*. The effect is enhanced by the enjambement between 1 and 2, and the emphatic positioning of *non* at the beginning of 2. Cinna's 'children' are not *liberi* for two reasons: (1) the term properly refers to one's own children; cf. Cic. *Nat. d.* 2.62 *ex nobis natos liberos appellamus*, (2) *liberi*, from *liber* 'having the status of a free man' (*OLD* 1), normally refers to the offspring of a legitimate union between free persons: cf. Suet. *Diff.* 277.13–278.2 R *liberi autem non dicuntur nisi qui ab ingenuis nascuntur.*

non: the use of *non* to negate a single substantive is rare: cf. Grewing *ad loc.*

3   nec est amici filiusue uicini: stresses that the fathers of Marulla's offspring are not of her class, but there is also an amusing implication that her adultery might be condoned if they were. Certainly a woman who took a lover of equal status was less severely condemned than one whose lover was of lower rank, especially a slave (Edwards (1993) 52). Severe penalties were imposed by a Claudian *senatus consultum* on a free woman who had a child by a slave: see Gardner (1986) 141.

4   grabatis: a type of bed used by the very poor (**64**.11 n.).

tegetibus: the *teges*, a piece of rush matting used for lying on or as a cover, was a mark of extreme poverty: 11.32.2, Prop. 4.5.69, Juv. 9.140. The reference to *grabati* and *tegetes* is principally a sneer at the servile status of Marulla's lovers, but it also implies that she has behaved like a prostitute: cf. Juv. 6.117 (*teges* of bedding used by *meretrices*).

5   materna produnt...furta   'betray by their features their mother's secret liaisons'. For a child's resemblance to a low-class lover as evidence of a wife's adultery, cf. Juv. 6.80–1 *ut testudineo tibi, Lentule, conopeo | nobilis Euryalum murmillonem exprimat infans.* Conversely, the likeness of children to their father was routinely cited as proof of a woman's chastity (cf. Hor. *Carm.* 4.5.23, M. 6.27.3–4 quoted on 9). Cf. the story in Macrob. *Sat.* 2.5.9 that Augustus' daughter Julia took lovers only when pregnant, with the unexpected result that all her children looked like their father Agrippa.

capitibus: all the physical traits exhibited by the offspring are associated with the head, the most visible part of the body.

6   hic qui retorto crine Maurus incedit   'that one who struts about, a Moor with curly hair'.

retorto crine: an unusual expression which refers to the tightly curled hair characteristic of black Africans: cf. *Moretum* 33 *torta comam labroque tumens et fusca colore*, M. *Spect.* 3.10 *tortis crinibus Aethiopes.*

Maurus: a native of Mauretania ('Moor'), here a synonym for *Aethiops* (= 'negro': cf. Snowden (1970) 11–12): black immigrants from Ethiopia formed part of the population of ancient Mauretania (J. Carcopino, *Le Maroc antique* (Paris, 6th edn 1943) 20–3).

incedit: he struts about in the haughty manner of an aristocrat. *incedere* refers to a stately walk (Serv. *Aen.* 1.46 *incedere proprie est nobilium personarum, hoc est cum aliqua dignitate ambulare*), but is often used pejoratively of those who parade before the public in an arrogant fashion: cf. Sall. *Jug.* 31.10 [*nobiles*] *incedunt per ora uostra magnifici.* The verb nicely conveys the incongruity between the Moor's upper class bearing and his demonstrably servile origins.

7   subolem: an ironically high-style word to describe the offspring of a union between mistress and slave.
   Santrae: for the name see on **32**.1.

8 The pure choliambic verse (**32**.22n.) suits the highly insulting character of its contents.
   sima nare, turgidis labris 'with snub nose and swollen lips': this could be a pejorative description of the negroid flat nose and large lips, which the Romans viewed negatively: cf. Petr. 102.15 *labra . . . tumore taeterrimo, Moretum* 33 *labro . . . tumens*, Snowden (1970) 33–99. But a black slave has just been mentioned (6–7), and in view of the father's profession (*palaestritae* 9n.), it might be preferable to see an allusion to the squashed features of a boxer: cf. M. Dickie, *Nikephorus* 6 (1993) 142.

9   ipsa est imago Pannychi: an amusing inversion of a common marital ideal exemplified in 6.27.3–4 *est tibi, quae patria signatur imagine uultus,* | *testis maternae nata pudicitiae.*
   Pannychi: the name, literally 'all night long' suits Pannychus' rôle as his mistress's lover.
   palaestritae: a type of slave kept in wealthy households to help his master exercise by wrestling with him, to act as a masseur and to put on exhibitions of boxing and wrestling (cf. Dickie (8n.) 141–4). The slave's profession suits his erotic servicing of his mistress, wrestling being a common sexual metaphor in Greek and Latin (14.201, Adams, *LSV* 157–8).

10   pistoris 'the offspring of the *pistor*': for the construction, cf. 18–19. A wealthy household would have a *pistor* (speciality pastrycook) as well as a *coquus* among the slaves employed as kitchen staff: cf. 11.31.8–14, Garrido-Hory (1981 b) 135.

11   quicumque lippum nouit et uidet Damam 'whoever knows this *lippus* individual [the son] and looks at Damas [his father]'.
   lippum: logically, there is no reason why a child raised by a nobleman like Cinna should suffer from chronic *lippitudo* (running, bleary eyes): remedies were readily available for this common disease (see Cels. 6.6).

But his condition provides telling proof of his paternity, being commonly connected with persons of low moral character and slaves: cf. Petr. 28.4, **20**.14n.

Damam: a common slave name. At Pers. 5.76–7 it also refers to a slave who is *lippus*.

12 **cinaeda fronte:** a brow of the type exhibited by *cinaedi* (effeminate men): the son has inherited this trait from his father, who is Cinna's *concubinus. cinaedi* were thought recognisable by physical peculiarities, several associated with the facial expression (cf. Gleason (1990) 394–6, Courtney on Juv. 2.17). For the brow in particular, cf. *Script. physiogn.* 2.208 Foerster *si uides uirum fronte arta, oculis multum fulgurantibus . . . noli dubitare eum cinaedum esse.*

candido uultu: pale skin, a female trait, was characteristic of catamites: cf. Stat. *Silu.* 2.1.41 (of the *delicatus* Glaucias) *o ubi purpureo suffusus sanguine candor?* Here it is derogatory, implying effeminacy: λευκός, 'white' was similarly used of pathics; cf. Henderson (1991) 211.

13 **concubino:** Lygdus, father of Marulla's fourth son, is also the bedmate of her husband. For a married couple sharing the same slave partner, cf. 12.91, Petr. 75.11 *tamen ad delicias ipsimi annos quattuordecim fui. nec turpe est quod dominus iubet. ego* [Trimalchio] *tamen et ipsimae satis faciebam.*

Lygdo: the name is used elsewhere by M. of a boy-love (6.45.3, 11.73, 12.71). It is appropriate for its historical resonances (a favourite eunuch of the younger Drusus was called Lygdus: Tac. *Ann.* 4.10), as well as its etymological connection with λύγδος, a kind of Parian marble noted for its whiteness: cf. *candido* 12.

14 **percide, si uis, filium: nefas non est:** a deliberately outrageous suggestion: it would not be a crime to bugger your 'son' because he is not in fact your offspring.

percide: a military metaphor (cf. Adams, *LSV* 146) used frequently by M. of anal penetration (e.g. 4.48.1 *percidi gaudes, percisus, Papyle, ploras*).

15–17 Several abnormalities are imputed to the fifth son: a pointed head, long mobile ears, a hump-back (*Cyrtae* 17n.), and mental deficiency (the comparison to an ass, and a *morio* for father). Most of these features are consistent with a genuine medical condition. Syndromes involving physical deformity, especially of the head, are frequently accompanied by low intelligence (Warkany et al. (1982) 4). Given the epigram's emphasis on the resemblance of sons to fathers, it is relevant that many such syndromes are hereditary.

15   acuto capite: probably refers to the condition now known as oxycephaly or acrocephaly, in which the sufferer has an elongated, pointed head. It is characteristic of several diseases, e.g. Crouzon's syndrome, which also involves a high incidence of mental subnormality (Warkany et al. (1982) 130–2, 137–40).

auribus longis: large ears were thought a sign of stupidity (e.g. *Anon. physiog.* 47 *magnae aures stultitiae . . . sunt indices*, 16n.), but the description is also consistent with oxycephaly (previous n.), which often goes with abnormal size of the external ear.

16   quae sic mouentur ut solent asellorum: for the mobility of asses' ears cf. Ov. *Met.* 11.176–7. This detail is probably not based on physiological reality, but rather a way of suggesting stupidity: to impute this to someone, Romans put the thumb to the temple and moved the other fingers in imitation of the ears of the proverbially stupid ass (Otto, *Sprichw.* s.v. *asinus*).

17   morionis: *moriones* were half-wits kept to provide amusement at dinner parties by their clownish antics: cf. Sen. *Ep.* 50.2, Plin. *Ep.* 9.17, Garland (1995) 46–8. For an affair between a mistress and a *morio*, cf. *Philogelos* 251.

Cyrtae: cf. κυρτήν = *gibbus*, a hump. The name implies that the father, and perhaps the son as well, is a hunch-back. Skeletal anomalies are often linked with defects of the head, as in the Hurler syndrome, the most striking characteristics of which are scaphocephalic head, mental retardation and gibbus formation (Warkany et al. (1982) 394–5).

18   sorores: after the masc. *filius* in 3, the female offspring come as a surprise. They prepare for the comparison in 20 with Niobe, whose children included girls as well as boys.

nigra 'black-haired', as at Petr. 43.7, to balance *rufa* (foll. n.), rather than the usual meaning 'dark-skinned' (Grewing). Both hair colours would have been considered un-Roman (Thompson (1989) 31–3).

rufa: red hair was not merely regarded as a flaw (Ter. *HT* 1061–2, 2.33.2 *cur non basio te, Philaeni? rufa es*), but was particularly associated with slaves: Πυρρίας, 'Redhead' was a generic name for these, and *serui* in Roman Comedy wore a red wig.

19   Croti: a common slave name. It might suggest a percussionist rather than a *choraules* (κρότος = a rattling or clashing noise), but in mythology Crotus was the son of Pan, inventor of the pipes.

choraulae: a wind-player who accompanied a group of singers at public functions or private dinner parties. He is probably a slave member of the household, as at Petr. 53.13. For a *choraules* among the humble lovers favoured by *matronae*, cf. Juv. 6.76–7. The wife of the Emperor Pertinax was in love with a citharode (SHA *Pertinax* 13.8).

Carpi: for this as a slave name, see Petr. 36 and 40, *CIL* vi index s.v. The name (καρπός 'produce') suits his profession of *uilicus*.

20   Niobidarum grex 'a brood as numerous as Niobe's', *grex* being used contemptuously, as often. In the most common version of the myth, Niobe had seven children of each sex. M. means that if Coresus and Dindymus had not been *spadones*, Cinna would have had twice as many children, the implication being that Marulla favoured eunuchs over other lovers (see next n., W. Tränkle, *WS* 109 (1996) 138–9).

21   si spado ... non esset: because Coresus and Dindymus were infertile, Marulla's sexual relationships with them occasioned no increase in the number of Cinna's 'children'. Women were thought to favour eunuchs as lovers for just this reason: cf. 6.67 *cur tantum eunuchos habeat tua Gellia, quaeris,* | *Pannyche? uult futui Gellia nec parere,* Juv. 6.366–8. Sex was not a physiological impossibility for a *spado*: cf. 6.2.6, Kay on 11.81.3, P. Guyot, *Eunuchen als Sklaven und Freigelassene in der griechisch-römischen Antike* (Stuttgart 1980) 37–42, 63–6.

spado: strictly speaking a male whose testicles have been 'dragged' (σπάω) from the scrotum, *spado* can in practice refer to any kind of eunuch.

Coresus Dindymusque: the names of the eunuchs are well chosen. Coresus might suggest κόρη ('girl'). Dindymus is a mountain range in Asia Minor associated with Cybele, whose priests practised self-castration; it is used elsewhere by M. of eunuchs (11.81.1), *delicati* and *cinaedi* (5.83.2, 10.42.6, 11.6.11, 12.75.4).

45   (= 2.89)

'Gaurus, your drinking late into the night can be excused by the example of Cato, your composition of miserable verse by that of Cicero, your vomiting and gormandising by Antony and Apicius respectively. But what precedent can you invoke for being a *fellator*?'

In ironically forgiving each of Gaurus' vices by appealing to historical precedent, M. draws on the rhetorical technique of invoking *exempla* from history to back up an argument. Normally *exempla* are cited as instances of virtues to be emulated or vices to be avoided, but they can also be used, as here, to justify a *uitium*. Seneca, for example, in arguing that occasional indulgence in *ioci* is necessary for relaxation, invokes the gambling of Socrates, the drinking of Cato and the dancing of Scipio (*Dial.* 9.17.4); cf. Hor. *Carm.* 3.21.11−2 *narratur et prisci Catonis | saepe mero caluisse uirtus.*

Often when multiple historical precedents for various vices are cited, it is to establish a maxim of universal validity, as in the following instances, Sen. *Contr.* 2.4.4 *nemo sine uitio est: in Catone moderatio, in Cicerone constantia, in Sulla clementia* [*desideratur*] and 9.2.19 *illum locum pulcherrime tractauit, quam multa populus Romanus in suis imperatoribus tulerit: in Gurgite luxuriam, in Manlio impotentiam . . . in Sulla crudelitatem, in Lucullo luxuriam.* M. however, in cataloguing precedents for a variety of shortcomings, ostensibly in order to exculpate Gaurus, in fact contrives to imply that he is a repository of sundry vices − including one for which no justificatory precedent can be invoked, *fellatio*: for who would admit to being a *fellator*?

Further reading: Bonner (1949) 62, Nordh (1954)

1   nimio . . . uino: whereas a modest intake of wine to induce a pleasantly relaxed state was socially acceptable, drinking to excess was frowned upon: the drunkard is a common satirical type (Citroni on 1.11).

noctem producere 'to prolong the night', i.e. spend the whole night: cf. Stat. *Theb.* 8.219 *uario producunt sidera ludo.* In Roman society, where the main meal began in mid-afternoon, drinking throughout the night was a sign of a dissolute lifestyle: cf. Suet. *Iul.* 52.1 *Cleopatram, cum qua et conuiuia in primam lucem saepe protraxit*, Sen. *Ep.* 83.14.2, M. 1.28.

2   uitium . . . Catonis: although both the Elder and the Younger Cato were famous as heavy drinkers, M. is probably thinking of the latter, whom he mentions often. For his drinking, cf. Plut. *Cat. Min.* 6 'as time went on, he allowed himself to drink heavily, so that often he lingered over his cups till dawn', Plin. *Ep.* 3.12.2 with S-W.

Gaure: the name, used several times by M. in different contexts (**22.**1 n.), suggests pomposity (γαῦρος 'haughty': cf. 5.82 with Howell).

3   Musis et Apolline nullo: abl. abs. 'with the Muses and Apollo being absent', i.e. poetic inspiration being non-existent: cf. Var. *Men.* 52

Cèbe *cum Quintipor Clodius tot comoedias sine ulla fecerit Musa.* For the idiomatic use of *nullus* 'absent', cf. Ter. *Eun.* 345, Ov. *Ep.* 10.12 *perque torum moueo bracchia: [Theseus] nullus erat!*

4   laudari debes: heavily ironical.

hoc [sc. uitium] **Ciceronis habes:**   Cicero had a reputation as an execrable poet: cf. Sen. *Contr.* 3 *praef.* 8, Juv. 10.122–4 *'o fortunatam natam me consule Romam': | Antoni gladios potuit contemnere, si sic | omnia dixisset,* Tac. *Dial.* 21.6. Such criticism may have originated with adversaries of Cicero whose objection was to the sentiments, rather than the style, of some of his verses. For modern attempts to rehabilitate his poetry cf. G. Townend in T. A. Dorey, ed., *Cicero* (London 1965) 109–34, W. Ewbank, *The poems of Cicero* (London 1933) 27–39, W. Allen, *TAPhA* 87 (1956) 130–46.

5   quod uomis, Antoni refers to a famous occasion, narrated with relish by Cicero: *tantum uini in Hippiae nuptiis exhauseras ut tibi necesse esset in populi Romani conspectu uomere postridie ... in coetu uero populi Romani negotium publicum gerens, magister equitum, cui ructare turpe esset, is uomens frustis esculentis uinum redolentibus gremium suum et totum tribunal impleuit* (*Phil.* 2.63; cf. 2.76, 84, Plut. *Ant.* 9.6). Antony's notorious bibulousness was later exploited in Octavianic propaganda, provoking in reply a pamphlet from Antony *De ebrietate sua:* cf. K. Scott, *CPh* 24 (1929) 133–41.

quod luxuriaris, Apici: M. Gauius Apicius (*PIR* G91), a wealthy gourmet in the time of Tiberius, was a byword for *luxuria*: cf. Sen. *Dial.* 7.11.4, 12.10.8–12, Ath. 7a–d. According to a well-known anecdote (cf. 3.22), he spent vast sums on his feasts, and, on discovering that he had only ten million sesterces left, poisoned himself rather than live in a state of 'starvation'. (N.B. the collection of gourmet recipes under the name of Apicius belongs to the fourth century).

6   quod fellas: a surprise conclusion, introducing a *uitium* which would be more at home in graffiti or invective than a rhetorical list of moral failings: cf. *CIL* xi 6721.9a *salue Octaui felas* with J. Hallett, *AJAH* 2 (1977) 151–2, Krenkel (1980b) 85–7. Accusations of practising oral sex were regularly levelled against prominent Romans, e.g. Sextus Clodius (Cic. *Dom.* 25, 47, *Cael.* 78, *Har. resp.* 11) and Tiberius (Suet. *Tib.* 45) but no famous person was known as a *fellator*, unless we count the grammarian Q. Remmius Palaemon (Suet. *De gramm. et rhet.* 23.7 with Kaster).

uitium, dic mihi, cuius habes?   a rhetorical question: no precedent exists, implying that this *uitium* is unforgivable.

dic mihi: the expression has a colloquial flavour (Citroni on 1.20.1).
It often introduces a rhetorical question which forms the culmination of an
attack: cf. 9.47.8 *dic mihi, percidi, Pannyche, dogma quod est?*, 10.56.8 *qui sanet
ruptos, dic mihi, Galle, quis est?*

46   (= 9.67)

'I possessed all night long a girl whose lack of inhibition knows no bounds.
Exhausted by coupling in countless positions, I asked to make love to her
like a boy. I had barely begun my request when she granted it. Embarrassed
and blushing, I asked for something naughtier still. She promised it without
hesitation. But for me she remained unsullied. She will not so remain for
you, Aeschylus, if you want to receive the same favour on dubious terms.'

This, like many obscene epigrams of M., is thoroughly obscure. The main
difficulty lies in the final couplet, in particular what is meant by *pura* and *mala
condicio*. At least five solutions have been proposed: the least unsatisfactory
are listed here to provoke discussion. Housman, *CPh* 725, argued that the
girl consents to fellate M. as long as he agrees to reciprocate by performing
cunnilinctus upon her (*mala condicio*). M. declined and consequently was
not fellated (*sed mihi* [*ore*] *pura fuit*). Aeschylus, by contrast, will accept –
gladly: cf. 9.4 *Aureolis futui cum possit Galla duobus | et plus quam futui, si totidem
addideris: | aureolos a te cur accipit, Aeschyle, denos? | non fellat tanti Galla. quid ergo?
tacet.* Killeen, likewise invoking 9.4 as evidence of Aeschylus' addiction to
cunnilinctus, takes Aeschylus to be a *cunnilinctor* who indulges his tastes when
his partners are menstruating (cf. Sen. *Ep.* 87.16 *Natalis, tam improbae linguae
quam impurae, in cuius ore feminae purgabantur*). Aeschylus is prepared to lay out
a large price (so *mala condicio* is interpreted) for what others would regard
as disgusting. Schuster contended that M., agreeing to lick the girl's *cunnus*,
did not defile her, because he was no *fellator* of males, unlike the corrupt
Aeschylus. But one cannot easily imagine M. admitting to cunnilinctus, an
activity which he despised (cf. Krenkel (1981) 52). It is better to suppose that
the *puella* readily agreed to fellate M., and did so, but in the case of Aeschylus
insisted on a *quid pro quo* in the shape of cunnilinctus. In performing the
latter, Aeschylus, *ore pollutus*, as his name suggests (7 n.), in turn defiled her.

Further reading: Housman, *CPh* 725, Killeen (1967), Krenkel (1980a) and
(1981), Prinz (1930), Schuster (1928)

1   Lasciuam tota possedi nocte puellam: cf. Paul. Silent. *AP* 5.283.1–2 'all night long I embraced upon my bed the lovely Theano'. *nox* has the specialised sense 'a night of love making': cf. 9.2.7, Cic. *Att.* 1.16.5 *noctes certarum mulierum*, O. Hey, *ALL* 11 (1900) 531–2. The lower genres are given to first-person accounts of purported sexual escapades, e.g. Catull. 32, 56, Archil. fr. 188a W.

possedi 'I possessed sexually': cf. 9.32.5–6 *poscentem nummos et grandia uerba sonantem | possideat crassae mentula Burdigalae.*

puellam: a polite designation for a prostitute: cf. Adams (1983a) 344–8.

2   cuius nequitias uincere nemo potest 'whose naughtinesses none can exhaust'. For *uinco* in this sense: cf. Sall. *Cat.* 20.12 *summa lu-bidine diuitias suas uincere nequeunt.* Lindsay's preference for the *nulla* of the second family over the *nemo* of the first and third seems uncalled for.

3   fessus mille modis illud puerile poposci: *illud puerile* is anal intercourse, the usual way of making love to boys; cf. Plaut. *Cist.* 657 *puerile officium.* References to heterosexual anal intercourse are not uncommon (Apul. *Met.* 3.20 *mihi iam fatigato de propria liberalitate Fotis puerile obtulit corollar-ium*, Ath. 602d, *PGM* 4.350–1, 11.104.17–18) but even prostitutes, it appears, only granted it as a special favour, (cf. Ar. *Plut.* 149–52, Machon 226–30 and 327–32 Gow). This is why the *puella*'s ready compliance (4) is noteworthy, and why M.'s next request can be styled *improbius*, 'more naughty still'.

fessus: less common than *lassus* in descriptions of sexual exhaustion (Adams, *LSV* 196).

mille modis: *mille* = 'countless', as often. *modus* = 'sexual position': cf. Ov. *Am.* 2.8.27–8 *quoque loco tecum fuerim quotiensque, Cypassi, | narrabo dominae quotque quibusque modis*, Tib. 2.6.52 with Murgatroyd.

illud 'that well known'.

4   ante preces totas: before I could even finish my request she readily complied. *totas*, the reading of the MSS, is preferable to Ker's jejune *totum.*

5   improbius quiddam: *fellatio.* Literary texts routinely bring vagi-nal, anal and oral intercourse (sc. fellation) into association as the three recognised ways of having sex: cf. D. Bain, *CQ* 41 (1991) 59. *improbius* neatly captures the feelings of ambivalence which Greek and Roman males enter-tained towards *fellatio*: it was something which they ardently desired, while simultaneously feeling that it degraded the female who thus obliged them (Krenkel (1980a)).

ridens rubensque 'with a shamefaced laugh'. *rubere* is used of blushing with embarrassment at things of a sexual nature; cf. *AP* 5.74.4, [Tib]. 3.4.31–2 *ut iuueni primum uirgo deducta marito | inficitur teneras ore rubente genas,* M. 4.17.1–2, 5.2.6–8.

6   luxuriosa: wanton as she was, she promised without hesitation.

7   sed mihi pura fuit: on the interpretation of this phrase, see intro.

Aeschyle: the name has associations with oral sexuality; its first element αἰσχ- (*aesch-*) regularly serves as shorthand for this kind of activity: cf. Ar. *Eq.* 1284–5 'for he outrages his own tongue with shameful (*aeschrais*) pleasures, in the brothels licking up the spat-out dew (i.e. vaginal secretions)', Diog. Laert. 1.5, Machon 410 with Gow, Krenkel (1980a) 77–8.

8   hoc munus: identical with *improbius quiddam* (5).

condicione mala: conditions which are imposed by the *puella* upon the beneficiaries of her favours (cf. *rogaui, poposci* and *munus*). Given the context, it is noteworthy that *condicio* can sometimes bear the sense 'sexual union': cf. 3.33.1–2 *ingenuam malo, sed si tamen illa negetur, | libertina mihi proxima condicio est,* A. Ernout, *RPh* 23 (1949) 107–19.

mala: if the *condicio* is correctly identified as *cunnilinctus* (cf. above) then it is *mala* because the activity was felt to degrade the male who performed it: cf. **59**.2n., Krenkel (1981) *passim.*

47   (= 3.75)

'Lupercus, you have long been impotent, but like a fool still strive to achieve an erection. But a whole battery of aphrodisiacs has no effect. You have begun to pay money for persons to fellate you to arousal – without success. Who could believe it, Lupercus, that what does not stand, stands to cost you so much?'

Impotence is a frequent comic and satiric theme, generally appearing in one of two guises: either a lover experiences a humiliating sexual failure, notwithstanding his urgent desire (cf. *AP* 5.47, Ov. *Am.* 3.7, *Priap.* 83 Büch., Petr. 126–8), or else, as here, the subject gives rise to mockery of an individual's vanished sexual powers: cf. Ar. *Vesp.* 1379–81, *Lys.* 598–601, *AP* 11.30.5–6, 12.240 and Juv. 10.204–9, a savage account of senile impotence,

nam coitus iam longa obliuio, uel si | coneris, iacet exiguus cum ramice neruus | et,
quamuis tota palpetur nocte, iacebit. | anne aliquid sperare potest haec inguinis aegri |
canities? quid quod merito suspecta libido est | quae uenerem affectat sine uiribus? M.
was particularly fond of mocking the impotent: other instances are 2.45,
3.73, 9.66, 11.46, 11.71, 13.34 *cum sit anus coniunx et sint tibi mortua membra,*
| nil aliud bulbis quam satur esses potes, where, as here, the sufferer resorts to
aphrodisiacs in an unavailing attempt to cure his erectile dysfunction.

Further reading: Licht (1926) 228–9 and (1928) 248–9, McMahon (1998),
Sharrock (1995), Stroh (1991)

1   Stare ... mentula: the verb is commonly used of the erect penis;
cf. Apul. *Met.* 2.7 *steterunt et membra quae iacebant ante, Priap.* 73.2.

Luperce: a real name (Kajanto 318), but here attached to a fictitious
addressee on account of its comic inappropriateness: the festival of the
Lupercalia was closely associated with the promotion of fertility: cf. Ov.
Fast. 2.425–52 with Bömer. 4.28 also plays on the name (cf. intro. 15,
A. W. J. Holleman, *Latomus* 35 (1976) 861–5).

iam pridem: Lupercus has 'long since' lost his virility. This suggests
a sufferer from senile impotence: cf. Juv. 10.204 cited intro., L. Houdijk and
P. Vanderbroeck, *WZRostock* 36 (1987) 58.

desît: cf. 6.26.3, **73**.9. For contracted third pers. sing. of the perfect indicative, see N–W III 446–8. There are numerous examples in
M. (Friedländer on *Spect.* 16.1).

2   demens: the *iam pridem* of the previous line provides the reason
for this epithet.

arrigere: sc. *penem.*

3–4   Lupercus attempts without success to produce an erection using
three well-know aphrodisiacs.

3   erucae: rocket (εὔζωμον), a herb belonging to the mustard family,
was celebrated for its alleged capacity to produce sexual arousal: cf. Col.
10.108–9, Ov. *Rem.* 799 with Lucke. The herb owed its reputation either to
its heat-producing capacities, impotence being often attributed to inguinal
'chill' (Plin. *NH* 19.154–5), or because it stimulated the production of semen
(Gal. 6.639 Kühn, Cels. 4.28).

bulbique: the most commonly mentioned of all ancient erotic stimulants, *bulbi* is a collective term for bulbous plants such as onions and garlic

(*RE* iii 669 s.v. βολβός). For their supposed aphrodisiac qualities, cf. Ath. 63e–64d, Ar. *Eccl.* 1092, Petr. 130, E. Csapo, *Phoenix* 47 (1993) 116. The operative principle behind their alleged powers seems to have been the visual resemblance to human testicles, especially when growing in pairs: cf. J. Winkler in C. Faraone and D. Obbink, *Magika Hiera* (Oxford 1991) 220–2. Also pertinently, they were, like *eruca*, allegedly 'productive of semen' (Ath. 64a).

salaces: active, 'producing sexual arousal' (Ov. *Ars* 2.422 *herba salax*, *Priap.* 51.20), and going with both nouns in line 3.

4   improba 'lust-provoking'; cf. Ov. *Ars* 3.796 *nec taceant mediis improba uerba iocis.*

nec prosunt iam: the time has passed when such remedies could avail.

satureia: the neuter form *satureia, -orum*, only elsewhere at Ov. *Ars* 2.415, is a contamination of *satureia, -ae* f., savory, a harmless condiment never found in lists of amatory stimulants, and the famed aphrodisiac σατύριον, Lat. *satyrion, satureum*: cf. J. André, *REL* 38 (1960) 169–71. The latter derived its purported powers from a semantic link with the lecherous Satyrs and the resemblance of its root to human testicles or a phallus: cf. Plin. *NH* 26.96, Dioscor. *Mat. med.* 3.126. *satyrion* seems to have belonged to the family *Orchidaceae*, but cannot be more closely identified.

5   coepisti puras ... corrumpere buccas: in an attempt to re-store his powers, Lupercus has resorted to having himself fellated, a widely touted remedy for impotence: cf. Nov. ap. Fest. 34–5 L *quid ego facerem? otiosi rodebam rutabulum*, 11.46.5–6 with Kay.

puras: 'when Martial uses *purus* suggestively (with 'impurity' in mind), he is usually alluding to oral sex' Adams, *LSV* 199. Cf. 6.66.5, **46**.7, 14.70.2.

corrumpere: used in two senses, 'corrupt sexually' (*TLL* iv 1056.35–1057.15) and 'bribe with money' (*opibus*: cf. *TLL* iv 1057.16–1058.32).

6   sic quoque non uiuit sollicitata Venus: the second remedy is as unavailing as the first.

non uiuit 'doesn't come to life': cf. 11.46.6 *summa petas: illic mentula uiuit anus*, Ov. *Am.* 3.7.60. Impotence is penile 'death': cf. *AP* 11.29.3–4 'for it, more droopy than a vegetable, that previously was alive and unbending, has completely disappeared within my thighs', M. 11.46.4, 13.34.1–2, Petr. 129.

sollicitata: referring to physical stimulation of the limp penis, usually by manual means (Ov. *Am.* 3.7.73–4, Adams, *LSV* 184), here orally.

Venus: *mentula*; cf. Lucr. 4.1269–70, M. 1.46.1–2 *cum dicis 'propero, fac si facis', Hedyle, languet | protinus et cessat debilitata Venus*, Adams, *LSV* 57.

8   quod non stat, magno stare, Luperce, tibi: what fails to stand, *magno stat*, 'costs' Lupercus a great deal (*OLD* s.v. 23), in his unavailing search to recover his virility. The poem ends with ring-composition of *stare* and with a pun, as often in M.: cf. Siedschlag (1977) 86–92, Joepgen (1967) *passim*.

48   (= 6.26)

'Our friend Sotades' *caput* is in danger. Do you suppose him to be on trial? Not so. He has become impotent, and is reduced to using his tongue.'

This epigram turns on a pun, utilising a favourite effect of M., whereby a key word or phrase is discovered in the concluding verse to have a second sense which completely redefines the meaning of the epigram and gives it its point (cf. Siedschlag (1977) 89). The pun here is on *caput* in the twin senses of 'life', *periclitari capite* in a judicial context signifying to be at risk of the death penalty, and *caput* in its literal sense of 'head', i.e. 'mouth' (cf. *Priap.* 22.2, Suet. *Tib.* 45.1, Grewing on **48**.1), the danger to which Sotades is exposed being oral rather than capital (3n.): because of impotence (3), Sotades has had to resort to *cunnilinctus* (*lingit*). The expectation that Sotades is standing trial for his life is encouraged not only by the question *reum putatis esse Sotaden?*, but also by the fate of the best-known Sotades (cf. 2.86.2), who, according to Ath. 620f–621a, was put to death at the behest of Ptolemy II on account of his notorious verse criticising the marriage of Ptolemy to his sister Arsinoe, 'you are thrusting your prick into an unholy hole' – a line which gives ironic colour to the present joke on Sotades' sexual shortcomings: cf. Launey (1945). It has been further suggested that obscene double entendres were integral to Sotades' work (A. Bettini, *MD* 9 (1982) 66–9); if this was so, M. may have chosen the name of his target with this feature in mind.

The name Sotades may have other associations which are none the less integral to the humour of the epigram. Names beginning with Σω- or Σο- (from a Greek root meaning 'safe') were often borne by doctors as healers of the sick: cf. *Sotae fili clinici* 4.9.1, 'Sotades of Crete, a physician' (*SEG* xxix

227), Solin (1995) 134 with n.61. If the Sotades of this poem is a doctor, a dual irony is at work. Not only is an individual whose name suggests the idea 'safe' far from being so (*periclitatur capite*), but given his dysfunctional *mentula* he represents a conspicuous example of a physician who is unable to heal himself, an idea which gains in probability from M.'s taste for attacking doctors on the grounds of incompetence (**60** intro.). He can hardly have been unaware of the paradox that a doctor who was infirm was unlikely to inspire others with confidence in his ability to heal them (cf. Hippocrates, IX 204 Littré, Sidon. Apoll. *Ep.* 1.8.3, Luxorius, *Anth. Lat.* 304 SB).

Further reading: Küspert (1902–3), (1905–6), Launey (1945), Solin (1995)

1–3   Sotades... | ...Sotaden... | ...Sotades: for the triple anaphora, cf. Anacr. fr. 359 Page 'I am in love with Kleuboulos, | I am mad about Kleuboulos, | I look earnestly at Kleuboulos', 12.16.1–3, Wills (1996) 285–6.

1   Periclitatur: it appears at first that Sotades' 'danger' is judicial in character; cf. Sen. *Dial.* 10.2.4 *hic aduocat, hic adest, ille periclitatur, ille defendit, ille iudicat.*

   capite 'of [losing] his life'. The equation of *caput* with *uita* stems from the fact that the head governs intelligence and sentience and thus in a sense one's very existence (Küspert (1902–3) 47). In judicial contexts the word normally refers to capital punishment: cf. Fest. 277 L *probrum uirginis Vestalis ut capite puniretur*, Cic. *Verr.* 2.2.99, Petr. 132.8 (also a pun on *caput*).

   Sotades noster 'our friend Sotades'. M. engages the reader's attention by suggesting that 'Sotades' is known to M. and reader alike.

3   The risk faced by Sotades is now revealed as quite different from that hitherto suggested: pollution of his 'head', i.e. mouth; cf. 11.25 *illa salax nimium nec paucis nota puellis | stare Lino desît mentula. lingua caue.* It was widely thought that the impotent resorted to *cunnilinctus* as an alternative sexual outlet: cf. 11.25, 12.86, SHA *Commod.* 5.11, and also that *cunnilinctores* were exposed to oral pollution and even disease of the tongue: cf. Krenkel (1981), Grewing on 6.44.6, 11.61, 85.

   arrigere desît posse Sotades: impotence is a common subject of satiric humour (**47** intro.). The sexual nature of Sotades' infirmity is consonant with his name, the homonymous poet being notorious for his use of obscenity: cf. I. H. M. Hendriks et al., *ZPE* 41 (1981) 76–8.

   desît: for the contraction, cf. **47**.1 n.

lingit sc. *cunnum*: cf. 3.96.1 *lingis non futuis meam puellam*, Adams, *LSV* 134–5.

49   (= 8.31)

'It isn't pretty what you confess about yourself, Dento, in soliciting from the emperor so persistently the *ius trium liberorum* despite taking a wife. You had better desist and return home at last. Otherwise your neglect of your spouse in pursuit of three children may result in the production of four.'

Although he has married, Dento is continually petitioning the emperor for the *ius trium liberorum*, 'the right of three children', an honour which enabled the childless, who would otherwise be penalised under the Augustan marriage laws, to be counted as parents of three fictitious offspring (**9a** and **b** intro.). The *ius* was normally granted to individuals whose marriages, through no fault of their own, had failed over time to produce progeny (cf. **9a**.5n.). M. implies that Dento, recently married (*coniuge ducta* n.), does not fall into this deserving category and so should give up a petition which must inevitably prove fruitless. But the primary thrust of the epigram is sexual satire: Dento, by seeking the 'right of three children' so insistently without waiting to test the fertility of his marriage, is effectively confessing something embarrassing about himself (cf. 1 n.).

   The concluding joke, that if Dento lingers too long away from home he will return to find that he has not three but four children, both builds upon and expands the mockery of Dento in lines 1–4. By deserting his wife for so long in his pointless quest, Dento will not only encourage her to seek consolation with more virile lovers, but will find his own marital shortcomings made public in the most tangible way possible.

Further reading: Raditsa (1980); see also bibliography for **9a** and **b**.

1   **Nescio quid . . . non belle . . . fateris:**   Dento is mocked for disclosing a shameful secret. As often in epigrams on sexual themes, the aberration is merely hinted at (cf. 2.28.5–6 *ex istis nihil es fateor, Sextille: quid ergo es? | nescio, sed tu scis res superesse duas*). Dento may be impotent: cf. 9.66 where M. satirises Fabullus for requesting the *ius trium liberorum* when he has a young attractive wife (*quod petis . . . | tu dabis ipse tibi, si potes arrigere*). Alternatively, Dento may have a distaste for 'normal' sex and a preference for passive activities either with his wife (n. on Dento) or with male partners.

Nescio quid has an insinuating tone: cf. 3.72.2 *nescio quod magnum suspicor esse nefas*, 3.77.9, 5.61.3.

non belle: ironic understatement.

Dento: Dento, literally 'Toothy', is a real but uncommon name: cf. Kajanto 238. In contrast to 5.44 (Dento likes to chew), the rationale for the name is not obvious here, but there may be an implication that Dento is a *cunnilinctor*, since such individuals were often described as 'eating' the female *pudenda* (**59**.2n.), and cunnilinctus was viewed by M. as a passive sexual alternative for those who *non futuunt* (cf. Kay on 11.25).

fateris: cf. 1.81 *a seruo scis te genitum blandeque fateris, | cum dicis dominum, Sosibiane, patrem.*

2   coniuga...ducta 'although you have taken a wife': the phrase suggests that Dento's marriage is not of long standing.

iura paterna: the *ius trium liberorum*. On the reasons for requesting this, see **9a** and **b** intro.

petis: the *ius trium liberorum* was normally obtained by petitioning the emperor directly: cf. *dominum* 3; **9a**, **9b**.1–3, 10.60.1, Plin. *Ep.* 2.13.8, 10.94.

3   supplicibus...libellis: *libelli* were written requests to the emperor for favours of various kinds. Except in the case of persons of high standing, petitioners were required to present their requests in person – hence Dento's absence from home (4): cf. Millar (1977) 240–52, 537–49.

dominum: Domitian (**10**.4n.).

lassare continues the critical tone of *supplicibus*: Dento, undeterred by lack of success, wearies the emperor with his repeated approaches: cf. 4.29.1–2 *obstat...nostris sua turba libellis* ('epigrams') | *lectoremque frequens lassat...opus.*

4   in patriam serus ab urbe redi: in order to approach the emperor in person (3n.), Dento has travelled some distance from home and has been staying in Rome for a considerable time.

serus 'at long last'.

5–6   'for while, abandoning your wife, you seek far off and for such a long time three children, you are likely to find four' (but not, of course, your own). Cf. Nicarchus, *AP* 11.243.

5   deserta puts Dento further in the wrong: by abandoning his wife for so long he can be held responsible for her infidelity.

6   A neatly balanced punchline, with the key words *tres* and *quattuor* placed emphatically at the beginning of each half of the pentameter.

50   (= 7.67)

'Philaenis the tribad penetrates both boys and girls, engages in sport and gymnastic exercises, drinks and vomits up copious amounts of wine and consumes huge quantities of athletes' food. When after this her thoughts turn to sex, regarding fellation to be insufficiently masculine, she devours girls' middles. May you continue in your perverse ways, Philaenis, deluded as you are into thinking cunnilinctus a mannish activity.'

This epigram attacks the female homosexual Philaenis, who, by her sexual practices, athletic endeavours, and drinking and eating habits seeks to outdo any male. This is one of three epigrams by M. on the topic of Lesbianism (cf. 1.90 and 7.70), a subject of which we hear relatively little in classical antiquity, almost all of it hostile. The basic objection against such females is that they act in a manner contrary to nature, by usurping male sexual and social prerogatives. Cf. Sen. *Ep.* 95.20–1, in many ways the best commentary on the present poem: *non mutata feminarum natura, sed uicta est; nam cum uirorum licentiam aequauerint, corporum quoque uirilium incommoda aequarunt. non minus peruigilant, non minus potant, et oleo et mero uiros prouocant; aeque inuitis ingesta uisceribus per os reddunt et uinum omne uomitu remetiuntur; aeque niuem rodunt, solacium stomachi aestuantis. libidine uero ne maribus quidem cedunt, pati natae, di illas deaeque male perdant! adeo peruersum commentae genus impudicitiae uiros ineunt.* Juvenal's mannish female (6.419–33) also acts in a manner very similar to Philaenis, although her disgusting behaviour is not specifically linked by the satirist to sexual inversion.

Further reading: Hallet (1989), Harris (1972), Krenkel (1980a), Lilja (1983)

1   **Pedicat pueros:**   Philaenis engages in anal intercourse with boys, a practice elsewhere confined to males, but consonant with ancient views of Lesbian physiology. Certain women, it was believed, had an over-developed clitoris (Cael. Aurel. *Gyn.* 2.112, M. 3.72.6) which could supposedly be used as a surrogate penis in Lesbian coitus or, as here, to practise sodomy. Cf. Howell on 1.90.7, and n. on 3.

  tribas: the *uox propria* for a Lesbian, literally 'she who rubs'. The word 'Lesbian' in classical antiquity refers not to female homoeroticism, but to the practice of *fellatio*: see H. D. Jocelyn, *PCPhS* 26 (1980) 12–66, A. C. Cassio, *CQ* 33 (1983) 296–7.

Philaenis: a name with pejorative and erotic associations (**84**.1 n.). The female pornographer Philaenis is said to have practised tribadism ([Lucian], *Am.* 28).

2   tentigine saeuior mariti = *tento saeuior marito. tendo* and *tentigo* are often used of male erection.

saeuior: of unbridled lust; cf. Hor. *Carm.* 1.25.13–15 *cum tibi flagrans amor et libido | ... | saeuiet circa iecur ulcerosum.*

3   undenas dolat in die puellas: such improbable feats of sexual athleticism are normally a male accomplishment: cf. Catull. 32.7–8 *paresque nobis | nouem continuas fututiones*, Hopfner (1938) 259–60.

dolat: literally 'chips, hews'; one of several words belonging to the semantic field 'cut, beat', which are used of sexual penetration (Adams, *LSV* 146): cf. Pompon. 78 Frass. *dolasti uxorem.* M. applies to Philaenis a term suggestive of male sexual dominance. Lesbians are frequently accused of confounding nature by adopting the active, masculine rôle in intercourse: cf. 1.90.8 *mentiturque uirum prodigiosa Venus*, Hor. *Epod.* 5.41–2, Lucian, *Dial. meret.* 5.2.

4–7   Philaenis establishes her masculinity by indulging in sporting pursuits which, despite limited participation by women (H. M. Lee, *Nikephoros* 1 (1988) 117 n.36), were seen as a male preserve. Cf. the tribad Megilla of Lucian, *Dial meret.* 5.3, who, doffing her wig, 'revealed the skin on her head which was shaved close like the most manly of athletes', and a hostess who, like a man, takes exercise before her bath (Juv. 6.419–33).

4   harpasto: the ball used in the game of *harpastum* or *phaininda*, which seems to have involved two teams of two in which one player sought to pass the ball to his fellow player using feints, jostling the opposition and shouting instructions: cf. S. Mendner, *Gymnasium* 66 (1959) 517–24; Harris (1972) 88–90. The game called for much violent exertion (Athen. 14f–15a). In Ovid's day at least, *puellae* did not take part in ball games (cf. Ov. *Ars* 3.381–6).

subligata: either 'with her clothes girt up', to facilitate ease of movement while exercising, or 'wearing a loin-cloth', *subligar*, which may have been part of the attire worn by female athletes: cf. Lee cited on 4–7, **29**.4n.

5–6   Philaenis effortlessly rotates weights which would tax even a strong man. *halteres* light enough for female use have been discovered (cf. N. B. Crowther, *G&R* 24 (1977) 118); Philaenis, with her unnaturally developed musculature, has no need of such.

5   **flauescit:**   cf. Ov. *Met.* 9.35–6 *ille cauis hausto spargit me puluere palmis | inque uicem fuluae tactu flauescit harenae.*

   haphe: properly sand sprinkled on wrestlers, to allow them to get a grip (ἀφή) on each other (Sen. *Ep.* 57.1), but in view of the mention of wrestling (7), the word cannot have that meaning here: it must re- fer to the sand on the floor of the courtyard, part of the bath-complex, where Romans exercised. Philaenis becomes dirty from this as she works out.

   grauesque draucis 'heavy even for strong-men'. *draucus* = 'one who performs feats of strength in public' (Housman, *CP* 1166–7). Since *drauci* were also in demand for their supposed sexual endowments (Kay on 11.72.1), M. may be implying that Philaenis is a female equivalent.

6   **halteras facili rotat lacerto:**   *halteres* (from Gk ἅλμα, 'leap') were cylindrical lumps of stone or metal used either to impart impetus when jumping, or, as here, swung in the hand like dumb-bells to develop the shoulder muscles: cf. Sen. *Ep.* 56.1 *cum fortiores exercentur et manus plumbo graues iactant*, Harris (1972) 150.

7   **putri lutulenta de palaestra:**   before exercising, wrestlers oiled their bodies, which became dirty both from a preliminary roll in the *ceroma*, the clay floor of the wrestling ring, and subsequently from the contest proper: cf. 11.47.5 *luteum ceromate corpus*, 14.50.1, O. W. Reinmuth, *Phoenix* 21 (1967) 191–5. The surface was soft and crumbly (*putri*), easily rubbed off on the body: cf. 4.19.5, 7.32.9, *AP* 12.192.3 'the crumbly dirt on a boy wrestler'.

8   **uncti . . . magistri:**   a major function of the athletic trainer (*mag- ister*) was to massage his charges with oil, hence his alternative designation of *aleiptes*, lit. 'anointer'. In so doing he becomes himself *unctus*. Sen. *Ep.* 15.3 describes trainers as *pessimae notae mancipia in magisterium recepta, homines inter oleum et uinum occupati*; cf. Quint. *Inst.* 1.11.15.

   uapulat: the 'pummelling' that Philaenis gets in the course of a mas- sage following exercise: cf. Sen. *Ep.* 56.1 *cum in aliquem inertem et hac plebeia unctione contentum incidi, audio crepitum inlisae manus umeris, quae prout plana peruenit* *aut concaua, ita sonum mutat.* Verbs of striking are often used metaphorically of sexual acts (Adams, *LSV* 145–9): *uapulat* may conceal an obscene double entendre, as masseurs were accused of stimulating sexually their female clients: cf. Juv. 6.422–3, Clem. Alex. *Paed.* 3.5.32.

9–10   Philaenis reclines at table after imbibing then vomiting up huge quantities of wine. There are numerous references to such behaviour: cf. Plin. *NH* 14.139, 29.26, Sen. *Dial.* 1.3.13. The practice was adopted for medical reasons, either to stimulate the appetite (Sen. *Dial.* 12.10.3), or to purge the stomach (Ath. 665d–e), but M.'s point is that the woman is behaving disgustingly: cf. Juvenal's graphic account of a wine-bibbing hostess (6.425–33). Excessive drinking by women was frowned upon, an attitude going back to the absolute prohibition in Rome's earliest days on the consumption of alcohol by females (L. Minieri, *Labeo* 28 (1982) 150–63).

10   **septem ... deunces:** a *deunx* was a measure of eleven *unciae*: the usual measure was four (approx. 1/3 pint: cf. 1.106.8, 4.82.5). Philaenis is represented as drinking seven servings of wine, each nearly three times the normal size – a total of over 6 pints! Similar excess is attributed to Zoilus (**56**.29).

uomuit: a surprise for *bibit.*

meros: the wine is both 'undiluted', suggesting heavy drinking, and 'undigested' i.e. is vomited straight up again after swallowing: cf. Sen. *Dial.* 1.3.13 *hi quidquid biberunt uomitu remetientur, Ep.* 95.21 (intro.).

11   **ad quos ... redire:** cf. Plin. *NH* 29.26 *potus deinde ieiuniorum ac uomitiones et rursus perpotationes.* The process of drinking deep, then vomiting, might be repeated several times (Plin. *NH* 14.139).

fas: Philaenis establishes her own standards of what is right and wrong at table.

12   **colyphia:** *colyphium* (κωλύφιον) is a cut of meat, probably the haunch, eaten by athletes, diet being an important part of the athletic regimen (*RE* VII 2026–30). *colyphium,* rather than MS *coloephium,* is the correct form (J. André, *RPh* 40 (1966) 48–9). The second syllable is long in Latin but short in Greek.

comedit: the prefix has an intensifying force, underlining the point made by *sedecim,* that her appetite is excessive, presumably in imitation of athletes, who ate heavily (Sen. *Ep.* 15.3). For intensifying *com/con,* cf. Juv. 6.100–1 *illa maritum | conuomit.*

13   post haec omnia cum libidinatur: her sexual appetite is aroused by all the wine which she has consumed: cf. Arist. *Probl.* 10.3, Apul. *Met.* 2.11 *Veneris hortator et armiger Liber*, Gerber (1988).

14   non fellat – putat hoc parum uirile – : *fellatio* was widely imputed to effeminate males (Krenkel (1980a) *passim*), and therefore cannot be countenanced by the ultra-virile Philaenis.

15   plane 'simply', strongly colloquial in flavour.
  medias: a common euphemism for the genitalia in contexts of oral sex: cf. 2.61.2 *lambebat medios improba lingua uiros*, Kay on 11.61.5, Adams, *LSV* 46–7.
  uorat: a vulgar metaphor for oral sex: cf. Catull. 80.6 *grandia te medii tenta uorare uiri*, Tertull. *Apol.* 9.2, **59**.2n.

16–17   M. amusingly wishes upon Philaenis a continuation of her present disgusting behaviour: cf. 7.24.7–8 *hoc tibi pro meritis et talibus imprecor ausis, | ut facias illud quod, puto, lingua, facis*, Symm. *Ep.* 4.48 *dii illos mentibus suis puniant*. Humorous curses are often sexual in character (Watson (1991) 142–56).

17   Far from being manly as Philaenis apparently thinks, cunnilinctus is, in M.'s view, a thoroughly unmasculine activity (cf. 2.84, **69**.14–15), since it involves the man's servicing the female and thus abandoning the dominant rôle played by the Roman male in sexual relations. In general, M. treats cunnilinctus as a sordid and illiberal activity: cf. 9.92.11, Citroni 1.77 intro., Krenkel (1980a) 85.

51 (= 12.20)

'You are wondering, Fabullus, why Themison has no wife. He has his sister.'

On Themison, who sleeps with his sister and so has no need of a wife. The epigram is one of three in M. dealing with the subject of incest: cf. 2.4 and 4.16 (the latter deals with 'incest' between stepmother and stepson: the Roman definition of *incestum* in the sense of a prohibited sexual union was much wider than ours and included a number of relationships by marriage: cf. A. Guarino, *ZRG* 63 (1943) 175–267). Accusations of incest were traded in a range of contexts: cf. Hippon. fr. 12.2 W, W. Süss, *Ethos* (Leipzig 1910) 249–50, Krenkel (1980a). But the primary inspiration for the present epigram comes from Catullus. Not only is the addressee's name Catullan (**31**.4n.), but Catullus, who made much of the incest-theme, devoted especial attention to that between brother and sister: cf. in particular 79.1–2 *Lesbius est pulcher. quid ni? quem Lesbia malit | quam te cum tota gente, Catulle, tua,* alluding to the rumours of a sexual relationship between Clodia/Lesbia and her brother P. Clodius Pulcher: cf. Krenkel (1981) 47. The thrust of the Catullan accusations is that incest is a barbarous practice, and implies an offensive assumption that no one outside the family is worthy of union: cf. poem 90, Eur. *Andr.* 173–6 with Stevens, Hopkins (1980), Rankin (1976) 120. The points which M. is making are less serious. First, Themison, whose name suggests that he is a doctor (2n.), is satirised for the corrupt sexual practices to which physicians were allegedly prone. Second, there is an ironic play on his name: Themison (cf. Gk *themis*, 'right') is manifestly acting παρὰ τὰ θεμιτά, 'contrary to what is right and proper', by sleeping with his sister.

Although M. is primarily drawing on Catullus, accusations of brother–sister incest were widespread: cf. Lys. *Contr. Alcibid.* 1.28, Plut. *Cim.* 4.6–8, 15.2–3, Suet. *Cal.* 24.1, SHA *Commod.* 5.8. Marriage between siblings was forbidden in Roman law: cf. Gaius, *Inst.* 1.61 *sane inter fratrem et sororem prohibitae sunt nuptiae,* FIRA 1 99.23 (contrast Athens, where a man could marry his half-sister by a common father).

Further reading: Dolderer (1933), Hanard (1986), Hopkins (1980), Rankin (1976), Römer (1990), Solin (1995)

1   **Fabulle:** **31**.4n.
    quaeris: a regular opening gambit, e.g. 6.67.1–2 *cur tantum eunuchos habeat tua Gellia quaeris, | Pannyche?,* 10.22.3.

2   **Themison:** a common Greek name, particularly associated with the medical profession, possibly in imitation of Themison of Laodicea, an important figure connected with the methodist school (L. Edelstein, *Ancient medicine* (Baltimore 1967) 73–8). For doctors bearing this name, cf. Juv. 10.221, Solin (1995) 126–8, Römer (1990) *passim.* If Themison is a physician, then he is transferring to his sister the sexual attentions which doctors were notorious for bestowing on female patients: cf. 6.31 *uxorem, Charideme, tuam scis ipse sinisque | a medico futui,* 11.71, Plin. *NH* 29.20, Dolderer (1933) 27–9).
    habet sororem 'he "has" his sister' (not 'he has a girlfriend', rightly rejected by Housman, *CPh* 734–5). *habeo* is used in the dual sense of 'has'

and 'possesses sexually'. For the latter, cf. Ov. *Met.* 9.497 *di nempe suas habuere sorores*, Adams, *LSV* 187.

52   (= 3.65)

'All the most fragrant smells that one can imagine, such are your kisses, Diadumenus. What would they be like if you granted them willingly?'

As in the closely related 11.8, M. illustrates the fragrance of a boy's kisses by a series of comparisons with sweet odours of various kinds. Both epigrams end with a surprise twist: in this case, a complaint that the boy is grudging in bestowing these kisses. M. addresses Diadumenus twice elsewhere, also on the theme of kisses: 6.34, and 5.46 where, in striking contrast to the present epigram, M. declares that he deliberately arouses the boy's anger because he only enjoys kisses given under duress.

Sexual relationships between free men and boys of servile origin were widely accepted in Roman society, provided that such a relationship maintained the social hierarchy, the older man assuming the active (dominant) rôle and the young slave or freedman the passive (subservient) rôle: cf. Sen. *Contr.* 4 *praef.* 10 *impudicitia* [sc. playing the rôle of *pathicus*] *in ingenuo crimen est, in seruo necessitas, in liberto officium*; Petr. 75.11, Garrido-Hory (1981a) 300–6, Verstraete (1980), Williams (1995). The epigram, then, has a basis in reality, though this does not necessarily mean that Diadumenus was real. It is also grounded in literary tradition: love poems to boys are an integral part of the epigrammatic genre, e.g. Strato's *Musa puerilis* and Catullus' Iuventius-poems. But whereas epigrammatists such as Meleager and Catullus treated both pederastic and heterosexual relationships, in M. the absence of corresponding love poems addressed to women is striking and may suggest a preference on the part of the real M. for boy love (cf. intro. 6).

The *cumulatio* technique used here, consisting of a series of examples linked by anaphora, is a particular favourite of M.: cf. Kay on 11.21 intro. In the present case it is especially effective because of an artful variation in the length of the individual *exempla*, the subtlety of many of the fragrances, well suited to the gentle perfume of the boy's kisses, and the vividness of images such as the young girl biting an apple, sheep cropping the grass, or the reaper in Arabia harvesting his spices.

The association of pleasant smells with eroticism had been traditional since Homer, *Il.* 14.170–8. The fragrance of the kisses or the breath of young persons of both sexes is often referred to in amatory contexts: cf. *Anacre-ontea* 43.8–9 'and with her a soft-haired boy with sweet-smelling mouth', *AP* 5.118, 305.1–2, Stat. *Silu.* 2.1.46 *osculaque impliciti uernos redolentia flores*, Lilja (1972) 120–4.

Further reading: Garrido-Hory (1981a), Grewing (1996), Lilja (1972), Obermayer (1998) 66–9, Verstraete (1980), Williams (1995)

1   Quod spirat tenera malum mordente puella: a particularly effective opening image, appropriate in several ways: (1) apples exude a subtle fragrance when bitten; (2) *tenera puella* evokes the youthful freshness of the boy's kisses; (3) apples are a common erotic symbol: cf. E. S. McCartney, *TAPhA* 56 (1925) 70–81, A. R. Littlewood, *HSPh* 72 (1968) 149–59.

quod spirat: for the opening, cf. 11.8.1 *lassa quod hesterni spirant opobal-sama dracti.*

2   quod de Corycio . . . croco: sc. *spirat*, 'the fragrance which per-fume that comes from Corycian saffron exhales'. *Corycius* is a stock epithet of saffron, the choicest type of which came from Mt Corycus in Cilicia (Plin. *NH* 21.31): cf. Hor. *S.* 2.4.68 *Corycioque croco.* M. may have in mind the spraying of saffron-water in the theatre: cf. 11.8.2 with Kay. On saffron cf. Lilja (1972), 92–3, 196, L. Robert, *REA* 62 (1960) 333–5. In this pederastic context, it may be relevant that Crocus was a beautiful youth turned into the homonymous flower (Ov. *Fast.* 5.227, *Met.* 4.283).

aura: lit. 'breeze', refers to the sweet 'odour' exhaled by the saffron: cf. Virg. *G.* 4.416–7 *at illi* | *dulcis compositis spirauit crinibus aura.*

3   uinea quod primis cum floret cana racemis: the pleasant aroma emitted by the vineyard when the anther of the vine blossom, which is white, appears: cf. V. Picón, *EClás* (1980) 105–6.

cum floret: *floret cum*, the reading of C, is preferred by some editors on the grounds that a monosyllable in the second half of the third foot of the hexameter can only precede a spondaic word if there is strong break in sense (cf. F. Marx, *Molossische und bakcheische Wortformen* (Leipzig 1922), 215). But the rule does not always apply, and in cases like this where the clause is introduced by a conjunction is usually not observed [EJK].

4   gramina . . . quae modo carpsit ouis: the association of the smell of new cut grass with animals cropping the grass is original to M.

5   quod myrtus: sc. *olet*; for the sweet scent of the myrtle, cf. Hor. *Carm.* 2.15.6 with N–H, Ov. *Ars* 3.690, Lilja (1972) 175n. It was especially associated with Aphrodite (Plin. *NH* 15.120), making it an apt subject of comparison here.

messor Arabs 'the Arabian harvester'; cf. [Tib.] 3.8.17–18 *metit quidquid bene olentibus aruis | cultor odoratae diues Arabs segetis*. Arabia was famous for its spices, especially balsam, frankincense and myrrh, gathered by tapping the bark of the tree and collecting the juice exuded: see Plin. *NH* 12.58–60, J. I. Miller, *The spice trade of the Roman empire* (Oxford 1969) 101–5. In the process the *messor* would become imbued with their fragrances.

sucina trita: amber, the fossilised resin of an extinct species of conifer, exudes a piny smell when 'rubbed'. It was a favourite luxury item of Roman ladies who carried lumps of the substance as a perfume: cf. 11.8.6, Juv. 6.573–4, P. Watson, *LCM* 17 (1992) 1–4.

6   pallidus: pale yellow; cf. Ov. *Met.* 11.110 *saxum quoque palluit auro*. The flame takes on the amber hue of the frankincense, *tus*, for the colour of which cf. Pind. fr. 107 Bowra 'amber tears of yellow frankincense'; Moldenke (1952) 57.

Eoo: from Arabia, home of frankincense (Plin. *NH* 12.51; Virg. *G.* 2.117 *solis est turea uirga Sabaeis*).

ignis olet: frankincense gives off a strong balsamic odour when burned (Moldenke (1952) 57). Incense was burned in various contexts (Lilja (1972) 31–47, 50–2). M. no doubt has in mind its sympotic/erotic associations, for which cf. Plaut. *Men.* 353–4 *sternite lectos, incendite odores, munditia | illecebra animost amantium.*

7   gleba quod [olet] ... imbre: cf. Pacuv. fr. 412 D'Anna *terra exhalat auram ad auroram humidam.*

leuiter: because summer rain was light (Nissen I 391).

8   madidas nardo passa corona comas: a garland, a traditional accoutrement of the symposium, impregnated with the perfume which was poured over the hair at drinking parties: cf. Hor. *Carm.* 1.4.9–10 with N–H, Ov. *Am.* 1.6.38 *madidis lapsa corona comis.* The unusual *passa*, lit. 'having undergone', may be chosen for the sake of a gratuitous verbal play with *madidas*, 'drenched': another meaning of *passus* is 'dry'.

nardo: an unguent made from spikenard, a perennial herb of the valerian family, with strong and pleasant-scented roots (Moldenke (1952)

148–9). It was often used to perfume the hair: cf. Tib. 2.2.7 *illius puro destillent tempora nardo*, Ov. *Ars* 3.443, Lilja (1972) 84–7.

9   tua . . . basia fragrant: a young lover's kisses were traditionally fragrant (see intro).

   saeue 'cruel', because reluctant to bestow kisses (cf. 10). Iuventius is accused of *saeuitia* for similar reasons (Catull. 99.6).

   Diadumene: from Greek διαδούμενος 'binding one's hair', a common servile name, and an appropriate appellation for a young *delicatus*, since it suggests the famous Διαδούμενος of Polyclitus (cf. C. Picard, *Manuel d'archéologie grecque* (Paris 1939) II 1.287–300), a statue of a youth with his hair bound back, noteworthy for the beauty of its subject and his youthful appearance: cf. Lucian, *Philopseud.* 18, Plin. *NH* 34.55 (Polyclitus) *Diadumenum fecit molliter iuuenem*.

10   quid si . . . dares: a veiled imperative.

   tota 'in their fulness' (SB) i.e. with his whole mouth, like the lovers' kisses satirically described by Lucretius (4.1194) *et tenet assuctis umectans oscula labris*. Diadumenus apparently gives M. kisses of the type mentioned at 2.10.1 *basia dimidio quod das mihi, Postume, labro.*

   sine inuidia 'without reluctance': a slave was unable to refuse the sexual advances of his master, but M. would prefer Diadumenus' willing obedience rather than his grudging compliance. Paley and Stone and SB less attractively treat *sine inuidia* as a calque on ἀφθόνως, i.e. 'unstintingly', 'in generous quantities'.

53   (= 7.87)

'If certain friends and acquaintances of mine delight in a variety of bizarre and improbable pets, surely [my] Babyrtas with his winning countenance is not too odd to love?'

M. rationalises his affection for Babyrtas by appealing to the strange *deliciae* in which his acquaintances take great, even passionate, delight – exotica such as a fennec, an ichneumon, an ape, a black African, a pet snake and a *pica* with its astonishing power of imitating human speech. The lap-dog (3) and the nightingale (8) might appear out of place in such a list, but the idea seems to be that they are remarkable not so much *per se* but for the extravagance of the affection showered on them by their owners.

These pets are collectively defined as *monstra* 'freaks' in 10 and it is a logical inference that Babyrtas is likewise an oddity of some sort, possibly an intellectually impaired dwarf: both dwarfs and *fatui* were often kept as *deliciae* (9n.).

Since 1–8 describe relations between owner and pet, 9–10 must by extension deal with a similar relationship: that between M. and his slave Babyrtas. We might therefore have expected *amem* rather than *amet* in 9. The difficulty is solved either by understanding 'my' i.e. 'why should anyone who sees these *monstra* pleasing their owners not love the winning face of my Babyrtas?' or, perhaps better, by taking M. to refer to himself in the third person 'why should not he who sees [i.e. I, Martial] ... not love ... ?'

Further reading: Friedrich (1913), Herrlinger (1930)

1   meus ... Flaccus: Flaccus is one of the commonest of M.'s addressees, evidently a close friend (Pitcher (1984) 414–23); he is mentioned at 10.48.5 along with Canius, the subject of the next verse.

lagalopece lit. 'hare-fox' (λαγώς, ἀλώπηξ) has generally been adopted since Schneidewin for MS *lagagopece* or *-cepe*. It is recommended by *aurita*, which suits an animal resembling a hare; cf. Virg. *G.* 1.308 *auritos ... sequi lepores*. *lagalopece* is thought to refer to a fennec, a small North African fox noted for its huge pointed ears. Most of the individuals in this epigram exhibit some resemblance to their pets and Flaccus (lit. 'floppy eared') is a suitable owner for a fox with large ears like a hare. The hybrid form, which underlines the creature's oddity, recalls composite names such as χηναλώπηξ 'goose-fox', and στρουθοκάμηλος 'sparrow-camel', ostrich.

2   tristi: gloominess was not especially associated with Ethiopians, but two statuettes of the Hellenistic period show black Africans with plaintive expressions (G. H. Beardsley, *The negro in Greek and Roman civilisation: a study of the Ethiopian type* (Baltimore 1929) figs. 214, 223).

Canius: M.'s close friend and fellow-Spaniard (1.61.9 with Howell).

Aethiope: '"Aethiops" ... designates a particular human somatic type that might today be described as "black African"' (Thompson (1989) 57). The Aethiops may have been a *delicium*, a bed-mate of Canius (Thompson (1989) 147): for such *Aethiopes capillati* cf. Petr. 34.4, for *fruor* 'enjoy sexually' see Adams, *LSV* 197–8. Whether or not this is correct, M. feels it improbable that Canius should take pleasure in an individual whose gloominess was temperamentally alien to him (1.69, 3.20.21).

3   Publius: a friend of M. mentioned several times: cf. Howell on 1.109.

exiguae ... catellae: Issa, the *deliciae Publi* whose charms are celebrated in 1.109, almost certainly a Maltese lapdog, a 'tiny' breed and a popular pet among both Greeks and Romans: cf. Ath. 518e, Ael. *NA* 7.40, Orth, *RE* VIII 2552. Epitaphs for canine pets survive (Herrlinger (1930) 182); Theophr. *Char.* 7.34 and *AP* 7.211 mention inscriptions or tombs being set up for Maltese dogs. Cf. Toynbee (1973) 108–22.

flagrat amore 'is ablaze with passion', suggesting a degree of extravagance in Publius' feelings for a mere lapdog.

4   Cronius: the MSS are divided between *Cronius* and *Chronius*. Both names are found elsewhere, and false aspiration and false psilosis are frequent in the MSS of M., making a decision difficult. *Cronius* creates a better alliterative effect with *cercopithecon*, thus reinforcing aurally the resemblance between master and pet.

similem: sc. *sibi*: cf. 6.77.8 *quaeque uehit similem belua nigra Libyn*. To compare someone to an ape was a common insult: cf. Cic. *Fam.* 5.10.1, 7.2.3, Hor. *S.* 1.10.18, Suet. *Nero* 30.2.

cercopithecon: a generic name for an ape with a tail (κέρκος). Although there is considerable evidence for apes as pets (W. C. McDermott, *The ape in antiquity* (Baltimore 1938) 131–40), the 'love' which Cronius feels is nonetheless paradoxical: the creatures were notorious for their ugliness and bad character: cf. Ennius *apud* Cic. *ND* 1.97 *simia ... turpissima bestia* with Pease, Simon. fr. 7.73 W, W. C. McDermott, *TAPhA* 67 (1936) 148–67.

5   delectat Marium: it is unclear whether Marius is real, or whether, given that his pet is a natural killer (*perniciosus*), the name is chosen to recall the bloody career of Gaius Marius.

perniciosus ichneumon: a weasel-like North African animal related to the Indian mongoose, which preys upon all sorts of four-footed creatures, birds and reptile eggs. Notwithstanding its aggressiveness, it is even in modern times often kept tamed (Keller (1909) 158–60).

6   pica salutatrix: a magpie (or jay: Thompson (1936) 146–8) which gives a salutation. Its uncanny imitative capacities are often remarked (e.g. Ov. *Met.* 5.299 *imitantes omnia picae*), and it could be taught to utter various forms of greeting: cf. Macrob. *Sat.* 2.4.30, Petr. 28.9, M. 14.76.1 *pica loquax certa dominum te uoce saluto*. According to Plin. *NH* 10.118 it was even more articulate than a parrot.

Lause: Lausus features in the adjacent poems 7.88 and 7.81, apparently as a friendly critic. The name was Spanish (*CIL* XIV 3795, Schulze (1904) 85); possibly Lausus, like Canius and perhaps Glaucilla (n. *ad loc.*), was a compatriot.

7   si gelidum collo nectit ... draconem: cf. Suet. *Tib.* 72.2 (a pet snake which fed out of Tiberius' hand), Sen. *Dial.* 4.31.6 *aspice ... repentes inter pocula sinusque innoxio lapsu dracones,* Toynbee (1973) 224. Nevertheless to drape (*nectere*) a snake round one's neck seems an act of singular bravado.

gelidum: like *frigidus* and ψυχρός, a stock epithet to describe the purportedly cold and clammy feel of snakes' skin; cf. Luc. 6.488, 12.28.5 *ceruinus gelidum sorbet sic halitus anguem,* A. Sauvage, *RPh* 49 (1975) 248.

Glaucilla: the MSS are divided between Gladella, Gadilla, Gedilla and Glacia. Glaucilla, the suggestion of Heinsius, would forge another connexion between pet and owner: the epithet γλαυκός is applied to snakes in Greek. Friedrich (1913) 273–4 makes a plausible case for Claudilla; Heraeus proposed Cadilla, a name known in Hispania Ulterior (*CIL* II 971), which would make the lady a fellow-Spaniard like Canius and, putatively, Lausus.

8   luscinio: the nightingale was kept as a caged pet (Nemes. *Ecl.* 2.60–6, Toynbee (1973) 276–7) on account of its song, which was widely accounted the most beautiful among birds: cf. Plin. *NH* 10.81–3, Sauvage (1975) 195–6.

tumulum: there seems to have been a fad, particularly in Imperial times, for the burial of pets, including birds (Ael. *NA* 7.41, Ov. *Am.* 2.6.59–62, Plin. *NH* 10.121–3, Stat. *Silu.* 2.6.20). The practice may have been given an impetus by the custom of burying the emperor's horse: cf. Plin. *NH* 8.155, Herrlinger (1930) 10–12.

9   blanda Cupidinei ... ora: if, as argued below, Babyrtas was a *morio,* the phrase may suggest that, as in 12.93, he was also a dwarf, a popular kind of *delicium* (Garland (1995) 46–8). Intellectual impairment is a feature of certain types of dwarfism (V. Dasen, *Dwarfs in ancient Egypt and Greece* (Oxford 1993) 12–15), and proportionate short-stature dwarfism is characterised by doll-like, childish features (Dasen 12–13 with pl. 1.4), for which *blanda Cupidinei ... ora* would be an eminently suitable description.

Cupidinei: elsewhere this epithet = 'belonging to Cupid', but the sense required here is 'Cupid-like'; Scàndola's *seducente come Cupido* catches the sense nicely.

Babyrtae: suggested by Friedrich (1913) 275–6 as a plausible alternative to the reading of B *Labyrtae* (superior to C's *Labycae*: names in -υρτας are commoner than those in -υκας: cf. C. A. Lobeck, *Pathologiae sermonis Graeci prolegomena* (Leipzig 1843) 331, 397). The name Labyrtas is elsewhere unknown, whereas Babyrtas (cf. *baburrus* = *stultus* (Isid. *Orig.* 10.31, *CGL* IV 589.4)) could designate a *morio*, which would fit the idea that this person is treasured by M. despite manifest short-comings. For *moriones* as *delicia*, see **44**.17n.

10   monstra 'freaks', τέρατα, for which there was a specialised market in Rome (Plut. *De curios.* 10). On the term see Cl. Moussy, *REL* 55 (1977) 345–69.

54   (= 2.16)

'Zoilus is unwell. It is his luxury coverlets that are responsible. How could he show these off unless he affected illness? You have no need of doctors. Do you want to recover? Take my [miserable] bedclothes.'

An attack on Zoilus, who pretends to be ill in order to display to sick-visitors his luxurious bedclothes. **54** is the first of seventeen epigrams on this fictitious individual, whose character is developed at far greater length than any other in M.: see further intro. 14–15. Zoilus is a common slave name (*CIL* IV index s.v.); the name was also borne by a notoriously unpleasant Homeric critic of the fourth century BC (see Kay on 11.12 intro.). Both details suit M.'s Zoilus, who is an unwholesome parvenu, i.e. a person of humble, often servile, origins, who has risen dramatically in the world.

Further reading: Duff (1928), Meyer (1913), Ransom (1905), Sebesta (1994)

1   faciunt...stragula febrem: it is not illness, but the desire to show off his coverlets, that make Zoilus take to his bed.

stragula: the various draperies placed over the bed, which among the wealthy were often elaborate and expensive: cf. Tib. 1.2.77, Lucr. 2.34–6 (cf. 6n.). Zoilus has *stragula* of both scarlet (2) and embroidered purple (3).

2   si fuerit sanus 'if he recovers'.
coccina 'scarlet materials'. Scarlet dye (*coccus*) was obtained from an insect living on the kermes-oak. Along with amethyst and purple, scarlet was especially associated with luxury (Plin. *NH* 21.45–6, Suet. *Nero* 30.3).

quid facient? 'what will be the good of?', a colloquial use of *facio*, which is often found in medical contexts and is thus neatly ironic: cf. Citroni on 1.59.2, *OLD* s.v. 30b.

3   torus a Nilo: lit. 'a mattress/bed from the Nile', apparently refers to a *torus* with embroidered coverlets of the type known as 'Alexandrina' or 'polymita': cf. 14.150.1–2 [*Cubicularia polymita*] *Haec tibi Memphitis tellus* (sc. Egypt) *dat munera: uicta est | pectine Niliaco iam Babylonos acus*, Plin. *NH* 8.196, and for *torus* used with reference to the coverlets, cf. Prop. 1.14.20 *ostrino... toro*. Some interpret *torus a Nilo* as a mattress either stuffed with papyrus, or imported from Egypt and filled with cotton, or encased in Egyptian linen, but these explanations do not do justice to the emphasis on the luxurious appearance of Zoilus' bed.

Sidone tinctus olenti: a coverlet dyed with Tyrian purple (*Sidone* n.). Of the various types of 'purple' material, the most highly prized was the Tyrian. Its distinctive deep-red shade was obtained by dipping the cloth first in the dye obtained from the sea-purple (*pelagium*) and then in that derived from the whelk (*bucinum*): see Plin. *NH* 9.135. The ultimate in luxury, Tyrian purple was especially popular in wealthy households for coverings of beds and dining couches; cf. Tib. 1.2.75 *Tyrio... toro*, Virg. *G.* 3.306–7.

Sidone: Sidonian purple. Although the Phoenician town of Sidon had its own dyeing industry, 'Sidonian' is probably a synonym for the more famous 'Tyrian', Tyre and its neighbour Sidon being closely associated (see Kay on 11.1.2).

olenti 'strong smelling'. Tyrian purple had a pungent odour (*uirus graue* Plin. *NH* 9.127), because the dye was obtained from decaying shell-fish (Lilja (1972) 136). This disadvantage was overlooked by those who prized it as a luxury item, but in satirical contexts its smell is emphasised to illustrate the folly of *luxuria*.

4   ostendit stultas quid nisi morbus opes?: like all parvenus, Zoilus acquires luxuries not for their own sake but to show off his wealth, in this case to the friends who visit him in his sick-chamber, an important duty of *amici* (J. C. Yardley, *Phoenix* 27 (1973) 283–8).

5   Machaonas: doctors; cf. Ov. *Pont.* 3.4.7 *firma ualent per se nullumque Machaona quaerunt*. Machaon was a healer, like his father Asclepius, god of medicine: along with Podalirius, he attended to the wounded Greeks at Troy. M. likes to use mythical prototypes to represent different classes of people (H. Szelest, *Eos* 62 (1974) 297–310).

6   stragula sume mea: poor bedclothes such as M.'s own would effect Zoilus' speedy recovery, since he would no longer have the motivation for feigning illness.

55   (= 2.29)

'Rufus, you see that man sitting prominently in the equestrian rows at the front of the theatre, decked out in the richest and most luxurious fashion? Although he tries to pass for a knight by giving the impression that he is not merely wealthy but also of superior breeding (7–8), he is in fact an ex-slave, as you will see if you remove the "beauty spots", which hide the marks of slavish punishment.'

Under the *Lex Roscia theatralis* of 67 BC, the first fourteen rows in the theatre behind the orchestra were reserved for the equestrian class: cf. E. Scamuzzi, *RivStClass* 17 (1969) 133–65, Reinhold (1971) 281. Widespread abuse of the edict by persons not technically qualified to occupy these seats led Domitian to reinforce it (Suet. *Dom.* 8.3) around AD 89: there are frequent allusions to the subject in book 5, published in that year. Domitian's action was directed against (1) those without the equestrian census of 400,000 sesterces: cf. 5.23, 27; (2) freedmen who possessed the census but were disqualified by birth from enrolment among the *equites*, freeborn status going back three generations being a prerequisite: cf. Plin. *NH* 33.32, T. P. Wiseman, *Historia* 19 (1970) 67–83, Reinhold (1971) 275–302. The subject of the present epigram belongs to the second category.

In the above, it is assumed that M.'s object of attack is attempting to pass himself off as a knight of patrician stock, whose distinctive footwear he has appropriated (cf. 7–8nn.). SB and others, however, argue that the freedman wants to be taken for a senator. This involves understanding *prima subsellia* as the senatorial seats in the orchestra at the front of the theatre, and 7–8 as referring to the senatorial shoe, which was similar to the patrician shoe (Diocletian's edict (*CIL* III suppl. 5.6) gives separate prices for *calcei patricii* and *calcei senatorii*, but it is unclear exactly how they differed). It seems improbable, however, that someone would be able to masquerade as a member of the senatorial class, which was small enough that an intruder would be obvious. Furthermore, the epigram predates Domitian's reinforcement of the theatre edict by only a few years, and the situation to which the edict gave rise – the usurpation of equestrian privileges by imposters – was no doubt already a topical issue. For this same reason, the epigram is not to be taken as an attack, fuelled by snobbish resentment at social mobility, on a freedman who had been awarded a special grant of equestrian status: for two opposing views on the frequency of such grants, see P. R. C. Weaver, *P&P* 37 (1967) 3–20 and N. Purcell, *PBSR* 38 (1983) 125–73.

Further reading: Meyer (1913), Reinhold (1971) 281

1   Rufe: 'Rufus' often serves M. as addressee.

uides illum: for similar introductory formulae, cf. 4.53.1–2 *hunc quem saepe uides intra penetralia nostrae* | *Pallados*, 1.24.1 *aspicis incomptis illum, Deciane, capillis?*, 8.59.1–2. Cf. also Horace's *uidesne* (*Epod.* 4.7).

subsellia prima: the front of the fourteen rows assigned to the knights in the theatre (cf. intro.): cf. Hor. *Epod.* 4.15–16 *sedilibusque magnus in primis eques* | *Othone contempto sedet*, 5.14.1 *sedere primo solitus in gradu semper*.

terentem 'frequenting'. The verb (lit. 'wear down by repeated rubbing') suggests that the parvenu is in the habit of occupying the front rows.

2   et hinc lucet: the gleam of the parvenu's bejewelled hand can be seen even from where M. and Rufus are imagined as sitting, i.e. towards the back of the fourteen rows which, as a knight, M. was entitled to occupy.

lucet: cf. Juv. 6.381–2 *densi radiant testudine tota* | *sardonyches*.

sardonychata manus: he wears a sardonyx ring or rings. Sardonyx, a banded chalcedony (agate) containing at least one red layer, was an expensive stone often used for signet rings: cf. Plin. *NH* 37.86–9, F. H. Marshall, *Catalogue of the finger rings, Greek, Etruscan and Roman, in the British museum* (Oxford 1907/1968) index of materials s.v. *sardonyx*. Ostentatious rings are often affected by parvenus, e.g. Petr. 32 (Trimalchio), 11.37 (Zoilus), Juv. 1.27–9 (Crispinus).

sardonychata: adjectives in *-atus* are common in invective; cf. Cic. *Red. sen.* 13 *cur in lustris et helluationibus huius calamistrati saltatoris tam eximia uirtus tam diu cessauit?*, Sen. *Ep.* 62.3. M. often uses them of pretentious or hypocritical persons whose outward appearance conceals their true nature, e.g. 1.96.5–9 *[ille] baeticatus atque leucophaeatus* | *...galbinos habet mores*, 2.57, 5.35.2. Cf. T. Adamik, *AUB* (class) 7 (1979) 72.

3–4   *lacernae* and *toga* go with *lucet* (2). For the 'gleam' of Tyrian purple, cf. Plin. *NH* 9.135; for that of a toga see 4n.

3   Tyron: as at Stat. *Silu.* 3.2.139–40 *quo pretiosa Tyros rubeat, quo purpura suco | Sidoniis iterata cadis,* 'Tyre' stands for Tyrian purple, on which see **54**.3n., Kay on 11.39.11. The wearing of a *lacerna* treated with expensive Tyrian purple advertises the parvenu's new-found wealth: Tyrian garb is likewise worn by Trimalchio (Petr. 30) and Crispinus (Juv. 1.27).

totiens: a sarcastic exaggeration: garments were double-dyed to produce the rich hue characteristic of Tyrian purple (**54**.3n.).

epotauere: an unparalleled form, only the past participle of this verb being in regular use. For garments 'drinking deep' of dye, Plin. *NH* 9.139 *[amethystum] inebriatur Tyrio,* where, as here, there is a suggestion of luxury and excess.

4   non tactas uincere iussa niues: lit. 'bidden to surpass untouched snow', i.e. made whiter than untrodden snow. *iussa* suggests the process of fulling, whereby a toga could recover its pristine appearance: cf. Non. Marcell. 34 *qui* [sc. *fullones*] *poliendo diligenter uetera quaeque quasi in nouam speciem mutant,* **36**.8n. Because the toga was expensive both to purchase and to clean (cf. Vout (1996)), a gleaming white toga symbolised wealth, e.g. 9.49.4–5 *in hac ibam conspiciendus eques, | dum noua, dum nitida fulgebat splendida lana*; cf. Juv. 3.149–52.

5   olet toto pinguis coma Marcellano: he wears so much unguent on his hair that it can be smelt all over the theatre of Marcellus. Over-lavish use of perfumes was associated with dandyism and effeminacy: cf. Ov. *Ars* 3.443 *nec coma uos fallat liquido nitidissima nardo,* 11.39.11, V. Tracy, *EMC* 20.2 (1976) 61. The potent smell of ancient cosmetics is often remarked: cf. 3.55.1, Lilja (1972) 86–7.

pinguis: greasy with unguent.

Marcellano: the *theatrum Marcelli,* also known as the *theatrum Marcellianum* (Suet. *Vesp.* 19.1, *CIL* vi 33838a) was the largest of the three permanent stone theatres. Built by Augustus and dedicated in 13 BC to the memory of his nephew Marcellus, it was restored by Vespasian (Suet. *Vesp.* 10.1); see Richardson 380.

6   splendent: cf. Juv. 9.13–14 *nitor in cute, qualem | Bruttia praestabat calidi tibi fascia uisci* [Bruttian pitch was used as a depilatory].

uulso bracchia trita pilo: arms made smooth by removal of body hair, an action suggestive of foppishness or effeminacy: cf. 2.62, 3.63.6 *[bellus homo] mouet in uarios bracchia uulsa modos,* Juv. cited prev. n., Hagenow (1972) 51–3.

uulso: *uellere* is a generic term for the removing of body hair, whether by the use of *uolsellae*, tweezers, or by means of depilatories, the preferred method: cf. Auson. 13.100.1–2 Green *inguina quod calido leuas tibi dropace, causa est:* | *irritant uulsas leuia membra lupas*.

7 non hesterna . . . lingula: a brand new shoe lace.

lunata . . . planta: lit. 'on his crescent-decorated sole' (i.e. shoe). The *calceus patricius*, worn by patricians and magistrates, had an ivory crescent sewn on the top of the instep: cf. Stat. *Silu.* 5.2.27–8 *sic te, clare puer, genitum sibi curia sensit* | *primaque patricia clausit uestigia luna*, Isid. *Orig.* 19.34.4 *patricios calceos Romulus reperit . . . assutaque luna*, A. Alföldi, *Der fruhrömische Reiteradel und seine Ehrenabzeichen* (Baden-Baden 1952) 67–8, N. Goldman in Sebesta and Bonfante (1994) 120–1.

8 coccina . . . aluta: the *calceus patricius*, or *mulleus*, was made of red leather (cf. Plin. *NH* 9.65). M. describes the shoe as 'scarlet' because this colour had associations with luxury: cf. **54**.2n.

non laesum: because the patrician shoe, being expensive, was of superior quality leather, thus affording the wearer greater protection from chafing.

pingit 'bedecks'.

9–10 A slave convicted of theft or running away had the name of the offence tattooed or branded on his forehead (Jones (1987) 154). As a former slave, this man bears such marks of punishment and in order to hide them he plasters his forehead with beauty spots, which he hopes will be taken as a mark of affectation in keeping with his foppish appearance. Parvenus are often alleged to have been good-for-nothing slaves: cf. Aesch. *Fals. leg.* 76, Lucian, *Timon* 23, Hor. *Epod.* 4.11–12, M. 3.29 and 11.37.

9 numerosa: the freedman's face carries the traces of repeated punishments, much as the backs of bad slaves are scarred from frequent floggings (cf. Plaut. *Pseud.* 133–6, *Rud.* 753–4). Alternatively, he bears a single inscription so large that several patches are needed to cover it. Cf. Petr. 103: to disguise his companions as slaves, *impleuit Eumolpus frontes utriusque ingentibus litteris et notum fugitiuorum epigramma per totam faciem . . . duxit.*

stellantem: proleptic. The patches give his brow the appearance of the sky dotted with stars. The application of the epic *stellans* to *frons* is strikingly unusual, but ties in with the other allusions in the epigram to gleaming brightness (*lucet, non tactas niues, splendent*).

splenia: decorative patches (cf. 8.33.22 *talia lunata splenia fronte sedent*). Regulus wore a white one on his eyebrow in court, perhaps for luck: cf. Plin. *Ep.* 6.2.2 with S-W.

frontem: cf. Petr. 103 cited above, 3.21.1 *famulus...fronte notatus*, Jones (1987) 143.

10   quid sit 'what he is' rather than 'what is the reason' sc. for his wearing the patches. The emphasis is on the man's servile origins, for which no amount of wealth can compensate: cf. Hor. *Epod.* 4.6 *fortuna non mutat genus.*

splenia tolle, leges: Rufus will read the letters *FVR* or *FVG* [*itiuus*]. In reality, such marks could be removed by specialist doctors (**6.**26n.); M., for satiric purposes, simply takes no account of this possibility. Less attractive is the suggestion of Jones (1987) 144 n.24, that the allusion is to scars left by an operation to remove the letters: *leges* suggests that the words are clearly visible.

56   (= 3.82)

'Anyone who can bear to be Zoilus' guest could eat and drink with the filthiest of prostitutes. His behaviour, as host, combines vulgarity, ostentation, and ill manners. He and his household get the best of food and drink; we his guests must put up with inferior beverages and minuscule quantities of perfume. And when he falls asleep in a drunken stupor we are bidden not to disturb his repose. Nor can we revenge ourselves with a gesture of contempt on this arrogant upstart: he sucks.'

The rich upstart Zoilus (**54** intro.) is here depicted in his capacity as appalling host. The vulgarity and social ineptitude of such individuals is often viewed through the eyes of their dinner guests: cf. Petronius' *Cena Trimalchionis*, a major model for **56**. In the present epigram, emphasis is placed on the ostentatious luxury of the host's lifestyle, the preciousness of which is underscored by M.'s sarcastic use of unusual vocabulary (e.g. *tractatrix, sciscitator,* and *capillare*) and by the hyperbolic picture of Zoilus surrounded by a bevy of slaves serving his various bodily needs (8–17). The theme of *luxuria* is closely integrated with accusations of effeminacy, a typical trait of the parvenu (cf. **55**.5–6), culminating in the *fellatio*-joke at the conclusion of the poem, which serves to explain why Zoilus' unfortunate guests cannnot revenge themselves upon their host, as their fellow victims do at the conclusion of the *cena Nasidieni* (Hor. *S.* 2.8) and the *cena Trimalchionis.*

A further dimension of the attack on Zoilus is the depiction of him in 18–29 as the stingy host who entertains himself better than his guests – a typically epigrammatic–satiric motif having roots in contemporary practice: cf. 2.19, Juv. 5, Plin. *Ep.* 2.6, Lucian, *Sat.* 17, 22, Kay on 11.31 intro. The particular twist here given to the theme is that Zoilus' slaves and even his dogs dine better than his so-called guests.

The poem is in the choliambic metre (scazons), which is especially associated with invective: see intro. 28.

1–4   Anyone who can bear to dine with Zoilus would not baulk at eating or drinking with the most degraded of prostitutes (2–3); indeed, to be his guest involves even greater pollution (4).

1   **quisquis ... potest** 'whoever can bring himself to', cf. Cic. *Sest.* 106 *nemo illum foedum uultum aspicere, nemo furialem uocem bonus audire poterat. quisquis* turns out unexpectedly to include M. himself (n. on *contendo* 4).

2–3   **cenet ... bibat:**   potential subjunctives.

2   **Summemmianas ... uxores:**   a colourful appellation for prostitutes who plied their trade near (*sub*) the *lupanaria Memmiana*. As the cheapest class of whore (**64**.22), notorious for *fellatio* (11.61.2 *Summemmianis inquinatior buccis*), they would pollute the mouth of anyone who ate and drank with them. On the topography and spelling of *Summemmianas*, see Kay on 11.61.2 and Citroni on 1.34.6.

3   **curtaque Ledae sobrius bibat testa:**   one would normally 'drink from Leda's broken wine jar' only if too inebriated to worry about what one was doing; cf. Cic. *Mur.* 13 *nemo enim ... saltat sobrius.*

   curta ... testa: Leda is so poor that she possesses no drinking cups and her guest has to drink straight from her wine container (cf. Hippon. fr. 14 W): this is broken (a sign of poverty: cf. **64**.13n.) and worse, because owned by a *fellatrix* (next n.), polluted by contact with her mouth.

   Ledae: a typical prostitute name (cf. Kay on 11.60.1 and 61.4), used here, the context shows, of a *fellatrix*, as at 4.4.9 and 11.61.4.

4   **hoc:**   i.e. the eating and drinking mentioned in the previous two lines. Dining with *fellatrices* ought to represent the *ne plus ultra* in degradation, but to be Zoilus' guest is even worse.

   leuius 'less intolerable'.

purius 'more pure', used by humorous paradox for 'less impure'. It was thought that the mouth was corrupted by imbibing from a vessel which had been used by a practioner of oral sex: cf. 2.15, 4.39.10, 12.74.10, Kay on 11.11.3, Grewing on 6.44.6. The comparison with *fellatrices* (2–3) hints that Zoilus is likewise a *fellator*, thus preparing for the concluding joke (*fellat* 33).

contendo: M. claims to speak from personal experience.

5   iacet, for the more usual *accubat*, 'reclines at table', has connotations of an unseemly or drunken sprawl: cf. Var. *apud* Serv. *Aen.* 3.631 *in lectu temulentos iacere, sobrios cubare consuescere*, Petr. 83.10.3.

occupato 'taken over' to the exclusion of others (*OLD s.v. occupo* 2). There were three diners to a *lectus*, but Zoilus (6) acts as if he were the sole occupant, a piece of unmannerliness on a par with assigning a single couch to oneself (Cic. *Pis.* 67).

galbinatus: the wearing of green was a sign of effeminacy: cf. 1.96.8–9 with Citroni, Stat. *Silu.* 2.1.133, Juv. 2.97. On the suffix *-atus*, see **55**.2n.

6   cubitis ... trudit: Zoilus rudely elbows aside his neighbours to left and right (*hinc et inde*). The detail indicates that Zoilus occupies the central place on the *lectus* – a social *faux pas*, since the host should properly take the first position on the lowest of the three couches (Plut. *Quaest. conu.* 619d). The boorish Nasidienus (Hor. *S.* 2.8.23) and Trimalchio (Petr. 31.8 with Smith) likewise occupy places other than the usual one for the host.

7   effultus ostro Sericisque puluillis 'propped up on purple and on cushions of silk'. Cushions were provided to support the guests, who reclined on their left elbow, their feet facing away from the table, which occupied the centre of the U-shape described by the three dining couches.

ostro: a symbol of luxury (**54**.3n.). *effultus* suggests that the reference is to cushions which are covered in purple material. M. may have in mind Petr. 38.5, where it is asserted that all Trimalchio's cushions were stuffed with purple or scarlet.

Sericis: silk, another luxury item, used *inter alia* to cover couches and cushions: cf. Hor. *Epod.* 8.15–16 *sericos ... puluillos*, Prop. 1.14.22. On silk in classical antiquity see S. Lieberman, 'Contact between Rome and China' (Dissertation Columbia 1953) 1–95.

8   exoletus: the term, which properly describes a male prostitute past the age of adolescence, is used insultingly of a slave *concubinus*. An *exoletus* might play either the receptive or insertive rôle in penetrative acts (Williams (1999) 83–6) – here, in view of Zoilus' effeminacy, the latter.

ructanti 'when he belches', suggests excessive consumption of drink or food: cf. Sen. *Thy.* 910–11 *uino grauatum fulciens laeua caput. | eructat,* Lucian, *Sat.* 21. The juxtaposition in **56** of belching and snoring with drunkenness and sexual debauchery may be indebted to Cael. fr. 17 Malcovati *ipsum* [sc. *C. Antonium*] *offendunt temulento sopore profligatum, totis praecordiis stertentem, ructuosos spiritus geminare, praeclarasque contubernales ab omnibus spondis transuersas incubare.*

9   pinnas ... cuspidesque lentisci: both feathers and *cuspides lentisci,* pieces of mastic wood sharpened to a point, were used as toothpicks: cf. **24.**3n. Zoilus' ostentation is underlined by having a slave offer him a choice of toothpicks, and by the highly visible character of the *pinnae* (next n.). For the same reason, Trimalchio uses a silver toothpick (Petr. 33.1).

rubentes: the bright red or pink feathers of a flamingo (*phoenicopterus*): cf. 3.58.14 *nomenque debet quae rubentibus pinnis,* 13.71. Red was a symbol of luxury (**54.**2n.). The flamingo also has associations with sumptuous dining (Thompson (1936) 305–6, Toynbee (1973) 246).

10   aestuanti 'when he sweats'.
tenue 'gentle'.
uentilat frigus 'blows a cool draught of air', internal accusative: cf. Woodcock §13 iii.

11   supina 'lying on her back'. The adjective has connotations of languorousness and sexuality which suit her role as *concubina*: cf. Adams, *LSV* 192. The presence at dinner of a *concubina* may seem surprising given the stress on Zoilus' effeminacy. In Roman society, however, pathic males engaged in passive sexual activities with partners of either sex. Cf. Williams (1999) 197–203.

prasino ... flabello: in Rome, the fan was a woman's accessory; cf. Ter. *Eun.* 595, Prop. 2.24.11. It originated in the East, where public attendance of a fan-bearing slave symbolised royal status. Its use thus implies both effeminacy and oriental luxury. The first point is also suggested by the green colour of the *flabellum* (cf. on *galbinatus* 5).

12   fugat ... muscas ... puer: one of a slave's duties was to brush away flies from his master: cf. Cic. *De orat.* 2.247 *puer, abige muscas.* Sometimes a peacock's feather was used (14.67), here, a myrtle branch, perhaps for its association with Venus. There may be a further suggestion of Oriental-style luxury: Assyrian kings were commonly attended by a eunuch bearing a flyswat: cf. D–S II 1149 s.v. *flabellum*.

13   tractatrix 'masseuse'. The word is found also at *CIL* VI 37823. Massaging had dubious associations: cf. Sen. *Ep.* 66.53 *an potius optem, ut malaxandos articulos exoletis meis porrigam? ut muliercula aut aliquis in mulierculam ex uiro uersus digitulos meos ducat?* Presumably the woman's skill at manipulation extends further than the joints: *tractare* can have a sexual flavour (Adams, *LSV* 186, Kay on 11.29.1).

14   spargit has the unusual sense 'send a single object or person to several places in turn'; cf. Sen. *Dial.* 12.6.6 *mobilis enim et inquieta homini mens data est, nusquam se tenet, spargitur.*

15–17   The use at table of a *matella* (urine flask) was not considered objectionable *per se*: cf. *CLE* 932 *miximus in lecto; fateor, peccauimus, hospes. | si dices quare, nulla matella fuit,* 6.89 quoted below. Likewise, the snapping of the fingers (*digiti crepantis*), which might be thought imperious, was the usual means of summoning a slave to bring a chamber pot: cf. Petr. 27.5, 6.89.1–2 *cum peteret seram media iam nocte matellam | arguto madidus pollice Panaretus,* 14.119. What singles out Zoilus is the fact that his slave has not only to bring the pot, but to assist his drunken master in using it.

15   eunuchus: a eunuch also holds a *matella* for Trimalchio to urinate into at Petr. 27.5.

16   delicatae sciscitator urinae: *sciscitator,* from *sciscitari* 'make enquiries, get to know about', is a parodic coinage on the analogy of words in *-tor* (e.g. *obsonator, pistor, dispensator*) describing a slave's specific function in the household. This slave's job consists of familiarising himself with his master's urinary habits. The urine is described as 'pampered' in having a specialist slave to guide it into the receptacle. 'It is also extra-selected, being generated by rare vintages (24n.)' [EJK].

17   bibentis: he takes in liquid at the same time as he voids it.
   ebrium . . . penem: *ebrium* is to some extent a transferred epithet (cf. Petr. 79.9 *ebrias manus*); but since the organ is often portrayed as having a life of its own (**38**.3n.), the adjective conjures up an amusing picture of the penis flopping around drunkenly, unable to aim without help.

18   ipse 'the master' (*OLD* 12). The term is often applied sarcastically to boorish hosts: cf. Hor. *S.* 2.8.23, Petr. 29.8, Juv. 5.114.

retro flexus ad pedum turbam: Zoilus leans backwards to distribute food to the crowd of slave attendants who were stationed behind his feet at the back of the couch: cf. 3.23.2, Lucillius, *AP* 11.207.2, Petr. 58.1 *Giton qui ad pedes stabat* with Smith. *pedum* is best taken as a compressed expression for *seruorum ad pedes*, slave attendants at dinner: (cf. 12.87.2 *ad pedes uernam*). For a similar piece of compression, cf. Cic. *Deiot.* 2 *qui ... seruum corruptum praemiis ad accusandum dominum impulerit, a legatorum pedibus abduxerit*, where *pedes = serui a pedibus* i.e. *pedisequi*.

19   catellas ... lambentes: table scraps were thrown to dogs (**32.**17n.); these pets, however, receive choice delicacies (next n.) – a further sign of the host's extravagance, and implying that even Zoilus' dogs eat better than his guests.

anserum exta: *foie gras*, a luxury item: cf. Juv. 5.114 *anseris ante ipsum magni iecur*, André (1981) 129–30.

20   apri glandulas 'sweetbreads of boar': a choice part of a choice animal: see André (1981) 115.

palaestritis: 44.9n.

21   turturum nates: another luxury; cf. 3.60.7 *aureus inmodicis turtur ... clunibus*, André (1981) 121. Given the association of turtle doves with Venus, and the sexual connotations of *natis*, they are an appropriate offering to a *concubinus*.

22–5   Zoilus, in the typical fashion of bad hosts, drinks better wine than his guests: cf. Plin. *Ep.* 2.6.2, Juv. 5.30–51, Lucian, *Sat.* 22, *Merc. con.* 26.

22   Ligurum ... saxa: wine from the Alps in the modern region of Piedmont, home of the Ligures: for the metonymy, cf. 14.118.1 *Massiliae fumos* of Massilian wine. The resinated Ligurian wine was considered unpalatable (Strabo 202, Plin. *NH* 14.124).

23   cocta fumis musta Massilitanis: literally 'grapejuice fermented over Massilian smoke'. This wine is both young (cf. 13.120.2 for *musta* in this sense), in contrast to the aged 'Opimian' drunk by the host, and of poor quality, the wine of Marseilles being known for its unpleasantly smoky taste: cf. 10.36.1 *improba Massiliae quidquid fumaria cogunt*. Wine jars were placed near hearth smoke to assist the ageing process, but too much smoke could compromise the flavour: cf. Col. 1.6.20.

24   Opimianum ... nectar: 'Opimian', which properly refers to the famous vintage laid down in the consulship of Opimius (121 BC), stands, as elsewhere in M., for vintage wine of the highest quality: cf. 1.26.7 with Citroni. Genuine Opimian would be undrinkable by M.'s time (Plin. *NH* 14.55). *nectar* reinforces the idea of quality: the noun is not just a synonym for *uinum* (*OLD* 2a), but signifies a very fine wine: cf. Theoc. 7.153, 13.108.1 *nectareum ... Falernum.*

morionibus: 44.17n.

25   crystallinisque murrinisque 'in vessels made of rock-crystal and fluorspar'. Imported from the East, these were both expensive and exotic: cf. Juv. 6.155–6 *grandia tolluntur crystallina, maxima rursus | murrina* with Courtney, Plin. *NH* 37.18–29.

propinat 'drinks to pledge the health of': the *propinatio* involved drinking a toast which one had proposed, then passing the cup to the person whose health was being drunk. Zoilus insults his guests not only by drinking better wine than them (*Opinianum* 24n.) but by sharing it with his slaves, and his idiot slaves at that.

26   Cosmianis ... ampullis: vials of 'Cosmian' i.e. high quality perfume: Cosmus was the greatest supplier of perfume of M.'s day.

fusus 'drenched' (cf. Tib. 1.7.50 *multo tempora funde mero*), is preferable to the alternate reading *fuscus* adopted by SB. It was usual to pour perfume over one's hair at a dinner party: cf. Hor. *Carm.* 2.3.13, 11.15.6 with Kay, but *fusus* here underlines the contrast between the host, who uses copious amounts of the best perfume, and the guests, who must share a small amount of inferior ointment (28). Zoilus' excessive use of perfume is also linked to his effeminacy and Oriental-style luxury: cf. Virg. *A.* 4.215–17 *et nunc ille Paris cum semiuiro comitatu, | Maeonia mentum mitra crinemque madentem | subnexus,* D. Potter, 'Odor and power in the Roman empire', in J. Porter, ed., *Constructions of the classical body* (Ann Arbor, Michigan 1999) 175–6.

27   murice: large shells were used for holding ointment (e.g. Hor. *Carm.* 2.7.22–3 *funde capacibus | unguenta de conchis,* Hilgers (1969) 50), but the use of the diminutive murex-shell for such a purpose is unparalleled. The luxuriousness of the container (*aureo* n.) is at odds with the paucity and poor quality (*pauperis* 28) of the unguent which Zoilus unblushingly dispenses.

aureo 'gilded', not 'gold-coloured': cf. 9.42.10 *cornibus aureis iuuencum.* The shell of the *murex brandaris*, to which the Latin *murex* normally refers, is salmon pink: cf. B. Grzimek's *Animal life encyclopedia* (New York 1972-) III 71.

28   moechae 'prostitute': cf. Adams (1983a) 350–1.

capillare sc. *unguentum*, perfume for the hair. The word is found only here. Prostitutes would need this as a tool of trade (cf. Lilja (1972) ch. 4 on the connexion between fragrances and eroticism): that used by a *moecha pauper* would be of the cheapest quality.

29   septunce multo ... perditus 'done for by many a half-pint': for both the construction and the hyperbolic use of *perdere* cf. Catull. 14.4–5 *nam quid feci ego ... | cur me tot male perderes poetis?* A *septunx* was a measure of seven *unciae*, almost double the usual serving (cf. **50**.10n.).

deinde: scanned as a disyllable by synezesis, which M., in contrast to other Latin poets, allows in his scazons: Pelckmann (1908) 54.

stertit: Zoilus' drunken snoring echoes that of C. Antonius (8n.).

30   silentium: Servius, commenting on *Aen.* 1.730 *tum facta silentia tectis*, alludes to a custom at banquets of having silence after the first course, followed by a libation to the gods, who are honoured through the silence. There may be an implication that Zoilus is arrogantly usurping divine prerogatives.

rhonchis (Gk ῥέγκος)**:** a very rare word, used for derogatory effect; in its proper sense 'snore' it is found only here. It is probably a vulgarism (Citroni on 1.3.5).

31   iussi: presumably by a slave; cf. Petr. 30.5. This is the climax of a series of actions infuriating to the guests: their host neglects them by falling asleep, he subjects them to loud snoring, and finally they are ordered by an underling to maintain silence.

nutibus: perhaps a grotesque variant on lovers' furtive communications at the dinner table: cf. Ov. *Am.* 1.4.17–18 *me specta nutusque meos uultumque loquacem: | excipe furtiuas et refer ipsa notas.*

propinamus: when offering the cup to the person toasted in the *propinatio* (24n.), one said *tibi propino* or the like: cf. Cic. *Tusc.* 1.96 *propino ... hoc pulchro Critiae*, Mau, *RE* IV 614. The injunction to keep silent reduces the *propinatio* to a dumb show (*nutibus*).

32   Malchionis 'a Malchio': pointedly reminiscent of Petronius' Trimalchio (lit. 'thrice, i.e. very much, a Malchio'). The term, which is attested in Latin inscriptions as a name for slaves and freedmen, may be derived from a Semitic root meaning *rex* (S. Priuli, *Ascyltus: note di onomastica Petroniana* (Brussels 1975) 35–6). In view of the diminutive suffix in -ιών it is thus the equivalent of *regulus*, and suggests both the overbearing deportment of the parvenu and his Eastern origins. A Roman reader would also think of the Greek μαλακός = 'effeminate'.

improbi 'shameless', both in his general behaviour and in the treatment of his guests.

33   uindicari: middle, 'avenge ourselves'.

Rufe: 55.1 n.

fellat: as often in M., the joke is reserved for the last word of the epigram. Zoilus' guests are unable to gain their revenge on their insufferable host. Why? *fellat*. The word reveals both the nature of the revenge envisaged – *irrumatio* – and the reason why this would be ineffective in the present case: '*irrumatio* holds no terrors for the *fellator*: he regards it not as *irrumatio*, but as *fellatio*, which he enjoys' (Adams, *LSV* 126). The idea of *irrumatio* as punishment/revenge might come from Catull. 16.1 *pedicabo ego uos et irrumabo*; cf. Adams *LSV* 128–9, who points out that it was normally a verbal threat, not meant to be carried out in reality. The humour here lies in taking the idea as a literal possibility.

57   (= 9.73)

'A one-time shoemaker, you now possess the Praenestine estate of your late master, in which you scarcely deserved a tiny room. You drunkenly serve hot Falernian in crystal cups, thereby cracking them, and you sleep with your ex-master's catamite. But *my* parents ensured that I had a good education – foolishly. Why be a poet, when the profession of cobbler is so much more lucrative?'

In voicing indignation that a former slave has inherited his *patronus'* estate, M. reflects the typical attitude of members of the upper classes to the acquisition of wealth by freedmen: cf. Hor. *Epod.* 4, *Catal.* 10.1–2 and 23–4, Sen. *Ep.* 27.5 *et patrimonium habebat libertini et ingenium; numquam uidi hominem beatum indecentius*, Duff (1928) 67–8, Meyer (1913) *passim*. Resentment of successful ex-slaves was redoubled if they had previously practised one of the banausic professions upon which the aristocracy looked with lofty disdain: this included all forms of manual labour, as well as a number of other occupations: see Joshel (1992) 62–9, A. Burford, *Craftsmen in Greek and Roman*

society (London 1972) 39–41. In this epigram, M.'s displeasure is exacer-
bated by the fact that his own modest income is eclipsed by the freedman's
new-found wealth. This is brought out especially in 7–10 where he protests
that poets receive inadequate rewards by comparison with more lucrative
professions requiring little formal education: cf. esp. Juvenal 7 *passim*, M.
5.56, 6.8, 10.74, 76.

M. selects a cobbler as an especially striking instance of an ex-slave
made good, because even among manual occupations the profession suffered from particularly low esteem. The tanning and footwear industries
were despised because of the contact with foul-smelling animal hides, and
the job of cobbler was the lowliest of all, symbolic of humble status and
poverty: cf. Lucian, *Catapl.* 20, *Menipp.* 17, Juv. 3.293, Knox and Headlam
(1922) xlviii–xlix, Lau (1967) 41–4. None the less, a cobbler might in exceptional circumstances improve his social standing. One instance was
the ex-slave Felicio (M. Charlesworth, *JRS* 27 (1937) 60–2). A cobbler
called Vatinius acquired such wealth as a court *scurra* under Nero that
he could give a gladiatorial show at Beneventum (Tac. *Ann.* 15.34, Juv.
5.46, M. 10.3, 14.96): M. may have been thinking of this individual in three
poems of book 3 attacking a former *sutor* who presented gladiatorial shows
at Bononia.

M. implies that the ex-slave graduated directly from cobbling to becoming an heir of his master (10) – a most improbable contingency. A more
realistic scenario would see a slave rising from the position of cobbler to
that of overseer of his master's footwear business, then, after acquiring his
freedom, continuing as business partner of his *patronus*, and on the latter's
death, inheriting part of the estate (3n.): there is ample evidence for slaves
and freedman as successful business managers (P. Garnsey, *Klio* 63 (1981)
359–71, S. Treggiari, *Roman freedmen during the late republic* (Oxford 1969) 91–
106). Irrespective of whether this was what M. had in mind, for M. the
cobbler remains essentially a cobbler and therefore is unworthy of his new
position, an attitude that is brought out by describing the subject's quondam work in the most degrading terms (1–2), by *decepti* (3n.) and *cella* (4n.),
and by returning to the cobbler's banausic occupation in 10, where the
pejorative term *sutor* is pointedly used.

Further reading: Lau (1967), Parroni (1979); for bibliography on parvenus,
see on **54**

1–2   antiquas ... | ... uetusque: the adjectives make it clear that
these lines refer to shoe repairing rather than shoe making. Shoe repair

was the job of the *sutor ueteramentarius* or cobbler, who occupied the lowest rank in the hierarchy of the footwear industry: cf. intro.

1   Dentibus antiquas solitus producere pelles: apparently refers to the same procedure as 2, sc. stretching the sole with the teeth while refastening it to the upper. Lau (1967) 44, 72 fig. 3 thinks that M. describes a process of shoe repair whereby the leather fastenings attaching the sole to the upper part of the shoe or boot were drawn with the teeth through holes, but surely new, not 'old', leather would be used for this, and in any case Lau's evidence comes from an Egyptian tomb of 1450 BC.
   producere: cf. Lucian, *Gall.* cited on 2 and the German proverb 'Der Schuster hat zwei lange Zähn, damit er kann das Leder dehn', 'the cobbler has two long teeth, which which he can stretch the leather'.
   pelles: shoes were made of leather (*corium, scortum, aluta*) rather than *pelles*, which properly refers to untanned skin, but the term is deliberately chosen because of its associations with smelly animal hides.

2   mordere ... solum: the sole was apparently held taut in the teeth while being fitted and refastened to the upper part of the shoe; cf. Lucian, *Gall.* 28 '[a cobbler] will ... gnaw around the leather soles as he stretches them out'. The contact of the cobbler's mouth with the sole epitomises the lowliness of his job: cf. 12.59.7 where a cobbler *modo pelle basiata* appears in a list of persons engaged in dirty and smelly pursuits. Perhaps the proverbial connexion of leather-gnawing with dogs (**6.**31–2n.) contributed to the degrading associations of the activity.
   luto putre: Lucian, *Catapl.* 20 and *Menipp.* 17, dealing with the cobbler's trade, similarly speaks of 'rotting shoes'. Shoe-leather would easily perish in the muddy and insanitary streets of Rome: cf. Scobie (1986).

3   Praenestina ... regna: Praeneste, about twenty miles southeast of Rome in the Apennines, was a popular site for the villas of the wealthy: cf. Hor. *Carm.* 3.4.22–4 *seu mihi frigidum | Praeneste seu Tibur supinum | seu liquidae placuere Baiae*, Juv. 3.190, Balsdon (1969) 198. The estate is probably to be regarded as the freedman's share of his *patronus'* properties: in the absence of children, a man might appoint a *libertus* as co-heir (Champlin (1991) 132).
   tenes decepti regna patroni: *decepti regna*, the reading of B, is preferable to the blander *defuncti rura* of the other MSS. His former master's 'realm' (*regna:* cf. **20.**19n.) has been taken over (*tenes*) by the one-time cobbler. *decepti* suggests that the master was deceived as to his slave's true

nature (parvenus are invariably represented as being of bad character). Shackleton Bailey (1989) 141 suggested 'cheated of one's expectation of life', 'prematurely dead', but the parallels he cites for *deceptus* in this sense, unlike here, contain an explicit reference to death.

patroni: former master; manumission is to be imagined as taking place before the master's death, rather than in his will: cf. Champlin (1991) 137.

4   **in quibus indignor si tibi cella fuit** 'in which I hold it a disgrace that you had even a closet' – let alone ownership of the whole estate. *si* is virtually equivalent to 'that' (*OLD* s.v.12).

cella: a derogatory term, used *inter alia* of rooms occupied by slaves (cf. Cato, *Agr.* 14.2) and of humble urban garrets (**32**.21 n.).

5   **rumpis ... ardenti ... crystalla Falerno:**   you crack your crystal cups by drinking from them Falernian mixed with hot water. Roman diners had their wine diluted with cold or hot water according to taste (K. M. Dunbabin, *JRA* 6 (1993) 116–41); it was recommended that crystal cups be avoided in the latter case, because they could split: cf. 10.14.5, 12.74.6, 14.94.2, Plin. *NH* 37.26 [*crystallum*] *caloris impatiens nisi in frigido potu abdicatur*, G. Agosti, *Aufidus* 25 (1994) 65–70. The ill-bred freedman gets drunk (*madidus*) and fails to treat his expensive crystal with due care and respect.

madidus: parvenus are given to unseemly intoxication. Cf. **56**.17, Petr. 78 *ibat res ad summam nauseam, cum Trimalchio ebrietate turpissima grauis*.

crystalla: **56**.25n.
Falerno: generally reckoned the finest of Italian wines.

6   **pruris ... cum:**   lit. 'feel desire with', a euphemism for intercourse: cf. Catull. 88.1–2 *Quid facit is, Gelli, qui cum matre atque sorore | prurit et abiectis peruigilat tunicis?*, **86**.6–7.

Ganymede: although slaves did bear this name (e.g. 11.22.2), Ganymede here signifies a boy-catamite, like the Trojan Ganymede, who was spirited to heaven to perform that function for Zeus, and from whose name Latin *catamitus* is derived.

7   **litterulas stulti docuere:**   lit. 'foolishly taught me my ABC', i.e. 'had me educated'. The contemptuous diminutive expresses M.'s disgust at the inability of education to generate a decent income, *stulti* his protest at the naivety of his parents in thinking that it would do so: cf. Parroni (1979).

8   quid cum grammaticis rhetoribusque mihi? 'what use to me
are . . . ?' Cf. 5.56, where M. ruefully advises Lupus not to entrust his son
to *grammatici* and *rhetores*, but rather have him study the lucrative *artes* of the
citharoedus, choraules, praeco or *architectus*.

grammaticis rhetoribusque: teachers of the two advanced stages
of education, grammar/literature and rhetoric: cf. Bonner (1977) 189–211,
250–327. In Spain, where Roman education had long flourished (Bonner
(1977) 135, 158), M. would have had access to teachers of the highest quality.

9   frange . . . calamos et scinde . . . libellos: since literary pursuits fail to provide a reasonable living: cf. Calp. Sic. 4.23–7 *frange puer
calamos et inanes desere Musas . . . quid enim tibi fistula reddet | quo tutere famem?*,
Juv. 7.27–8 *frange miser calamum uigilataque proelia dele, | qui facis in parua sublimia
carmina cella.*

leues: reed pens (*calami*) are literally 'light', but the adjective also
suggests the generic 'lightness' of epigram as well as the insubstantiality of
the rewards accruing to literary men.

Thalia: properly the Muse of Comedy (Roscher v 449–54), Thalia
can represent any of the less elevated genres which do not have their own
special Muse (cf. Virg. *Ecl.* 6.2, *Culex* 1): in this capacity she is often associated
by M. with his epigrams: cf. 7.17.3–4 *inter carmina sanctiora si quis | lasciuae
fuerit locus Thaliae*, 4.8.12, 23.4, 9.26.8.

10   si dare sutori calceus ista potest: an exaggeration: see intro.
ista: with an implied criticism, as often, 'those things of yours'.

58   (= 2.26)

'Just because Naevia behaves like a consumptive, Bithynicus, do you think
you've got it made? You're wrong: she's wheedling, not dying.'

Naevia pretends to be terminally ill in order to encourage the attentions
of the *captator* Bithynicus. The figure of the *captator* (inheritance or legacy
hunter) receives its first extended treatment in Hor. *S.* 2.5, and subsequently
becomes prominent in the writers of the Empire, notably M., Petronius,
Juvenal, and Lucian. His particular target is the rich and childless personage. Often such individuals are old, but it seems unlikely that Naevia is
envisaged thus, since she feigns tuberculosis, a disease normally associated
with the young (see Jackson (1988) 180–1, 186). The *captator*'s aim is to induce his victim to leave all his or her money to him, i.e. outside the family
in defiance of testamentary proprieties. In pursuance of this aim he deploys

several strategies – giving gifts, heaping praise or flattery on the target, and providing *officia* of various kinds, including attendance upon the sick-bed and sexual services.

For their part, the *captati* use their considerable testamentary power to prey in turn on the *captatores*, particularly by pretending to be sick (*simulatus aeger* Sen. *Dial.* 10.7.7, M. 2.40, 5.39.5–6), so as to elicit gifts and solicitous attention from the *captator*, whose hopes are raised by the seeming imminence of the captated person's death. These hopes are usually foiled: either the 'sick' person recovers, or the *captator* dies before the aged invalid, or he is simply cut out of the will altogether.

Further reading: Champlin (1991) 87–102, Hopkins (1983) 238–42, Tracy (1980)

1–2   In view of her symptoms – wheezing breath, chronic cough, and bringing up of sputum – the illness Naevia is faking is evidently pulmonary tuberculosis: see Grmek (1989) 177–97. The context in which she does this is presumably sick-visiting, this being a key *officium* of *captatores*: cf. Champlin (1991) 90.

1   **querulum ... acerbum:**   neut. acc. of adjective used adverbially. Cf. Catull. 51.5 *dulce ridentem* 'laughing sweetly'.

querulum spirat: *querulum* refers primarily to the 'wheezing' breath characteristic of consumption (cf. *Hippoc.* 5.378 Littré 'within she wheezed huskily along the windpipe and throat') but there is also a suggestion of its literal sense 'plaintive', the implication being that Naevia breathes in such a way as seemingly to bemoan the imminence of her death. Cf. the *simulatus aeger* of Lucian, *Dial. mort.* 15.16 'and, whenever I (the *captator*) entered, moaning and croaking faintly ... so that I, thinking that he would any moment now climb into the tomb'. The play on the dual senses of *querulus* has a parallel in Sen. *Thy.* 766–7 *illa [uiscera] flammatus latex | querente aeno iactat*, where *queror* suggests both the 'hissing' of the pot and its 'lamenting' the fate of Thyestes' children, whose entrails are being cooked within it.

acerbum ... tussit 'has a dreadful cough'. For *acerbus* of severe physical ailments, cf. Cels. 2.7 *capitis acerbissimi dolores*. Since the adjective is also used of untimely death (*OLD* 4), it is further implied that Naevia is coughing in such a way as to suggest that her symptoms will prove fatal.

tussit: a cough is one of the things which attract the attentions of *captatores*: cf. Hor. *S.* 2.5.106–7, Petr. 117.9, M. 1.10 *petit Gemellus nuptias Maronillae | ... quid ... in illa petitur et placet? tussit.*

2   inque tuos mittit sputa subinde sinus: the phlegm which
Naevia repeatedly deposits in Bithynicus' lap is another manifestation of
her pretended tuberculosis: cf. *Hippoc.* 2.608 Littré 'the patients frequently
coughed up ... sputa'. The unpleasantness of the picture is well captured by
the sputtering 's' sounds. The *captator* needed a strong stomach for the job: cf.
Epictet. 4.1.148 'who could endure you loving old women ... and wiping
their noses and washing them ... and simultaneously attending on them
like a slave when they are sick while praying for them to die?', Champlin
(1991) 90.

3   iam te rem factam ... credis habere? 'do you think you've got
it made now?', a colloquial expression: cf. 6.61.1 *rem factam Pompullus habet,
Fausline: legetur | et nomen toto sparget in orbe suum.* Questions in the penultimate
line are a feature of M.'s style: see intro.

Bithynice: Bithynicus reappears in 9.8 (9) as a duped *captator*. The
name suggests foreign or servile origins: *captatores* are often represented as
persons of humble stock making their way in the world by such dubious
means; cf. Lucian, *Timon* 22, Champlin (1991) 95.

4   erras: the strong sense break after the first foot throws the verb
into relief.

blanditur: paradoxical, since *blandimenta* are usually applied by the
captatores to the *captati*, e.g. Cic. *Off.* 3.74 *mihi quidem etiam uerae hereditates non
honestae uidentur, si sunt malitiosis blanditiis, officiorum non ueritate, sed simulatione
quaesitae.* Naevia turns the tables by 'leading on' Bithynicus through the
seeming imminence of her death and the hopes which she thereby raises
in him. Her motivation may be simply to receive gifts and attention, but
in view of the erotic associations of *blandior*, it is likely that she wishes
to arouse Bithynicus sexually by the prospect of inheriting: cf. 11.29.5–8
*blanditias nescis: 'Dabo' dic 'tibi milia centum | et dabo Setini iugera certa soli; | accipe
uina, domum, pueros, chrysendeta, mensas.' | nil opus est digitis: sic mihi, Phylli, frica.*

59   (= 9.80)

'The impoverished starveling Gellius married a rich elderly woman. Now
he maintains himself by satisfying her every sexual need.'

The *locuples anusque* of this poem is a composite of two related characters, the
γραῦς καπρῶσα or sex-crazed elderly female, and the *uxor dotata*, the rich
wife whose wealth permits her to behave in a domineering and exacting

fashion towards her long-suffering husband. The γραῦς καπρῶσα is constantly mocked for her unseasonable desire, notably in Old Comedy, satire, iambic and epigram: cf. Kay on 11.29 intro. Such women were prepared to pay for the services of their lovers: cf. Ar. *Plut.* 975–8, *AP* 11.73.1–2 'the old woman was of course beautiful when young. But in those days she used to ask for money: now she is willing to pay for the ride,' Hor. *Epod.* 12, Juv. 1.39–41, M. 10.75, 11.29, Richlin (1984) 75.

A partial gloss of respectability could be placed on these – to the Greeks and Romans – reprehensible sexual desires by formalising the situation i.e. by marriage between the lover and his elderly *belle*, who in the present epigram assumes the mantle of a second stock figure, the *uxor dotata*. Mockery of such women is particularly associated with Roman Comedy, but the type is also represented in M.; cf. 8.12 and **63** intro. *uxores dotatae* are commonly represented as no longer young (cf. Plaut. *Aul.* 158–9, *Most.* 280–1, Schumann (1977) 59), are invariably unattractive to their husbands (e.g. Plaut. *Cas.* 584, *Asin.* 894–5), but, like the *locuples anusque* of the present poem, sexually demanding: cf. Plaut. *Most.* 703–7 *si qui' dotatam uxorem atque anum habeat | neminem sollicitat sopor: omnibus | ire dormitum odio est, uelut mihi | exsequi certa res est ut abeam | potius hinc ad forum quam domi cubem.*

The male protagonist of the epigram is an equally conventional figure, the man who is forced by poverty and starvation (*esuriens . . . pauper*) to service the sexual needs of, or, what amounts to the same thing, to marry an elderly female: cf. Pompon. *Atell.* 37, Ar. *Plut.* 975–8, *AP* 11.65 'the choice between starvation and an old woman is difficult. It is a terrible thing to go hungry, but to sleep with an old woman is even more painful. When Phillis was hungry, he prayed for an old woman. When he was sleeping with her he prayed for starvation: the dilemma of a son without an inheritance!', Lucian, *Rhet. praecept.* 24, M. 11.87. In this state of mutual exploitation both parties are ridiculous.

Further reading: Schumann (1977)

1   Duxerat esuriens locupletem pauper anumque: an elegant line, with neatly interwoven word-order. *esuriens* both characterises Gellius and gives the reason for his marriage. To *esurire* was synonymous with poverty: cf. Tert. *Adu. Marc.* 4.14 *non sunt alii esurientes quam pauperes et mendici.* The theme of hunger anticipates the sexual humour of 2.

2   uxorem pascit Gellius: as the following *futuit* indicates, *uxorem pascit* must conceal a crude joke. The logic of the poem ought to require that Gellius is forced at his wife's insistence to do something which, like *fututio* of an old woman, he would not do of his own free will. This seems to rule out the interpretation of SB that Gellius 'feeds' his wife by inserting his penis into her mouth: for *irrumatio* was viewed as 'the summit of male sexual cravings' (Krenkel (1980b) 83). It is better, therefore, to imagine Gellius as engaging in cunnilinctus, which was regarded as a demeaning and subservient activity (**50**.17n.): *pascit* will then have the meaning 'feeds on', a rare but well-authenticated sense: cf. Tib. 2.5.25 *tunc pascebant herbosa Palatia uaccae*, [Quint]. *Decl. mai.* 12.3 (*cadaueribus pasti*) *nos interim cibos ex malis inuenimus, et fames se ipsa pauit, et miseriae nostrae crudeles factae sunt.* Cunnilinctus is often described as 'eating' or 'feeding on' the female genitalia: cf. **50**.15, *Priap.* 78.1, Auson. 13.82 Green, Arist. *Eccl.* 470, *Pax* 716–17, Adams, *LSV* 129. In this context of *ad hoc* sexual jesting, it also pertinent that *pasco* was in origin a pastoral term (C. Moussy, *RPh* 43 (1969) 239–48), and that the female pudenda were often described metaphorically as a field, meadow or plain: cf. Adams, *LSV* 82–4, Henderson (1991) 135–6.

Gellius: possibly named after Catullus' Gellius, who was a practitioner of oral sex (poem 80).

futuit: it is no accident that the poem opens and closes with *duxerat* and *futuit* respectively: for Gellius' wife the two things are synonymous.

60   (= 6.53)

'Andragoras was with us at the baths and cheerful enough at dinner, and yet he was found dead next morning. Do you ask the reason for so sudden a death, Faustinus? He had seen Dr Hermocrates in a dream.'

The poem is based on an epigram of Lucillius, *AP* 11.257:

> Ἑρμογένη τὸν ἰατρὸν ἰδὼν Διόφαντος ἐν ὕπνοις
> οὐκετ' ἀνηγέρθη, καὶ περίαμμα φέρων.

'Hermogenes the doctor was seen by Diophantus while dreaming. He never woke up again, even though he was wearing an amulet.'

Mockery of doctors, often as death-dealing, is a long-standing satirical theme, frequent in M.; cf. 1.30 *Chirurgus fuerat, nunc est uispillo* (undertaker) *Diaulus.* | *coepit quo poterat clinicus esse modo*, 1.47, 5.9, **61**, 11.71, 11.74, Brecht (1930) 45–6. Such mockery is often characterised by hyperbole: cf. *AP* 11.123 (the mere sight of Agis the doctor killed Aristagoras), 118 (a man died through simply remembering a doctor's name), Grewing on **60** intro.

Satire of this kind reflects not only the relatively undeveloped state of medicine in the Greco-Roman era, but also the fact that no licence was needed to practise, and prosecution for incompetence a phenomenon of the distant future: cf. Plin. *NH* 29.18 *nulla . . . lex quae puniat inscitiam capitalem, nullum exemplum uindictae . . . medicoque tantum hominem occidisse impunitas summa est*. In Latin writers, attacks on doctors arise also from a prejudice against Greeks, practitioners of medicine at Rome being almost invariably Greek or of Greek descent.

Further reading: Dolderer (1933), Jackson (1988) 56–85, Scarborough (1969–70)

1–2 For a similarly sudden death due to unnatural causes, cf. Cic. *Cluent.* 27 *puer, cum hora undecima in publico ualens uisus esset, ante noctem mortuus*. The form of expression may be indebted to Callim. *AP* 7.519.1–3 'Who knows adequately tomorrow's fate when you, Charmis, whom we saw with our own eyes yesterday were buried by us with weeping on the next day?'

1 Lotus nobiscum est, hilaris cenauit: Andragoras went through the normal late afternoon routine in Rome – a visit to the baths followed by dinner. The point of *nobiscum*, as of *hilaris*, is that there was nothing obviously amiss with him at that stage.

idem 'and yet he'. *idem* is used idiomatically to convey two apparently irreconcilable facts: cf. Catull. 22.14–17 *infaceto est infacetior rure, | simul poemata attigit, neque idem umquam | aeque est beatus ac poema cum scribit. | tam gaudet in se tamque se ipse miratur* with Fordyce.

3 M. likes to pose a question in the penultimate verse which is answered in the concluding punch-line: often, as here, this contains a surprise. Cf. Grewing on 6.36.

subitae: M. often builds epigrams around sudden changes of situation: see Grewing *ad loc*.

Faustine: a wealthy patron of M. (**4**.6n.). As here, he often serves as the addressee of an epigram which has no bearing on him personally – unless, as Grewing thinks, *nobiscum* (1) is meant to include Faustinus.

requiris: M. adopts the epigrammatic device of putting a question in the mouth of an interlocutor: cf. Catull. 85 *odi et amo. quare id faciam, fortasse requiris? | nescio, sed fieri sentio et excrucior*.

4   in somnis medicum uiderat Hermocraten: merely dreaming of Hermocrates was enough to kill Andragoras. The medical context and the dream motif suggest a further association, incubation, whereby a patient would spend the night in a temple of Asclepius in the hope of being healed by a dream vision of the deity who either effects a cure or advises on treatment (cf. E. and L. Edelstein, *Asclepius: a collection and interpretation of the testimonies* (NY 1975), Jackson (1988) 144–8). Here, by an ironic reversal, the vision of Asclepius' functionary kills rather than cures.

in somnis 'in a dream', Lucillius' ἐν ὕπνοις: cf. Virg. *A.* 2.270–1 *in somnis, ecce, ante oculos maestissimus Hector | uisus adesse mihi.*

Hermocraten: recalls the Hermogenes of M.'s Greek model. The doctor's deadly nature, and the Hermes element in his name, suggests an association with Hermes ψυχοπομπός, who conducted the souls of the dead to the underworld: Nicharchus, *AP* 11.124 compares a lethal doctor to this divinity.

61   (= 8.74)

'Though once an oculist, you now replace
    your lancet by the gladiator's lance.
The change of weapon makes no difference,
    you still administer the coup de grâce'.
        R. H. P. Crawfurd, 'Martial and medicine', *The Lancet* 6 Dec. 1913

A satire on an incompetent physician whose change of profession has made no material alteration in what he does for a living (cf. 1.30 and 47). The target of the poem is an *opthalmicus*, 'eye doctor', who in his reincarnation as an *oplomachus* wields his lance with the same deadly effect as he once wielded a surgical instrument. His social status is also unchanged: gladiators were of the lowliest class (**26** intro.) and two thirds of the twenty-seven *medici ocularii* in the inscriptions assembled by Nutton (1972) were of servile origin. For doctors as objects of satire, see **60** intro., and for eye doctors in particular, cf. Nicharchus, *AP* 11.112 and 115, *AP* 11.117, 126.

As was the case with doctors in general, lampoons on incompetent eye specialists have a basis in reality. The widespread incidence of eye disease in ancient Rome made the profession popular, but no formal qualifications were needed to practise, and two tomb inscriptions for *ocularii* in their teens show that training and experience could be minimal (Jackson (1988) 83).

In addition, operations, such as that for the removal of cataracts, could go disastrously wrong, not entirely through the fault of the physician: cf. Celsus (7.7.14c) *a posteriore parte caput eius, qui curabitur, minister contineat, ut immobile id praestet: nam leui motu eripi acies* ('eyesight') *in perpetuum potest.*

Further reading: Jackson (1988) 82–3, 121–3, Köhne and Ewigleben (2000), Nutton (1972), Watson (1982) 73–4

1   Oplomachus (ὁπλομάχος): the *hoplomachus* (here spelt without the '*h*' to match *opthalmicus*) was a gladiator whose equipment of spear, short sword and round shield resembled that of the Greek hoplite (Robert (1940) 131–2, Ville (1981) 307 n.191, Köhne and Ewigleben (2000) 51–6). M. chose this type of gladiator partly for the sake of the word play, but also in view of the resemblance between the *hoplomachus*' lance and the needle used by eye surgeons (2n.).

opthalmicus (ὀφθαλμικός): an eye surgeon (Gal. XII 786 Kühn). The Greek term is used for the sake of the play with *oplomachus*, instead of the Latin (*medicus*) *ocularius* found in inscriptions.

2   fecisti medicus quod facis oplomachus: *oplomachus* and eye doctor both wield a sharp implement with disastrous results. In performing cataract operations a needle was inserted into the eye (Cels. 7.7.14); cf. J. S. Milne, *Surgical instruments in Greek and Roman times* (Oxford 1907) 21–2, plate 16.2, 7, E. Künzl, *Medizinische Instrumente aus Sepukralfunden der römischen Kaiserzeit* (Bonn 1983) 26–7, 61–6. Given the visual similarity between the surgical needle and the *hoplomachus*' lance, one might expect M. to be saying that both gladiator and eye doctor put out eyes with a sharp instrument. This is not, however, the case. The *hoplomachus* fought against the *murmillo* or the Thracian, both of whom had their face protected by a visored helmet with small eyeholes; blows were directed at the uncovered upper torso rather than the head (Köhne and Ewigleben (2000) 40). Nor was the helmet easily dislodged: artistic depictions of fallen gladiators invariably show the helmet in place, and it was not removed even when a defeated gladiator received the *coup de grâce*. Moreover Galen, who worked as physician to the gladiatorial school at Pergamum, mentions wounds to gladiators' limbs, but never to the eyes. The comparison between *hoplomachus* and eye doctor is in consequence not exact: the former inflicts wounds by piercing bodies, the latter pierces eyes. This lack of exactness need cause no concern: M. is frequently interested more in rhetorical effect than precise logic.

medicus: i.e. *medicus ocularius.*

62   (= 9.15)

'Accursed Chloe had the following inscribed on the tombs of her seven husbands: "Chloe was responsible." What could be plainer?'

This and the following epigram are the most concise and witty of several poems on the murder of a husband by a wife or vice versa. In **62**, M. suggests that by placing on the tombs of a series of husbands the inscription *Chloe scelerata feci[t]*, Chloe is openly admitting to having done away with them. The wit of the poem relies on a series of double entendres: see nn. on *scelerata, se fecisse* and *quid pote simplicius.*

Juvenal suggest satirically that the murder of husbands by wives was a routine occurrence in Rome (6.655–6 *occurrent multae tibi Belides atque Eriphylae | mane. Clytaemestram nullus non uicus habebit*).

Further reading: Veyne (1964)

1   **Inscripsit** 'had inscribed', sc. by a professional inscriber: cf. Courtney (1995) 11–12.
        tumulis septem . . . uirorum: for other serial spouse-murderers, cf. 9.78 *funera post septem nupsit tibi Galla uirorum, | Picentine: sequi uult, puto, Galla uiros,* 4.69.3. Seven is commonly used in M. as shorthand for a large figure: cf. 9.78 cited above, 7.58.1, 9.87.1,11.12.1. The exaggeratedly large number of Chloe's late husbands prompts the suspicion that their deaths were the result of foul play.
        scelerata 'accursed', part of the inscription rather than a comment by M. Terms like *sceleratus, impius* and *crudelis* often appear on epitaphs as a form of self-reproach by the survivor for having outlived the dead person: e.g. *CIL* vi 15160 *filiis suis infelicissimis . . . fecit mater scelerata,* Veyne (1964). After the opening *inscripsit tumulis,* this meaning of *scelerata* is to the fore. M., however, intends the reader to think of a second sense, 'criminal'.

2   **'se fecisse'** echoes both an epitaphic and a legal formula. Chloe's inscription may have read either *Chloe fecit* (cf. *CIL* vi 15160, cited above) or *Chloe feci* (cf. *CIL* vi 16610 *DM | Croco con | iugi bene | merenti feci | Euporia uix | annis L*). The surface meaning is 'Chloe set up this monument', the underlying sense 'Chloe committed this crime'. For the latter use of *facio,* cf. Juv. 6.638–9 *sed clamat Pontia 'feci, | confiteor, puerisque meis aconita paraui'*

with Courtney and the expression *fecisse uidetur* which was employed in delivering a verdict of guilty, e.g. Cic. *Pis.* 97.

Chloe is mainly attested as a slave name (cf. *CIL* VI index), but since slaves could not legally marry, this Chloe is envisaged as free.

quid pote simplicius? 'what could be plainer'? Ostensibly this refers to the simplicity of the inscription *Chloe scelerata feci[t]*, but *simplex* also suggests the sense 'honest, straightforward' (cf. Hor. *S.* 1.3.63): in expressing herself thus, Chloe is, according to M., admitting quite openly that she did away with the occupants of the tombs.

pote: for *potest.* Cf. Catull. 17.23–4 *nunc eum uolo de tuo ponte mittere pronum, | si pote stolidum repente excitare ueternum.*

63   (= 10.16 (15))

'Aper shot his wealthy wife through the heart, but only while playing at sport. Aper certainly knows how to play.'

As in **62**, an accusation of murder is presented obliquely. The same technique is employed in both: the first line and a half state the facts, but in such a way as to suggest foul play; in the final half line the poet's ironic comment on these makes this hint a certainty. The suggestion that Aper murdered his wife is conveyed by the strategic placement of *dotatae*, implying a possible motive for homicide; the final half line, congratulating Aper for his skill with the bow, affirms the suspicions earlier insinuated.

The legal realities underlying the marital relationship here depicted could give a husband a motive for murdering his wife. Although a husband enjoyed use of his wife's dowry, he could not legally alienate her property without her permission, and after divorce the dowry could be reclaimed by the wife: cf. Treggiari (1991) 329–31, Gardner (1986) 103, 112. In theory, a well-dowered wife could keep her husband in line by threatening to divorce him and so deprive him of a lucrative source of income – hence the literary topos of the *uxor dotata* who lords it over her husband (cf. **59** intro.). Under these circumstances, a husband would be better off with his wife dead: not only would he be relieved of a tiresome mate, but he would in most cases enjoy unhindered possession of her dowry: cf. Gardner (1986) 10–17.

Dowries could be of considerable size (Treggiari (1991) 344–8), but if, as R. P. Saller (*CQ* 34 (1984) 195–205) argues, the practice of giving very large dowries was less common under the Empire, the *uxor* of the epigram may be based on a comic topos rather than on contemporary reality.

Further reading: Schumann (1977)

1   Dotatae: the prominent position of *dotata* ('possessing a large dowry') immediately hints at murder by implying possible motivations: see intro.

cor ... fixit: the piercing of a vital organ implies premeditated murder on Aper's part.

harundine: Aper shot his wife with an arrow. The setting of the 'accident' is unclear. Perhaps Aper is to be imagined as shooting his wife during target-practice close to the villa on his estate: this was a pastime of Domitian at his Alban retreat (Suet. *Dom.* 19). Another possibility is the hunt, where the bow was used (cf. Plin. *NH* 8.114, D. B. Hull, *Hounds and hunting in ancient Greece* (Chicago 1964) 7–8), but the presence of a wife on such an occasion is unlikely, although the elegist Sulpicia ([Tib.] 4.3) does employ the topos of hunting with the beloved. An archery contest seems ruled out, these being effectively confined to epic poetry: cf. E. N. Gardiner, *Athletics of the ancient world* (Oxford 1930) 27.

2   sed ironically modifies the impression given by the first line that Aper murdered his wife: he killed her, says, M. but it was an accident while he was at sport.

dum ludit: for the verb in a similar context, cf. Ov. *Met.* 10.200–1 *nisi si lusisse uocari | culpa potest* (the accidental death of Hyacinthus by discus). Misadventures of this kind occurred in real life, giving Aper's 'accident' a semblance of plausibility: see *CLE* 1198 *bis mihi septenos aetas ostenderat annos | ... | cum subito mortis ... causa fuisti | lusus ... nam temere emissus non ad mea funera clauus (= claua?) | haesit et in tenero uertice delituit.* The fictional case in Antiphon, *Tetral.* 2 of a boy accidentally killed by a javelin may also reflect the occurrence of such incidents in reality.

ludere nouit Aper: M. comments wryly that Aper 'certainly knows how' to play sport, since his skill with the bow results in a most convenient accident. Cf. 2.52 *Nouit loturos Dasius numerare: poposcit | mammosam Spatalen pro tribus: illa dedit.*

64 (= 12.32)

'What a shameful sight I saw on the first of July, Vacerra, when you and your family were evicted from your lodgings for non-payment of rent. Your wife, sister and mother could be seen on the street carrying such of your possessions as the landlord had deemed too worthless to expropriate in lieu of rental. They looked like Furies just emerged from the darkness of Hades, you yourself like a latter-day Irus. Your pathetic goods and chattels bore detailed and vivid witness to your utter destitution. Why attempt to rent another apartment for which you will equally be unable to pay? You and your family can be lodged for free – on the open streets as beggars.'

This poem documents with cruel precision the expulsion of Vacerra and his family from their apartment for falling two years behind in their rent. In the ancient world, destitution usually elicited not sympathy but contempt (cf. Tyrtaeus fr. 10.3–12 W, Sen. *Clem.* 2.6.2, A. R. Hands, *Charities and social aid in Greece and Rome* (London 1968) 62–76), or even savage mockery, e.g. Ar. *Pax* 739–40, *Eq.* 1268–73, *Vesp.* 1265–74, *Thesm.* 948–52, *Ach.* 855–9, esp. *Plut.* 535–47: 'well, what "benefit" could you [Poverty] bestow except blisters from the bath-house and a noisy rabble of old women and starving little children? And a mass of lice and gnats and fleas . . . which irritate you by buzzing about your head, waking you up and saying "get up, or you will starve". And in addition to this rags instead of a cloak, and instead of a proper bed a mattress stuffed with straw and bugs, . . . for food, not bread, but shoots of mallow, and instead of barley-cake, withered radish leaves: and instead of a stool the top of a broken jar, and instead of a wine jar for kneading dough, a rib from a cask, and broken at that?'

M. often exploited the humorous possibilities of impoverishment: cf. esp. 6.82, 11.32; cf. Juv. 3.147–50; 52–3 *materiam praebet causasque iocorum | . . . si foeda et scissa lacerna, | si toga sordidula est et rupta calceus alter | pelle patet; nil habet infelix paupertas durius in se, | quam quod ridiculos homines facit.* M.'s inspiration derived above all from Catullus and the Neoterics. In particular, several details in **64** are drawn from Catull. 23, in which Furius and his kin are ironically congratulated on their impoverished condition. These include lack of servants or a hearth fire, bodily desiccation, perpetual hunger and the presence of unwholesome relatives.

The catalogue of Vacerra's paltry possessions (11–22) also incorporates certain details – the humble bedding, the items of furniture which lack one of their supports, the recycling of broken pottery, the meagre rations – which recall genre scenes such as are found in Ovid's Philemon and Baucis (*Met.* 8.618–724), Callimachus' *Hecale*, or the story of Molorchus from the beginning of *Aetia* 3: on this so-called *parua casa*-motif, cf. E. J. Kenney, *The ploughman's lunch. Moretum* (Bristol 1984) xxx–xxxiv. But the ethos of these texts, with their sympathetic portrayal of rural poverty, is radically different from M.

In Alexis, fr. 167 K–A, an account of impoverishment similar to **64**, the speaker and her family are Phrygians living abroad, probably in a Greek city. A good case can be likewise made for Vacerra and his family being Celtic immigrants living in Rome in straightened circumstances. ('Celtic' is understood to embrace not only Gauls, but also Germans and Britons, a common piece of ethnic confusion in ancient writers). The arguments for this hypothesis are as follows:

1 The name Vacerra could be a Romanisation of a Celtic one: names in Vac(c) are typically Celtic, and include Vacirro, Vagiro, Vaccurra and Vaccurro: cf. Holder (1907) 69–71, E. Evans, *Gaulish personal names* (Oxford 1967) 457–6.

2 Vacerra's wife is red-haired, one of the most frequently remarked characteristics of Northerly races: see on *rufa* 4.

3 Vacerra's sister is *ingens* (5). The great size of Gauls or Germans of both sexes was often remarked (cf. 8.75.5–6 *quid faceret Gallus, qua se ratione moueret?* | *ingenti domino seruulus unus erat*, Caes. *BG* 1.39.1, Tac. *Ann.* 1.64.2 with Goodyear), and the observation has been confirmed by skeletal remains: cf. R. Much, *Die Germania des Tacitus* (3rd ed., Heidelberg 1967) 96–7.

4 The *septem crines* of Vacerra's wife (4) might reflect some characteristically Celtic way of styling the hair. A statue of a god from Euffigneix, Haute Marne, France, has seven locks or curls, with three strands on each side of a central curl which descends vertically to the nape: cf. A. Cremin, *The Celts in Europe* (Sydney 1992) 85.

5 Vacerra's female relatives carry their possessions (4–5): this could comport with the belief that Celtic women were not inferior to their husbands in size and strength (cf. Strab. 197 'in regard to matters relating to [Gaulish] men and women, tasks are apportioned in a fashion which is the direct opposite of that found among us)'.

6 The comparison of Vacerra's female relatives to Furies calls to mind Tac. *Ann.* 14.30, on female Britons, *in modum Furiarum, ueste ferali, crinibus deiectis faces praeferebant* and in general the typically unkempt hair of Northern races (Tac. *Germ.* 38.3, Plin. *NH* 2.189).

7 The pallor of Vacerra and his relatives (5–9) may suggest their ethnic affiliation: Northerners were typically palefaces (Thompson (1989) 64–6).

If Vacerra is an immigrant, the epigram not only exemplifies the traditional mockery of the poor discussed earlier, but also, given its juxtaposition with **17**, where M. celebrates his easeful retirement in his Spanish homeland, reflects the *Schadenfreude* and sense of superiority entertained by a successful immigrant to Rome, as he smugly contemplates those who have met with disaster in the metropolis where he had so conspicuously made his mark.

Further reading: Frier (1977) and (1980)

1   Iuliarum . . . Kalendarum: the rental year usually began on the first of July (Petr. 38.10–11, *CIL* IV 138, Suet. *Tib.* 35.2). Vacerra has been served notice to quit on that day for non-payment of rent, one of the reasons for which a tenant could legally be evicted (Frier (1980) 73–5).

dedecus: the shameful and undignified spectacle presented by the evicted Vacerra, his female entourage, and pathetic possessions.

2   uidi, Vacerra . . . uidi: M. has seen the grotesque sight with his own eyes. 'A slightly richer pattern is created by the interposition of a short element into the gemination, for example Sen. *Phaedr.* 862 *iam perge, quaeso, perge*' (Wills (1996) 91).

Vacerra: the name has Gallic affiliations (intro.), but also possesses contextually appropriate connotations of folly, as in the other epigrams where it appears (8.69, 11.66, 11.77); cf. Fest. 513.6–7 L *Alii dicunt maledictum hoc nomine* [*Vacerra*] *magnae acerbitatis, ut sit uecors et uesanus.*

sarcinas 'baggage, movable goods and chattels' (cf. Courtney on Juv. 6.146), refers to the tenant's own possessions which he moved into the rental property (Dig. 13.7.11.5, Juv. 3.198).

3   quas non retentas pensione pro bima: *retinere* is a technical term for 'impound' (Crook (1967) 154). As security against non-payment of rent, *pensio*, the landlord had a lien on the furniture and moveables which the tenant had introduced into the property (Frier (1977) 29–30). Vacerra's possessions were, however, so valueless as not to be worth appropriating.

pensione pro bima: leases on rented accommodation normally ran for a year or multiples of a year. The rent was payable at the expiry of the lease; this is how Vacerra comes to be two years behind. The system posed the risk that poorer renters would be unable to find the required lump sum when the day of reckoning arrived: a risk particularly acute in Rome, where rental costs were exorbitant. Cf. Frier (1977), L. E. Dearns, *AJAH* 9 (1984) 163–4.

4   portabat: not owning a slave (a sign of great poverty), Vacerra's wife, mother and sister act as porters.

rufa: describes hair of a dull reddish-yellow hue (André (1949) 80–2), associated particularly with Northern tribes: cf. W. Sieglin, *Die blonden Haare der indogermanischen Völker des Altertums* (Munich 1935). The colour was not admired and was widely accounted a sign of bad character and servile origins: cf. **44**.18n., **74**.1 n.

crinibus septem: for the possible Celtic affiliations of the phrase, see intro. Neither of the two usual explanations is satisfactory: (1) Vacerra's wife has just seven hairs i.e. is bald. This is illogical after *rufa*, M. does not use seven to signify 'only seven', and *crines* does not mean individual 'hairs' but 'locks'; (2) *septem crines* is a botched version of the *seni crines [quibus] nubentes ornantur* mentioned by Festus 454.23–4 L. But M. is talking about a wife, not a bride, and there is no evidence for how the *seni crines* were arranged: cf. L. La Follette in Sebesta and Bonfante (1994) 54–64.

5   cum sorore ... ingenti 'huge' (cf. intro.). Like *rufa* and *cana*, the adjective is insulting, excessive tallness in a woman being considered undesirable (Alexis, fr. 103.10 K–A, Lucr. 4.1163, Ov. *Ars* 2.645–6).

cana: a colour contrast with *rufa* and a proof of age. Elderly parents are a pathetic detail in some accounts of the beggar's existence, but *cana* here is a sneer: cf. 14.27, 3.43.3.

6   Furias putaui nocte Ditis emersas: Vacerra's female relatives issuing forth from their lodgings resembled the Furies just emerged from the darkness of Hades. The comparison is inspired by their pallid appearance (8): cf. Ar. *Plut.* 422–3 (Chremes) 'and who may you [Poverty] be? For you look pallid (ὠχρά) to me.' (Blepyrus) 'Perhaps a Fury from a tragedy'. It is also relevant that the Furies were tall (cf. *ingenti* 5, *LIMC* III 2 s.v. *Erinys* fig. 1) and, like Vacerra's relatives, numbered three (Roscher I 1310 s.v. *Erinys*).

nocte Ditis emersas: the Furies dwelt in Hades. The analogy suggests the squalid and ill-lit conditions in which Vacerra's family had been living: cf. Juv. 3.223–5, 3.30.3 *unde tibi togula est et fuscae pensio cellae?*, McKay (1975) 88.

7   frigore et fame siccus: a common alliterative combination; cf. Ov. *Ib.* 318 *sit frigus mortis causa famesque tuae*, Liv. 27.44.8 *maiorem partem militum fame ac frigore ... amisisset.* Cold and hunger were thought to dry out the body: cf. Catull. 23.12–14 *atqui corpora sicciora cornu | aut siquid magis aridum est habetis | sole et frigore et esuritione.* According to Cic. *ND* 2.137, unexcreted food is converted into blood by the liver, which disseminates this through-out the body (Hagen (1961) 38): insufficiency of food suspends this process, resulting in desiccation; cf. Sil. 2.464–5 *et exurit siccatas sanguine uenas | per longum celata fames.*

frigore: the upper floors of urban apartment blocks, where the poorer tenants were housed, lacked a source of heat (cf. Packer (1971) 72–3). Absence of fire signifies destitution (Catull. 23.1–2 *Furi, cui neque seruus est... | ...neque ignis*, 11.32.1 with Kay), although there were also practical reasons for not kindling fires in tenement buildings (**65** intro.).

8   et non recenti pallidus magis buxo: *pallor*, an unhealthy sal-low discoloration of the complexion, is often compared to boxwood (cf. Ov. *Met.* 4.134–5 *oraque buxo | pallidiora gerens*), which 'when first cut... is pale yellow, but the colour mellows on exposure to light and air' (A. Jackson and D. Day, *Collins good wood guide* (London 1996) 60 with pl.).

pallidus: the typical *pallor* of the undernourished (*fame* 7): cf. [Quint.] *Decl. mai.* 12.7 *exspectant pallidi exsanguesque ciues tui* (the inhabitants of a famine-stricken town).

9   Irus tuorum temporum: Irus, the unsavoury beggar of Hom. *Od.* 18, became a proverbial representative of the type (5.39.9, *AP* 7.676, 9.209, Lucian, *Nekuom.* 15). The original 'stood out for his ravenous belly, eating and drinking unceasingly' (*Od.* 18.2–3), an ironic comment on his counterpart's starveling condition.

sequebaris: Vacerra brings up the rear, an idea underlined by post-ponement of the verb till sentence-end.

10   migrare cliuum crederes Aricinum: Vacerra and his rela-tions resembled a mass departure by the beggars who haunted the base of the slope by which the Via Appia descended into Aricia, an old Latin town, some sixteen miles from Rome: cf. 2.19.3–4, Juv. 4.117 *dignus Aricinos qui mendicaret ad axes* with Courtney.

migrare: the usual word for moving lodgings (Frier (1980) 92), ap-plied ironically to the homeless whose ranks Vacerra is about to join.

11–22: A comic inventory of Vacerra's possessions, seen processing (*ibat*) through the streets.

11 **tripes grabatus et bipes mensa:** a bed/table with a damaged or missing leg is a traditional symbol of indigence: cf. Catull. 10.21–3 *at mi nullus erat nec hic neque illic, | fractum qui ueteris pedem grabati | in collo sibi collocare posset*, Ov. *Met.* 8.661–2.

grabatus (κράββατος)**:** the bed of the poor: cf. *Moretum* 5, 1.92.5 *sed si nec focus est nudi nec sponda grabati*, 11.56.5, Callim. *Hecale* fr. 240 Pf./29 Hollis.

bipes mensa: the table, like the bed, is missing one of its legs: three was the normal number.

12 **corneoque cratere:** the mixing bowl is made of the cheapest material. Cornel-wood is poorly rated by Plin. *NH* 16.206; cf. Theophr. *HP* 3.12.1–2, Blümner, *Technologie* II 270.

13 **matella curto rupta latere:** the use or recycling of broken vessels is a hallmark of poverty (**56**.3n.).

matella 'urine flask', a flagon with a narrow neck for use by males (Hilgers (1969) 217), an undignified word to suit the context: cf. Juv. 10.62– 5 *ardet adoratum populo caput et crepat ingens | Seianus, deinde ex facie toto orbe secunda | fiunt urceoli, pelues, sartago, matellae*.

curto: the adjective, avoided in high poetry (Citroni on 1.92.6), is appropriate to the unsavoury context.

meiebat: an imaginative way of saying 'leaked' or 'dribbled', inspired by the *matella*'s function as a urine receptacle. For other transferred uses of *meiere* cf. Adams, *LSV* 142. The alliteration *matella . . . meiebat* and play on bodily functions recall proverbial usages like *Mentula moechatur. moechatur mentula? certe | hoc est quod dicunt ipsa olera olla legit* (Catull. 94) and *Romae . . . mures molas lingunt* (Sen. *Apocol.* 8.3).

14 **foco:** i.e. *foculo*, a portable stove: cf. Sen. *Ep.* 78.23 *quia non circa cenationem eius tumultus cocorum est ipsos cum opsoniis focos transferentium*.

uirenti: stained with verdigris (cf. 10.33.5 *uiridi tinctos aerugine uersus*), suggesting both age and lack of use (cf. 11.56.4 *tristis nullo . . . tepet igne focus*).

suberat amphorae ceruix: what function the *amphorae ceruix* served is unclear. It might have been employed as a support for the portable stove: the necks of the rounder, squatter types of *amphora* would, if broken off, suit such a purpose (cf. D. Peacock and D. Williams, *Amphorae and the Roman economy* (London 1986), esp. classes 25–37). But the *amphorae ceruix* may just have been another piece of trash which Vacerra could not bear to discard.

15 fuisse: there are no fish in sight: only the odour remains. *fuisse* stands for *adfuisse/fuisse inibi*, a usage normally found in late Latin: cf. Querolus 44.16 Peip. *silentium est ingens, nemo est*, E. Löfstedt, *Philologischer Kommentar zur Peregrinatio Aetheriae* (2nd ed., Uppsala 1936) 117–27.

gerres aut . . . maenas: *gerres* and *maenae*, here unusually not treated as synonyms (cf. Thompson (1947) 155), are small worthless fish which, like most Roman fish, were pickled in brine: cf. Plin. *NH* 31.83, R. J. Curtis, *Garum and salsamentum* (Leiden 1991). They were held in poor esteem: cf. 3.77.7–10 *teque iuuant gerres et pelle melandrya cana, |... ut quid enim, Baetice, saprophagis?*

inutiles 'unsalubrious' i.e. indigestible: cf. Plin. *NH* 26.86 *sed stomacho non inutile*. Pickled fish were widely regarded as bad for the stomach: cf. Ath. 120c, Xenocr. *apud* Oribas. *Collectiones medicae* 2.58.13.

16 odor impudicus 'the filthy smell', a unique use of the epithet. For the stench of pickled fish and the receptacles in which they were preserved, cf. Ath. 356c, 6.93.6 [*tam male Thais olet quam*] *amphora corrupto ... uitiata garo*, Lilja (1972) 100–5.

urcei: a storage jar for for pickled fish (Hilgers (1969) 84–5).

fatebatur 'showed': cf. Juv. 10.172–3 *mors sola fatetur | quantula sint hominum corpuscula*.

17 qualis marinae uix sit aura piscinae: B^A reads *qualis... uissit*, which is generally emended to *uix sit*, C^A *qualem ... uissit*, 'farts', printed by SB. But '*aura uissitur, non uissit*' (Housman, *CP* 1102). And the remark that the fishy smell of the *urceus* outdoes (*qualis uix sit*) even that of a *piscina* is in the style of M. when describing foul smells: cf. 4.4.1, 3, 12 *quod ... redolet ... | piscinae uetus aura quod marinae | mallem quam quod oles olere, Bassa*. See Lilja (1972) 166 for a scientific explanation of why a *piscina*, 'marine fish pond' (cf. 4.30) should smell so foul.

18 nec . . . deerat: implying that many other necessities were missing.

quadra 'a slice': cf. 9.90.18 *secta plurima quadra de placenta*. The word here suggests a meagre ration: cf. Sen. *Ben*. 4.29.2 *quis beneficium dixit quadram panis?*, Fordyce on Virg. *Aen*. 7.115, W. Bellardi, *AION* 5 (1963) 77–90.

casei Tolosatis: unlike other highly rated Gaulish cheeses (cf. *RE*
VII 648), that from Toulouse, mentioned only here, is plainly of poor quality.
Cheese often features in accounts of unpretentious meals, e.g. 11.52.10, Ov.
Met. 8.666; cf. *Moretum* 57.

19   quadrima nigri nec corona pulei: Var. *apud* Plin. *NH* 20.152
states that a garland of pennyroyal (*puleium*), an aromatic plant of the mint
family, *capitis dolores … dicitur leuare, quin et olfactu capita tueri contra frigorum aes-
tusque iniuriam et ab siti traditur.* As its efficacy depended upon its fragrance,
a 'four year old' specimen would have been utterly worthless. On pennyroyal in medicine, cf. Plin. *NH* 20.152–7, J. Scarborough in C. Faraone and
D. Obbink, *Magika hiera* (Oxford 1991) 144–5.
  nigri: discoloured with age.

20   caluaeque restes alioque cepisque: the fibrous tops of garlic
and onions, another useless item; cf. Plin. *NH* 20.51 [*alium*] *tostum cum restibus
suis.* Garlic was the food of the poor (Gowers (1993) 289–92). So were onions:
cf. 3.77.5, *Moretum* 82 with Kenney.
  caluae 'bare of', abl. sep.: cf. Cato, *Agr.* 33.3 *si uinea a uite calua erit.* Only
the inedible part is left.

21–2   nec plena… |…uxores: sc. *nec derat olla matris plena turpi
resina* etc. Among the items carried out from Vacerra's house is a jar of
resin, used by his mother for genital depilation (21 n.), such as was practised
by female prostitutes, *Summemmianae uxores* (**56**.2n.), to enhance their erotic
attractiveness: cf. Auson. 13.100.1–2 Green, D. Bain, *LCM* 7.7 (1982) 7–10,
M. Kilmer, *JHS* 102 (1982) 104–12.

21   plena: for once stocks are not depleted: it may be implied that
the resin is used, then recycled.
  turpi…resina: resin (*resina*) is one of a number of substances used
for depilation, especially of the *pudenda*, whence *turpi*: cf. 3.74.1, 6 *psilothro
faciem leuas et dropace caluam … hoc fieri cunno, Gargiliane, solet,* Hagenow (1972).
  matris: very pointed in view of *cana* 5. The implication is that
Vacerra's mother has no business plying the prostitute's trade at her age: cf.
10.90.1–3 *quid uellis uetulum, Ligeia, cunnum? | … | tales munditiae decent puellas.*
  olla: a jar for cosmetics or medicines (Hilgers (1969) 114).

23   uilicosque derides: 'by asking to rent a lodging without money
to pay for it' (SB). The *uilicus* supervised the letting of an apartment building
on behalf of the owner: cf. Juv. 3.195, Frier (1980) 30.

24   **habitare gratis:**   on the streets as a beggar: cf. *ponti* 25. For the phrasing, cf. 11.83.1 *nemo habitat gratis nisi diues et orbus apud te.*

   o Vacerra: the reversion to the second-person mode of address and repetition of *Vacerra* signals the denouement.

25   **haec sarcinarum pompa:**   *pompa*, properly a dignified cere-monial procession, is grotesquely combined with *sarcinarum*, referring to the pathetic train of possessions which Vacerra has paraded through the streets. For a similarly deflating use of *pompa* cf. [Tib.] 3.1.3–4 *uaga nunc certa discurrunt undique pompa | perque uias urbis munera perque domos.*

   conuenit ponti: such *sarcinae* would best grace one of Rome's bridges, the traditional haunt of beggars (**8.**3n.).

65   (= 3.52)

'You bought a house for 200,000 sesterces, Tongilianus, but it burned down – a misfortune all too common in Rome. Your friends contributed five times that amount. One might almost suspect that you lit the fire yourself.'

Juvenal no doubt had this epigram in mind in a well-known passage from the third Satire: *si magna Asturici cecidit domus, horrida mater, | pullati proceres, differt uadimonia praetor; | tunc gemimus casus urbis, tunc odimus ignem. | ardet adhuc, et iam accurrit qui marmora donet, | conferat impensas: hic nuda et candida signa, | hic aliquid praeclarum Euphranoris et Polycliti, | haec Asianorum uetera ornamenta deorum, | hic libros dabit et forulos mediamque Mineruam, | hic modium argenti: meliora ac plura reponit | Persicus orborum lautissimus et merito iam | suspectus, tamquam ipse suas incenderit aedes* (212–22). In both cases a householder is suspected of having burned down his own home, in the expectation of profiting thereby from the donations of self-interested 'friends' who, as Plin. *Ep.* 9.30.2 complains, *iis potissimum donant, qui donare maxime possunt* – to persons in fact such as Persicus, *orborum lautissimus.*

   The beauty of Tongilianus' crime is its utter undetectability. Fires were a routine occurrence in ancient Rome (*nimium casus in urbe frequens*); cf. Strabo, 235, Plut. *Crass.* 2.5. Apart from the great fire of Rome in Nero's reign and the equally important one under Titus, there were numerous major conflagrations, in some of which whole districts suffered extensive damage. The Domitianic period saw large-scale rebuilding of public works previously destroyed by fire, as well as further outbreaks (cf. 5.7, Werner (1906) 31–4). Deprecations against fire were inscribed upon walls (Plin. *NH* 28.20, Fest. 17.16 L), each year on 23 August the *Volcanalia* were celebrated to keep off fires, and Domitian erected altars in every region of the city *incendiorum arcendorum causa* (*CIL* vi 826 = 30837).

But such precautions were largely in vain. There were many reasons for this: the density with which buildings were packed close together (Tac. *Ann.* 15.38–9), the lighting of domestic fires which could easily get out of control (Mackay (1975) 86), the height of *insulae*-style buildings which made fires, once started, difficult to fight (Yavetz (1958) 511), the erection of flimsy illegal buildings such as shanties and outhouses in public spaces (Johnstone (1992) 54), and, above all, the sheer combustibility of most buildings in which wood was extensively employed (Gell. 15.1.2–3, Dig. 9.2.27.8). A special fire hazard were the wooden partitions, *craticii*, which divided rooms on the upper floors of multiple dwelling houses (Vitr. 2.8.20).

Further reading: Johnstone (1992), Mackay (1975), Werner (1906), Yavetz (1958)

1 Empta ... fuerat: more emphatic than *empta erat*: Tongilianus' house is now a thing of the past.

domus: a free-standing house for owner-occupation, as opposed to an apartment block (*insula*) purchased for the rental income which it would yield: for the distinction, see Tac. *Ann.* 6.45, 15.41, Suet. *Nero* 38.

tibi: dative of agent.

Tongiliane: Tongilianus reappears at 12.88. The name is attested elsewhere, but not frequently (*CIL* vi index, Schulze (1904) 455).

ducentis: sc. *milibus sestertium.* 200,000 sesterces was a very modest price for a house in Rome, where not many could afford to purchase property. Already in the late Republic luxury houses on the Palatine fetched between 3.5 and 14.8 million (R. Duncan-Jones, *PBSR* 33 (1965) 225). Tongilianus has bought a cheap property with the intention of setting it on fire, in order to build a better one with donations from friends.

2   abstulit hanc nimium casus in urbe frequens: an ironic expression of sympathy.

casus: lit. 'misfortune', but with a concomitant pun on the tendency of buildings on fire to collapse (cf. Juv. 3.212–4, Yavetz (1958) 508–11).

urbe: Rome (**8**.3n.).

collatum amusingly cancels out *abstulit* (2). For such contribution by self-seeking friends, cf. Juv. 3.216–20. In the case of large-scale fires, the financial losses of the victims were sometimes made good by imperial donations (Tac. *Ann.* 6.45, Suet. *Tib.* 48, Dio Cass. 59.9.4).

deciens: sc. *centena milia sestertium*, 1 million sesterces; cf. Howell on 1.99.1.

3–4   rogo, non potes ipse uideri | incendisse tuam... domum? In typical fashion M. insinuates what he evidently believes to be the unedifying truth. Juvenal is more straightforward (3.221–2 cited intro.).

rogo: 68.9n.

non = *nonne* (cf. K–S II 2.516–7).

66   (= 3.57)

'Recently at Ravenna a cunning innkeeper tricked me. When I asked for wine mixed with water, he sold me unmixed wine.'

This distich enlists a piece of local topography, Ravenna's celebrated shortage of drinking water, to coin an ingenious variation upon the notorious propensity of innkeepers to cheat their customers by over-watering their wine (1–2 n.). Ravenna, a city of the Po delta which became an important town and naval station after Actium, lay in ancient times in a marshy and lagoonal setting, and suffered frequent inundations from both sea and muddy rivers (Strabo 213), with the consequences described by Sidonius Apollinaris, *Ep.* 1.5.6 *in medio undarum sitiebamus, quia nusquam uel aquaeductuum liquor integer uel cisterna defaecabilis uel fons integer uel puteus inlimis.* The same marshy and alluvial ambience was also responsible for the remarkable fecundity of Ravenna's vines (Strab. 214), with the result that the town was much better supplied with wine than potable water (cf. 3.56, *sit cisterna mihi quam uinea malo Rauennae,* | *cum possim multo uendere pluris aquam*): hence the *copo*'s deception, a 'falsification en sens inverse' (Kleberg (1957) 111).

Further reading: Kleberg (1957), Nissen II.1 251–5

1–2   Wine in antiquity was normally drunk diluted with water, but innkeepers were often over-liberal in their use of water in order to economise on wine. Cf. Dio Chrys. 31.37 'the innkeepers who cheat on their measures, whose income derives precisely from base profiteering', Petr. 39.12 with Smith, M. 1.56, 9.98, *CLE* 930 *talia te fallant utinam me(n)dacia, copo.* | *tu uendes acuam et bibes ipse merum,* Kleberg (1957), 111–13. Here the *copo* remains true to the ways of his profession by cheating M. (*callidus, imposuit*),

but, on account of Ravenna's physical setting, the fraud in question is the
reverse of normal.

1   nuper: epigrams often commence with an adverb indicating some
recent occurrence: cf. 4.61.2, 8.9.1 (*nuper*), 7.79.1, 9.44.1, Lucill. *AP* 11.148.1,
Nicarchus, *AP* 11.113.1, 169.1, 330.1.

2   mixtum: i.e. *uinum cum aqua mixtum*. Cf. **32**.19n.

   merum: the wine which the *copo* sells is no doubt the local product,
of which, in contrast to water, there was an abundance (cf. intro.). It was
the normal practice in hostelries to serve *vin du pays*: cf. *CLE* 931, Kleberg
(1957) 108.

67   (= 6.72)

'A notorious thief who wished to rob a garden which contained nothing but
a statue of Priapus, unwilling to leave empty-handed, stole the Priapus.'

One of four poems on the subject in book 6, this and the following epigram
are concerned with Priapus, the uncouth and ridiculous ithyphallic god,
one of whose functions was to protect gardens and orchards. The thief was
a favourite epigrammatic character (cf. Kay, intro. to 11.54), while thefts
had long been a subject for humour in the popular literary genres: cf.
Watson (1991) 137–8, Brecht (1930) 68–70, L. Koenen, *ZPE* 26 (1977) 78–
80, Grewing on 6.72 intro. The topic was exploited by Catullus (12, 25, 33,
59): the inspiration for *fur notae ... rapacitatis* (1) may have come from 33.6–7
quandoquidem patris rapinae | notae sunt populo. Of particular interest for the
present poem is a body of Greek epigrams in which a thief purloins a statue
of a god, an idea possibly originating in the comic motif of the priest who
steals offerings from a deity (e.g. Ar. *Plut.* 676–81, *AP* 11.324). There are four
poems on the subject by Lucillius, *AP* 11.174–7. In the fourth Eutychides
filches Phoebus 'the detector of thieves', who singularly fails to do his job,
just as Priapus, the god who protects gardens against birds and thieves, is
powerless to prevent his own theft. Other pieces in which a god's statue is
subject to theft include Lucian, *AP* 16.238, noteworthy for its similarity to
M.'s poem: 'in this empty spot for custom's sake Eutychides set me, Priapus
to guard the pathetic shrivelled vine-shoots. I protect a sheer crag. But
whoever comes upon me, has nothing to steal except me the guard.'

Further reading: Herter (1932), Willenberg (1973) 338–42

1   notae nimium rapacitatis: the first instance of the alliteration
which is a pronounced feature of this poem. For the genitive of quality, cf.
6.66.1 *famae non nimium bonae puellam.*

  rapacitatis 'thievishness', a rare word, found again at 12.53.7 *dirae
filius est rapacitatis.*

2   compilare 'rob', looks forward to the theft of Priapus' statue (6),
since the verb is often used of robbing *sacra, fana* or the like.

  Cilix 'a Cilician', rather than an individual's name, as SB believes.
Cilicians were notorious for robbery and bad character (Σ to Juv. 8.94
piratae Cilicum: spoliatores latronum, AP 11.236, Hesych. s.v. κιλικίζεσθαι, Suda
κ 324). For Cilicians living in Rome, cf. 7.30.2.

3-4   ingenti sed erat . . . | . . . Priapum: Priapus is clearly not do-
ing his job. It was his task not only to protect gardens against thieves
(*AP* 6.21.9, M. 6.49, Virg. *G.* 4.110 *custos furium atque auium*), but also to promote fertility therein (Cornut. *Theol. comp.* 27). Such incapacity on Priapus'
part is not unusual: cf. Hor. *S.* 1.8, Herter (1932) 209–11; indeed he often
connives at theft in order to exact sexual retribution from the perpetrator
(cf. *Priap.* 5 with Goldberg).

3   ingenti: the size of the garden is in pointed contrast to its emptiness
(4). *ingenti . . . horto* is intended as a surprise: in Priapic contexts it is usually
the disproportionately large member of the grossly ithyphallic god that is
'huge'; cf. Herter (1932) 169, 175–6.

  Fabulle: the choice of addressee for a poem on Priapus no doubt
came from Catull. 47.3–4 *uos Veraniolo meo et Fabullo | uerpus praeposuit Priapus
ille?* Given that the penis is Priapus' dominant characteristic and that there
was a well-established association between noses and penises (J. N. Adams,
Glotta 59 (1981) 250, C. Brown, *QUCC* 14 (1983) 87–90), it may also be
relevant that another Catullan poem to Fabullus ends with the sentiment
deos rogabis, | totum ut te faciant, Fabulle, nasum (13.13–14).

4   marmoreum . . . Priapum: statues of Priapus were normally of
wood (*AP* 9.437, M. 8.40, Herter (1932) 163–4), in keeping with the god's
uncouth appearance (*Priap.* 39.5) and with ancient usage: as a deity of
the countryside he will originally have been carved from a bifurcated tree
branch (Herter (1932) 4–5). But statues of the god were sometimes made
of more expensive materials, marble included: cf. Virg. *Ecl.* 7.35–6 *nunc
te* [*Priapum*] *marmoreum pro tempore fecimus; at tu, | si fetura gregem suppleuerit,*

aureus esto, Herter ch. 4 *passim*. The costlier substance from which the statue is fashioned makes it a more tempting target for the thief.

5–6   For the idea, cf. 8.59.13–14 *si nihil inuasit, puerum tunc arte dolosa | circuit et soleas surripit ipse suas*, which also refers to a theft motivated by a *fur*'s wish not to go home empty handed.

5   dum: explanatory, 'seeing that' (*OLD* s.v. 4).

6   ipsum surripuit Cilix Priapum: cf. Lucian, *AP* 16.238 (intro. n). Priapus is made a fool of by being stolen from the garden which he is supposed to protect. This is in keeping with the treatment of the god in Latin poetry, where – in contrast to Greek poetry – he is almost invariably a figure of fun (Herter (1932) 30).

68   (= 3.44)

'Would you like to know, Ligurinus, why everyone flees your approach? You are too keen on reciting your verses. This is a disastrous vice which provokes greater terror than the most dangerous of wild creatures. No matter what I am doing – standing, sitting, running, shitting, swimming, dining, sleeping – you recite to me, and I cannot shake you off. Don't you realise the damage you are doing? Although a man of unblemished character, you inspire universal fear.'

On Ligurinus, a compulsive reciter who forces his bad verses on unwilling listeners in every place and on every occasion, who, once he has caught you, will not let you go: he reappears in 3.45 and 50 as a host who invites guests in order to subject them to a reading of his poetry. Under the Empire recitations were one of the nuisances attendant upon life in the city: cf. Juv. 1.1–14, M. 9.83, Phaedr. 4 epil. 8–9, Dio Chrys. 27.6, L. Friedländer, *Roman life and manners* (7th ed. tr. L. Magnus, New York 1968) III 39–40. For the most part these were arranged in advance and took place either in private houses or else in auditoria specially rented or let for the purpose (Sen. *Suas.* 6.27, Plin. *Ep.* 8.12.2, Juv. 7.39–47, Tac. *Dial.* 9.3). Ligurinus, however, like Petronius' manic poetaster Eumolpus, is of the peripatetic variety, which makes him more pernicious because more difficult to avoid.

1–4   Occurrit tibi nemo quod libenter, | . . . | . . . | quid sit 'why it is that nobody likes to meet you'. M. often begins his epigrams with a *quod* clause, e.g. 1.8.1, 95.1 with Citroni, 2.11.1, 6.22.1.

2–3   ingens | . . . solitudo 'a great emptiness', strikingly captures the scattering of potential listeners before the approach of Ligurinus.

2   quod, quacumque uenis: cf. 3.55.1 *quod, quacumque uenis, Cosmum migrare putamus.*

fuga est: a common reaction to a poetaster bent on foisting his verse upon others: cf. 3.45 (also Ligurinus), *AP* 11.133, 135, Hor. *Ars* 474 *indoctum doctumque fugat recitator acerbus.* The elision of the concluding syllable of *fuga* mimics the disappearance of the intended victims, an effect made more striking by the rarity of elision in M.'s hendecasyllabics.

3   circa te, Ligurine: the placing of the caesura after the third syllable, instead of the usual fifth or sixth, has the effect of isolating Ligurinus within the verse, suggesting the empty space which surrounds him.

Ligurine: an uncommon, and ironic name for a bad poet (3.50.9 [*Ligurini*] *scelerata poemata*). λιγυρός in Greek characterises the clear sweet sound of poetry or song: cf. Hom. *Od.* 12.183 λιγυρὴν δ' ἔντυνον ἀοιδήν, 'raise the clear strain', Hes. *Op.* 695, Phanocles, fr. 1.19 Powell. Petronius' wretched versifier Eumolpus (lit. 'Melodious') similarly bears an amusingly inapposite name (κατ' ἀντίφρασιν).

4   nimis: uncommon with a substantive: cf. Stat. *Ach.* 2.37–8, Apul. *Met.* 7.21.

poeta: for M., being a poet and reciting were effectively synonymous; cf. 2.88 *nil recitas et uis, Mamerce, poeta uideri.* | *quidquid uis esto, dummodo nil recites.*

5   hoc ualde uitium periculosum est: the prosaic language (*ualde, periculosus*) contrasts with the mock elevation of 6–8.

periculosum: similarly in Juv. 3.8–9 *Augusto recitantes mense poetas* climax a list of *pericula saeuae | Vrbis.* By comparable hyperbole, reciters are described as 'lethal' (Hor. *Ars* 475 *occiditque legendo, AP* 11.135.4, 'slain by a versy death'): cf. also Catull. 14.17–19 and 44 *passim* for the injurious effects of bad literature.

6–8   Ligurinus is feared more than the most savage or venomous creatures. The comparison is inspired by Ov. *Ars* 2.373–7 *sed neque fuluus aper media tam saeuus in ira est, | fulmineo rabidos cum rotat ore canes, | nec lea, cum catulis lactantibus ubera praebet, | nec breuis ignaro uipera laesa pede | femina quam socii deprensa paelice lecti;* Hor. *Ars* 472–4 compares a *recitator* to a dangerous bear which has escaped from its cage.

6   non tigris catulis citata raptis: tigresses were notoriously protective of their cubs and correspondingly ferocious if they were stolen: cf.
8.26.1–3, Stat. *Theb.* 4.315–16 *raptis ueluti aspera natis | praedatoris equi sequitur
uestigia tigris.*

   citata 'roused' sc. to pursuit of the thief. Cf. [Sen.] *HO* 1238 *citatam
gressibus...feram.*

7   dipsas: a mottled snake identified with the *Cerastes uipera* (Gossen-
Steier, *RE* II 1.530–1). It was so named because its potentially fatal bite
caused intolerable thirst (δίψα): cf. Lucian, περὶ διψάδων 4, Nic. *Ther.*
334–58, Luc. 9.737–60.

   medio perusta sole: the *dipsas* was indigenous to Libya, where the
midday sun would be especially fierce: cf. Luc. 9.754 *dipsas... terris adiuta
perustis.* M.'s phrase implies that the snake's temper is roused by the heat of
the sun and reflects a false etymology which derived its name from the heat
and thirst which it supposedly experienced: cf. Luc. 9.610 *in mediis sitiebant
dipsades undis.*

8   nec sic scorpios improbus timetur: *improbus* = 'pitiless, ruth-
less'. The scorpion, many varieties of which were known in classical antiquity (Nic. *Ther.* 769–804), was notorious for aggressiveness (Plin. *NH* 11.87).
Cf. S. Eitrem, *SO* 7 (1928) 53–82, W. Deonna, *Latomus* 17 (1958) 641–58, 18
(1959) 52–66.

9   rogo: a colloquial way of pointing a question, often used by M.;
cf. Hofmann (1951) 105–6.

   quis ferat...?:   i.e. no one would put up with L., if he gave his
listeners any choice in the matter.

   labores: the 'sufferings' (*OLD* s.v. 6a) entailed in listening to
Ligurinus.

10   et stanti legis: sc. *mihi*, as shown by the sequence of first person
verbs in 12–16.

11   currenti: running was a popular form of exercise among the
Romans (**21**.3–4, 7.32.11, Cels. 4.9, Gal. VI 144 Kühn). As it was not normally done with any great vigour (Sen. *Ep.* 83.4–5, 15.4), it will have been
easy for Ligurinus to keep pace with M. as he jogged.

   legis cacanti: 'a bathetic conclusion to an elegant and alliterative
chiasmus' (R. George). Reciting all the while, Ligurinus instals himself in

the seat next to M. as the latter relieves himself: cf. 11.98.21–2 *basium* . . . |
dabit cacanti. As most Roman households lacked sanitation facilities, public
latrines, often located in baths and theatres, were heavily patronised. Cf.
Scobie (1986) 429 'a Roman *forica* where as many as 60 or more people,
men and women, sitting on stone or wooden seats, relieved themselves in
full view of each other', Hodge (1992) 270–2.

12   in thermas fugio: if the public latrine in 11 is part of a bath
complex, M. depicts himself as hastily taking refuge in the nearest available
building.

   thermas: 21.13n. For unsolicited recitations in the baths, cf. Hor. *S.*
1.4.74–6, Petr. 91.3, 92.6.

   sonas ad aurem: *ad* implies an unwelcome contiguity: cf. 3.63.8
atque aliqua semper in aure sonat. Since *sonare* is associated with the production
of elevated poetry (**15.**4n.), there may be a further implication that Ligurinus
is a pretentious epic versifier.

13   piscinam peto: non licet natare: still within the bath complex, M. makes for the swimming pool, *piscina*, where his attempts to swim
are frustrated by Ligurinus' appropriation of much of the available space:
the *piscina*, generally situated in the *frigidarium,* was often quite small: cf. *RE*
XXII 1785–7 s.v. 2.

14   ad cenam propero: dinner normally followed directly after the
bath; cf. Kay on 11.52.3, Marquardt-Mau 269–70. *propero* suggests both M.'s
eagerness to shake off Ligurinus (cf. Hor. *S.* 1.9.8–9) and that, thanks to L.,
he is late for his *cena*.

   tenes euntem: cf. Hor. *Ars* 475 *quem uero arripuit* [*recitator acerbus*], *tenet
occiditque legendo*.

15   The dinner party was a popular place for recitations (Hor. *Ep.*
2.1.109–10, Plut. *Q. conu.* 621 B–C, 11.52.16 with Kay), often unwanted
(5.78.25, *AP* 11.10, 136) and often given by hosts, Ligurinus included (3.45,
50), who issue dinner invitations solely in order to inflict their poems upon
their guests (cf. *AP* 11.137, 394). This could be the situation here, but it seems
more in keeping with Ligurinus' glue-like adhesiveness that he pursues M.
to dinner at someone else's house.

15   lectum: R. Mayer, *CQ* 43 (1993) 504–5, rightly describing the
repetition of the transmitted *cenam* in 15 as 'pointless', suggests *mensam* or,

better, *lectum*, implying that Ligurinus shares the same couch, so that there is no escape.

fugas edentem: the *sedentem* of the MSS is maladroit after *sedenti* (10); Ramirez de Prado's *edentem* is surely right.

16 Having been relentlessly pursued by Ligurinus all day, M. is tired out (*lassus*) and wants to go to bed, but even there he cannot escape the reciter's unsolicited attentions.

17 uis, quantum facias mali, uidere? echoes syntactically *quid sit scire cupis?*, in an effect of ring composition.

18 The most cogent demonstration of Ligurinus' perniciousness is the paradox that, although of unimpeachable character, he is the object of universal fear. He may be a *uir bonus* but he is certainly not *dicendi peritus*!

uir ... probus ... timeris: an ironic inversion of *nec sic scorpios improbus timetur* (8).

<h2 style="text-align:center">69 (= 7.95)</h2>

'It's mid-winter and the weather is freezing, yet you dare to detain all comers with your chilly kiss, Linus, and kiss everyone in Rome. What more cruel revenge could you take if you had been beaten up? In this cold I wouldn't even want my wife and winsome daughter to kiss me, yet you are no doubt more agreeable and more elegant, with a filthy icicle hanging from your nose and your beard as stiff as a goat's. I would rather meet 100 cunt-lickers or a eunuch priest. So if you have any sense of decency, put off your wintry kissings till the beginning of spring.'

The theme of the inveterate kisser is treated several times by M.: 11.98 and 12.59 are general attacks on the type; a series of epigrams in book 2 (10, 12, 21-3) is directed against a single representative of the class, whom M. calls Postumus. For M., such persons are a menace because they are invariably unwholesome in some way. Here the theme is given an original twist: Linus is repulsive, not through any defect of character or physique, but because he persists in his osculations in the depth of winter, when an icicle of congealed mucus hangs from his nose and his beard is frozen stiff: at such a season even the kisses of family members would be unwelcome.

Kissing as a form of greeting had earlier been confined to the nobility (cf. Plin. *NH* 26.3, Suet. *Tib.* 34.2, Krenkel (1981) 49); but 12.59.4-7, which lists among *basiatores* individuals engaged in banausic professions, suggests that by M.'s time the custom had spread to persons of all classes. Are M.'s attacks on those who kiss everyone they encounter indiscriminately, then, simply a snobbish reaction to the fact that the practice had become so widespread among the general community that one was constantly in danger of being kissed by undesirable types? Possibly so, but he may have in his sights false friends, or parasites who kiss all they meet in the hope of obtaining a patron.

Further reading: Kroll in *RE* Suppl. v 514–15 s.v. *Kuss*, Moreau (1978), Sittl (1890) 38

1   riget: lit. 'is stiff with cold'; cf. *riget...barba* 11. Poetic winters are conventionally freezing: cf. Hor. *Carm.* 1.9 with N–H, though there may be some basis in reality: see 11 n.

horridus December: the coldest time of year: **14**.5n.

2   audes tu tamen 'yet *you* have the effrontery'. Linus is not deterred by the weather: cf. 11.98.8 *et aestuantem basiant et algentem.*

3   obuius hinc et hinc: cf. 11.98.2–3 *[basiatores] occurrunt | et hinc et illinc, usquequaque, quacumque.*

4   totam...Romam: typical Martialian hyperbole.

Line: a rare name (only four examples in *CIL* vi). It is used several times by M.; here it may have been chosen for a pun on *lino*, the idea being that Linus 'besmears' everyone with his kisses: cf. 8.33.11 *hoc linitur sputo Iani caryota Kalendis.*

5–6   If you had been physically attacked by someone, what worse revenge could you take than planting chilly kisses on them?

grauius: the adjective is often associated with the idea of punishment or retribution e.g. Cic. *Mur.* 47.1 *poena grauior.*

7–8   In such cold as this I would not want to be kissed either by my wife or charming daughter. Normally, the kisses of one's children were desirable (cf. Lucr. 3.895–6 *nec dulces occurrent oscula nati | praeripere*, Virg. *G.* 2.523 *interea dulces pendent circum oscula nati*), kisses exchanged between father and daughter especially so because of the particular bond of affection which prevailed between the two (Ov. *Met.* 1.485 *in...patris blandis haerens ceruice lacertis*, J. P. Hallett, *Fathers and daughters in Roman society* (Princeton 1984)

76–110). The lines have sometimes been read as evidence of M.'s marital status: this is unnecessary.

8   rudis 'innocent': cf. Luc. 4.396 *iam coniunx natique rudes.*

labellis: the diminutive has both literal and emotive force; cf. Catull. 61.212–13 *dulce rideat ad patrem semihiante labello.*

9   sed tu dulcior elegantiorque: highly sarcastic. Linus regards himself as more appealing than wife and daughter to kiss. This misguided belief recalls the self-delusion of many would-be *urbani* in Catullus.

10   liuida: refers to the greenish yellow colour of the solidified nasal mucus of which the icicle is composed: cf. Cels. 2.8.23 *si pus est liuidum et pallidum.*

caninis: presumably an allusion to the wetness of dogs' muzzles, though 'dog-like' nostrils are normally associated with keen-scentedness, e.g. Lucr. 1.404–5, Ov. *Met.* 7.806–7 *naribus acres | . . . canes.* The detail anticipates the animal comparison of 12–13.

11   dependet glacies: Linus has an icicle hanging from his nose; cf. **82**.5, 11.98.7 *nec congelati gutta proderit nasi.*

dependet glacies rigetque barba: reminiscent of Virgilian descriptions of Atlas, both man and snow-covered mountain (*glacie riget horrida barba, A.* 4.251), and of Scythia (*stiriaque impexis induruit horrida barbis, G.* 3.366); cf. also Ov. *Tr.* 3.10.21–2 on Tomi *saepe sonant moti glacie pendente capilli | et nitet inducto candida barba gelu.* But such descriptions, at home in northerly climes, are absurdly hyperbolic when transferred to a Roman setting: the city was not known, even in antiquity, for the severity of its winters (**79** intro.). On the other hand, in view of references to nasal icicles twice in the seventh book (cf. **82**), and to cold winter rains in **14**, it is possible that Rome experienced an unusually severe winter in 92, and that these poems reflect the fact.

12–13   Linus' beard, stiff with cold, resembles that cut from a goat, not only because goat hair is comparatively stiff, but because the shearing of goats took place in winter: cf. Longus, 3.3, Virg. *G.* 3.311–13. The double meaning of *forfices* (scissors/shears) and *tonsor* (barber/shearer) facilitates the comparison. Hair from long-haired goats (mohair) was used among other things for ship's tackle, tents, clothing for sailors and footwear (14.141 *udones Cilicii*). The beard, which is especially prominent and elongated in such animals (cf. *McGraw-Hill encyclopedia of science and technology* (6th edn 1987) XI 296 s.v. *Mohair*), was shorn along with the rest of the animal: cf. Virg. *G.* 3.311–13 *nec minus interea barbas incanaque menta | Cinyphii tondent hirci saetasque comantes | usum in castrorum et miseris uelamina nautis*, 14.141.1.

12   forficibus 'shears': cf. Calp. Sic. 5.72–4 *sed tibi cum uacuas posito uelamine costas | denudauit ouis, circumspice, ne sit acuta | forfice laesa cutis.*

13   Cinyphio ... marito: billy-goats are often referred to by poets as the 'husband of the flock' e.g. Theoc. 8.49, *AP* 9.99.1, Virg. *Ecl.* 7.7. For *maritus* by itself in this sense, cf. Hor. *Carm.* 1.17.7 *olentis ... mariti* where, as here, the sense is made clear by the accompanying epithet.

   Cinyphio: the Cinyps was a river in Africa, near the Syrtes, in the vicinity of which were found especially hairy goats; cf. Virg. *G.* 3.311–13 cited above, Plin. *NH* 8.203, M. 8.51.11.

   Cilix: from Cilicia, a province of Asia Minor, where long-haired goats were bred (Plin. *NH* 8.203). Hence goat-hair fabric was called *cilicium*. In modern times mohair wool is obtained from the angora goat, named from its place of origin Ankara, the modern name for Cilicia.

14–15   Meeting Linus would be even worse than encountering numerous practioners of oral sex whose kisses would be especially repulsive: cf. 12.59.10, Sen. *Ben.* 4.30.2 *cuius osculum etiam impudici denotabant.*

14   centum: a hyperbolic contrast with the sole *basiator* Linus. *centum* stands for any large number.

   cunnilingis: it was believed that this practice, like *fellatio*, resulted in a foul-smelling mouth; cf. 12.85 *pediconibus os olere dicis. | hoc si, sicut ais, Fabulle, uerum est, | quid tu credis olere cunnilingis?, AP* 11.220.1–2. The kisses of those who practised oral sex were thought polluting as well as malodorous: cf. Catull. 99.9–10, Krenkel (1981) 42–3, Obermayer (1998) 214–24.

15   Gallum: a person who has been initiated by self-castration as a priest of Cybele. Here it stands for *fellator, fellatio* being regarded by M. as the appropriate sexual activity for such eunuchs: cf. 3.81.1–2 *quid cum femineo tibi, Baetice Galle, barathro? | haec debet medios lambere lingua uiros.* Galli and the closely related eunuch priests of the Syrian Goddess were frequently accused of passive homosexual practices including *fellatio* (Apul. *Met.* 8.26–9; cf. Suet. *Aug.* 68, [Lucian] *Onos* 35, Juv. 2.112, H. Graillot, *Le cult de Cybèle* (Paris 1912) 305, P. Maas, *RhM* 74 (1925) 432–6).

recentem: the point seems to be that one who has been freshly castrated performs his new sexual activities with special fervour and so is a particularly obnoxious type of *fellator* to encounter. SB translates 'fresh from action', thinking perhaps of 12.59.10 *fellatorque recensque cunnilingus*, but *recens* here must mean fresh from the activity with which he is particularly associated, i.e. self-emasculation.

17   basiationes 'kissifications', a Catullan coinage, here used in a considerably less salubrious context than the original (7.1–2 *quaeris, quot mihi basiationes | tuae, Lesbia, sint satis superque*).

18   in mensem...Aprilem: i.e. the time when the winter cold gives way to warmer weather, cf. Ov. *Fast.* 4.87–9 *nam quia uer aperit tunc omnia, densaque cedit | frigoris asperitas, fetaque terra patet, | Aprilem memorant ab aperto tempore dictum*, Var. *L.* 6.33 [*mensem secundum*] *puto dictum, quod uer omnia aperit, Aprilem*, Virg. *G.* 1.217–18.

70   (= 3.8)

' "Quintus loves Thais." "Which Thais?" "One-eyed Thais." "She is blind in one eye, he in both." '

This distich is a witty variation on the erotic commonplace of the lover's blindness, suggesting with typically Martialian hyperbole that Quintus must be truly blind to love the repulsive Thais. The notion that the lover is metaphorically 'blind' to his beloved's physical shortcomings goes back at least to Plato, *Leg.* 731e, resurfaces in Theocritus (*Id.* 10.19–20: cf. 6.18–19), and attains prominence in the late Republic: e.g. Hor. *S.* 1.3.38–40 and Lucr. 4.1153–70, which begins *nam faciunt homines plerumque cupidine caeci | et tribuunt ea quae non sunt his commoda uere. | multimodis igitur prauas turpesque uidemus | esse in deliciis summoque in honore uigere*: cf. Brown *ad loc.* Cf. also Hor. *S.* 1.2.90–3 and Ov. *Ars* 2.641–62, advising the *amator* to *deliberately* overlook his girl's physical deficiencies by attaching to them hypocoristic names.

In other instances of the *amor caecus* theme, the beloved's *uitia* are sometimes, as here, of the ocular variety: cf. Lucr. 4.1161, Ov. *Ars* 2.659, Hor. *S.* 1.3.44–5 *strabonem | appellat paetum pater* and Cic. *ND* 1.79 (Roscius, the beloved of Lutatius Catulus, had *peruersissimi oculi*). But the amusing play in the present epigram on literal and metaphorical blindness and the notion of making the beloved actually blind in one eye (*lusca*) seems original to M.

70 is in dialogic form – rare in M., but widespread in Greek epigram, particularly of the sepulchral or declamatory kind: cf. Raschke (1910) 6–16. Such epigrams incline to the brief question and answer format adopted here, e.g. 5.55, Callim. *Ep.* 34 Pf. ' "I, a branch of oak, was dedicated to you, O lion-throttling swine-slaying lord, by – " "Whom?" "Archinos." "Which Archinos?" "Archinos the Cretan." "I accept.",' *AP* 5.46, 101, 267 ' "Why are you groaning?" "I am in love." "With whom?" "With a girl." "Is she attractive?" "She appears so to my eyes";' cf. Rashke (1910) 40–2, Pfeiffer on Callim. fr. 114. 4–7.

Further reading: Buchheit (1964), Ogle, (1920), Peek (1941), Rashke (1910), Watson (1982)

1   **'Thaida Quintus amat':**   the style is that of graffiti: cf. *CIL* IV 3131 *Pigulus amat Iudaia*, 7086 *Marcus Spedusa amat*, Lucian, *Dial. mer.* 4.3. Quintus and Thais reappear in 3.11, on Quintus' indignant reponse to the present epigram.

   Thaida: Greek accusative singular. *Thais* is a common prostitute's name, hence the need to enquire 'which Thais?'. Cf. Kay on 11.101.1.

   luscam: *luscus* can mean either 'blind in one eye' or 'having one eyeball missing'. The condition was obviously disfiguring, which is why Quintus must be 'blind' to overlook it: cf. 2.33.3, 12.22 *quam sit lusca Philaenis indecenter | uis dicam breuiter tibi, Fabulle? | esset caecior decentior Philaenis.* Witticisms at the expense of *lusci* constituted the lowest kind of humour (Watson (1982) 71): M. uses the theme twelve times in all, a reflection of the taste of epigram for mocking physical deformities.

2   **'unum oculum Thais non habet, ille duos':**   Thais is literally blind in one eye, Quintus metaphorically in both, if he cannot see how ugly Thais is: cf. Joepgen (1960) 81–2.

71   (= 4.87)

'Your acquaintance Bassa, Fabullus, is forever cuddling a baby and calling it her darling. The odd thing is that she is not baby-minded. The reason? She is given to farting.'

On Bassa, who has an embarrassing habit of farting, and hugs babies to give the impression that the smell emanates from the latter. Farting was an established subject for humour in the lower genres. M. himself remarks *pedere te mallem: namque hoc nec inutile dicit* | *Symmachus et risum res mouet ista simul* (7.18.9–10: cf. 12.77.3–4). Aristophanes treats farting as an established comic routine (*Ran.* 1–10), as does Petronius (117.12–13). The plays of the former are filled with jokes on the sound and smell thereof (cf. esp. *Plut.* 693–706, McDowell on *Vesp.* 394), and the topic receives an airing in other comic writers (e.g. *Com. Adesp.* fr. 168 K–A 'there is no nose that could withstand the stench of the fart') as well as Greek satiric epigram (*AP* 11.241–2, 415) and the Mime, which even assigned a rôle to a personified Fart (*P. Oxy.* 413).

While the stratagem adopted by Bassa to cloak her borborysms is novel and ingenious, she herself is far from novel. The inveterate farter is a butt of comedy: examples include Ar. *Ach.* 254–6, *Eccl.* 78, Timocles, fr. 23.6–7 K–A, Eupolis, fr. 99.5–10 K–A and the significantly named Pediata of Hor. *S.* 1.8.38–9. Farting is the sign of a coarse or uncouth person (Ar. *Plut.* 705, Catull. 54.3, Petr. 47, 117.12–13); it is hardly surprising that to fart publicly was regarded as a *faux pas* in a woman (Plato, *Com.* fr. 62 K–A, Machon 156–62 Gow) – hence the need for Bassa to lay the blame for her intestinal indiscretions elsewhere.

Like a number of M.'s epigrams, e.g. **31**, the present piece is indebted to Catull. 13. There the addressee Fabullus will be treated to a smell so delightful that he will 'ask the gods to make him all nose': here Fabullus' friend Bassa emits the opposite. In addition, the first element of his name may be contextually significant: *fabae*, beans, were notoriously productive of intestinal gas; cf. Ov. *Med.* 70, Cic. *Diu.* 1.62 with Pease.

Further reading: Hosek (1962) 160–74 and 220–2 (German summary), Manson (1978), Radermacher, *RE* xxii 235–40 s.v. πορδή, Sedgwick (1928)

1–2   Infantem secum semper . . . | **collocat:** *secum collocat*, 'she places in her lap', is found only here in classical Latin. Either Bassa keeps one particular baby constantly with her, or, more probably, she snatches up any conveniently to hand, thus giving the impression, contradicted in 3, that she is *infantaria*, 'baby-mad'. In an upper-class Roman household, Bassa's stratagem would be facilitated by the presence of slave children and the practice, affected by many Roman women, of keeping young slave *delicia*, 'pets' whom they liked to fondle: cf. Watson, (1992) 261, W. J. Slater, *BICS* 21 (1974) 133–40.

1   Infantem: used in its strict sense of a young baby: cf. Var. *L.* 6.52 *fatur is qui primum homo significabilem ore mittit uocem. ab eo, antequam ita faciant, pueri dicuntur infantes.* By M.'s day, *infans* had become the preferred term for a very small child, replacing the earlier *paruus* and *paruulus* (Manson (1978) 269–74).

semper: constantly, because her farting is also habitual (4).

tua Bassa 'your friend Bassa': cf. Catull. 13.7 *tui Catulli*. M, like Catullus, uses the possessive adjective to establish a relationship between the addressee of the poem and its subject (e.g. 6.6 *comoedi tres sunt, sed amat tua Paula, Luperce, | quattuor: et* κωφὸν *Paula* πρόσωπον *amat*). Fabullus is evidently rather taken with Bassa and needs to be disillusioned [EJK].

Bassa: the name is used by M. several times, at 4.4 also of a lady with a smell (of unspecified origin). It has a somewhat aristocratic flavour which is at odds with Bassa's unsalubrious behaviour: the cognomen Bassus, frequent under the Empire, was borne by a number of consulars (Schulze (1904) 350).

2   lusus deliciasque uocat 'calls it her plaything and her darling'. Bassa employs the sort of language that one uses of pets, human and animal: cf. 7.14.2 *amisit lusus deliciasque suas*.

3   et, quo mireris magis, infantaria non est 'and what you will find even more surprising, she is not a woman who is crazy about babies'.

quo mireris magis: cf. Sen. *Ep.*17.7 *haec omnia passi sunt pro regno, quo magis mireris, alieno*.

infantaria: evidently coined by M. for comic effect and not found elsewhere, *infantaria* must mean 'baby-mad, a lover of babies', not 'a woman who looks after babies' (*OLD, TLL*), an explanation based on the use of terms in -*arius*/-*a* to refer to practioners of an art or trade. But the suffix is often used colloquially in the sense 'keen on': e.g. Cic. *Att.* 2.7.3 *sanguinaria iuuentus*. M. coined several other such words e.g. *carnarius, pinguiarius, calcularius* and *glabraria*. See also E. W. Nichols, *AJPh* 50 (1929) 40–63.

4   ergo quid in causa est? 'so what's the reason?' Cf. Sen. *Dial.* 10.3.4 *quid ergo est in causa?*, *Dial.* 12.7.8.

pedere Bassa solet: Bassa's scheme for cloaking her smells is certainly plausible: Soranus, *Gynaec.* 2.30–1 advises attending to a baby's sanitary needs once a day and never at night, a regime which, if followed, would certainly produce a malodorous infant. Ancient jokes on breaking wind tend to stress sound as well as smell (Radermacher, *RE* xxii 236). M. is probably suggesting that the likelihood of an audible emission on the baby's part provides Bassa with a second line of defence.

pedere: a coarse word, used six times by M. (Adams, *LSV* 249).

72   (= 6.74)

'That individual who occupies the guest of honour's place, who attempts to hide his baldness by smearing unguent across his pate, and uses a fancy toothpick on his slack jaws, is practising deceit: he has no teeth.'

A brief squib against a vain individual who attempts ineffectually to disguise loss of both hair and teeth. Baldness and toothlessness were favourite targets of satiric humour. Aristophanes makes the chorus praise him 'for not mocking baldies', as his rivals did (*Nub.* 540): he was himself laughed at by Eupolis on this score (fr. 89 K–A). Cf. also Plut. *De exilio* 607 A. Epigram seized on the opportunities for humour suggested by a bald pate or attempts to conceal this (cf. *AP* 11.68, 310, 5.76, 7.401) and the topic is decidedly prominent in M. (2.41.10, 5.49, 6.12, 6.57, 9.37.2, 10.83, 12.23, 12.45, Grewing intro. to 6.12 and 6.57). This has been thought surprising given Domitian's supposed touchiness about his own baldness (Suet. *Dom.* 18.2, Szelest (1974) 113). But perhaps M. felt that the topic was so hackneyed as to preclude any risk, nor is it clear that Domitian was as sensitive as Suetonius alleged: cf. Morgan (1997).

   Equally trite is the theme of toothlessness, which is not infrequently coupled with hair-loss as a marker of old age: cf. Lucian, *Dial. mort.* 19, 3.93.1–2 *cum tibi . . . Vetustilla,* | *. . . tres capilli quattuorque sint dentes,* 9.37.2–3. Numerous variations are rung, in sceptic writings, upon the topic of dental deficiencies. The teeth may be black, few in number, loose, missing altogether, or simply false: cf. Howell on 1.19. Such jests, however conventional, none the less reflect dental realities: cf. Gell. 4.12 *eum uero cui dens* [collective sing.] *deesset, Seruius redhiberi posse respondit, Labeo in causa esse redhibendi negauit; 'nam et magna' inquit 'pars* [sc. *hominum*] *dente aliquo carent, neque eo magis plerique homines morbosi sunt',* Jackson (1988) 119–21, Heyne (1924).

Further reading: Heyne (1924), Morgan (1997), Szelest (1974)

1   Medio recumbit imus ille qui lecto: of the three dining couches, the *medius* was reserved for the most distinguished guests (Plut. *Brut.* 34): on it the most honorific position was the *imus*, the so-called *locus consularis*; cf. Plut. *Q. conu.* 619 B–F, Becker, *Gallus* 473–4, Marquardt-Mau 303–4. M.'s point is presumably the contrast between the guest's occupation of the place of honour and his ridiculous and demeaning attempts to disguise his capillary and dental deficiencies.

ille: often used deictically by M. at the beginning of a scoptic epigram to identify his target: cf. Grewing *ad loc.*

2   caluam trifilem semitatus unguento 'having streaked with unguent his bald pate with only three hairs remaining'. The evidence of 6.57.1–2 *mentiris fictos unguento, Phoebe, capillos | et tegitur pictis sordida calua comis* suggests that the reference is to 'hairs' smeared on with unguent and describing paths across the individual's almost totally bald pate (*trifilem*), not to three remaining hairs plastered across his skull so as to give the impression that he has more thatch than he really has. The absurdity of the picture is enhanced by a markedly original mock-elevation of language and syntax: *semitatus* is best explained as a Greek poetic middle, a dignified usage, while the compound *trifilis* is M's own coinage.

trifilem: three and four are the numbers of choice for describing a few remaining hairs or teeth: cf. Lucian, *Rhet. praecept.* 24, 2.41.6–7, 3.93.2 (intro.), 8.57.1, *Priap.* 12.8–9.

3–4   A second piece of deception, forming the climax of the poem and nullifying any possibility that the guest of honour can enjoy the food: cf. Juv. 10.200 *frangendus misero gingiua panis inermi*, Paulin. Nol. *Ep.* 23.9 *eum fratris Victoris coquina et adsueto cibo ut ex rusticis hominem et apto ut edentulum saginauit.*

3   foditque tonsis ora laxa lentiscis: the guest employs a toothpick to give the false impression that he has teeth. Toothpicks were made from quills or pieces of mastic wood (*lentiscum*) sharpened to a point, the latter being regarded as superior: cf. **56**.9, **24**.3 nn.

tonsis 'cropped' of leaves, which were removed from the twig of mastic before it was pressed into service as a toothpick: cf. Leary on 14.22.1. *tonsis* makes sly allusion to the guest's baldness: his toothpicks may be 'shorn', but his hairless pate needs no such ministrations: cf. 6.57.3–4 *tonsorem capiti non est adhibere necesse. | radere te melius spongea, Phoebe, potest.*

ora laxa: the slack jaws of the toothless: cf. 8.57.1–4 *tres habuit dentes, pariter quos expuit omnes | ...Picens... | collegitque sinu fragmenta nouissima laxi | oris.*

4   mentitur: simulate the possession of missing attributes: cf. 6.57.1 (2n.) with Grewing.

Aefulane: for the *nomen*, apparently derived from the Latin township of Aefula (E. Hübner, *Hermes* 1 (1866) 426), cf. Plin. *Ep.* 5.16, *CIL* vi 10606, xi 670.

73 (= 7.39)

'Unable any longer to tolerate the early morning rounds of the *salutatio*, Caelius simulated a crippling attack of gout: he even went to the length of bandaging his feet and walking with a painful gait. It is astonishing what artifice can achieve. From being a pretended sufferer from gout, Caelius became a real one!'

Much was written in classical antiquity on the subject of gout, which 'is due to a metabolic disorder caused by an excess of uric acid in the blood. This results in the deposition of urate crystals in the joint tissues, which gradually degenerate, with consequent destruction of the joint surfaces. The victim experiences swelling, inflammation, pain, and frequently restricted use of the hands and feet' (Jackson (1988)). The illness was particularly associated with the latter, whence its name *podagra* (Greek πούς/ποδός 'foot'). In addition to technical discussions of its symptoms and cure, the pathology of the disease being already understood by the first century AD (Aretaeus, *Acut. morb.* 4.14), literary texts have much to say on the topic. In particular, gout is the target of satire and of moralising writers on account of its not undeserved association with luxurious living: cf. Brecht (1930) 81–2, Juv. 13.96 *locupletem ... podagram* with Mayor. Other literary treatments include *AP* 11.403 and 414, Catullus 71, *P. Oxy.* 2532, a few lines of an elegiac poem jeering at the tendency of sufferers from gout to disguise the true nature of their illness, and Libanius, *Ep.* 1380 (Foerster XI 366–7), a witty response to a comic treatment of gout by a friend and fellow-sufferer. Most expansive of all are Lucian's paratragic *Tragoedopodagra* and the ironically named pseudo-Lucianic *Ocypus* ('Swiftfoot'). The attitude of mockery which animates all such treatments is summed up in *Trag.* 332–3 'and let every one of the sufferers endure being joked at and taunted: for such is the nature of this thing'. M.'s epigram evinces a similar spirit of mockery, but, in his original way, he has combined the theme of gout with one of his favourite topics, the burdensome and disagreeable nature of the *salutatio*.

Further reading: Grmek (1989) 72–3, Jackson (1988) 177–9, Zimmermann (1909)

1   Discursus uarios: clients had to 'rush hither and thither' all over the city because of the number of patrons who had to be visited at the morning levée: cf. 12.29.1–3, Sen. *Dial.* 10.14.3 *isti, qui per officia discursant ... cum* *omnium limina cotidie perambulauerint*, Lucian, *Nigrin.* 22, *Merc. con.* 10. The distances involved could be considerable: cf. 1.108.5 with Citroni.

uagumque mane 'the morning with its roving about [from house to house]'; cf. 4.78.3–4 *discurris tota uagus urbe, nec ulla cathedra est | cui non mane feras irrequietus 'haue'*. The use of *mane* as a substantive is not uncommon (e.g. 1.49.36, 3.36.3), but only here in classical Latin is it a direct object.

mane: the *salutatio* began at sun-up: cf. 4.8.1 *prima salutantes atque altera conterit hora*, 3.36.3 *ut primo . . . te mane salutem*. This made it necessary to rise at daybreak (Lucian, *Merc. con.* 10, Stat. *Silu.* 4.9.48, Mayor on Juv. 5.19–23) or even before (10.82.2, Plin. *Ep.* 3.12.2 *officia antelucana*, Lucian, *Nigrin.* 22), with consequent loss of sleep (12.29.7–8, **25**, Lucian, *Merc. cond.* 24).

2   et fastus . . . potentiorum: complaints about the arrogance of patrons are frequent apropos of the *salutatio*: cf. Hor. *Epod.* 2.7–8 *superba ciuium | potentiorum limina*, Sen. *Dial.* 10.2.5. Such disdainful behaviour could assume several forms: the offensive gradation of clients at the morning levée according to their standing (Sen. *Ben.* 6.34.1), the barest acknowledgement of the client's greeting (Sen. *Dial.* 10.14.4 *uix alleuatis labiis insusurratum milies nomen oscitatione superbissima reddent*, Juv. 3.184–5), and refusal of admittance (5.22, 9.6, Lucian, *Merc. cond.* 10), sometimes compounded by the slave-doorkeeper's aping the arrogant demeanour of his master (Marquardt-Mau 259 nn.10–11).

aue potentiorum: the client's greeting (**23**.1 n.) was reciprocated by the patron: cf. Auson. 2.4.4–6 Green *habitum forensem da, puer. | dicendum amicis est 'aue | ualeque', quod fit mutuum*. For *aue* as a substantive, cf. 1.55.6, 4.78.4 and 5.51.7. SB treats line 2 as a hendiadys and translates 'the haughty salutations of the powerful'.

3   perferre patique: the two verbs are often found in alliterative combination: cf. Lucr. 5.314, Hor. *Ep.* 1.16.74, 1.15.17 *rure meo possum quiduis perferre patique*.

5   dum: used with causative force (**67**.5n.).

6   sanas linit: Caelius 'smears' perfectly healthy feet. The reference is to the pain-relieving salves which were applied to the feet of *podagrici*: cf. Lucian, *Trag.* 268–9, 291–2, Cels. 4.31, Marcell. Empir. 36.1, whose preferred word for applying such a balm is *illinere*.

obligatque plantas: a second, related, remedy for gout was to bandage the feet of sufferers. The method was apparently to smear the salve on rags (*panni*) and then to bind the feet with these: cf. Marcell. Empir. 36.5, 13.

7   inceditque gradu laborioso: Gellius mimics the difficulty experienced in walking by a sufferer from gout, graphically described by a recovered victim: 'no longer can I be seen crab-footed, nor walking as though on sharp thorns' (*IG* II^2 4514 para. 3.24–5): cf. *Pod.* 217–18, 221–40, Marcell. Empir. 36.3, a remedy so efficacious that *qui usus fuerit etiam ambulare possit.* In severe cases walking might actually become impossible (Aretaeus, *Acut. morb.* 4.12, *AP* 11.414.3, Lucian, 64–8, 183–4, *Ocypus* 70–3).

laborioso: both 'effortful' and 'painful': Greek πόνος similarly means both 'toil', and 'suffering' caused by disease.

8–9   Caelius' desire to make his fiction credible (*dum uult nimis approbare ueram* 5) has led to such realistic simulation of the symptoms that he has succumbed to the actual disease (it is thus ironic that even a genuine attack of gout would not necessarily be accepted as an excuse for shirking one's social obligations: cf. Lucian, *Merc. cond.* 31). The idea that nature can replicate the effects of art humorously inverts the familiar topos of art imitating nature (cf. 1.109.21–3, 3.41, 6.13, 7.44, A. Oltramare, *REL* 19 (1941) 88–101).

8   cura 'cultivation' (SB).

ars contains, as often, an implication of deceit or pretence: cf. Sen. *NQ* 4a. *praef.* 11 *ubi artem simulationemque non redolet*, Luc. 4.744 *simulatae nescius artis.*

9   desît fingere Caelius podagram: cf. 4. M., like Catullus, often concludes a poem by echoing the opening line or a verse from the early part of the poem: cf. Friedländer on 2.7.7.

desît: for the contraction, cf. **47**.1 n.

74   (= 12.54)

'Zoilus, with all your bodily shortcomings, it would be a miracle if you were a good person.'

The idea that moral and physical characteristics were closely related is common in Greek and Roman writers, commencing with Homer's Thersites (*Il.* 2.211–21), and forms the basis of physiognomy, a 'science' which enjoyed especial popularity in the late first and second centuries AD: cf. E. C. Evans,

TAPhA 72 (1941) 96–108, Garland (1995) 87–104, Vlahogiannis (1998) 13–36. The *physiognomici* focused on one physical feature at a time, which might be either good or bad, and deduced from it various mental characteristics. But Zoilus exhibits such a complex of undesirable corporeal attributes that the conclusion must be that he is wholly vicious: cf. 11.92.2 *non uitiosus homo es, Zoile, sed uitium*. The impression that Zoilus is anomalous is enhanced by giving him two features – red hair (a 'Northern' trait) and dark skin (a 'Southern' trait) – which are elsewhere mutually exclusive, making him into some kind of improbable and loathsome hybrid. Apart from physiognomic lore, another factor may be at work in the epigram: Zoilus is a freedman (see **54** intro.) and at least two of the flaws attributed to him, red hair and black skin, are associated with slaves. M. may be suggesting that Zoilus' servile features are an outward manifestation of the moral turpitude which was commonly associated with persons of slave status.

Further reading: Garland (1995), Gleason (1990), Thompson (1989)

1 A line notable for its artistry, containing 2 × 2 adjective–noun pairs, each arranged in chiastic order, balancing weak and strong caesurae in the first and third and second and fourth feet respectively, and, unusually, a sequence of five dactylic feet, giving the impression of skipping through a lengthy catalogue of flaws. Perhaps the metrical abnormality of the line also reflects Z's abnormal appearance.

Crine ruber: for red hair as a physical defect, see **44**.18n. It was thought to signify undesirable character traits: cf. *Anon. physiog.* 73 *qui* [sc. *capilli*] *uehementer rubicundi sunt ... repudiandi sunt: nam et auarum et ferum et indocilem significant*, **64**.4n. Since red hair was associated with slaves, there is also a jibe at Zoilus' servile origins (intro.).

niger ore: dark skin was considered a flaw: cf. Ov. *Ars* 2.657–8 *no-minibus mollire licet mala: fusca uocetur,* | *nigrior Illyrica cui pice sanguis erit*, Lucr. 4.1160 with Brown, Pl. *Rep.* 474d, Thompson (1989) 105–6, 110–13. According to *Anon. physiog.* 79 *color niger leuem, imbellem, timidum, uersutum indicat*.

breuis pede: abnormal feet were associated with defects of character (*Anon. physiog.* 72 *crassi pedes et breues admodum ferinos mores indicant ... pertenues et breues malignum produnt*); the unpleasant Thersites of Hom. *Il.* 2.217 is 'lame in one foot'.

lumine laesus: Zoilus has some disfigurement of the eye, either con-genital, or the result of injury or disease. Given that chronic *lippitudo* had servile and morally questionable associations (**44**.11n.), M. probably has in mind one of the deformities caused by that disease, such as abnormal smallness of the eye (cf. Cels. 6.6.14) or protrusion resulting from rupture of the eyeball (Cels. 6.6.1 d).

2   rem magnam praestas, Zoile, si bonus es: lit. 'you exhibit a great thing if you are good': i.e. it would be a miracle if you were a man of moral worth. For *magna res* cf. Citroni on 1.17.2.

   Zoile: **54** intro.

75   (= 3.34)

'Your name is both suitable and unsuitable, Chione ("Snow White"): you are frigid and dark-skinned.'

The epigram, one of several which turn on the meaning of a Greek name (**76** intro.), concerns a black or dark-skinned prostitute, Chione, whose name (cf. χιών, snow) is dramatically at odds with her appearance. Such amusingly inapposite names (κατ' ἀντίφρασιν) are often heard of, particularly in connexion with slaves: cf. Plin. *NH* 7.75, Juv. 8.32–4 *nanum cuiusdam Atlanta uocamus, | Aethiopem Cycnum, prauam extortamque puellam | Europen.* In the case of a pet slave such names might be humorously affectionate (cf. Thompson (1989) 47–8), but here the effect of is one of ridicule, as in 6.77.7 and Juvenal (cited above); cf. Lucian, *Imag.* 2. Here, unusually, Chione's name is not only laughably unsuitable, but also unexpectedly appropriate, in that her name, with its suggestion of cold, suits her sexual frigidity (cf. 11.60.7–8 *at Chione non sentit opus nec uocibus ullis | adiuuat, absentem marmoreamue putes*).

   The distich is noteworthy for its neatly balanced structure: *frigida* and *nigra* respond in both sound and sense to *digna* and *indigna*: the former are picked up chiastically by *es* and *non es*. In typically Martialian fashion, the point is not disclosed until the conclusion of the epigram, with the postponement of the addressee's name to the final position.

Further reading: Joepgen (1967) 57–8

2   frigida: cold, like snow, i.e. sexually unresponsive: cf. Ov. *Am.* 2.1.5 *me legat in sponsi facie non frigida uirgo.*

   nigra: a dark complexion was regarded as undesirable (**74**.1 n.). Chione does not possess the snow-white complexion suggested by her name and often lauded in the beloved. Cf. 4.42.5 *niue candidior*, 5.37.6, 11.22.1 with Kay.

non es et es: such paradoxes are frequent in M., e.g. 4.71.6 *non dat, non tamen illa negat*, 8.20.2 *non sapis atque sapis*.

Chione: 29.1 n.

76 (= 3.78)

'You pissed once as the ship was speeding along, Paulinus. Do you want to piss a second time? That will make you a Palinurus (lit. "he who urinates again").'

M. is fond of jokes on names, often involving contrived Greek etymologies: cf. 3.67.10 (on slow rowers) *non nautas puto uos, sed Argonautas*, 4.9 *Sotae filia . . .* ἔχεις ἀσώτως, Joepgen (1967) 116–21, Grewing (1998a) 340–5. His most notable forerunner in the use of innovatory puns, especially puns involving names, was the Rome-based Greek epigrammatist Marcus Argentarius: one of his distichs, *AP* 5.63 [*GP* 1311–12] 'Antigone, you were previously a Sicilian for me, but after you became an Aetolian (αἰτέω 'ask for'), look, I have become a Mede (μὴ δός 'don't give')', depends, like the present epigram, on the idea that people's names may change to suit their circumstances. Further instances in M. of this conceit are 9.95 *Alfius ante fuit, coepit nunc Olfius esse,* | *uxorem postquam duxit Athenagoras* and 6.17.

The background to the epigram is unspecified. Book 3 was composed and sent to Rome while M. was staying in Cisalpine Gaul: cf. 3.1.1–2, 3.4. Sullivan (1991) 31 and 157 hypothesises a specifically Gallic setting for **76**, but this contributes nothing to our understanding of the poem, the main point of which is the etymological pun.

Further reading: Grewing (1998), Joepgen (1967)

1   Minxisti: a mild obscenity. The MSS here, as in other classical authors, vary between *mix-* and *minx-*, making it unclear whether M. wrote *minxisti* or *mixisti*: see Adams, *LSV* 245–6.

currente . . . carina: poetic language, preparing for the epic allusion in the next line, and amusingly juxtaposed with the undignified *minxisti*. For *curro* in verse referring to the movement of ships, cf. Ov. *Am.* 2.11.24, Virg. *A.* 5.862 *currit iter tutum non setius aequore classis* (part of the Palinurus story). *carina* is an epic word, used by M. most commonly in stylistically elevated passages. The combination of *currens* with *carina* involves an etymological pun (Isid. *Orig.* 19.2.1 *carina a currendo dicta, quasi currina*), thus anticipating the use of a pun in the next line.

Pauline: the name, unusual in M., is chosen for the alliterative play with Palinurus.

2   iam: inferential, 'then surely'.

Palinurus eris: in the *Aeneid*, Palinurus is the chief helmsman of the Trojans. The circumstances of his death after falling overboard are described at *Aen.* 5.833–71. M. jokingly derives the name from πάλιν 'again' and οὐρεῖν 'to urinate' rather than πάλιν 'back' and οὖρος 'watcher', the correct etymology, 'he who keeps watch at the back' (R. Merkelbach, *ZPE* 9 (1972) 83, A. Dihle, *Glotta* 51 (1973) 268–74).

77   (= 7.79)

'Recently I drank "consular" wine. Do you ask how old it was and how noble? It was laid down in the consulship of the host: but the host who served it was consul.'

The joke turns on *consulare*. The epithet describes things associated with the consulship, e.g. a consular province or a consular army; in the case of wine, the reader naturally thinks of the custom of identifying vintage wine by the name of consul for the year when the wine was cellared (e.g. 'Opimian'): the phrase *uinum consulare* would thus be read as an original expression for aged wine. This impression is reaffirmed by *quaeris quam uetus atque liberale*, and is not contradicted by the first part of M.'s reply – that the wine was laid down in the consulship of the very man who gave the dinner party – since the phrase *ipso consule conditum* implies that the consulship in question took place some years previously (3n.). *But*, M. continues, the host was currently consul. The wine, then, was indeed 'consular', not in the sense that it was of vintage quality, but in the literal sense of 'belonging to a consul'.

Housman (followed by SB) argued that the Latin *consulare uinum* can only mean 'wine drunk at a consul's table', but that since line 1 would on that reading anticipate the meaning of 4, thereby preempting the joke, editors tried to avoid this difficulty by inventing an impossible sense for *consulare uinum*, 'vintage wine'. He therefore emended *ipso consule* to *prisco consule*. The meaning would then be 'recently I drank wine at a consul's table. Do you ask how old it was? It was laid down in the consulship of Priscus.' The point of the epigram now turns on the double sense of *priscus*: after *quam uetus*, one expects it to mean 'of olden times', but instead discovers that the word is a proper noun.

There may have been a consul called Priscus in 93, the year after M.'s epigram was published (cf. Tac. *Agr.* 44.1). But authorities other than Tacitus give the consul's name as Priscinus; moreover, the point of the epigram is that the wine served was new, which would be an insult to Priscus if, as Housman argues, the poem was written in honour of a patron's coming consulship.

There are more serious objections to Housman's emendation. First, it is unnecessary: the dogmatic assertion that *consulare uinum* cannot mean 'vintage wine' ignores M.'s predilection for novel expressions (intro. 24), and in any case, Housman's own translation equally stretches the meaning of *consularis*. A more serious objection to the emendation, however, is that it ignores the internal dynamic of the epigram by shifting the focus from *consulare* in 1 to *prisco* in 4. The novel *consulare uinum* sets up an expectation that the phrase will be of crucial importance in the denouement of the epigram, an expectation which is duly answered by the revelation that the wine is 'consular' in an entirely different sense from that initially anticipated. The technique here is identical to that of **2**: see discussion *ad loc.*

Further reading: Housman, *CPh* 721–2, 816

1   consulare uinum: lit. 'wine associated with a consul', a phrase which at this point appears to refer to an old vintage. Wine for cellaring, as opposed to *vin ordinaire* for immediate drinking, was matured in *amphorae*, the necks of which were often inscribed with the names of the two consuls for the year (see M. H. Callender, *Roman amphorae* (Oxford 1965) 5–6, *ILS* 8578–83). Old wine of special quality, however, tended to be associated with the name of a single consul, e.g. Opimian (see on **56**.24) or Anician (Cic. *Brut.* 288); see also Hor. *Epod.* 13.6 *tu uina Torquato moue consule pressa meo, Carm.* 3.8.11–12.

2   uetus 'aged': wine was at its best between five and twenty-five years: see Ath. 26c–27b, Gow on Theoc. 7.147. By contrast, wine of the current year, which is what the 'consular' wine turns out to be, was poorly regarded: cf. A. Tchernia, *Le vin de l'Italie romaine* (Rome 1986) 28–37.

liberale 'of noble quality' to partner *uetus*.

3   ipso consule conditum: *condo* refers to the process of putting the wine into *amphorae* after its initial fermentation in a vat, 'bottled' as we might say. The combination with *ipso consule* encourages the supposition that the wine served to M. was a *grand cru* (cf. 3.62.2 *sub rege Numa condita uina*, 13.111.2), but the reverse proves to be the case.

ipse 'the host'; cf. **56**.18n.

4   ponebat = *apponebat* 'served'.

Seuere: a frequent addressee in M.: see Howell on 5.11, Kay on 11.57. There is a touch of deliberate paradox in addressing a poem on wine to a Severus, since the adjective is often used of water drinkers: cf. Catull. 27.5–7 *at uos quo lubet hinc abite, lymphae,* | *uini pernicies, et ad seueros* | *migrate.*

78   (= 2.80)

'While fleeing an enemy, Fannius committed suicide. What madness, to kill oneself in order to avoid being killed!'

This distich, commenting on the story, elsewhere unattested, of Fannius' suicide while fleeing an enemy, is one of a small number of epigrams taking as their theme an *exemplum* from Roman history: for details, see Howell on 1.13 intro. In every other case, however, a historical incident is related either as a paradigm of virtue or, less commonly, of vice: here, by contrast, a historical *exemplum* serves to illustrate a philosophical commonplace on the topic of suicide.

The epigram has its basis in a well-known paradox, going back to Democritus, fr. 68 B 203 D–K, 'men seek after death while fleeing from it', where the philosopher comments on the folly of actively seeking death through fear of it. The idea is particularly, but not exclusively, associated with the Epicureans: cf. Sen. *Ep.* 24.23 (Epicurus) *dicit: 'quid tam ridiculum quam appetere mortem, cum uitam inquietam tibi feceris metu mortis'? his adicias et illud eiusdem notae licet, tantam hominum imprudentiam esse, immo dementiam, ut quidam timore mortis cogantur ad mortem,* Lucr. 3.79–82. The Stoic Seneca equally embraces the sentiment (*Ep.* 70.8 *stultitia est timore mortis mori*), and it was also, according to Dio Chrys. *Or.* 6.42, espoused by the Cynic Diogenes, whose example of suicide from fear interestingly involved the case of one surrounded by enemies.

M.'s treatment of the theme is typically epigrammatic. The bipartite structure is characteristic of M. (see intro. 15–18). Also typical is the use of a rhetorical question to point the moral. The closing *sententia*, with its use of word-play, is a fine illustration of the epigrammatist's art. Finally, whereas in most other occurrences of the same topic the paradox is presented in a general form, M. gives it greater immediacy by focusing on a single concrete example, which is used to illustrate the philosophical point.

There are several recorded instances of persons who took their own life to avoid death at the hands of assassins; these include C. Gracchus, Mutilus (proscribed under Sulla) and, during the Second Triumvirate, Cestius and Statius: see Van Hooff (1990) 90. But none of our sources on Fannius Caepio, the presumptive subject of this epigram (1 n.), attributes his death to suicide, although they do associate that death with flight from an enemy. This discrepancy is surprising: normally when dealing with famous historical incidents M. does not depart in essential details from the vulgate tradition. Perhaps M. is confusing Fannius with Cestius, who fled after being proscribed and who, on seeing armed centurions approaching with the heads of those fugitives who had already been caught and executed, killed himself in terror of suffering the same fate (App. *BC* 4.26). *hostem* (1), which most naturally suggests a military context, would suit this possibility.

Further reading: Griffin (1986), Grimal (1989),178, Van Hooff (1990)

1 Fannius: usually taken to refer to Fannius Caepio, the instigator of a conspiracy against Augustus, who was condemned by Tiberius, and was killed while attempting to flee (Dio Cass. 54.3.4, Vell. Paterc. 2.91.2, Suet. *Tib.* 8, Macrob. *Sat.* 1.11.21). For the difficulty with this identification, see intro.

2 hic, rogo, non furor est?: for this verdict, cf. Sen. *Ep.* 24.23 and 70.8 cited above; according to Sen. *Dial.* 7.19 the Epicurean Diodorus was accused by some of *dementia* for committing suicide.

rogo: see **68**.9n.

ne moriare, mori 'to die in order to avoid dying': a brilliantly alliterative paradox.

79   (= 4.18)

'Where there is a constant drip from the gateway adjacent to the Vipsanian columns, a falling icicle fatally pierced the throat of a boy as he was passing beneath its archway. Our lives are entirely subject to Fortune's caprices, and death is evidently ubiquitous, when even water can inflict a lethal wound.'

Authentic Greek and Roman epitaphs often record the manner of a person's death if it was unusual or noteworthy (Lattimore (1962) 151–3). But the primary inspiration for the present poem stems from the fictional epitaphs of Greek literary epigram, which frequently recount bizarre and extraordinary deaths, sometimes in extremely graphic terms. Many examples occur in *AP* 7 and 9, where they represent a specialised instance of the grotesquerie which is a pronounced feature of Hellenistic poetry: cf. Watson (1991) 181–7. Closest to M. are *AP* 7.402 (Antipater) 'when winter snow had melted about the lintel, a house collapsed and killed old Lysisice', featuring the common epitaphic motif of death by falling object, and a pair of epigrams by Statilius Flaccus and Philip of Thessalonica, *AP* 7.542 and 9.56, 'when the water of Thracian Hebrus was bound by winter cold, a child stepped upon it and could not escape death. After he had slipped on the surface of the river which was now thawing, his tender neck was cut right through by the ice. The rest of his body was dragged down, but his face, all that was left of him, had perforce the travesty of a funeral. Unhappy mother! The child whom she bore has been divided between fire and water, and seeming to belong to both, belongs entirely to neither.'

As in M., the victim is a child, death occurs from the piercing of his throat by ice, and the poem ends with a paradox. An important difference, however, is that M.'s epigram is set in Rome, and concludes by drawing a moral from the event. Both features are typical of M.'s pieces on unusual occurrences: cf. Szelest (1976).

Thrace, the setting of *AP* 9.56, was notoriously cold; the same cannot be said of Rome. Does M.'s epigram therefore describe a fictional event? People can undoubtedly lose their lives in this bizarre way: cf. *The independent international* for 24 December 1997–6 January 1998 'one person [in Russia] has been killed by a falling icicle'. But it is questionable whether such an occurrence could take place in the temperate region of central Italy. It is sometimes argued that the climate of Rome was colder in classical antiquity than now (Nissen I 400–2), Le Gall (1953) 26–7), but such claims are largely based on reports of abnormally severe winters in historians such as Livy, or on conventional allusions in the poets to winter cold. On the other hand, poems 2–3 of the present book, with their mention of snow and frost, could suggest that there was a particularly severe winter in Rome about this time. So M. might be embellishing epigrammatically an actual event.

Further reading: Le Gall (1953), Szelest (1976)

1–2 The reference is to the overflow from an aqueduct, but the topographical details are bedevilled by uncertainty: see below.

1   **pluit:**   of drips 'raining down'; cf. 3.47.1 *Capena grandi porta qua pluit gutta*. Line 2 repeats the image.

Vipsanis . . . columnis: generally thought to refer to the *Porticus Vipsania*, begun by Vipsania Polla, the sister of Agrippa, in the *Campus Agrippae*, which formed part of the *Campus Martius*: cf. Richardson, Platner–Ashby s.v. 'Porticus Vipsania'.

porta: usually explained as an archway, doubling as a gate, over which passed an aqueduct, possibly the *Aqua Virgo*: city gates, town walls and the arches of aqueducts were closely associated in ancient Rome (J. A. Richmond, *JRS* 23 (1933) 152–6). Excavations have, however, made it doubtful that the *Aqua Virgo* could be described as *uicina* to the *Porticus Vipsania* (cf. Howell on 1.108.3); the identity of the aqueduct is therefore best left open. The gate in question may be the *Porta Quirinalis* or the *Porta Salutaris* (Richardson *loc. cit.*): it is unlikely to be the Arch of Claudius, as claimed by Prior (1996) 127–8, not least because this does not seem to have been near the *Porticus Vipsania*: cf. F. Castagnoli, *Athenaeum* 28 (1956) 72.

2   **et madet assiduo lubricus imbre lapis:** aqueducts ran twenty-four hours a day (*assiduo*) and leakage was a constant problem. This might come either from the terminal *castellum*, distribution reservoir, as in the case of the *Aqua Marcia*, which entered the city above the Capenian Gate (cf. Juv. 3.11), or from above ground arches whose channels had been blocked by calcium carbonate deposits: cf. E. B. Van Deman, *The building of the Roman aqueducts* (Washington 1934) 141, 415 n.16, D. N. Wilkes in R. Stilwell, ed., *Antioch-on-the-Orontes: the excavations 1933–6* (Princeton 1938) 49–56, esp. pl. 5.

lubricus: slippery with water.

3   **iugulum:** cf. *iugulatis* 8.

roscida tecta 'dewy arch' SB.

4   **hiberno praegrauis unda gelu:** a highly poetic periphrasis for an icicle.

5   **cumque peregisset . . . fata** 'and when it had accomplished the death'.

miseri: often used of the victim in sepulchral epigram, e.g. *CLE* 447.5, 466.5 *quem mater miserum fleuit*.

crudelia fata: more epitaphic language; cf. *CLE* 1484 *si non ante diem crudelia fata fuissent,* | *hic pater et mater debuit ante legi*, 1213.1.

6   tabuit in calido uulnere mucro tener: such unpleasant details
are a feature of Hellenistic epigrams on bizarre deaths (intro.), but are also
found in genuine sepulchral inscriptions, e.g. an epitaph for a boy who fell
from a tree 'and broke his skull, wetting the bosom of his father with streams
of blood piteously and fatally shed as the child quitted life' (Vérilhac (1978)
no. 61).

    tener: because the ice-blade melts in the warm blood. The adjective
forms an oxymoron with *mucro* and plays on the fact that in epitaphs the
prematurely dead are often styled *tener*: cf. *CLE* 1198.9–10 *nam temere emis-
sus . . . clauus | haesit et in tenero uertice delituit*, 1164.3–4 *hic etenim puer . . . | inuida
quem tenerum Parca tenax rapuit*.

7   Fortune conventionally controls all human destiny, an idea by
no means confined to sepulchral epigram: cf. Men. fr. 482.4–5 Kock
'Fortune . . . is what governs everything and overturns or preserves it', Sall.
Cat. 8.1 with Vretska, Sen. *Dial.* 11.16.5, *CLE* 409.8–9 *actumst, excessi, spes et
Fortuna ualete, | nil iam plus in me uobis per saecla licebit.*

    saeua: a stock epithet of *Fortuna* (Kajanto, *ANRW* xvii 1.531), common
in epitaphic contexts: cf. *CLE* 980.3 *saeua parentibus eripuit Fortuna me[is] me*,
Kaibel, *Epigr. Graec.* 334.16, B. Lier, *Philologus* 62 (1903) 460–1, 473–7. In
Menander Rhetor's prescriptions for the funerary oration he advises 'right
at the very beginning one should berate the gods and unjust fate' (iii 435
Spengel).

8   aut ubi non mors est, si iugulatis aquae?   death's ubiquitous-
ness is another conventional idea, enlivened by the paradoxical *si iugulatis
aquae*: cf. 4.60.5–6, Sen. *NQ* 6.2.6 *cum mors ubique praesto sit et undique occurrat
nihilque sit tam exiguum, quod non in perniciem generis humani satis ualeat.*

    si iugulatis aquae 'if you waters cut throats'. The verb is used in its
literal sense of plunging a blade into a person's neck.

80   (= 4.44)

'Here is Vesuvius, not so long ago the site of flourishing vines, beloved of
Bacchus and the Satyrs. Here too were cities sacred to Venus and Hercules.
Now everything lies buried beneath the ash: the gods would prefer not to
have had such destruction in their power.'

The poem was published ten years after the eruption of Vesuvius on 24–25
August AD 79 which overwhelmed Pompeii and Herculaneum. Although

the cities were never rebuilt, the fertility of the surrounding land, which M. here emphasises, was eventually restored (G. Soricelli, *Athenaeum* 85 (1997) 139–54). In 89, however, this was yet to take place.

The most important literary influence on M.'s poem is the epideictic epigram on the theme of a destroyed city. Such epigrams, which were popular in the first century AD (e.g. *AP* 9.28, 62, 101–4), are a type of ἔκφρασις τόπου, 'description of a place' (G. Kennedy, *A new history of classical rhetoric* (Princeton 1994) 206). Their focus was less on pure description than on soliciting an emotional response by a contrast between the present devastation and the prosperity of the town which once stood there (Goldhill (1994)). In emphasising the loss of former glories, such pieces are related to epitaphs, and in many examples the city speaks in the first person as if from the tomb; also epitaphic is the use of a formula such as κεῖμαι (cf. *AP* 9.103.5, 250.3). M.'s epigram, unusually, adopts the third, rather than the first or second person of the Greek epigrams. Another anomalous feature is that, whereas the Greek epigrams deal with cities whose glories were in the distant past, M. describes an area as it appeared in recent memory (*modo* 1); this engages the interest of readers who were personally familiar with the cities prior to their destruction. Finally, the descriptive element in M.'s poem is on a larger scale and bears a different emphasis from the corresponding Greek epigrams, M. focusing not so much on the lost cities as on Vesuvius itself.

This emphasis on Vesuvius is shared by accounts of the calamity, which became a common literary theme in M.'s day and shortly after. In one important respect, however, M.'s epigram differs from the rest. Elsewhere, Vesuvius is either shown as itself the aggressor (e.g. Stat. *Silu.* 4.4.79; cf. *Silu.* 3.5.72–3, 4.8.5), or else as part of the natural forces that destroyed the two cities and their environs. Here the volcano is presented, along with the two cities, as part of the devastated landscape, the innocent victim of an inexplicable act on the part of the gods. This is because M. is not describing the eruption itself, but adopting the perspective of a visitor to the Bay of Naples, whose attention is monopolised by the mountain, dominating the landscape and towering above the wasteland beneath.

The poem is on a higher artistic plane than its epigrammatic predecessors. The first part suggests happiness and prosperity, with its pastoral-style description of the shady vines on Vesuvius, its vivid evocation of Satyrs dancing on the slopes and its stress on the affection of the deities. The exuberant idyll forms a sharp contrast with the brief and stark *cuncta iacent flammis et tristi mersa fauilla* (7). The final comment on the reaction of the gods has been neatly prepared for by the emphasis on the numinosity of the place and on the love which the triad of deities felt for the three localities over which they presided.

Further reading: Descoeudres (1994), Goldhill (1994), Mau (1899), Peterson (1919), Renna (1992)

1   Hic est has an epitaphic character and confers a certain solemnity on the opening of the epigram: see Citroni on 1.1.1. In addition, the anaphora of *hic* (*hic . . . haec . . . hoc . . . haec . . . hic* 2–6) is common in the ἔκφρασις τόπου (e.g. Virg. *A.* 6.295–8, 580–2); it suggests that M. is standing looking at the scene and pointing out details which the reader is invited to imagine.

pampineis . . . umbris 'shady vines': cf. Virg. *Ecl.* 7.58 *Liber pampineas inuidit collibus umbras*. The allusion to the *Eclogues* sets the tone for the description of the one-time idyllic landscape.

uiridis 'verdant' with the vines which covered Vesuvius before the eruption. The concentration on the vine prepares for the emphasis in 3–4 on Vesuvius' slopes as a haunt of Bacchus and his retinue.

Vesbius: (Gk Βέσβιον), a popular form (Huisintveld (1949) 19), used for the metrically intractable Vesuvius.

2   presserat . . . madidos . . . lacus 'had loaded the vats to overflowing' (SB). *madidos* is proleptic and signifies 'abounding in liquid'; cf. Calp. *Ecl.* 1.2 *quamuis . . . madidis incumbant prela racemis*. *presserat* puns on the more common meaning of the verb, to 'press' grapes.

nobilis uua: the Aminean variety of grape was grown on the slopes of Vesuvius. *nobilis* alludes either to its superior quality (Plin. *NH* 14.22) or its fame (Col. 3.2.10). Plin. *NH* 14.70 does not share M.'s opinion of Pompeian wines.

lacus: the containers for the juice of the newly trodden grapes: cf. Cato, *Agr.* 25, Var. *R.* 1.54.3.

3   haec iuga . . . Bacchus amauit: the association of Bacchus with Vesuvius is depicted in a Pompeian fresco, discussed by M. Frederiksen, *Campania* (London: British School at Rome 1984) 6–12; cf. Descoeudres (1994) 39 fig. 29, Renna (1992) 43 fig. 5.

quam Nysae colles plus: Dionysus preferred Vesuvius to Nysa, the mountain where he was reared as an infant (*Hom. hymn.* 1.9) and which became the seat of his cult: cf. Eur. *Bacch.* 556 with Dodds.

colles . . . Bacchus amauit: adapts Virg. *G.* 2.112–13 *denique apertos | Bacchus amat colles,* Bacchus being here not a metonymy for vines, but the god of wine himself, who dwelt on the vine-covered slopes.

4   **Satyri** were associated with Dionysus from early times; they appear along with Bacchus in frescoes in the Pompeian Villa of the Mysteries and are in general common in Pompeian art. See Mau (1889) 440–1, 463.

choros: in artistic representations, Satyrs are often shown dancing (F. Brommer, *Satyroi* (Würzburg 1937) 20–2); they formed part of the Bacchic *thiasos*; cf. Hor. *Carm.* 2.19.1–4.

5   **haec Veneris sedes:**   Venus was the patron goddess of Pompeii (Peterson (1919) 246–54, Roscher VI 192–4 s.v. *Venus*). For iconography and symbolism, cf. J. P. V. D. Balsdon, *JRS* 41 (1951) 6. Her temple would have been among the first buildings sighted by those arriving by sea (Descoeudres (1994) 27). Venus, Liber and Hercules were all joined in a dedication in the suburban villa at Pompeii of N. Popidius Florus (Renna (1992) 96 n.220).

Lacedaemone gratior illi: in Sparta, Aphrodite was worshipped as 'Goddess of the Spear'. Cf. *AP* 9.320–1, Paus. 3.15.10, L. R. Farnell, *The cults of the Greek states* II (Oxford 1896) 653–4.

6   **hic locus Herculeo nomine clarus erat:**   Herculaneum was named after Hercules, its putative founder (Dion. Halic. 1.43). For the cult of the god there, see Peterson (1919) 284–5.

7   **cuncta:**   so completely were Pompeii and Herculaneum buried that 'those who came there by daylight felt ignorance and uncertainty as to where these had been situated' (Plut. *Pyth. orac.* 398E). Cf. Antipat. Sid., *AP* 9.151.5–6 'for not even a trace of you, ill-fated city [Corinth], is left, but war has snatched up and consumed everything'.

iacent: the verb, which has epitaphic associations, is often used of destroyed cities, e.g. Ov. *Ep.* 1.3 *Troia iacet,* Val. Max. 3.2 ext. 5 (Sparta). κεῖμαι is similarly used e.g. *AP* 9.250.3, 423.5–8.

flammis et . . . mersa fauilla: for the combination, cf. Lucr. 6.690 (Aetna). The eruption occurred in two main stages: during the first, airborne pumice, carried by the wind, settled on Pompeii, burying the city to a depth of up to 2.8 metres. In the second, lethal, stage eighteen hours later, a number of hot avalanches, consisting of ash, pumice and gases, moved rapidly down the mountainside, asphyxiating those inhabitants who had failed to flee and overwhelming Pompeii; Herculaneum was destroyed during this second phase. See H. Sigurdsson et al., *AJA* 86 (1982) 39–51, 315–16.

flammis: cf. Stat. *Silu.* 4.4.79–80 *fractas ubi Vesuius egerit iras,* | *aemula Trinacriis uoluens incendia flammis,* Sil. 17.593. Cf. Plin. *Ep.* 6.16.13, 18; 6.20.9, 16.

mersa 'sunk beneath'; perhaps more natural of *fauilla* than *flammis,* but for the use with fire cf. Stat. *Theb.* 6.225–6 *seu frena libet seu cingula flammis* | *mergere, Silu.* 3.3.34–5.

fauilla: the volcanic ash from the eruption of Vesuvius features in many accounts, e.g. Plin. *Ep.* 6.16 and 20, Val. Fl. 4.509 and (exaggeratedly) Sil. 17.595–6 *uidere Eoi, monstrum admirabile, Seres* | *lanigeros cinere Ausonio canescere lucos.*

8   'Not even the gods [although responsible for the destruction] would have wished to have had such power.' Instead of berating the gods for letting disaster happen, as is often done in epitaphic or related literature (Estève-Forriol (1962) 138–9), M. concludes with the paradox that while the gods caused the eruption, they regret having done so.

nec: 4.12n.

hoc licuisse: cf. 7.21.4 *debuit hoc saltem non licuisse tibi.* M. reflects the popular, as opposed to the scientific view of natural catastrophes, the former positing that these were caused by divine agencies, e.g. Pind. *Pyth.* 1.15–28, Lucr. 6.54–5, Cic. *Nat. d.* 2.14 with Pease, *Aetna* 29–35.

81   (= 4.59)

'As a snake was crawling along a poplar branch, a drop of amber flowed over it. Amazed to find itself stuck, it grew stiff, suddenly held tight in a chilly grip. Do not be too proud of your regal sepulchre, Cleopatra, when a snake lies in a more noble tomb.'

One of three epigrams on creatures preserved in amber: cf. 4.32 (a bee) and 6.15 (an ant). Amber inclusions came about when small animals, usually invertebrates, became enmeshed in the sticky resin of a species of conifer, which later became fossilised to form amber. Specimens would have been kept by rich Romans as curiosities. M.'s epigrams may have been inspired by seeing one or more such *objets d'art* in the home of a wealthy patron (cf. White (1974) 43 and n.12). In the case of the snake, however, it is debatable whether M. had encountered such a thing in reality or whether the poem

is a flight of fantasy. Certainly the description of the process by which
the snake becomes entombed is a fiction. Unlike an insect, a snake would
be strong enough to extricate itself from the sticky resin. Furthermore, M.
describes it as entrapped while crawling along a branch at full length, but to
fit inside a lump of amber the snake would have to be coiled (see on *uipera*).
No genuine cases of snakes preserved in amber are known, but Pliny's
mention in this connexion of lizards (*NH* 37.46) suggests that in Roman, as
in later times, inclusions of small vertebrates were faked by hollowing out
the amber, inserting the animal, and resealing (Grimaldi (1996) 133–41).
M. could conceivably have seen a piece of amber with a small coiled snake
inserted, though there are no recorded instances of forgeries involving a
snake. A viper (see on *uipera* 1) would certainly be able to be fitted by such
a process into a large piece of amber: Nero is reported by Plin. *NH* 37.46
to have possessed a specimen weighing 13 pounds. It is something of an
infelicity that the *uipera* is implicitly compared in line 6 to the 'asp' reputed
to have caused Cleopatra's death; this is generally agreed to be the Egyptian
hooded cobra (J. G. Griffiths, *JEA* 47 (1961) 113–18) – a very much larger
snake which by no stretch of the imagination could be encased in amber.
The points of interconnection between lines 1 and 6 are (1) the snake motif
and (2) the idea of a sumptuous tomb.

   The epigram takes the form of a narrative describing the circumstances
in which the creature came to be entombed in amber. It is thus to some
extent in the tradition of epigrams concerning the death of an animal in
unusual circumstances (cf. *AP* 9.86, Szelest (1976) 251–3).

Further reading: Grimaldi (1996), Poinar (1992), Ramelli (1997), Watson
(2001)

1   **Flentibus Heliadum ramis:**   i.e. the branch of a poplar, into
which Phaethon's sisters, the Heliades, were turned: their teardrops supposedly solidified into amber (cf. Ov. *Met.* 2.340–366). The legend might
have been suggested by the tear-like appearance of amber lumps.

   ramis = 'per ramos', ablative of space traversed, cf. Virg. *A.* 4.404 *it
nigrum campis agmen.*

   uipera: the common European viper, which, at 18–24 inches long
(*Encyclopaedia Britannica*, 13th ed., s.v. 'viper'), was small enough, if coiled,
to fit into a large lump of amber and was also, like Cleopatra's 'asp' (see
intro.) distinctly poisonous: cf. Virg. *G.* 3.416–7, Ov. *Rem.* 421 *parua necat
morsu spatiosum uipera taurum.*

2   obstantem: the snake was in the path of the amber drop.

    gutta: the MSS vacillate between *gutta* and *gemma*. The former should be read, as at 4.32.1 and 6.15.2 where the MSS are unanimous for *gutta*.

3–4   quae ... | ... gelu: cf. Plin. *NH* 37.46 *formicae culicesque et lacertae quae adhaesisse musteo non est dubium et inclusa durescente eodem remansisse,* Tac. *Germ.* 45.5. M. describes the process subjectively, from the animal's viewpoint (*dum miratur*) and for the sake of vividness, makes it instantaneous (*repente*).

3   pingui implying both 'glutinous' and 'rich/expensive'.

4   gelu: used metaphorically of petrifaction, but also suggesting the chill of death.

5–6   Cleopatra need not boast about her royal sepulchre since she is buried in a less splendid tomb than the type of creature responsible for her death.

5   ne tibi ... placeas: cf. Juv. 10.41–2 *sibi consul | ne placeat, curru seruus portatur eodem.*

    regali ... sepulchro: Cleopatra was buried at Alexandria in the Mausoleum (Florus, 2.21.11) which she had been building before her death; cf. Suet. *Aug.* 17.4. Her tomb, which was magnificent (Plut. *Ant.* 74.1), was a tourist attraction in M.'s day: cf. Stat. *Silu.* 3.2.119–20, I. Becker, *Das Bild der Kleopatra in der griechischen und lateinischen Literatur* (Berlin 1966) 169–72.

6   nobiliore: cf. 6.15.4 (of an ant in amber): *funeribus facta est nunc pretiosa suis.* Amber was extremely expensive: cf. Plin. *NH* 37.49.

82   (= 7.37)

'Castricus, a bizarre signal for sentence of death was devised by a quaestor. His orders were that whenever he blew his nose, this should serve as a fatal sign. In the chill and damp of December, an ugly icicle hung from his nostrils. His colleagues refused to assist. The result? He could not wipe his nose.'

The introductory *est operae pretium discere* suggests that Castricus is about to be regaled with the kind of amusing anecdote (αἶνος) which is recounted in a variety of texts. Examples include Archilochus, fr. 168 W, Catull. 56, which begins *o rem ridiculam, Cato, et iocosam,* several fables of Phaedrus, and numerous instances in the collection of funny stories known as the Φιλογέλως. Other epigrams of this type are: 3.24 and 91, risible accounts of unintended castrations, 6.66, and 12.77, an absurd tale of the professional diner-out Aethon, who farted in the temple of Iuppiter Capitolinus and was punished with a *trinoctiale . . . domicenium.*

The action of wiping/failing to wipe one's nose which provides this epigram with its plot-line has metaphoric resonances which assist with its interpretation. To have unwiped mucus about one's nostrils is to be like a child or an old person who cannot attend to his personal hygiene (cf. Lucian, *Dial. mort.* 16.2, Suet. *Claud.* 30) and thus to be, by extension, foolish or in one's dotage: cf. Pl. *Rep.* 343c, Lucian, *Alex.* 20, Hesych. s.v. λέμφος ('snotty'): 'it signifies a silly senseless individual'. Similarly, in Roman Comedy, to *emungere aliquem* is figuratively to wipe a person's nose i.e. to treat them like a drivelling idiot and hence to make a fool of them; cf. *OLD emungo* 2, Sittl (1890) 113 n.1. All this suggests that the concluding remark, that the poor wretch could not wipe his nose despite an urgent need to do so, is M.'s way of implying that the quaestor's unusual *mortiferum signum* was the foolish affectation of a figurative and literal driveller. Such a reading is in line with the tradition of the αἶνος, where the protagonist is regularly a stupid or silly individual.

The connexion of nasal mucus with the extinction of life may have been inspired by the pseudo-Hesiodic description of ' Αχλύς, a figure closely associated with death, as having 'mucus running from her nostrils' (*Scutum* 267).

While the literary background to the epigram is clear enough, its setting and content are remarkably unclear. Does the action take place in Rome or in the provinces (see 1 n.)? Are we to imagine a prisoner readied for execution, which will take place if the quaestor blows his nose? But if this is so, why should he not wish to blow it? Or is the *mortiferum signum* a sign, not for execution, but for passing the death sentence (cf. on *theta nouum* 2)? This might diminish somewhat the ghoulish humour of the epigram, but M. could well be thinking of the passing of sentence followed by summary execution. And who are the quaestor's *collegae?* The difficulty of establishing the type of quaestor in question (1 n.) makes this impossible to answer.

Further reading: Callahan (1964), Sittl (1890) 112–13

1   **mortiferum . . . signum** 'signal for execution.'

quaestoris: what kind of quaestor M. has in mind is unclear. In the absence of a clear location for the epigram, and in view of the intense debate about the number and functions of quaestors as the office developed and changed over the centuries, the solution of Friedländer, 'the *quaestor pro praetore*, who assisted the proconsul in senatorial provinces', and exercised criminal jurisdiction, seems as good as any. Another possibility is an ordinary provincial quaestor (i.e. not one acting *pro praetore*), since these often heard cases: Cic. *Fam.* 10.32.3 reports that the younger Balbus, when holding this office, executed a Roman citizen in Hispania Ulterior. Paley and Stone suggested one of the *quaestores parricidii*, but there is no evidence that this archaic office continued to exist so long. A municipal quaestor of the type met in many *municipia* and *coloniae* seems likewise improbable: such quaestors do not appear to have possessed judicial powers. The basic problem is that very little is known of the quaestors' role in carrying out punishments under the law (Mommsen (1899) 156), so that certainty is impossible.

Castrice: a poet friend of M. who appears also in 6.43, 6.68, 7.4, and 7.42.

2   est operae pretium discere 'it's worth your while to hear about' i.e. you will enjoy the anecdote which follows. For the formula, see Muecke on Hor. *S.* 2.4.63.

theta nouum: *theta* glosses *mortiferum ... signum*. A mark, widely interpreted by Roman writers as the Greek letter θ (*theta*), standing for θάνατος, 'death', was entered by the *iudex* beside the names of those sentenced to death (Isidor. *Orig.* 1.24); in military registers it indicated soldiers killed in action (ibid. 1.3.8; G. R. Watson, *JRS* 42 (1952) 56–62, J. D. Thomas, *ZPE* 24 (1977) 241–3).

nouum 'strange, unusual'. The gender is the regular one for Greek letter-names, which were normally treated as neuter and indeclinable: cf. A. Bain, *Latomus* 43 (1984) 598–9.

3   exprimeret combines the actions of squeezing the nose and blowing it to expel mucus. This was done with the fingers: cf. *AP* 11.268, Phaedr. *App.* 3.15, Theophr. *Char.* 19.4 with Steinmetz. Marcell. Empir. 10.78, which mentions using a sheet of papyrus, is anomalous.

rorantem frigore nasum: *rorare*, frequent in the higher poetic genres, is an ironically elevated word to use of nasal drip.

4   **letalem . . . notam** repeats *mortiferum . . . signum* in another form of words.

iuguli 'execution', σφαγῆς. The term is anatomically exact (*iugulum* lit. = 'throat'): executions were normally performed by beheading (Mommsen (1899) 916–18, 924).

5   **inuiso** 'hateful', on account both of its unwholesome appearance (cf. *turpis*) and the fact that it wielded the power of life and death.

pendebat stiria: cf. **69**.10–11 *cuius liuida naribus caninis | dependet glacies*, 11.98.7. The picture of frozen nasal discharge hanging from the quaestor's nose in icicle shape is absurd hyperbole.

6   cum flaret madida fauce December atrox: December is a byword in M. for cold and damp, e.g. 1.49.19–20, 4.19.3, **14**.5. The image of December blowing with damp throat is a creative adaptation of visual representations 'in which painters depict Boreas [and other wind-gods] emitting blasts from their own persons' (Arist. *Mot. anim.* 2.1): a splendid example in *LIMC* III 2.108 s.v. *Boreas*, from a vase in the Ashmolean museum, showing Boreas with open mouth and puffed-out cheeks blowing mightily upon Odysseus' craft.

madida fauce December: cf. 10.5.6 *illi December longus et madens bruma*. M. possibly had in mind the popular etymology of November and December, which derived these from *imber* (Isid. *Orig.* 5.33.11).

December atrox: the basic meaning of *atrox*, a high-style word often used to characterise storms or winter, is 'of sombre aspect', which suits its application to foul weather: cf. A. Debru, *RPh* 57 (1983) 271–83.

7   collegae tenuere manus: the quaestor's colleagues 'stayed their hands' i.e. refused to help him out of his absurd predicament. For this use of *tenere manus*, cf. Ov. *Am.* 1.4.10 *uix a te uideor posse tenere manus*, *Met.* 13.202–3. The translation 'they held his hands' (SB), sc. in an attempt to prevent him from giving a signal that would unintentionally condemn a man to death, has less to recommend it, since the following *non licuit* would then have to mean 'they didn't allow him', which would be superfluous.

quid plura requiris? 'what more need be said?'

8   emungi 'to wipe his nose' (middle voice): cf. Juv. 6.147 *iam grauis es nobis et saepe emungeris: exi.*

misero: mock-sympathetic.

non licuit 'it was not possible' for the quaestor to wipe his nose, lest his action be fatally misinterpreted.

83   (= 5.34)

'I entrust to your care, my parents, this small pet slave girl of mine, so that she won't be terrified of the darkness of the Underworld or Cerberus. She died at the end of the winter, just six days short of her sixth birthday. May she frolic in the company of such venerable patrons and chatter my name lispingly. May a turf that is not hard cover her tender bones nor, earth, be heavy on her: she wasn't to you.'

One of three epigrams on the death of M.'s slave Erotion. The second (5.37) is placed in close proximity and must be taken into account in considering the tone of the present piece (see below). In 10.61 M. entrusts the rites in Erotion's memory to the next owner of the land where she is buried, probably M.'s Nomentan farm, which he handed over to Marrius on his return to Spain (10.92).

M. has many epigrams on the theme of *mors immatura*. Frequently the persons commemorated are slaves, belonging either to M. himself (e.g. 1.88, 1.101, 11.91) or to patrons/friends (e.g. 6.28–9, 6.68). In expressing emotion at the deaths of young slaves, M. is not unusual. Despite a feeling that excessive grief for a slave merits an apology (cf. Cic. *Att.* 1.12.4), Roman masters *did* form sentimental attachments to slaves and lamented their demise, as shown by the many tomb inscriptions set up for slaves by their owners, and by the literary tradition: see Citroni on 1.88 intro.

The epigram differs from M.'s other funerary pieces in several respects: (1) There is a pronounced element of pathos, the poet dwelling for example on the dangers faced by the little girl's shade as she enters the Underworld. Elsewhere, the focus is on the virtues of the deceased, the death itself, or the poet's generosity towards the slave (1.88, 101); (2) Erotion held a special place in the poet's affections: she is entrusted to M.'s own deceased parents, and no other slave is honoured with three epigrams; (3) An element of light-heartedness can be detected amid the pathos, e.g. the picture of the little girl terrified by the Tartarean hound and the play on *sit tibi terra leuis*. Both can be paralleled in genuine epitaphs, but **83** must also be read along with the companion piece 5.37, in which a lengthy – and slightly parodic – display of mourning for Erotion is used as a peg on which to hang a surprise ending in the form of a reply to Paetus, whose criticism of the poet's excessive grief for a mere *uernula* and his own restraint in the case of his departed wife is shown to be hypocritical.

This combination of genuine grief and a tone of more detached amusement may reflect the rôle of Erotion as M.'s *delicium*, or pet slave; *delicia* of either sex were recipients of playful affection which could include a sexual element. See further Watson (1992). It has been suggested that Erotion was M.'s own (illegitimate) daughter. This is unnecessary as well as unprovable. A master could love a slave *delicium* like his own child: cf. Stat. *Silu.* 2.1.82–6 (Melior's freedman Glaucias who was both *delicatus* and child-substitute).

The epigram has close affinities both with genuine tomb inscriptions and with literary epitaphs and *epicedeia*. These include linguistic echoes of tomb inscriptions (*commendo* 2, *impletura* 5, 9–10nn.), as well as variations on traditional themes. For instance, the invocation to M.'s parents to look after the child Erotion resembles the summoning in epitaphs of infernal deities to receive children into the Underworld, e.g. *SEG* 8.799.5–6 'but you divinities of the Underworld . . . welcome Epichares and be kind to him'; cf. Vérilhac (1978) 44–6, (1982) 275, 277, Lattimore (1962) 62. The idea that M.'s parents will protect Erotion from the terrors of the Underworld recalls a topos of the literary *consolatio*, the reassurance that the deceased will not suffer such fears, e.g. Prop. 4.11.25 *Cerberus et nullas hodie petat improbus umbras*. Lines 5–6 reflect the epitaphic practice of expressing the exact age of the deceased and the common lament that they would have reached a certain age, had death not intervened: cf. *CLE* 501.5–6 *qui prope uicenos bis iam supleuerat annos,* | *ni Lachesis breuia rupisset stamina fuso*, 7.96.3. Finally, the notion that the dead will meet relatives in the Underworld (1–2, 7–8) is common both in consolation literature (e.g. Stat. *Silu.* 2.6.98–100) and in tomb inscriptions: cf. *IG* v.1.1222.1–2, Lattimore (1962) 59–62, Vérilhac (1978) 132–3, (1982) 275–8.

Further reading: Lattimore (1962), Toynbee (1971), Vérilhac (1978), (1982), Watson (1992)

1   Fronto pater, genetrix Flaccilla: M.'s deceased parents. M. came from a Spanish family who had taken Roman citizenship and Roman names (intro. 1). Fronto was a cognomen of M.'s *gens*, the Valerii; the name Flaccilla is attested in six inscriptions from Spain (Kajanto 240). It has been suggested (e.g. J. Mantke, *Eos* 57 (1967–8) 234–44) that Fronto and Flaccilla are Erotion's parents, but *patronos* (7n.) is not appropriate of a parent/child relationship.

2   oscula 'the object of my kisses'; cf. Plaut. *Poen.* 366 *meum sauium*.

   commendo: cf. *CLE* 1204.5–6 *infernae, uobis commendo uirtute satactam, | circa hoc tumulum quae cinis occulitur*.

   delicias: used as a term of endearment (**71**.2n.), but the technical sense of a slave *delicium* is also suggested (see intro.).

3   paruula: a diminutive with especially pathetic resonances; cf. Virgil's famous *paruulus Aeneas* (*A.* 4.328–9). The epithet is also common in verse epitaphs, e.g. *CLE* 1535a.4 *morte . . . heu rapitur paruulus iste puer*.

   nigras . . . umbras 'the shades of the Underworld', a variation on *infernae* or *Stygiae umbrae*, the usual epitaphic formulae. *nigrae* emphasises that Erotion, like any small child, is afraid of the dark. *nigrae . . . umbrae* could also have the secondary sense 'ghosts' (cf. *nigro . . . gregi* Hor. *Carm.* 1.24.18), in which case there would be the amusing idea that Erotion, though herself an *umbra*, is afraid of the other *umbrae*. But ghosts are normally described as *pallentes* or *exsangues* (e.g. Virg. *A.* 4.26, 6.401, Ov. *Met.* 4.443, Stat. *Theb.* 1.308).

   Erotion = Gk ' Ερώτιον: the name is not elsewhere attested in Latin. Greek diminutives in -*ion* were normally Latinised to -*ium*; the Greek form of Erotion's name may point to her being a *delicium*, since these often have Hellenic names (e.g. Amphion at 12.75.5).

4   ora . . . Tartarei prodigiosa canis 'the monstrous mouths of the Tartarean hound' (Cerberus), which might terrify Erotion by their barking: cf. Prop. 4.5.3–4 *Cerberus . . . | . . . terreat ossa sono. ora* is a genuine plural: Cerberus had multiple heads (N–H on Hor. *Carm.* 2.13.34); the *ora* are *prodigiosa* in terms both of number and size (cf. Virg. *A.* 6.417 *Cerberus . . . ingens*).

   Tartarei 'belonging to the Underworld': cf. Virg. *A.* 6.395 *Tartareum . . . custodem*, also of Cerberus.

5–6   'She would just now have got through the cold of her sixth winter had she not lived the same number of days less': a poetic periphrasis for 'she died in late winter just six days short of her sixth birthday'. The precision fits the tendency in cases of *mors immatura* to express the age of the deceased with great exactitude (see Citroni on 1.101.4). In the other two epigrams on Erotion M. similarly associates her death with the winter season: cf. 10.61.2, 5.37.15–16 *quam pessimorum lex amara fatorum | sexta peregit hieme, nec tamen tota.*

5   impletura fuit: more vivid than *impleuisset*. 'she was on the point of completing'. *impleo* and *totidem* (6) are both used in epitaphs, e.g. *CLE* 1055.5 *bis mihi iam senos aetas impleuerat annos*, *CLE* 528.3–4 *iste quater denis et quattuor mensibus annis | im [iam* Cagnat] *uixit totidemque dies.*

7   inter tam ueteres: *uetus* points a contrast with the extreme youth of Erotion, but beyond this the meaning is difficult to establish. *tam ueteres* might mean 'so old' in the sense that they have been ghosts a long time, or that they died at an advanced age. It cannot mean 'of such long standing' because M.'s parents have only just become her *patroni*. The same objection applies to Heinsius' *iam ueteres*, 'now of long standing'. SB prints *iam* and joins it with *ludat* 'let her now play', but the separation of *iam* from *ueteres* is forced.

   ludat: reflects the notion that the dead continue in the Underworld the activities that they had enjoyed in life, e.g. Virg. *A.* 6.653–4 *quae gratia currum | armorumque fuit uiuis, quae cura nitentes | pascere equos, eadem sequitur tellure repostos.* Cf. the common burial practice of placing in graves equipment (including children's toys) for the use of the dead (Toynbee (1971) 52–3).

   lasciua: could be used of a young child's frolicking play, but might also suggest the behaviour of a *delicium*: cf. Stat. *Silu.* 2.1.75.

   patronos: best taken as 'guardians', 'protectors' (cf. W. Neuhauser, *Patronus und orator* (Innsbruck 1958) 117–18). Less probably, the noun has its technical sense 'the former master of a *libertus, -a*', such patronage being transferred from M. to his dead parents, who will act *in loco patronorum*. But this would imply that Erotion was manumitted on her deathbed (cf. 1.101 with Citroni). There is however no evidence for Erotion's manumission, and the description of her as *uernula* in 5.37.20 tells against it.

8   blaeso . . . ore: *blaesus* is used of halting or lisping speech. In reality a six-year-old girl would speak clearly: M.'s description may be intended to arouse pathos by exaggerating her extreme youth.

   garriat: *delicia* were prized above all for their entertaining chatter; cf. Tib. 1.5.26 *garrulus in dominae [consuescet] ludere uerna sinu.*

9   mollia non rigidus caespes tegat ossa: a variation on the epitaphic *molliter ossa cubent*, for which cf. *CLE* 428.15, Ov. *Am.* 1.8.107–8 *saepe rogabis | ut mea defunctae molliter ossa cubent.* Erotion's *ossa* are also *mollia* because she died at a tender age (*mollis*).

ossa: after cremation came the *ossilegium* whereby burned bones, along with the ashes, were collected and put into a burial urn; cf. Virg. *A.* 6.228 *ossaque lecta cado texit Corynaeus aeno,* Toynbee (1971) 50.

9–10   nec illi, | terra, grauis fueris: non fuit illa tibi: a pithy variation on the epitaphic *sit tibi terra leuis*; cf. *CLE* 1313.3–4 *terra... sibi sit leuis oro, | namque grauis nulli uita fuit pueri.* M. may have in mind Meleager, *AP* 7.461 = *HE* 4688–9 'Hail Earth, universal mother: Aesigenes was previously not heavy on you, and may you now lie not heavily on him'. See further W. Hartke, 'Sit tibi terra leuis' (Dissertation Bonn 1901).

84   (= 9.29)

'Philaenis, Nestor's equal in length of life, have you been carried off so prematurely to Hades? You were not quite as old as the Cumaean Sibyl. Alas, what a tongue is silent! It could not be overwhelmed by the noise of the slave market, of Sarapis' worshippers, by a rabble of schoolboys, or the cry of cranes. Who now will draw down the moon, or offer sex for sale as a procuress? May the earth lie light on your bones – so that dogs may be able to dig them up.'

A mock-epitaph on old Philaenis which with transparent irony laments her death and bemoans the loss of her dubious accomplishments. Terminology and themes drawn from serious epitaphs are employed in an overtly parodic way to construct an attack which reaches its apogee with the wicked inversion of a funerary topos in the last couplet. The epigram is one of many satiric assaults by M. upon *uetulae*, his aversion to whom normally stems from their physical appearance, or their unseasonable sexuality. Here, however, the target is a procuress (*lena*) and witch, whose main failing is her deafening loquacity. The poem draws on the abuse of *lenae* which is widespread in Comedy and, above all, Roman elegy, where the rôles of witch and *lena* are often combined: the best known instances of such attacks are Prop. 4.5 and Ov. *Am.* 1.8.

The name Philaenis is used by M. on several other occasions, almost always with reference to women represented as physically or morally repulsive. In the present epigram it is especially appropriate: (1) the name, which may be interpreted as meaning 'lover of talk' (φιλεῖν, 'to love', αἶνος, 'tale', 'story'), suits a woman renowned for the power of her *lingua*; (2) Philaenis is a prostitute's name (Lucian, *Dial. het.* 6.1, *AP* 5.186, 202.3): this suits the addressee's profession of *lena*, since *lenae* were usually ex-courtesans; (3) applied to an old *lena*, a character who is often depicted as passing on her knowledge to younger women, the name suggests the notorious Philaenis, reputed authoress of a didactic treatise on sex, who apparently also lived to an advanced old age (cf. B. Baldwin, *CL* 6 (1990) 1–8).

Further reading: Lattimore (1962), Myers (1996), Tolman (1910)

1   Saecula Nestoreae permensa . . . senectae 'who completed the centuries of old Nestor' i.e. lived as long as Nestor, proverbial for longevity. According to Homer (*Il.* 1.250–2), Nestor was king among a third generation of men, and *saeculum* can have the sense 'generation', but the hyperbolic tone and a Roman tendency to exaggerate Nestor's age make it likely that *saeculum* here = a period of 100 years, making Philaenis, absurdly, a multi-centenarian: cf. Var. *L.* 6.11 *seclum spatium annorum centum uocarunt*, Ov. *Met.* 12.187–8, Hor. *Carm.* 2.9.13–14 with N–H. In comparing Nestor to Philaenis on grounds of age, M. expected readers to make a further connexion between them, their loquacity.

permensa: *per* intimates that Philaenis has attained the full measure of Nestor's years.

2   rapta es . . . tam cito?: M. applies parodically to an old person the epitaphic topos of *mors immatura*: cf. *CLE* 1187.1 *prima aetate tua rapta es*, 1.88.1 *Alcime, quem raptum domino crescentibus annis*. The interrogative, unusual in such contexts, sarcastically suggests incredulity that Philaenis was 'carried off' so soon. Also ironic is M.'s use of the second-person address, which normally implies more heartfelt grief on the part of the epitaph-speaker than the third person (Tolman (1910) 1).

ad infernas . . . Ditis aquas: *rapio* + *ad* may reflect epitaphic style; the collocation is frequent in the *CLE*. Cf. 1219.1–2 *uiginti duo erant anni . . . | cum me florentem rapuit sibi Ditis ad umbras.*

tam cito: frequent in epitaphs, sometimes in conjunction with *rapio* (*CLE* 647.3), more often alone (e.g. *CIL* IX 292, *CLE* 1035.6). From the mourner's point of view, death at even an advanced age might seem premature (cf. 10.71, *Eleg. in Maecenat.* 1.136–40), but after the exaggeration of *saecula Nestoreae permensa senectae*, the phrase sounds ludicrous.

3–4   Euboicae nondum numerabas . . . Sibyllae | tempora: the grotesque overstatement of Philaenis' age is continued in a parallel with the Sibyl: for comparable exaggeration of an old woman's longevity, cf. **86**

intro. The *Euboica...Sibylla* is the Sibyl of Cumae, best known from *Aeneid* 6. Cumae was a colony of Chalcis in Euboea (Virg. *A.* 6.2 *Euboicis Cumarum adlabitur oris*). Popular accounts of the Sibyl made her so old that she eventually dwindled away into virtual nothingness (Petr. 48.8, Serv. *Aen.* 6.321).

numerabas...| tempora 'you had [not yet] completed the years', again epitaphic language: cf. *CLE* 1967.1–2 *Flauius hic situs est proauus qui tempora uitae | plura senex numerans meruit hoc saepe uocari*, ibid. 7. For *numero = compleo*, cf. also *CLE* 1260.2 *nondum ter denos numerabat temporis annos*.

3   nondum: the mock-sympathetic observation that Philaenis had not yet attained the age of the Sibyl parodies the widespread use of the adverb in verse epitaphs for the prematurely dead: cf. *CLE* 398.1 *quae nondum septem compleuerat annos*, 1260.2.

4   maior erat mensibus illa tribus: M. ironically expresses regret over the fact that Philaenis fell three months short of the Sibyl's lifespan, a thousand years according to Ov. *Met.* 14. 144–6. The numerical precision spoofs the propensity of real inscriptions to give the age of the deceased exactly (in the form *uixit ann...men...dieb...*). Cf. *CLE* 489, **83**.5–6 *impletura fuit sextae modo frigora brumae | uixisset totidem ni minus illa dies* and 5.37.15–16 for the same exactitude.

5   heu quae lingua silet!: epitaphs commonly celebrate the deceased's virtues, and lament the loss of these to the world. M. sends up the convention by attributing to Philaenis various undesirable characteristics of which a noisy tongue is the most expansively developed.

heu: the word, rare in prose, belongs to the impassioned style; it is frequent in versified laments. Cf. *CLE* 412.1 *heu iuuenis tumulo qualis iacet abditus isto*, Catull. 101.6.

quae: for the exclamation, cf. *CLE* 1057.11 *quanta iacet probitas, pietas quam uera sepulta est*.

lingua: the *lena* usually deploys her tongue to undermine female chastity (cf. Ov. *Am.* 1.8.19–20 *haec sibi proposuit thalamos temerare pudicos; | nec tamen eloquio lingua nocente caret*), but the reference here is to the loudness (5–8) of Philaenis' chatter. Juvenal condemns a clever woman for her loud voice (6.434–43), and epitaphs for females sometimes praise the deceased for not speaking overmuch, e.g. *CLE* 1988.11 *exiguo sermone irreprehensa manebat*.

silet suggests two ideas: (1) her voice is stilled in death: cf. Sextilius Ena, *FLP* fr. 1 Courtney *deflendus Cicero est Latiaeque silentia linguae*, *CIL* VI 10096.16–17; (2) she no longer deafens people with her prattle.

mille: *mille* = 'countless', as often. In this and the following examples Philaenis' tongue outdoes in volume things whose intrinsic loudness is compounded by large numbers (cf. *caterua . . . turba . . . grex*).

catastae: *catasta*, a platform on which slaves for sale stood for inspection, here stands by metonymy for the slave auction, which would have been a noisy occasion, the general hubbub of the milling crowd being interspersed with the announcements of the *praeco* and the sound of potential buyers testing the slaves' fitness by slapping them (Pers. 6.77) or getting them to jump up and down (Prop. 4.5.52).

6   quae turba Sarapin amat: Sarapis, a Ptolemaic amalgam of Apis and Osiris, had become especially popular in the late first century AD at Rome, where his cult was closely associated with that of Isis. The worship of both deities was a noisy affair: cf. Tib. 1.3.31–2 *bisque die resoluta comas tibi* [sc. *Isidi*] *dicere laudes | insignis turba debeat in Pharia*, Apul. *Met.* 11.9 and 20 with Griffiths.

7   matutini: school lessons began before daybreak (9.68.1–4).

cirrata 'curly-haired'. Cf. Pers. 1.29–30 *ten cirratorum centum dictata fuisse | pro nihilo pendas?* Prepubertal boys at Rome wore their hair long (cf. 10.62.2, D–S I 1370 n.278 s.v. *coma*, Jahn on Pers. *loc. cit.*), which would enhance the natural tendency of the locks to curl.

caterua magistri: a class of elementary school pupils. M. is thinking of the 'discordant concord of young voices, raised in a kind of sing-song as they repeated together . . . the words which their teacher uttered' (Bonner (1977) 166). As lessons were often given in the open air (**20.**5n.), the noise would have been a prominent feature of city life.

8   quae Strymonio de grege ripa sonat: the river Strymon in Macedonia was famous for the cranes that frequented it during their annual migration from East Africa: cf. Virg. *G.* 1.120 with Mynors. The cry of cranes was proverbially loud and raucous (Thompson (1936) 70).

de grege . . . sonat 'resounds with the flock'. The combination of *sonare* with *de* indicating source (cf. Plaut. *Truc.* 632 *nam mihi de uento miserae condoluit caput*) is unparalleled.

9–10   quae nunc Thessalico lunam deducere rhombo | . . . sciet?: like Propertius' and Ovid's *lenae* (intro.), Philaenis is a witch. To these was attributed the ability to draw down the moon from the sky; the feat was associated particularly with Thessalian women, whence *Thessalico*. Cf. Hill (1973).

9   rhombo: a term of disputed meaning, usually thought equivalent
to the *iunx* or magic wheel (see A. S. F. Gow, *JHS* 54 (1934) 1–13, Tupet
(1976) 50–5). The *rhombus* is usually associated with love-magic, which suits
Philaenis' profession of *lena*. For its use in drawing down the moon, see
20.17n.

10   hos illos . . . toros 'this bed or that'. For the unusual asyndeton,
cf. 12.60.11 *excipere hos illos*.
    lena: in apposition to *quae*, i.e. in her capacity as a *lena*.

11–12   The standard benediction in epitaphs, *sit tibi terra leuis* (11), is converted into a malediction by the following line, possibly under the influence
of the curse on a *lena* at Prop. 4.5.1–4. *ne*, which is common in funerary
inscriptions where the speaker desires to avert harm from the deceased's
remains (Lattimore (1962) 69 n.363), sets up a false expectation of good will
that is overturned by the following *non*. The benedictory formula is often
subject to witty exploitation; cf. *AP* 7.204, 11.226 'May the dust lie light
upon you, wretched Nearchus, when below the ground, so that the dogs
may easily dig you up', **83.**9–10n.

12   ne tua non possint eruere ossa canes: the possibility that
one's bones might be disinterred by scavenging dogs was very real (Scobie
(1986) 418).

85   (= 10.63)

'Passer-by, the marble tomb whose inscription you are reading is small, yet
not inferior to the Mausoleum and the pyramids. At two Secular Games
my life was approved and was in no way diminished up to the day of my
death: I bore five sons and five daughters, and all their hands closed my
eyes. Furthermore I attained rare glory in marriage and my chastity knew
but one cock.'

The epigram mocks the concept of the *uniuira*, the ideal Roman *matrona* who
has only one husband. It takes the form of a tomb inscription for one who is
the complete embodiment of the matronal ideal, not only in her chastity, but
also in her fertility and good fortune at being survived by all her offspring.
The parodic character of the piece only becomes explicit in the punch-
line, with the appearance of the inappropriate obscenity *mentula*, but has
already been prepared for through a series of hyperbolic and improbable

details which provoke suspicions that the epitaph is less than serious. The concluding *mentula* is, however, so outrageous that the surprise effect is not spoiled even for the reader sensitive to the hints of parody throughout the epigram.

The opening couplet contains the first of a series of pointers to the mock-seriousness of the epitaph. The contrast between the smallness of the tomb and the greatness of its occupant is a commonplace, but is normally used with reference to famous persons (1–2n.); in the mouth of an anonymous *matrona* it is laughably hyperbolic. The same applies to the claim that her tomb vies with the greatest sepulchral monuments of antiquity (*non cessura* 1 n.). The matron's appearance at the Secular Games is something of which a woman might reasonably boast (*mea...spectata est uita* 3n.), but her appearance at successive Games (*bis*) is almost too good to be true. Similarly the survival of all ten children and the neat balance between the sexes arouse suspicion (5–6nn.); comparable exaggeration is found in fictitious epitaphs such as *AP* 7.224 on Callicratia, who died at 105 after having 29 children, all of whom survived her.

The concluding joke, with its startling obscenity, is not just a parody of epitaphs for *uniuirae*. The ideal *matrona* was not merely a woman who was once-married, but also a paradigm of virtue and *dignitas* even within the marriage bed, the sort of joyless partner deplored in 11.104, whose capacity to express overt sexual desire was constricted by Roman notions of womanly propriety: cf. Jocelyn (1983). By characterising the woman's *uniuiratus* in explicitly sexual terms, M. hints that even one as virtuous as she enjoyed sex at least with her husband, thus ridiculing the notion that the ideal matron could really exist.

1–2   The modest size of the tomb is belied by the greatness of its occupant, which puts it on a par with proverbially imposing *sepulchra* such as the Mausoleum or the pyramids. Such claims are commonplace: compare the epitaphs in *AP* 7 for Homer, e.g. 2b 'wayfarer, though the tomb be small, pass me not by, but...venerate me as you do the gods. For I hold divine Homer the epic poet, honoured greatly by the Pierian Muses', Stat. *Silu.* 2.7.95 *angusto Babylon premit sepulcro* (of Alexander) with Van Dam.

non cessura...| Mausoli saxis pyramidumque: cf. *Spect.* 1.7 *omnis Caesareo cedit labor Amphitheatro*, where *omnis labor* describes architectural masterpieces, the pyramids and the tomb of Mausolus included, which are eclipsed by the Colosseum. Such a comparison, appropriate in the opening poem of the *De spectaculis*, with its flattery of the emperor Titus, might seem like self-aggrandisement in the mouth of a *matrona* who applies the notion to herself.

1   Marmora: the preferred material among the wealthier classes for their sepulchres (Toynbee (1971) 253, 270).

uiator: in sepulchral epitaphs the dead person often addresses a passer-by, reflecting the fact that tombs were erected beside major roads beyond the city boundaries, such as can still be seen on the Via Appia outside Rome.

2   Mausoli: Mausolus was a Persian satrap of Caria in the fourth century BC whose tomb, the Mausoleum, was famously grand: cf. S. Hornblower, *Mausolus* (Oxford 1982) 237–51. For the monument's size, see P. Zanker, *The power of images in the age of Augustus* (Ann Arbor 1988) 74.

3   refers to the Secular Games, an ancient ceremony marking the beginning of a new *saeculum*, or period of 110 years. The celebration took place in the *Campus Martius* at the spot known as Tarentum or Tarentos (cf. 4.1.8 *quae Romuleus sacra Tarentos habet*), here called *Romanus* to distinguish it from the town of the same name in Southern Italy. See further St. Weinstock, *Glotta* 21 (1932) 40–52.

bis: placed at the beginning of the line for emphasis. Participation in two Secular Games would have been decidedly unusual, though not wholly impossible: games were staged by Domitian in 88, only forty-one years after the previous celebration by Claudius in 47.

mea ... spectata est uita 'my life was held up to public scrutiny [and seen to be exemplary]'. An appearance by a *matrona* at the Secular Games represented an official acknowledgement of her qualities. At those held by Augustus in 17 BC, 110 chosen matrons offered banquets and prayers to Juno and Diana (cf. *ILS* 5050, 5050a). A prerequisite for selection will have been the matronal virtues of chastity and fertility, both of which are highlighted in Horace's *Carmen saeculare*, commissioned for Augustus' celebration of the Games (13–20, 57–9).

4   nihil extremos perdidit ante rogos: i.e. the *matrona*'s reputation remained unblemished right up to her death.

rogos: at this period in Rome, cremation rather than interment was the norm. See H. Nock, *HThR* 25 (1932) 321–59, I. Morris, *Death-ritual and social structure in classical antiquity* (Cambridge 1992) 31–69.

5   quinque dedit pueros, totidem mihi Iuno puellas: exceptionally fertile women, though rare, were not unknown: Cornelia, mother of the Gracchi, bore twelve offspring, Agrippina the Elder, nine; cf. Liv. 42.34.4, Plin. *NH* 7.34, 158. But the statistically improbable even distribution of the sexes is more difficult to credit.

Iuno: in her capacity as Juno Lucina, goddess of childbirth: cf. Catull. 34.13–14 *tu Lucina dolentibus | Iuno dicta puerperis.*

6   cluserunt omnes lumina nostra manus: it was customary for the nearest relative to close the eyes of the deceased. In this case, all ten children perform the service. The detail is hard to swallow, given the unlikelihood in ancient Rome of a woman's offspring all growing to adulthood, let alone outliving a mother who had attained old age (*bis* 3n.). Agrippina the Elder was survived by only four of her nine children; the emperor Commodus was the only survivor of his mother Faustina's twelve children. See further T. G. Parkin, *Demography and Roman society* (Baltimore/London 1992) 94, 113–14.

7   thalami: the genitive explains the source of her glory.

gloria: a common motif in sepulchral epigram: cf. *CLE* 2053 *si qua uerecunde uiuenti gloria danda est, | huic iuueni debet gloria digna dari.*

rara: sepulchral epigram characteristically represents the deceased as extraordinary in some way: cf. *CLE* 1508.1–3 *et quae rara fides toris habetur, | multos cum caperet superba forma, | blando iuncta uiro pudica mansit.*

8   una pudicitiae mentula nota meae 'only one cock was known to my chastity'. *mentula* is both shocking and amusing. Although the idea of marriage to a single partner is occasionally expressed in sexual terms (e.g. *CLE* 558.3 *matrona unicuba uniiuga, AP* 7.324), the characterisation of matronal chastity by means of a basic obscenity is grotesque in the extreme. The effect is enhanced by the fact that the woman is pronouncing her own epitaph: indecent language was considered unsuitable for *matronae*: cf. **41** intro., Adams, *LSV* 217.

nota: in the sense 'know sexually'; cf. *CIL* VI 12853.5 *dedita coniugi soli suo ignara alienum*, Plaut. *Most.* 894, Adams, *LSV* 190.

86   (= 10.67)

'Plutia, older than the oldest women of mythology, is laid to rest at last in this tomb – where she enjoys sepulchral sex with bald Melanthio.'

The inspiration for this brief poem is twofold: the language of sepulchral inscriptions, which is amusingly spoofed in lines 6–7, and late Hellenistic epigram, which provided its central strategy, the hyperbolic characterisation of old age in supposedly superannuated females by making them, fantastically, coevals or relatives of the earliest figures of Greek mythology. Among such epigrams, where some of the mythical families referred to in M.'s fictitious stemma already appear, are Myrinus, *AP* 11.67 (*GP* 2574–7) 'the letter *U* signifies 400: but you have twice as many years, wanton Lais, old as a crow or Hecuba (κορωνεκάβη), o nurse of Sisyphus and sister of Deucalion', Bassus, *AP* 11.72 (*GP* 1637–42) and Lucillius, *AP* 11.67 'Themistonoe, three times as old as crows, having dyed her hair, suddenly became not *nea* (young), but *Rhea* (wife of Kronos)', where, as here, old age fails to put a damper on the lady's sexual activity. None of M.'s Greek models is however quite as exuberant in its scurrilous mythologising of female decrepitude as the present epigram: nor are the other passages where M. appropriates mythology to characterise old age, sc. 3.32.3–4, **38**, 10.39, 10.90, and **84**.1–4, with nn. *ad. loc.*

1   Pyrrhae filia, Nestoris nouerca: i.e. old enough to be Pyrrha's daughter or Nestor's stepmother.

   Pyrrhae filia: Pyrrha symbolises the very beginnings of history (Lucian, *Rhet. praec.* 20, Juv. 15.30). Along with her husband Deucalion, she magically recreated mankind after the flood (Ov. *Met.* 1.313–415). Two of their daughters were Protogeneia ('Firstborn': Apollod. *Bibl.* 1.7.3) and 'Pandora . . . the first woman' (Eustath. *Iliad* 23.42): according to M., Plotia is their coeval. The era of Deucalion and Pyrrha serves in Greek epigram to characterise geriatric females: cf. *AP* 11.67.3 (intro.), 11.71.

   Nestoris nouerca: there may have been such a person (cf. *RE* XVI 2276–8, E. Curtius, *Gesammelte Abhandlungen* I (Berlin 1894) 459–64), but *Nestoris nouerca* simply stands for a representative of an era which predated even Nestor, who, like Laertes and Priam 3–4, belonged to a generation which was in its prime prior to the Trojan War.

**2   **'You were already grey-haired when Niobe was a mere slip of a girl.' As grandmother of Nestor (Apollod. *Bibl.* 3.5.6), Niobe lived several generations before the Trojan war.

   puella canam: pointed juxtaposition, repeated in *auiam senex* 3. *canam, nouerca, auiam, nutricem and socrum* are all variations on the same theme, that Plotia belongs to a period earlier than the oldest heroes and heroines of myth.

3   Laertes auiam senex uocauit: Plutia antedates Laertes, father of Odysseus, by two generations.

senex: beginning with Homer, Laertes is pictured as a very old man: cf. Ael. *VH* 7.5, Ov. *Ep.* 1.97–8, Sen. *Tro.* 698–700. If the aged Laertes could call Plutia his grandmother, she must be antiquated indeed.

4   nutricem Priamus: the wet-nurse of Priam (cf. *AP* 11.67.3 quoted above) would be of unimaginable antiquity. In both literature and art, *nutrices* are typically thought of as very old women (cf. Homer's Eurycleia, Eur. *Hipp.* 252, Virg. *A.* 7.1–2, *RAC* 1 381–3). The reason is that, on account of the close bond forged between wet-nurse and baby, she was frequently maintained in the house of the latter during her twilight years: cf. Dem. 47.55.

Priamus: Priam, like Laertes, is to be thought of as an old man (cf. Hom. *Il.* 22.37–76), again an implied comment on Plutia's age.

socrum Thyestes: the identity of Thyestes' mother-in-law is unknown and of no consequence. She merely stands for a female of remote antiquity.

5   iam cornicibus omnibus superstes: Plutia has 'outlived all the crows', paradigms of great longevity: cf. Hes. fr. 304.1–2 M–W 'the cawing crow lives nine generations of men in their prime', Hor. *Carm.* 4.13.24–5 *parem | cornicis uetulae temporibus Lycen*, Thompson (1936), s.v. κορώνη. Such reports are greatly exaggerated; they arise from the tendency of crows to persist from generation to generation in suitable territories (W. G. Arnott, *Tria lustra* (Liverpool 1993) 129). True or not, the belief spawned such sarcastic appellations for the elderly of both sexes as τρικόρωνος, 'three times as old as a crow', *AP* 5.298.1 and 11.69.1: cf. also 11.67.2 (intro.).

omnibus superstes: *superstes* takes the dative of the person outlived. Cf. *CLE* 844 *infelix annosa uiro nataeque superstes*, *OLD* s.v. 3b.

omnibus: including even the longest-lived members of the species.

6–7   prurit... | ...cum: a surprise for *iacet cum* or the like. *prurire*, lit. 'itch with lust', is a circumlocution for 'have sex with' (**57**.6n.). To be buried in the same tomb was a common amatory or marital ideal: cf. Eur. *Alc.* 365–8, *CLE* 367.8 *cum fatum tulerit, una eius mecum condere ossa loco*, Howell on 1.116.4. *prurit cum* mischievously puts a blatantly sexual construction on the idea that a shared tomb represents a perpetuation of the marital bed where husband and wife were once joined: cf. Kaibel, *Epigr. Graec.* 386.1–2 'I Amphia lie united (μίγα) with my husband here, | for in life we enjoyed this privilege together', Peek, *Griech. Versinschr.* 1718.3–4, *CLE* 1142.25–6, 1273.6, Treggiari (1991), 246. Prop. 4.7.94 *mecum eris et mixtis ossibus ossa teram* is an even more wicked spoof on the conceit.

6   hoc tandem sita prurit in sepulchro: cf. 3.93.20. Not only does Plutia exhibit overtly sexual behaviour, considered indecorous in a female (Plut. *Coniug. praec.* 140c, Treggiari (1991) 314–15, Jocelyn (1983) 54), but her desire is unseasonable. For elderly women sexual activity, it was felt, should be a thing of the past (Watson (1994)), a taboo which Plutia drastically violates by perpetuating her amorous activities in the grave. It is a neat irony that womanly chastity is often lauded in epitaphs e.g. *CLE* 368.1 *hic est illa sita pia frug(i) casta pudica.*

   tandem: her death was overdue: cf. Hor. *Carm.* 3.15.4 *maturo propior . . . funeri.* The comment wittily reverses the common epitaphic complaint that death has come too soon.

   sita 'laid to rest', an epitaphic term amusingly at odds with the vigorous activity implied by *prurit*: cf. *CLE* 539.2 *Heli<odo>rus sedibus his situs est miserabilis*, 1545.2. The formulation *hic situs/-a est* is particularly common.

7   caluo: primarily suggests that Melanthio is of an age when sexual activity should have ceased, but M. also has in mind the belief that bald men incline to lecherousness ([Arist.] *Probl.* 4.18). Baldness is a common butt of jokes (see on **72**).

   Plutia: *Plutia* b, *Plotia* Ital. The spelling *Plutia* has good inscriptional support (cf. Heraeus' *adnotatio critica* to 10.67, Dessau, *ILS* index), and should probably be preferred, especially since it permits a contextually appropriate pun on Pluto.

   Melanthione: both the Greek termination in *-io* and the name suggest servile status (the Melanthio of *CIL* III 4256 is unusual in being free-born). *Melanthus*, of which *Melanthio* is a derivative, is associated in inscriptions with *serui* and *liberti*: cf. *CIL* VI 24212.7, VIII 919, IX 4670, *ILS* 5644.

BIBLIOGRAPHY

1 EDITIONS AND COMMENTARIES

Bowie, M. N. R. (1988) 'Martial, book XII: a commentary.' Dissertation, Oxford

Bridge, R. T. and Lake, E. D. C. (1906–8) *Selected epigrams of Martial.* Oxford

Citroni, M. (1975) *M. Valerii Martialis epigrammaton liber primus.* Florence

Friedländer, L. (1886) Edition and commentary. Leipzig

George, R. G. (1994) 'Martial, book 3.1–68: a commentary.' Dissertation, Oxford

Grewing, F. (1997) *Martial, Buch VI: ein Kommentar.* Göttingen

Henriksén, C. (1998–9) *Martial, book IX: a commentary.* Uppsala

Howell, P. (1980) *A commentary on book one of the epigrams of Martial.* London
　(1995) *Martial, Epigrams V.* Warminster

Izaac, H. J. (1930–3) Budé edition. Paris

Kay, N. (1985) *Martial, book XI: a commentary.* London

Lindsay, W. M. (1903) *M. Val. Martialis Epigrammata.* Oxford

Paley, F. A. and Stone, W. H. (1881) *M. Val. Martialis epigrammata selecta.* London

Scàndola, M. (1996) Italian transl. with notes by E. Merli and introduction by M. Citroni. Milan

Shackleton Bailey, D. R. (1990) Stuttgart

Stephenson, H. M. (1907) *Selected epigrams of Martial.* London

2 WORKS CITED

Adamik, T. (1975) 'Martial and the "vita beatior"', *AUB (Class)* 3: 55–64

Adams, J. N. (1983a) 'Words for "prostitute" in Latin', *RhM* 126: 321–58
　(1983b) 'Martial 2.83', *CPh* 78: 311–15

Anderson, R. D., Parsons, P. J., Nisbet, R. G. M. (1979) 'Elegiacs by Gallus from Qaṣr Ibrîm', *JRS* 69: 125–55

André, J. (1949) *Études sur les termes de couleur dans la langue latine.* Paris
　(1981) *L'alimentation et la cuisine à Rome.* 2nd edn, Paris

André, J.-M. (1967) *Mécène: essai de biographie spirituelle.* Paris

357

Appel, G. (1909) *De Romanorum precationibus.* Giessen

Axelson, B. (1945) *Unpoetische Wörter.* Lund

Balsdon, J. P. V. D. (1969) *Life and leisure in ancient Rome.* London

Bardon, H. (1956) *La littérature latine inconnue.* Paris

Barry, W. D. (1996) 'Roof tiles and urban violence in the ancient world', *GRBS* 37: 55–74

Barwick, K. (1958) 'Zyklen bei Martial und in den kleinen Gedichten des Catull', *Philologus* 102: 284–318

(1959) *Martial und die zeitgenössische Rhetorik.* Leipzig

Baumgart, J. (1936) *Die römischen Sklavennamen.* Diss. Breslau

Birt, Th. (1882) *Das antike Buchwesen.* Berlin

Blümner, H. (1911) *Die römischen Privataltertümer.* Munich

Bonner, S. F. (1949) *Roman declamation.* Liverpool

(1977) *Education in ancient Rome.* Berkeley/Los Angeles

Bradley, K. R. (1984/7) *Slaves and masters in the Roman empire: a study in social control.* Oxford

Brecht, F. (1930) *Motiv- und Typengeschichte des griechischen Spottepigramms.* Leipzig

Bruun, C. (1991) *The water supply of ancient Rome: a study of Roman imperial administration.* Helsinki

Buchheit, V. (1964) '*Amor caecus*', *CM* 25: 129–37

Buckland, W. W. (1908) *The Roman law of slavery.* Cambridge

Burnikel, W. (1980) *Untersuchungen zur Struktur des Witzepigramms bei Lukillius und Martial.* Wiesbaden

Busch, S. (1999) *Versus balnearum. Die antike Dichtung über Bäder und Baden im römischen Reich.* Stuttgart/Leipzig

Cairns, F. (1975) 'Horace, Epode 2, Tibullus 1,1 and rhetorical praise of the countryside', *MPhL* 1: 79–91

Callahan, J. F. (1964) 'The figurative use of *emungere*', in *Classical Mediaeval and Renaissance Studies in Honour of B. L. Ullman* (Rome) 1: 67–78

Cameron, A. (1973) *Porphyrius the charioteer.* Oxford

Champlin, E. (1991) *Final judgements: duty and emotion in Roman wills, 200 BC–AD 250.* Berkeley

Citroni, M. (1968) 'Motivi di polemica letteraria negli epigrammi di Marziale', *DArch* 2: 259–301

(1969) 'La teoria lessinghiana dell'epigramma e le interpretazioni moderne di Marziale', *Maia* 21: 215–43

(1988) 'Pubblicazione e dediche dei libri in Marziale', *Maia* 40: 3–39

Coleman, K. M. (1998) 'Martial book 8 and the politics of AD 93', *PLLS* 10: 337–57

Cook, A. B. (1904) 'The European sky-god', *Folklore* 15: 264–315

Copley, F. O. (1947) '*Servitium Amoris* in the Roman Elegists', *TAPhA* 78: 285–300

Courtney, E. (1980) *A commentary on the Satires of Juvenal*. London
(1995) *Musa lapidaria*. Atlanta

Crook, J. A. (1967) *Law and life of Rome*. London

Curtius, E. R. (1953) *European literature and the Latin middle ages*. Tr. W. D. Trask. London

Damon, C. (1992) 'Statius *Silvae* 4.9: *Libertas Decembris?*', *ICS* 17: 301–8
(1997) *The mask of the parasite: a pathology of Roman patronage*. Michigan

D'Arms, J. H. (1970) *Romans on the bay of Naples*. Cambridge, Mass.

Darwall-Smith, R. (1996) *Emperors and architecture: a study of Flavian Rome*. Brussels

Daube, D. (1976) 'Martial, father of three', *AJAH* 1: 145–7

Davies, M. (1987) 'Description by negation. History of a thought-pattern in ancient accounts of a blissful life', *Prometheus* 13: 265–84

Desbordes, Fr. (1991) 'Latinitas: constitution et évolution d'un modèle de l'identité linguistique', in S. Saïd, ed. 'ΕΛΛΗΝΙΣΜΟΣ. *Quelques jalons pour une histoire de l'identité grecque* (Leiden) 33–47

Descoeudres, J.-P., ed. (1994) *Pompeii revisited*. Sydney

Dodge, H. and Ward-Perkins, B. (1992) *Marble in antiquity*. London

Dolç, M. (1953) *Hispania y Marcial*. Barcelona

Dolderer, A. (1933) *Über Martials Epigramme auf Ärtze*. Dissertation, Tübingen

Dominik, W. J. (1994) *The mythic voice of Statius*. Leiden

Duff, A. M. (1928) *Freedmen in the early Roman empire*. Oxford

Durand, R. (1946) 'In Martialem', *Latomus* 5: 257–61

Dziatzko, K. (1894) 'Autor- und Verlagsrecht im Altertum', *RhM* 49: 559–76

Edwards, C. (1993) *The politics of immorality in ancient Rome*. Cambridge

Estève-Forriol, J. (1962) *Die Trauer- und Trostgedichte in der römischen Literatur*. Dissertation, Munich

Evans, H. B. (1994) *Water distribution in ancient Rome: the evidence of Frontinus*. Michigan

Fagan, G. G. (1999) *Bathing in public in the Roman world*. Ann Arbor

Fantham, E. (1972) *Studies in republican Latin imagery*. Toronto

Faraone, C. A. (1990) 'Aphrodite's KESTOS and apples for Atalanta', *Phoenix* 44: 204–43

Fears, J. R. (1981) 'The cult of Jupiter and Roman imperial ideology', *ANRW* II 17.1: 3–141

Fehling, D. (1974) *Ethnologische Überlegüngen auf dem Gebiet der Altertumskunde.* München

Ferguson, J. (1963) 'Catullus and Martial', *PACA* 6: 3–15

  (1970) 'A note on Catullus' hendecasyllables', *CPh* 65: 173–5

Ferraro, V. (1988) 'Casca e la sua "pusa" nell' epigramma di Papinio (*FPL*, p. 54 Buechn. = p. 42 Mor.)' in V. Tandoi, ed. *Disiecti membra poetae* (Foggia) III 50–2

Fowler, D. P. (1995) 'Martial and the Book', *Ramus* 24: 31–58

Friedrich, G. (1913) 'Drei Epigramme des Martial', *RhM* 68: 257–78

Frier, B. W. (1977) 'The rental market in early imperial Rome', *JRS* 67: 29–37

  (1980) *Landlords and tenants in imperial Rome.* Princeton

Gardner, J. F. (1986) *Women in Roman law and society.* London

Garland, R. (1995) *The eye of the beholder. Deformity and disability in the Graeco-Roman world.* London

Garrido-Hory, M. (1981a) 'La vision du dépendant chez Martial à travers les relations sexuelles', *Index* 10: 298–315

  (1981b) *Martial et l'esclavage.* Paris

Garthwaite, J. (1990) 'Martial, book 6, on Domitian's moral censorship', *Prudentia* 22: 13–22

  (1993) 'The panegyrics of Domitian in Martial book 9', *Ramus* 22: 78–102

  (1998) 'Patronage and poetic immortality in Martial, book 9', *Mnemosyne* 51: 161–75

Gerber, D. (1988) 'The measure of Bacchus', *Mnemosyne* 41: 39–45

Giegengack, J. M. (1969) 'Significant names in Martial'. Dissertation, Yale

Gilbert, W. (1882) 'Zum ersten Buch Martials', *Philologus* 41: 359–66

Gleason, M. W. (1990) 'The semiotics of gender: physiognomy and self-fashioning in the second century C.E.', in D. M. Halperin, J. J. Winkler and F. I. Zeitlin, edd. *Before sexuality* (Princeton) 389–415

Gnoli, R. (1988) *Marmora Romana.* Rev. edn, Rome

Goldhill, S. (1994) 'The naive and knowing eye', in S. Goldhill and R. Osborne, edd. *Art and text in ancient Greek culture* (Cambridge) 197–223

Gowers, E. (1993) *The loaded table.* Oxford

Grassmann, V. (1966) *Die erotischen Epoden des Horaz.* Munich

Grewing, F. (1996) 'Möglichkeiten und Grenzen des Vergleichs: Martials *Diadumenos* und Catulls *Lesbia*', *Hermes* 124: 333–54

(1998a) 'Etymologie und etymologische Wortspiele in den Epigrammen Martials', in Grewing, F. ed. (1998b) 315–56

(1998b) ed. *Toto notus in orbe: Perspektiven der Martial-Interpretation.* Stuttgart

Griffin, M. (1986) 'Philosophy, Cato and Roman suicide', *G&R* 33: 64–77

Grimal, P. (1989) 'Martial et la pensée de Sénèque', *ICS* 14: 175–83

Grimaldi, D. A. (1996) *Amber: window to the past.* New York

Grmek, M. D. (1989) *Diseases in the ancient Greek world.* Baltimore

Haffter, H. (1956) 'Superbia innenpolitisch', *SIFC* 27/8: 135–41

Hagen, H. (1961) *Die physiologische und psychologische Bedeutung der Leber in der Antike.* Diss. Bonn

Hagenow, G. (1972) 'Kosmetische Extravaganzen', *RhM* 115: 51–9

Hallet, J. P. (1989) 'Female homoeroticism and the denial of Roman reality in Latin literature', *YJC* 3.1: 209–27 = J. P. Hallett and M. B. Skinner, edd. *Roman sexualities* (Princeton 1997) 245–73

Hanard, G. (1986) 'Inceste et société romaine: un essai d'interprétation ethno-juridique', *RBPh* 64: 32–59

Harcum, C. G. (1914) *Roman cooks.* Baltimore

Harris, H. A. (1972) *Sport in Greece and Rome.* Ithaca

Harris, W. V. (1989) *Ancient literacy.* Cambridge, Mass./London

Hehn, V. (1976) *Cultivated plants and domesticated animals in their migration from Asia to Europe.* New ed. by James P. Mallory. Amsterdam

Henderson, J. (1991) *The maculate Muse: obscene language in Attic Comedy.* 2nd edn, New York/Oxford

Henriksén, C. (1998) 'Martial und Statius', in ed. Grewing (1998b) 77–118

Herrlinger, (1930) *Totenklage um Tiere in der antiken Dichtung.* Stuttgart

Herter, H. (1932) *De Priapo.* Giessen

Heuvel, H. (1937) 'De inimicitiarum, quae inter Martialem et Statium fuisse dicuntur, indiciis', *Mnemosyne* 4: 299–330

Heyne, R. (1924) *Zähne und Zahnärztliches in der schönen Literatur der Römer.* Diss. Leipzig

Hilgers, W. (1969) *Lateinische Gefässnamen.* Düsseldorf

Hill, D. E. (1973) 'The Thessalian trick', *RhM* 116: 221–38

Hodge, A. T. (1992) *Roman aqueducts.* London

Hofmann, J. B. (1951) *Lateinische Umgangssprache.* 3rd edn, Heidelberg

Holder, A. (1896/1907) *Alt-celtischer Sprachschatz* I and III. Leipzig

Holzberg, N. (1986) 'Neuansatz zu einer Martial-Interpretation', *WJA* 12: 197–215
 (1988) *Martial.* Heidelberg
 (2002) *Martial und das antike Epigram.* Darmstadt
Hopfner, Th. (1938) *Das Sexualleben der Griechen und Römer.* Prague
Hopkins, K. (1980) 'Brother-sister marriage in Roman Egypt', *CSSH* 22: 303–54
 (1983) *Death and renewal.* Cambridge
Hosek, Radislav (1962) *Lidovost A Lidové Motivy in Aristofana.* Prague
Howell, P. (1998) 'Martial's return to Spain' in ed. Grewing (1998b) 173–86
Huisintveld, H. (1949) *De Populaire Elementen in de Taal van M. Valerius Martialis.* Diss. Nijmegen
Humphrey, J. H. (1986) *Roman circuses: arenas for chariot racing.* London
Jackson, R. (1988) *Doctors and diseases in the Roman empire.* London
Janson, T. (1964) *Latin prose prefaces.* Gothenburg
Jennison, G. (1937) *Animals for show and pleasure in ancient Rome.* Manchester
Jocelyn, H. D. (1983) 'Lucretius 4, 1263–77', *PACA* 17: 53–8
Joepgen, U. (1967) *Wortspiele bei Martial.* Diss. Bonn
Johnstone, S. (1992) 'On the uses of arson in classical Rome', in C. Deroux, ed. *Studies in Latin literature and Roman history* (Brussels) vi 41–69
Jones, C. P. (1987) 'Stigma: tattooing and branding in Graeco-Roman antiquity', *JRS* 77: 139–55
Joshel, S. R. (1992) *Work, identity, and legal status at Rome.* Norman/London
Keller, O. (1909/13) *Die antike Tierwelt.* 2 vols., Leipzig
Kenyon, F. G. (1951) *Books and readers in ancient Greece and Rome.* 2nd ed., Oxford
Kier, H. (1933) *De laudibus uitae rusticae.* Diss. Marburg
Killeen, J. F. (1967) 'Ad Martialis Epigr. ix 67', *Glotta* 45: 233–4
Kleberg, T. (1957) *Hotels, restaurants et cabarets dans l'antiquité romaine.* Uppsala
 (1992) 'Commercio librario ed editorio nel mondo antico', in G. Cavallo, ed. *Libri editori e pubblico nel mondo antico* (2nd ed., Rome/Bari) 25–80 = T. Kleberg, *Buchhandel und Verlagswesen in der Antike* (Darmstadt 1967)
Knox, A. D. and Headlam, W. (1922) *Herodas: The mimes and fragments.* Cambridge
Köhne, E. and Ewigleben, C. (2000) edd., *Gladiators and Caesars.* English version ed. by R. Jackson, British Museum Press
Konstan, D. (1997) *Friendship in the classical world.* Cambridge

Krenkel, W. A. (1980a) 'Sex und politische Biographie', *WZRostock* 29: 65–76

(1980b) 'Fellatio and irrumatio', *WZRostock* 29.5: 77–88

(1981) 'Tonguing', *WZRostock* 30: 5.37–54

Küspert, O. (1902–3/1905–6) *Über Bedeutung und Gebrauch des Wortes 'Caput'.* Programm des k. humanistischen Gymnasiums in Hof

Kyle, D. G. (1998) *Spectacles of death in ancient Rome.* London/NY

Lattimore, R. (1942) *Themes in Greek and Latin epitaphs.* Urbana, Illinois

Lau, O. (1967) *Schuster und Schusterhandwerk in der griechisch-römischen Literatur und Kunst.* Dissertation, Bonn

Launey, M. (1945) 'L'exécution de Sotades', *REA* 47: 33–45

Laurens, P. (1965) 'Martial et l'épigramme grecque du 1er siècle ap. J.-C.', *REL* 43: 315–41

Lausberg, M. (1982) *Das Einzeldistichon: Studien zum antiken Epigramm.* Munich

Le Gall, J. (1953) *Le Tibre fleuve de Rome dans l'antiquité.* Paris

Lefkowitz, M. (1981) *The lives of the Greek poets.* London

Licht, M. (1926/8) *Sittengeschichte Griechenlands, das Liebesleben der Griechen.* Dresden and *Ergänzungsband.* Zürich

Lilja, S. (1972) *The treatment of odours in the poetry of antiquity.* Helsinki

(1983) *Homosexuality in republican and Augustan Rome.* Helsinki

Litchfield, H. W. (1914) 'National exempla virtutis in Roman Literature', *HSCPh* 25: 1–71

Lyne, R. O. A. M. (1979) 'Servitium Amoris', *CQ* 29: 117–30

Manson, M. (1978) '*Puer bimulus* (Catulle 17.12–13) et l'image du petit enfant chez Catulle et ses prédecesseurs', *MEFRM* 90: 247–91

Mau, A. (1899) *Pompeii: its life and art.* Transl. F. W. Kelsey, London

McGinn, T. A. J. (1998) *Prostitution, sexuality and the law in ancient Rome.* New York/Oxford

McKay, A. G. (1975) *Houses, villas and palaces in the Roman world.* London

McMahon, J. (1998) *Paralysin caue. Impotence, perception and text in Petronius' Satyrica.* Leiden

Meyer, E. (1913) *Der Emporkömmling.* Dissertation Giessen

Millar, F. (1977) *The emperor in the Roman world.* London

Mohler, S. L. (1931) 'The *cliens* in the time of Martial', in G. D. Hadzsits, ed. *Classical studies in honor of John C. Rolfe* (Philadelphia) 239–63

Moldenke, H. N. and A. L. (1952) *Plants of the bible.* Waltham, Mass.

Mommsen, Th. (1899) *Römisches Strafrecht.* Leipzig

Moreau, Ph. (1978) 'Osculum, basium, savium', *RPh* 52: 87–97

Morgan, L. (1997) '*Achilleae comae*: hair and heroism according to Domitian', *CQ* 47: 209–14

Murgatroyd, P. (1981) 'Servitium Amoris and the Roman elegists', *Latomus* 40: 589–606

Myers, K. S. (1996) 'The poet and the procuress: the *lena* in Latin love elegy', *JRS* 86: 1–21

Nielsen, I. (1990) *Thermae et balnea: the architecture and cultural history of Roman public baths*. Aarhus

Nisbet, G. (1998) 'Greek skoptic epigram of the first and second centuries AD', Dissertation, Oxford

Nisbet, R. G. M. (1978) '*Felicitas* at Surrentum (Statius, *Siluae* II.2)', *JRS* 68: 1–11

Nordh, A. (1954) 'Historical *exempla* in Martial', *Eranos* 52: 224–38

Nutton, V. (1972) 'Roman oculists', *Epigraphica* 34: 16–29

Obermayer, H. P. (1998) *Martial und der Diskurs über männliche 'Homosexualität' in der Literatur der frühen Kaiserzeit*. Tübingen

Ogle, M. B. (1920) 'The lover's blindness', *AJPh* 41: 240–52

Oliver, Jr. A. (1977) *Silver for the gods: 800 years of Greek and Roman silver*. Toledo, Ohio

Packer, J. E. (1971) *The insulae of imperial Ostia*, *MAAR* 31, Rome

Parroni, P. (1979) 'Gli *stulti parentes* di Marziale e il prezzo di una vocazione (nota a Mart. 9,73)', in *Studi di poesia latina in onore di Antonio Traglia* (Rome) 833–9

Paukstadt, R. (1876) *De Martiale Catulli imitatore*. Dissertation Halle

Peek, W. (1941) 'Griechische Epigramme III', *MDAI(A)* 66: 47–86

Pelckmann, J. (1908) *Versus choliambi apud Graecos et Romanos historia*. Dissertation Kiel

Peterson, R. M. (1919) *The cults of Campania*. Rome

Pitcher, R. (1984) 'Flaccus, friend of Martial', *Latomus* 43: 414–23

Platner, S. and Ashby, T. (1929) *A topographical dictionary of ancient Rome*. Oxford

Poinar, G. O. (1992) *Life in Amber*. Stanford

Preston, K. (1920) 'Martial and formal literary criticism', *CPh* 15: 340–52

Prinz, K. (1930) 'De Martialis Epigr. IX 67', *WS* 48: 113–16

Prior, R. E. (1996) 'Going around hungry: topography and poetics in Martial 2.14', *AJPh* 117: 121–41

Purcell, N (1987) 'Town in country and country in town', in E. R. MacDougall, ed. *Ancient Roman villa gardens* (Dumbarton Oaks) 185–203

Raditsa, L. F. (1980) 'Augustus' legislation concerning marriage, procreation, love affairs and adultery', *ANRW* II 13: 278–339

Ramage, E. S. (1973) *Urbanitas*. Oklahoma

Ramelli, I. (1997) 'Il ΣΗΜΕΙΟΝ dell' ambra da Omero a Marziale (IV 32; IV 59; VI 15)', *Aevum (ant)* 10: 233–46

Rankin, H. D. (1976) 'Catullus and incest', *Eranos* 74: 113–21

Ransom, C. L. (1905) *Couches and beds of the Greeks, Etruscans and Romans*. Chicago

Rashke, G. (1910) *De Anthologiae Graecae epigrammatis quae colloquii formam habent*. Diss. Münster

Raven, D. S. (1965) *Latin metre*. London

Reinhold, M. (1971) 'Usurpation of status and status symbols in the Roman empire', *Historia* 20: 275–302

Renna, E. (1992) *Vesuvius mons*. Naples

Ribbeck, O. (1883) *Kolax: eine ethnologische Studie*. Leipzig

Richlin, A. (1984) 'Invective against women in Roman satire', *Arethusa* 17: 67–80

Rist, J. M. (1980) 'Epicurus on friendship', *CPh* 75: 121–9

Robert, L. (1940) *Les gladiateurs dans l'Orient grec*. Paris

Römer, C. (1990) 'Ehrung für den Arzt Themison', *ZPE* 84: 81–8

Rudd, N. (1986) *Themes in Roman satire*. London

Sáez, R. M. M. (1998) *La métrica de los epigramas de Marcial: esquemas rítmicos y esquemas verbales*. Zaragoza

Salemme, C. (1976) *Marziale e la 'poetica' degli oggetti*. Naples

Saller, R. P. (1982) *Personal patronage under the early empire*. Cambridge
  (1983) 'Martial on patronage and literature', *CQ* 33: 246–57
  (1991) 'Corporal punishment, authority, and obedience in the Roman household', in B. Rawson, ed. *Marriage, divorce and children in ancient Rome* (Canberra) 144–65

Sauter, F. (1934) *Der römische Kaiserkult bei Martial und Statius*. Stuttgart/Berlin

Sauvage, A. (1975) *Étude de thèmes animaliers dans la poésie latine*. Brussels

Scarborough, J. (1969–70) 'Romans and physicians', *CJ* 65: 296–306

Schönbeck, G. (1962) *Der Locus Amoenus von Homer bis Horaz*. Diss. Heidelberg

Schulten, A. (1955) *Iberische Landeskunde* I. Strasbourg

Schulze, K. P. (1887) 'Martials Catullstudien', *JKPh* 135: 637–40

Schulze, W. (1904) *Zur Geschichte lateinischer Eigennamen*. Berlin

Schumann, E. (1977) 'Der Typ der Uxor Dotata in den Komödien des Plautus', *Philologus* 121: 45–65

Schuster, M. (1928) 'Ad M.'s Epigr. IX, 67', *RhM* 77: 432

Scobie, A. (1986) 'Slums, sanitation, and mortality in the Roman world', *Klio* 68: 399–433

Sebesta, J. L. (1994) *'Tunica ralla, tunica spissa*: the colors and textiles of Roman costume', in Sebesta and Bonfante, edd. (1994) 65–76

Sebesta, J. L. and Bonfante, L., edd. (1994) *The world of Roman costume.* Wisconsin

Sedgwick, W. (1928) 'Babies in ancient literature', *The Nineteenth Century* 104: 374–83

Seel, O. (1961) 'Ansatz zu einer Martial-Interpretation', *AA* 10: 53–76 (excerpt in English tr. in J. P. Sullivan, ed. *Martial* (New York/London 1993) 180–202)

Shackleton Bailey, D. R. (1989) 'More corrections and explanations of Martial', *AJPh* 110: 131–50

Sharrock, A. R. (1995) 'The drooping rose: elegiac failure in Amores 3.7', *Ramus* 24: 152–80

Siedschlag, E. (1977) *Zur Form von Martials Epigrammen.* Berlin

Sittl, C. (1890) *Die Gebärden der Griechen und Römer.* Leipzig

Smith, R. E. (1951) 'The law of libel at Rome', *CQ* 1: 169–79

Snowden, F. M. (1970) *Blacks in antiquity: Ethiopians in the Greco-Roman experience.* Cambridge, Mass.

Solin, H. (1995) 'Die sogennanten Berufsnamen antiker Ärtze', in P. van der Eijk, H. Horstmanshoff and P. Schrijvers, edd. *Ancient medicine in its social and cultural context* I (Amsterdam/Atlanta) 119–42

Speyer, W. (1971) *Die literarische Fälschung in heidnischen und Christlichen Altertum.* München

Sposi, F. (1997) 'Archeologia e poesia in due epigrammi di Marziale (2,14; 7,73)', *A &R* 42: 16–27

Stambaugh, J. E. (1978) 'The function of Roman temples', *ANRW* II 16.1: 573–96

Starr, Raymond J. (1987) 'The circulation of literary texts in the Roman world', *CQ* 37: 213–23

Stroh, W. (1991) 'De amore senili quid ueteres poetae senserint', *Gymnasium* 98: 264–76

Strong, D. E. (1966) *Greek and Roman gold and silver plate.* London

Sullivan, J. P. (1991) *Martial: the unexpected classic.* Cambridge

Swann, B. W. (1994) *Martial's Catullus.* Hildesheim

Syme, R. (1977) 'Scorpus the charioteer', *AJAH* 2: 86–94

Szelest, H. (1963) 'Martials satirische Epigramme und Horaz', *Altertum* 9: 27–37

(1974) 'Domitian und Martial', *Eos* 62: 105–14

(1976) 'Martials Epigramme auf merkwürdige Vorfälle', *Philologus* 120: 251–7

(1980) '*Ut faciam breuiora mones epigrammata, Corde . . .* Eine Martial-Studie', *Philologus* 24: 99–108

Thompson, D'Arcy W. (1936) *A glossary of Greek birds.* London

(1947) *A glossary of Greek fishes.* London

Thompson, L. A. (1989) *Romans and blacks.* London/Oklahoma

Tolman, J. A. (1910) *A Study of the sepulchral inscriptions in Buecheler's Carmina Epigraphica Latina.* Chicago

Toynbee, J. M. C. (1971) *Death and burial in the Roman world.* London

(1973) *Animals in Roman life and art.* London

Tracy, V. (1980) 'Aut captantur aut captant', *Latomus* 39: 399–402

Treggiari, S. (1991) *Roman marriage.* Oxford

Tupet, A.-M. (1976) *La magie dans la poésie latine.* Paris

Turner, E. G. (1980) *Greek papyri: an introduction.* 2nd edn, Oxford

Van der Valk, H. L. M. (1957) 'On the edition of books in antiquity', *VChr* 11: 1–10

Van Hooff, A. J. L. (1990) *From autothanasia to suicide: self-killing in classical antiquity.* London/NY

Vérilhac, A.-M. (1978/1982) ΠΑΙΔΕΣ ΑΩΡΟΙ: *poésie funéraire* I Texts/II Commentary. Athens

Versnel, H. S. (1974) 'A parody on hymns in Martial v 24 and some trinitarian problems', *Mnemosyne* 27: 365–405

Verstraete, (1980) 'Slavery and the social dynamics of male homosexual relations in ancient Rome', *Journal of Homosexuality* 5.3: 227–36

Veyne, P. (1964) 'Martial, Virgile et quelques épitaphes', *REA* 66: 48–52

Ville, G. (1981) *La gladiature en Occident des origines à la mort de Domitien.* Rome

Vischer, R. (1965) *Das einfache Leben.* Göttingen

Vlahogiannis, N. (1998) 'Disabling bodies', in D. Montserrat, ed. *Changing bodies, changing meanings: studies on the human body in antiquity* (London) 13–36

Vout, C. (1996) 'The myth of the toga: understanding the history of Roman dress', *G&R* 43: 204–20

Ward, R. B. (1992) 'Women in Roman baths', *HThR* 85: 125–47

Warkany, J. R., Lemire, J. and Cohen, M. M. (1982) *Mental retardation and congenital malformations of the central nervous system*. Chicago/London

Waters, K. H. (1964) 'The character of Domitian', *Phoenix* 17: 49–77

Watson, L. C. (1991) *Arae: the curse poetry of antiquity*. Leeds

  (1994) 'Horace *Odes* 1.23 and 1.25: a thematic pairing?', *AUMLA* 82: 67–84

Watson, L. C. and P. A. (1996) 'Two problems in Martial', *CQ* 46: 586–91

Watson, P. A. (1982) 'Martial's fascination with lusci', *G&R* 29: 71–6

  (1992) 'Erotion: *puella delicata* ?', *CQ* n.s. 42: 253–68

  (1998) 'Ignorant Euctus: wit and literary allusion in Martial 8.6', *Mnemosyne* 51: 30–40

  (1999) 'Martial on the wedding of Stella and Violentilla', *Latomus* 58: 348–56

  (2001) 'Martial's snake in amber: ekphrasis or poetic fantasy?', *Latomus* 60: 938–43

  (2003) 'Martial's marriage: a new approach', *RhM* forthcoming

Weinreich, O. (1926) *Die Distichen des Catull*. Tübingen

  (1928) *Studien zu Martial*. Stuttgart

Werner, P. (1906) *De incendiis urbis Romae aetate imperatorum*. Diss. Leipzig

White, K. D. (1970) *Roman farming*. London

  (1975) *Farm equipment of the Roman world*. Cambridge

White, P. (1974) 'The presentation and dedication of the *Silvae* and the *Epigrams*', *JRS* 64: 40–61

  (1975) 'The Friends of Martial, Statius, and Pliny, and the dispersal of patronage', *HSCPh* 9: 265–300

  (1978) '*Amicitia* and the profession of poetry', *JRS* 68: 74–92

  (1982) 'Positions for poets in early imperial Rome', in B. Gold, ed. *Literary and artistic patronage in ancient Rome* (Texas) 50–66

  (1996) 'Martial and pre-publication texts' *EMC* 40 n.s. 15: 397–412

Wiedemann, T. (1992) *Emperors and gladiators*. London/New York

Wikander, Ö. (1988) 'Ancient roof-tiles – use and function', *OAth* 17: 203–16

Willenberg, K. (1973) 'Die Priapeen Martials', *Hermes* 101: 320–51

Williams, C. A. (1995) 'Greek love at Rome', *CQ* 45: 517–39

  (1999) *Roman homosexuality: ideologies of masculinity in classical antiquity*. Oxford

Williams, Gareth (1996) *The curse of exile: a study of Ovid's Ibis*. Cambridge

Williams, Gordon (1958) 'Some aspects of Roman marriage ceremonies and ideals', *JRS* 48: 16–29

(1959) 'Dogs and leather', *CR* 9: 97–100

Wills, J. (1996) *Repetition in Latin poetry*. Oxford

Yavetz, Z. (1958) 'The living conditions of the urban plebs in republican Rome', *Latomus* 17: 500–17

(1965) 'Plebs Sordida', *Athenaeum* 43: 295–311

Yegül, F. (1992) *Baths and bathing in classical antiquity*. New York

Zaganiaris, J. (1977) 'Le roi des animaux dans la tradition classique', *Platon* 29: 26–49

Ziegler, K. (1950) 'Plagiat', *RE* xx 2: 1956–97

Zimmermann, J. (1909) *Luciani quae feruntur podagra et ocypus: commentatio philologica*. Diss. Leipzig

INDEXES

References are to lemmata in the Commentary or page numbers in the Introduction.

2 GENERAL INDEX